Cultural Diversity, Governance and Policy
India-Australia

Cultural Diversity, Governance and Policy

India-Australia

Editors

D. Gopal

Alan Mayne

SHIPRA

Price: Rs. 895, US$ 45.00

ISBN: 978-81-7541-476-1

First Published in India in 2009

Cultural Diversity, Governance and Policy: India-Australia

Published by :
SHIPRA PUBLICATIONS
115-A, Vikas Marg, Shakarpur, Delhi-110092 (India)
Tel. : 91-11-65277210, 22500954, Fax : 91-11-22458662
Email : info@shiprapublications.com
www.shiprapublications.com

Contents

Preface

In the world of today, the notion of cultural diversity has become quite salient within and between nation-states. Currently witnessed process of globalisation undermining national and ethnic identities is raising concerns about the ability of nation-states to nurture differences in all aspects of cultural expression including language, creative expressions, values, ideas and histories. The importance of cultural diversity to social, economic and political agendas is, therefore, gaining momentum in policy-making. However, understanding of cultural diversities is at various levels between nations-states. This edited compendium of essays – *Cultural Diversity, Governance and Policy: India-Australia*—by specialists and scholars from India and Australia explores in-depth the multiple issues of multiculturalism confronted by both the countries.

The editors express their gratitude to each one of the contributors for extending their cooperation in the completion of the compendium. The editors owe their special thanks for the cooperation extended to them by Hon. Dr. Karan Singh, Member of Parliament (Rajya Sabha) & President, Indian Council for Cultural Relations (ICCR), Professor V.N. Rajasekharan Pillai, Vice Chancellor, Indira Gandhi National Open University (IGNOU), H.E. John McCarthy, Australian High Commissioner to India, New Delhi, and Dr. Kapila Vatsyayan, Founder and Former Director, Indira Gandhi National Centre for Arts, Delhi.

The editors thank the original conference sponsors, the Australian Studies Programme at Indira Gandhi National Open University (IGNOU) and the Australia-India Council (AIC), Australia High Commission, for making this volume possible.

The editors also record their gratitude to the Australia-India Council (AIC) for extending funding support for the publication of the volume. Without the active support of Ms. Asha Lele Das, Country Manager, AIC, this publication would not have been possible. No less, the editors thank Shipra Publications for meeting our demands.

1 January 2009
New Delhi

D. Gopal
Alan Mayne

Introduction

Cultural Diversity, Governance and Policy: India-Australia, was a significant conference (2007) because of its explicit linking of the concept and practice of cultural diversity with the mechanics of contemporary governance and policy-making. The Concept Note of the conference pointed out to participants that until recently attention with cultural diversity as a policy issue had been associated with immigrant-receiving societies. In these societies cultural diversity was debated in terms of ethnic and racial diversity, and applied to public policy mainly in order to mediate the effects of immigration upon the growing cultural heterogeneity of these societies. It further contended that the parameters of policy debate about cultural diversity have in recent years been repositioned as nation-states' attempt to nurture, and also to contain, diverse aspects of cultural expression within their societies, and the playing out of these cultural expressions across communal, regional and national boundaries. These changes have been driven by public policy considerations about national identity, security, trade, and social innovation. But for the most part, they concluded, this enlarged policy debate has yet to result in the delivery of sustained, effective, and equitable policies by governments. The Concept Note posed three questions:

- What are the sources and meanings of cultural difference in our societies?
- In what ways do institutions and policy makers deal with cultural diversity?
- Do these policy tools provide solutions for nurturing and managing cultural diversity, or are they themselves problem-ridden?

The eclectic nature of the following chapters highlights the diversity of viewpoints and opinions that are generated by these questions, but the book's contributors identify important common issues that policy makers must address in order for government inputs to achieve greater traction and deliver better outcomes than have been evident to date.

Before discussing these issues more fully, however, it is important to acknowledge what Bruce Bennett, in the first chapter of this book, calls the unique relationship that exists between India and Australia. This relationship provides a useful background context against which to consider the arguments presented in the later chapters. The modern histories of both nations have in common the experience of British colonialism. Moreover, in building modern nation-states India and Australia share overlapping post-colonial paths. It is worthwhile to consider briefly the changing nature of bilateral relations between India and Australia during the colonial and post-colonial periods, because they highlight the interplay between evolving public knowledge of cultural diversity, public policy, and social well-being.

Professor Alan Mayne, one of the editors, lives in Adelaide, from where he can easily fly to Indian cities, just as his friends and colleagues in India can visit him in Adelaide. The basis for these exchanges began some 130 years ago, but in very different circumstances. In 1879 the colonial government of South Australia passed a Northern Territory Indian Immigration Act to facilitate the use of 'Indian coolies' as a cheap and easily controlled labour force through which to develop northern Australia. When Queen Victoria, concerned that the legislation provided insufficient safeguards for the welfare of the Indian labourers, declined royal assent for the legislation, the South Australian government sent Major J. Fergusson to India in 1881 to negotiate with the British Viceroy about acceptable conditions for importing Indian labour. Enabling legislation was passed in 1882 and renewed by the Indian Coolie Immigration Amendment Act in 1891. Indian labour was used in northern Australia during the late nineteenth century in agriculture, mining, and railway construction. The reasoning of South Australian policy makers then, however, appears obnoxious to us today. Indian immigration was advocated in the past in order to build up a subordinate labouring class, and thereby block Chinese immigration and their potential competition with Europeans, in the Northern Territory.

Fergusson had reported to the South Australian government in 1882, 'The coolies are quiet patient workers, slow and plodding, ... but they are very easily managed, and if kindly treated will stick faithfully to their employers. They are wanting in ambition'. In this respect, he said, Indians were unlike the Chinese, and 'they may be depended upon to remain in the service of their employer, content if they are earning a trifle more than enough to secure the necessities of life, and delighted if they can save a small sum besides'.[1] Fergusson's opinion was endorsed in 1888 by a European missionary based in Calcutta, who confirmed that 'The coolies are very docile, and are essentially labourers and not capitalists. They do not enter into business, but work contentedly for less wages than the Chinese will accept, and in the course of years amass sufficient gold to return to India and live in independence'. The missionary advised that Indian labourers 'are docile and patient, without the secrecy and cunning of the Chinese'.[2]

These perverse and racially coloured characterisations of cultural difference have no place in Australian policy making today, and are contradicted by the multicultural realities of contemporary Australian society. As Graeme Hugo and Gouranga Dasvarma point out in their careful demographic analysis of recent Indian migration to Australia, later in this book, not only has the Indian community in Australia almost doubled in size during the last decade, but Indian immigration is distinguished by its disproportionately high proportion of skilled arrivals. Almost three quarters of Indian arrivals are skilled migrants. The old 'coolie' stereotypes have long since vanished from policy debate.

A second caveat should also be made. As the historical example from nineteenth-century South Australia illustrates, cultural diversity has long been recognised as a policy issue by governments, but it has usually been discussed hesitantly and translated into policy programmes largely in terms of containment and control. Policy makers have been reluctant to endorse diversity unconditionally and thus perhaps encourage dissent and internecine conflict. They question the consequences of fully unleashing the positive energies that, as Hugo and Dasvarma imply, flow from enabling pluralism and promoting inclusiveness. Liz Hall, in her analysis of the Australia industrial relations system, calls such policy initiatives 'capturing the diversity dividend'. We hope that this book will influence policy makers to take the necessary steps to earn that dividend.

Cultural diversity is now widely but cautiously acknowledged in terms of cultural 'performances'[3] (for example music, song, dance, theatre, art, and cuisine) that assist in building national identities, but the emphasis of government policy has been to harness such performances in order to build unity and consensus in communities and nation-states. These emphases are evident, for example, in Australian immigration and settlement policy since the Second World War, where even as assimilation policies that had been designed to protect a supposed monoculture eroded during the 1960s and 1970s and were replaced by multiculturalism during the 1980s and 1990s, the purpose of government acknowledgement of diversity was to ensure social integration and consensus, and to promote citizenship. These emphases are even more evident in India, where government, conscious that the achievement of nationhood in 1947 was accompanied by 'unclean massacres [repeated] a hundred times over' between Hindus and Muslims,[4] urgently promoted the conciliatory concept of unity in diversity.

The forced concessions by policy makers to the realities of cultural diversity in their societies can best be described as strategic interventions that pragmatically employed social engineering to achieve the goals of the nation-state.[5] The drive by policy makers to consolidate consensus, and their ambivalence towards subaltern cultural diversity, have recently been reinforced by popular reactions against globalisation, two trends that Kapila Vatsyayan, in the second chapter of this book, calls 'this twin phenomenon of coming together and falling apart'. Mass anti-globalisation demonstrations, beginning in Seattle during the World Trade Organisation meeting in 1999, forced the world's economic leaders to consider alternative viewpoints and tested the commitment of state authorities to maintaining democratic guarantees for the full expression of diverse points of view.

Democratic procedures for free expression and the protection of minorities within pluralistic nation-states have been further tested amid post 9/11 worries about international terrorism and internal extremist minorities. There has been deep soul-searching in Britain, for example, following the London '7/7' bombings in 2005, about the consequences for civil liberty of tightening surveillance and lengthening the allowable periods in detention for terrorist suspects. Civil society in Britain struggles to contain the anti-Muslim backlash that has been unleashed by revelations of internally generated terrorist activity. India is even more sensitive to the social and political tensions generated by religious, ethnic, caste, and regional diversity, and in this book Sudhir Jacob George draws attention to the alienation of north-east India as a result of interventions there by 'insensitive nation-states and their bureaucracies'.

Even in Australia, knee-jerk reactions by the federal government to cultural difference and diversity, and clumsy attempts to reinforce national consensus, resulted in the introduction during 2007 of a widely criticised citizenship test before the granting of Australian nationality to immigrants. In 2006 the first man jailed under Australia's tough new anti-terrorism legislation, the alleged al-Qaeda terrorist Jack 'Jihad' Thomas, was freed, much to the embarrassment of federal authorities, when the courts threw out as inadmissible the evidence collected against him. In 2007 the Australian government was further embarrassed when charges against the Indian doctor Mohammed Haneef for assisting terrorists (after his cousin in Britain, to whom he had given his mobile phone chip, rammed a burning jeep into a terminal at Glasgow airport), likewise fell apart and the Commonwealth Director of Public Prosecutions admitted that the doctor should never have been charged.

These frictions expose the weaknesses and deceits of public policy making, and the blind spots in public knowledge upon which policy is built. They highlight the shallowness of the assumptions about mainstream homogeneity and minority dysfunctionality upon which much policy formulation is based. They also suggest the wisdom of governments heeding, and channelling into lawful expressions, the full gamut of a nation's cultural diversity.

The contributors to this book understand culture holistically, as permeating social life and social action, rather than as a set of socially disengaged performances. This understanding of culture and diversity has much in common with that of the cultural anthropologist Clifford Geertz, who argued that 'man is an animal suspended in webs of significance he himself has spun, [and] I take culture to be those webs'.[6]

Cultural Diversity, Governance and Policy: India-Australia sustains three main lines of discussion and analysis.

The first is theoretical, and includes discussion of democratic process and pluralism (Subrata Mukherjee) and multiculturalism (Sushila Ramaswamy). This important strand in the book is summed up neatly by R. Narayanan's discussion of identity and cultural 'slippage', in which the example of the Indian diaspora is used to highlight the usefulness of post-colonial theoretical concepts in probing the permeability of state and cultural boundaries.

The second strand deals with issues of Indian cultural diversity. Kapila Vatsyayan provides an overview of the intrinsic cultural pluralism of India, which she juxtaposes with some policy makers' efforts to introduce 'a "fixity" and contrived uniformity'. Abdulrahim P. Vijapur compares cross-cultural tolerance in pre-colonial India with state-sanctioned discrimination against

Muslims and other minorities since Independence. Sailaja Gullapalli discusses Gandhian concepts of cultural pluralism and grassroots democracy. Sudhir Jacob George analyses marginalisation and unrest in north-east India. Satya Pattnayak rounds off these discussions, and interweaves them with the book's parallel discussions of social theory, in the last chapter. Like Narayanan he discusses the Indian diaspora, but within the context of the United States and the Caribbean, in order to highlight the dynamic qualities of cultural formation and hence the 'segmented ethno-cultural identities' of Indians overseas.

The third main line of discussion and analysis deals specifically with multiculturalism and identity. Sonu Trivedi provides a comparative assessment of multiculturalism in Australia and India. David Roberts focuses on the tensions within Australian multiculturalism, exploring the increasing responsiveness of public policy making to cultural diversity and sensitivity to social inclusiveness, but also emphasising the continuing marginalisation of Indigenous Australians. Andrew Hassam discusses Bollywood Down Under in order to critique multiculturalism and its undercurrent of elite cosmopolitanism. D. Gopal concludes this theme by carefully reviewing the evolution of multicultural policy in Australia and relating this to changing Australian identity and values.

There are three key points of confluence between these and the other chapters in this book. We urge policy makers to note and draw lessons from them, and researchers to study them further and make their findings widely available.

Firstly, public knowledge of cultural diversity and community tolerance of differences are mediated by the structures of power in a society. Hegemony is not an abstract concept; it conditions and frequently compromises day-to-day social understanding and social action. Alan Mayne demonstrates how homogenised representations of cultural differences (which he explains in relation to stereotypes about city slums and rural outstations) distance minority groups from decision-making and perpetuate social disadvantage. Sonu Trivedi likewise draws attention to the culturally homogenising effects of nation-building, and its marginalising effects upon minority groups. S. Ram Vemuri links the legacy of past interactions between colonisers and the colonised in Australia and India to post-colonial assumptions about core and peripheral groups in the new nation-states, and hence to the continuing economic marginalisation of Indigenous communities in both nations. Sally Percival Wood details the post-9/11 marginalisation of Arabic-speaking Australians as a result of the negative stereotypes carried in the mainstream media.

Secondly, public policy recognition of cultural diversity has consequently often had the effect (more often than not unintentionally) of entrenching cultural marginalisation, social discrimination, and political disempowerment. If multiculturalism is a policy of cultural recognition alone, then the question that needs consideration is whether or not should it come after the fight against social discrimination is the poser against which Priti Singh dwells at length on issues of socio-economic inequities of the tribal peoples in India. David Roberts highlights the disappointingly limited outcomes of multicultural policy in Australia for Indigenous communities. Shashi B. Upadhyay provides a historical perspective on the effects of British colonialism in India upon ongoing educational discrimination against Dalits. Swaraj Basu underlines how continuing discrimination against Dalits in India and Indigenous peoples in Australia has created a festering sore in both societies in terms of the marginalisation and injustice dealt out to these minority groups.

Thirdly, these mistakes in both public understanding and public policy are continually challenged by alternative subaltern points of view sustained by the very diversity of experience and belief that mainstream knowledge and policy making often attempt to undermine. The lesson for healthy democracies is plain: celebrate and perpetuate diversity, contain and harness in positive ways the arenas for conflict which multiplicity necessarily generates, and resolve social injustice. Amita Singh highlights both the challenges and the opportunities that lie ahead in her discussion of the ambivalent relationship between social justice programmes, governance, and new information and communications technology (ICT). She urges a better balance so that 'the voice of the poor and the oppressed does not get buried'. Other contributors, from Bennett to Upadhyay and Wood, develop similar arguments in relation to both social justice and cultural enrichment as they urge educational reform and better resourcing for language teaching. Such initiatives (and, as Mayne urges, the forging of genuine partnerships between governments and disadvantaged communities in pursuit of the United Nations Millennium Goals for global social justice and sustainability), provide the way forward to empower marginalised communities, and thus to ensure the general well-being of democratic societies.

India and Australia provide a good test case for our collective abilities, by underwriting cultural diversity, of ensuring a just and sustainable future for human society globally in the twenty-first century.

Endnotes

1. Major J. Fergusson to the Minister for Education), 2 March 1882, in State Records of South Australia, GRS 1 (Letters Received In The Office Of The Minister Controlling The Northern Territory), unit 18, item 117/1882.
2. *Adelaide Advertiser*, 23 June 1888, 'An Indian Native Pastor'.
3. We are influenced by the work of cultural anthropologist Victor Turner, who regarded the rituals of cultural performance as being inseparable from the ongoing dramas and tensions of social life. See, for example, his *On the Edge of the Bush: Anthropology as Experience* (Tuscon: University of Arizona Press, 1985), part two.
4. Nirad C. Chaudhuri, *Thy Hand, Great Anarch! India 1921-1952* (Reading, MA: Addison-Wesley, 1988), p. 829.
5. Alan Mayne developed this point further in 'What Immigration Policy for Australia?' *Overland*, no. 115 (1989): pp. 78–85.
6. Clifford Geertz, *The Interpretation of Cultures* (New York: Basic Books, 1973), p. 5.

1

Building the Australia-India Relationship

Bruce Bennett

The unique relationship between Australia and India provides opportunities for citizens of both countries to increase their awareness of cultural diversity. As a member of the Board of the Australia-India Council and a Professor of English, I am frequently engaged in programmes aimed at developing links between people and institutions in India and Australia in the perceived long-term interests of both countries.

The Australia-India Council (AIC) is a highly active bilateral council of the Australian Government's Department of Foreign Affairs and Trade which aims to increase Indian awareness of Australia and vice versa. The current AIC Board has selected five priority areas of funding of which Education is one. The others are the Arts (including film and literature), Society (including Health and Sport), Science/Technology and Environment and Public Policy (including media links). Focus areas, in addition to Australian Studies in the priority area of Education, include a 'train the trainers' program involving Australian and Indian doctors in the treatment of HIV/AIDS, a biotechnology/biomedical links program and a new focus on heritage and cultural conservation.

The Vital Role of English

English language and the cultural artefacts that grow from it are key elements in relations between Australia and India. It would be surprising if a Professor of English did not say this. Clearly, the ability to communicate in English that is shared by many leading figures in India and Australia enables levels of understanding and collaboration which would not be possible otherwise. Yet our assumed heritage of English can paradoxically work against higher levels of communication if our citizens fail to adequately develop their skills and adaptability in English. We are in danger of this happening. This applies to both countries. The urgency with which China has taken up the challenge of English as a new *lingua franca* by introducing its study nationally at Grade 3 level in schools challenges the lethargy in this area which sometimes prevails in Australia and India. The reading of complex texts is an aspect of the ability to 'read' people and situations. But satisfactory cross-cultural communication depends on such readers and it is one of our tasks to develop such readers in Australia and India.

If Australian educators work much harder at it, we can be a leading player in the growth of English as both a *lingua franca* and a source of social and cultural understanding in our region. To achieve this in Australia, we need a national strategy on English akin to that which grew from the recent National History Summit (but less politicised), which will recognise and reward excellence in English and put in place a curriculum framework which reinforces the priority of Australian English and its literature into the future. This should not be presented as an alternative to second and third language learning but as a necessary complement to it.

The tracking of languages other than English must also be strengthened in Australia too, with special reference to Asian languages such as Hindi, Mandarin and Bahasa Indonesia. Similarly, in the much more complex linguistic landscape of India, a firm sense of the value and utility of English must be translated into educative action. English is already widely reported to be the most common medium of communication in city schools in India and journalists from time to time exhort students to read widely and write 'simple and crisp' English. 'Fluency and flair' is encouraged in English language curricula and examinations. Perhaps through our more democratic means than China's centralized decision-making, Australia and India will both lift our games in English, as we need to do.

Role of the Australia-India Council

The Australia-India Council was established by the Australian Government in May 1992 to broaden and deepen Australia-India relations through contacts and exchanges in a range of fields which promote mutual awareness and understanding. As a member of this Council I am particularly interested in the links that can be developed and maintained through education and the arts, especially literature. But the AIC Board has seven members, all with differing interests and expertise across sport, politics, the visual arts, museums, business and medicine. Education is one of the priority funding areas. As mentioned earlier, the other areas are the Arts (including film and literature), Society (including Health and Sport, Science, Technology/Environment and Public Policy (including media links).

In the Australia-India Council, our role is not to be entrepreneurial on behalf of particular institutions, but rather to ensure that Australia remains on India's radar screen by assisting with the showcasing of Australian talent and expertise. We are concerned to 'sell' aspects of Australian culture in India while also welcoming aspects of Indian culture to Australia's shores. Getting this balance right is not an easy business. Our programs and activities are not designed as an aid to trade, but the so-called 'cultural industries' of art, music, dance and literature are enhanced by our support as are universities which participate in joint activities.

Conferences such as the one that first aired the papers in this volume on Cultural Diversity, Governance and Policy in Australia and India are important for both countries, for the themes they discuss and for the enhanced institutional links which they encourage. Similarly, a conference on Discourses of Development Studies and Democracy held at the University of Madras in January 2007 brought leading scholars from India and Australia together to consider an important theme in the literatures and cultures of both countries. The key to such events is the partnerships and continuing dialogues opened up between professors and students in India and Australia.

Such dialogues have been evident recently in lectures and visits to Australia by AIC-supported leading Indian thinkers. They have ranged across the sciences and the arts. For example, Professor K. Kasturirangan's public lecture at the Australian National University in 2006 on 'India's Space Enterprise' which was funded by the Australia-India Council, awakened many Australians to this developing field of science and communications and its policy implications. At the level of popular culture, a conference hosted by Monash University and the Australian National University in 2006 on 'Transnational Dialogues on Bollywood' brought Australian and Indian filmmakers and academics together in a quite different field of endeavour.

Australian Studies Initiatives

Australian Studies programs offer an umbrella under which a variety of important and worthwhile university-level interactions can occur. Such programmes have established a firmer grounding in the early twenty-first century than what they had achieved before.

The Indian Association for Studies of Australia (IASA) has been a landmark development. The Australia-India Council has supported our Indian partners in their desire to build IASA, whose foundation President is Professor Santosh K. Sareen from Jawaharlal Nehru University with Professor Darvesh Gopal from Indira Ghandhi National Open University as secretary and also a key player in this development. IASA has held three biennial conferences at the University of Madras, JNU and in Pune with a fourth planned for Kolkata in January 2008. In February 2007, a new Eastern Chapter of IASA was started in Kolkata. Seeds will thus have been planted in the south, north, west and east of India. These conferences have attracted on average over 200 members and visitors speaking on a variety of topics across disciplines such as literature, film, media, history, indigenous studies, geography, defence, security studies and international relations. IASA's newsletter and the publication of conference proceedings aid the recognition of Australian Studies and publish refereed scholarly papers which contribute to further learning. As a prelude to the Kolkata Book Fair in February 2007, a record number of seven books on Indo-Australian topics were launched.

One of the Australia-India Council's most successful initiatives to date has been the introduction of Australian Studies Visiting Fellowships. Managed for several years by a consortium led by Professor Richard Nile at Curtin University and including Monash University and the University of Queensland, the consortium has recently been strengthened by the addition of the University of New South Wales, the University of South Australia and the Australian National University. The scheme enables up to six Australian Studies Fellows each year – junior and senior – from Indian universities to visit Australia for 2–3 months to undertake research relevant to their own teaching or research. The AIC's Australian Studies Fellowships have set an example for the more recently introduced Endeavour India Research Fellowships which are supported by Australia's Department of Education, Science and Technology. Another complementary scheme is AusAID's Australian Leadership awards which are aimed at 'present and future leaders and personnel in corporate, academic, non-government and government services'. A major challenge for these schemes will be to develop an active corps of alumni who will keep alive their Australian interests and communications.

A Cultural Question: National Days and their Significance

National holidays in Australia and India serve to highlight their country's ideals and aspirations at a particular time. When I left Australia's capital city, Canberra, for India on 26 January 2007 it was Australia Day. When I arrived in India the same night, it was Republic Day. In Canberra, I had seen hot air balloons sailing over the city, lake and Parliament House. In Chennai, my first stop in India, I had to be content with comments from friends on the processions and celebrations together with television and newspaper reports.

I was struck by reports of a speech by Indian Prime Minister Manmohan Singh in which he referred, amongst other things, to the value of plurality of views and dissent in a democracy such as India's. But he also asked for recognition of the value of decision-makers who must take variety of views into account and then act in the perceived best interests of the country.[1] In making these two statements of value, the Indian Prime Minister brought together the two strands of the present volume and the conference from which it grew: he recognised the value of cultural diversity but also the necessity for proper governance and policy. Anyone who holds public office knows the difficulty of reconciling the diversity of viewpoints and values with the necessity of taking hard decisions which necessarily simplify these viewpoints into policy and modes of governance.

The Australian Prime Minister John Howard's Australia Day message also attempted to balance diversity and difference with a perceived national interest. His public statement emphasized shared values rather than diversity and difference: 'We are a people bound by common values which include respect for the freedom and dignity of the individual, a commitment to the rule of law, the equality of men and women and a spirit of egalitarianism that embraces tolerance, fair play and compassion for those in need'.[2] Should public rhetoric of this kind be relied upon when we ask questions about cultural diversity and its influence on policy and governance? To students of rhetoric, such statements have an intrinsic interest; to students of politics this may suggest the kind of 'spin' which is translated into policy frameworks and acts of governance. But reality checks must also be made with historians and country specialists – in this case, Indianists and Australianists. From this perspective, it will be seen that the diversity which Prime Minister Singh acknowledges is far greater than that faced by Prime Minister Howard. As Dr. Karan Singh has pointed out in this conference, the cultural diversity of India is akin to that of all countries in the European Union.

The Question of Patriotism: Does it diminish respect for diversity?

Attempts in both India and Australia to reinforce patriotism by invoking common values are instructive. In Australia, the flag is back in fashion with politicians of all complexions. As one of the Australia Day advertisements claimed, 'the raising of the flag ceremony will rouse the patriot in you'. The *Sydney Morning Herald's* cartoonist, Leunig, presented his own satiric response to such sentiments with a 'Dinkum Aussie Australia Day Diary':

8 am Woke up with an Aussie flag in my bed and made love to it. What a beautiful experience.
9 am Got up and ate two Aussie flags for breakfast. *Beautiful*!
10 am Raised Aussie flag on flagpole and wept uncontrollably. I'm in love.
11 am Got on the couch with another Aussie flag. Communicating together in silence. Awesome!
1 pm Lunch. Ate another three Aussie flags. Big ones. I love that flag!
2.30 Afternoon nap. I dreamed I was an Aussie flag and I met this other Aussie flag and we fell in love and did amazing things. What a horny dream. What a great day.[3]

Leunig's cartoon mixes irony with affection and in doing so reflects a typical attitude of Australians towards patriotism.

A similarly sceptical viewpoint about 'overcooked patriotism' was expressed by Tony Stephens who reflected nostalgically on a previous period when Australians 'wore their nationalism lightly':

> It wasn't that the people then lacked pride or pleasure in being Australian. It was more that they didn't feel the need to flaunt it. Some might have had in mind Samuel Johnson's words that patriotism is the last refuge of a scoundrel, or Albert Einstein's that nationalism is an infantile disease, the measles of mankind. Others had fled countries where anthems were sung with gusto and

> the people marched to war behind banners and flags. Still others were born here but had fought in those wars. Happy is the land not in need of flags.[4]

Patriotic feeling is not undermined by Stephens. On the contrary, he supports patriotism while criticizing its exhibitionistic forms of expression.

How may a country's leaders – both its intellectuals and its elected politicians – strike the appropriate balance in their ideas and policies for cultural diversity and their desire to achieve national harmony? Australian Booker Prize-winning author Thomas Keneally has criticised the 'ethnic hysteria' that has characterised some Australian reactions to Asia over the past century.[5] Keneally links anti-Asian reactions to racist attitudes towards Aboriginal people which he had observed in his childhood in country New South Wales and declares a continuing fascination with 'the way we decide whether another person belongs in our world or not'. Racial suspicion, in Keneally's view, is 'an opportunistic beast that grazes on one set of newcomers and then on another'.[6] Thus we come to believe that 'they (the new immigrants) live in ghettos, they refuse to learn English, they'll never be true Australians'. At the beginning of 2007, Keneally urges the value of 'a temperate attitude, of tranquillity rather than unnecessary racial fever'. He invokes an Australia that is not divided between Christian and Muslim but which accepts a cultural diversity wherein citizens respond with tolerance and sympathy towards new waves of immigrants.

Beyond Narrow Nationalism

From their different circumstances, two Indian Nobel Prize-winners, the economist Amartya Sen and poet Rabindranath Tagore have arrived at similar outlooks to those of Keneally. Tolerance for, and indeed pleasure in cultural diversity depends on a broad and inclusive notion of nation. Sen sees the antithesis of this attitude in the Hindutva policies of the BJP government which preceded the present Congress-led government in India.[7]

Drawing on Tagore's writing of seventy-seven years earlier, Sen recalls the Bengali poet's view that the idea of India itself must be capacious and that nationalist movements may prevent this. 'Patriotism cannot be our final spiritual centre', wrote Tagore in 1908. 'My refuge is humanity. I will not buy glass for diamonds, and I will never allow patriotism to triumph over humanity as long as I live'. 'To worship my country as a god', says one of his characters, 'is to bring a curse upon it'.[8]

Less emphatically but with the full force of his reason, the economist Sen asserts that 'the reach of Indian traditions, including heterodoxy and the celebration of plurality and scepticism, requires a comprehensive recognition (of India)'.[9] Against this, he sets the negative vision of 'a small India, bundled around a drastically downsized version of Hinduism'.[10] Nations need to be – and can be seen to be – conglomerations of citizens, not a 'collectivity of religious ethnicities'.[11]

Conclusion

The building of a stronger and deeper relationship between Australia and India is an important goal for Australians as the Australia-India Council recognises. In science, culture, sport and the arts, we will interact increasingly at personal and institutional levels and thereby strengthen the ties that a partially shared history has bequeathed us. Not least, Australians will learn about the benefits and tensions of massive cultural diversity in India, that we Australians, in smaller compass, also share. For Indian thinkers and policy makers, Australia also offers fresh fields of investigation and insights into shared problems including international security and alliances, safeguarding the natural environment and the development of English and other languages. Recent statistics showing a preference among Indian students for Australian universities over Europe's[12] indicate that Australia will continue to be a leading influence on Indian higher education. The Indian Association for Studies of Australia and similar groups thus have a crucial pioneering role to play in increasing knowledge and understanding of Australia in India. At the same time, Australians will become more curious about India in all its facets. In these circumstances, the arts, science, culture and history of India will add to the diversity Australians seek in their rapidly increasing involvement with the world at large.

Endnotes

1. 'Manmohan: Respect value of dissent', *The Asian Age* (Kolkata), 31 January 2007.
2. *Canberra Times*, 26 January 2007.
3. *Sydney Morning Herald*, 26–28 January 2007, p. 36.
4. Ibid.
5. 'Flattened by a falafel', *Australian Literary Review*, 2, 1, February 2007, pp. 3, 6.
6. Ibid, p. 6.
7. Amartya Sen, *The Argumentative Indian: Writings on Indian Culture, History and Identity*, Penguin, London, 2005, p. 72.
8. cited in *The Argumentative Indian*, p. 108.
9. Ibid, p. 72.
10. Ibid.
11. See Amartya Sen, *Identity and Violence: The Illusions of Destiny*, Allen Lane, 2006.
12. See *The Times of India* cited in *The Australian*, 12 February 2007, p. 3.

2

Plural Cultures, Monolithic Structures

Kapila Vatsyayan

On the one hand, it is said that everyone is coming closer and that we are all members, equal or otherwise, of a single global family – 'global village' we call it. On the other hand, perhaps never before, have so many big or middling wars been fought on the basis of race, colour, ethnicity, language, religion and cultural identity. By some accounts ten times more people have been killed in these wars than during the Second World War. Every moment there are clashes between groups, adjacent and remote, not explicitly on the basis of political ideology but on the basis of race, colour, ethnicity, language and religion. A second deeper look invariably brings to surface the economic inequalities and motivations of power: these are neatly camouflaged. These are the implicit and explicit levels of tension and conflict. It would appear that just at the moment of the shrinking of all differences into a single homogenized village without differentiation, there is an outburst of intolerance and violence with each other and against each other. Most parts of the world appear to have been affected by this twin phenomenon of coming together and falling apart. Also, it would appear that the countries which were erstwhile colonies and are now political independent nation-states, are more inflicted with this malady, of course with outstanding exceptions.

It is against the background of this consciousness, as also the awareness of the monolithic or certainly single models of development that have been adopted, that one is obliged to ask the question whether there is an intrinsic inability of clearly defined cultures to live with each other in harmony. Or, are the tensions and conflicts the result, in part if not whole, in the imposition or acceptance of models of development and governance which are uniform, fixed, rigid, linear and unidimensional? Is the problem with 'cultures' or is it with structures of governance?

Underlying this paper is an attempt to try and comprehend the characteristics of societies with plural cultures – clearly distinguished them from those others which are today called multi-cultural on account of recent immigration, but were and are basically mono-cultures. It is also an attempt to identify once again the texture of these plural-culture societies which have existed for centuries as a network of honeycombed units, clear and distinct but in a relationship of give and take. Was there co-existence or was there always a confrontation between the several groups called tribes in Africa? Did the Tutus and Tutsi always fight? Was this the case of several groups of Indonesia and of course, the countless groups and communities in India? Were the Kukis always at war with the Meiteis? Even a minute's attention will reveal that there was space for a fluidity of identities.

Without elaborating upon other parts of world, relevant as their situation is to ours in India, let me begin with ourselves; all those who have lived and been part of the civilization called Indian, and those who are now citizens of the nation-state called India. I shall attempt to identify the diverse levels of this plurality as also refer to the measures adopted to categorise this plurality for purposes of territorial demarcation, administrative boundaries and citizenship rights and duties, education, economic and social development. In the very exercise of the descriptive account there are bound to emerge a number of issues which are relevant for our purpose of understanding both the cultures, as also the yardsticks for classification evolved for governing these societies.

II

Primary and self-evident is the physical, geographical entity known as India. Its very land mass is so situated that a natural boundary as also paths of communication are created. The youngest of the geological mountains, the Himalayas, are both a natural boundary as also a natural pathway. More, this is a unique continuous range from the northwest to the southeast. Here there is immense bio-diversity. While plurality through mobility from the north-south movement was facilitated, there was as much geo-physical and cultural movement from the northwest to the southeast. This is as true of the flora, fauna, and high altitudes, the forest covers, as also the people: the Gujjars Bakarwalas and the Kirats and Nishadas of ancient India. Perhaps nowhere else as many rivers flow from a single mountain system.

The river systems give rise to the civilizations which develop from them, today identified by their popular and debatable terms – Indus, Ganges and now Saraswati. The rivers and the foothills of the mountains provide the geo-physical basis of agricultural societies of great antiquity. Again the movement is from the northwest to the southeast generally. Through their meandering paths at different tributaries to make confluences and meeting of different tributaries to make confluences (*Sangam*) Prayag, is a common phenomenon. The people who have lived along these rivers have similarly led distinct lifestyles; they have come together to mingle, co-exist and then move on their different paths. Further south, the landscape has provided the space and place for contrasting groups of people and their lifestyles shaped by environment and agriculture function. The desert dwellers comprise numerous groups but they are not 'static' forever. They move from desert lands to fertile lands, from the west to the east, from the west to the Southwest. Middle India, with its extensive forests, is again both a place for meeting as also mobility. Further south the Vindhyas once again become a natural demarcation, as also a route for communication. The same is true of the seas that surround us on the east and west. The oceans provide the boundaries, and are also the channels of communication both with the West and the East.

Altogether each geo-physical region of India is an eco-zone closely connected with others, adjacent and remote. The consciousness of the connection between the mountains and the oceans, the forests and the rivers, the deserts and the marshlands has been responsible for a large body of literature which has conceived of the land as a large coherent unit with plurality and inter-dependence. The very ecology of the country has been responsible for the development of major concepts of unity and multiplicity, of interdependence of one region with the other. Major myths revolving around the ocean, the mountains, the rivers, the forest and the flora and fauna evolved. The one message was interconnectivity.

All this description of primary and self evident geo-physical landscape would be an irrelevant exercise were it not for the fact that the non-cognizance of the eco-zones, the plurality of the methods by which eco-balances were maintained has been the cause of much disruption. Our first paradox of plural cultures and monolithic structures appears here. The history of the non-cognizance of the plurality as also of interdependence of regions is rather long. It cannot be elaborated upon here. Nevertheless let me draw attention only to one or two aspects of the recent debate on issue of environment: the natural and human landscape and the processes of development.

We are all aware of humanity's concern with the threat to the environment. Conferences have been held in Stockholm, Rio de Janeiro and now Japan. Issues of greenhouse effect, global warming, depletion of the ozone layer have been raised. Alternate sources of energy have been discussed. However, few have identified in these conferences that underlying this situation of imbalance in the environment is not only the fact of an unequal distribution of natural resources but also the more basic question of man's attitude to Nature. The modern world has believed and subscribed to the view that man is the most important and dominant species of the universe. This is a fundamental philosophic premises built on the basis of a progressive evolutionary model and a deterministic science. A mighty edifice of a modern civilization has developed on this premise. Man is considered as the most dominant amongst life forms, and thus the most empowered to exploit and modify natural rhythms.

In clear contrast to this view, among large parts of humanity largely from all those cultures which are considered underdeveloped or developing and those with plural societal structures, there was the faith and assertion that man is one amongst all life forms. He is not dominant, even if he/she is special. Flora, fauna, even stones and inanimate life are as important. This is patently clear from the myths and legends of the people of America, Africa, Asia, the aborigines of Australia and of course India. In India whether at the highest textual tradition of the Vedas or the myths – legends of the Nagas, the Marias and Murias, the Mukkuvars, the Bhils or Santhals, the Ho's, Oraons and Saoras, there was and continues to be an acute consciousness of Man-Nature relationship. Man identified and communicated with oceans, mountains, rivers, forest plants and animals and birds. He considered it his sacred duty not to assault Nature. Understandably all these perceptions were couched in a multiplicity of vocabularies and lifestyles directly related to the environment.

Though not couched in scientific terms and, therefore, often dismissed as superstition, it was a lay person's or collective community's understanding of the two issues which we discuss today in international forums: bio-diversity and ecological balances. Many strategies were identified to ensure both bio-diversity and ecological balances. After a detour through mono-models of cultivation, single seed plantation, water management through construction of large dams and other monolithic structures of development, some scientists and planners have realized that there was some sense in the affirmation of these cultures in plural ways in the principle of bio-diversity and in maintaining eco-balances through a variety of strategies. Now there is a cry for conserving bio-diversity, plural methods of water conservation and all that we understand by the term alternate models of development. Each of these recent recommendations refers to sustainable development. Basic to all suggested alternate paradigms of development there is the concern for maintaining eco-balances and protecting the environment.

It is in this context of environment and need for sustaining eco-balances that the Indian worldview and the commitment of small cohesive groups become again relevant. India believed, and continues to do so, that man was only one amongst all life forms; that there were multiple ways by which an order could be sustained. Further, that nothing was absolute or static. Negation of these perceptions in the actual organization of land distribution and management has created serious disruptions. The common land, the fallow land, the common water resources were the responsibility of all. Certain locations both of land and water were considered scared. In this connection, let me draw attention to a recent study on Bio-diversity Management sponsored by UNESCO. This global study comes to the conclusion that many cultures in all their plurality evolved certain notions of the sacred. These notions of the 'sacred' were the strategies for conserving bio-diversity. Many traditional societies all over the world value a large number of plant species from the wild for a variety of reasons, for food, fibre, shelter or medicine. Arising out of the close forest-human linkage, the protected refugia of the natural ecologies in a given region has existed as sacred groves. These groves are managed through a variety of ways in different parts of India. The concept of the sacred grove ranges from identifying a species, for example the peepal (*ficus religiosa*) and tulsi to a given eco-system and human made agro-ecosystems and village eco-systems.

In turn all this leads to the concept of the sacred landscape. One of the best examples of this sacred landscape was that can be recognized along the course of the Ganges, originating from the high mountains of the Garhwal Himalayas in the northwest, traveling through the plain of Uttar Pradesh and West Bengal and draining into the Bay of Bengal. The plains with human habitation represent a set of inter-connected eco-system types bound together by the river. The humans are or should be only one part of the integral eco-systems. We know that non-recognition of this aspect has resulted in the pollution of the Ganges and the degradation of forests and lands. Mindless, unilinear progress or haphazard industrialization has led to a situation where human survival is threatened. Inability to comprehend the integrated system has caused major malfunctions. The Bio-sphere Reserve concept of UNESCO is actually a modern version of the sacred landscape concept of small cohesive societies of the so-called underdeveloped world. It is know as much to the Australian aborigines as to the Native Americans as to the countries of the Mediterranean, Africa and Meso-America, as to the countless groups called tribal and village societies in India. The question to be asked is, was cognizance taken of their consciousness in development models? The answer is a clear 'No'. The disruptions caused are both obvious and alarming.

III

The plurality of natural landscapes is matched by the plurality of human landscapes, and indeed the human species itself. Elementary and self-evident is not only the plurality but the plurality of criteria adopted to classify and categorise this plurality. Of course, there is a staggering plurality of racial types; this is all too well known. However, we have also to recognize that often we have continued to adopt nineteenth century anthropological yardsticks. We have spoken not only of the evolution of man, but have divided the human race according to physiognomy, blood groups and the rest. This is well known in the discipline of physical anthropology. These theories of racial distinctions were not restricted to physical characteristics but they went further to identify character. Racial discrimination and the appellation of the white, black, brown and yellow races were a logical corollary of theory in the evolution and legitimization of power structures. India accepted the criterion, even if with modifications and protests. It is not at all necessary even to mention Gandhiji's being thrown out of the train on account of pigmentation and power. There is then the classification which implies history and linguistic grouping. The earlier debate on the Aryans, and the recent discourse on the Aryans and their homeland is one outstanding example. In addition to speaking about the Australoids, Mongoloids, Negriods, we speak about Aryans and Dravidians. The very mention of the division evokes a vision of many centuries, with an unsaid acceptance of racial distinctions. This is closely linked to the plurality of linguistic grouping and family of languages. We shall speak about this later.

Next, we classify all these or some racial groups according to social structure, broadly following the *Varna* and *jati* grouping of some ancient Indian texts. Further the social structure is quantified on the basis of 'caste', again a term of recent origin, and categorise the population of practically the whole land on the basis of caste and those outside the caste system. Further the same population is classified in terms of functions but implied in the classification is an evolutionary evaluative criterion based on some historical notions of civilization. Hunters, gatherers, village societies (*grama*), city (*nagar*) and mega cities – denote a hierarchy, not merely the differentiation of life-functions, modes of agriculture, and trade. The same population is then classified on the basis of languages and what are termed as dialects. The history of the classification of languages and dialects also carries with it a special type of discourse on linguistic structures.

We further divide the same population on the basis of 'religion', that is, institutional religion and arrive at a demographic profile of Hindus, Muslims, Sikhs, Zoroastrians, Christians, Jews and so on. To all these classifications is added understandably the economic criteria, and, therefore, the division into the below poverty line, above property line, lower and higher income groups. The same population is as naturally classified into the illiterate and literate, implying a stage of evolution from pre-literature to literature societies. The gender demographic classification is natural and basic.

Can any statistical exercise of numbers set up a one to one correspondence between one category and another? For example, are all Aryans Brahmins and all Dravidians non-Brahmins or shudras of the social system? Do all forest-dwellers speak the same language? The absurdity of these questions is as patent as the complexity of defining what constitutes the total cultural identification of an individual or a group. We are back to our initial statement of the geophysical landscape and the human landscape. Each local space and place, each region has its own very special processes of overlapping categories, symbiosis or semiotics. A distinctive personality can be identified by taking all these factors into account. However, the acceptance of any single yardstick immediately results in distortions of reality.

This jigsaw puzzle of plurality and the yardsticks of adopting criteria for measuring plurality is an issue which has not been addressed with the sophistication that it deserves. It appears that there is both an element of generalizing and essentialising a single criterion of race, language, social structure or religion. The essentialising has resulted in some major disruptions – not only at the political level but also at the social level. Each individual or group comprised multi-identities; also the identities were fluid and changing. This allowed for co-existence and reciprocity. Any external categorisation, or attempt to give or demand a single identity on the basis of either race or language of religion meant that there was no room for accommodation or manoeuvre. The situation worsened because the structures correlated identity with fixed territory and privileges. On the one hand nation-states are theoretically constructed on the basis of individual rights, eschewing all classification on the basis of caste, creed, race, language, spoken or written, and of course religion. On the other, these very identities have been used to demarcate 'place' and privilege one group above another. Naturally tensions and conflicts have increased.

As illustration let us take the case of social structure and the volatile question of 'caste' and the categories called SC, ST and OBC. Only two questions may be asked amongst many others. First, was the *Varna* system an absolute fixed system in the original concept, and was there was any possibility of inter-connection and mobility, and even transgression? Second, that as and when any hierarchical rigidity manifested itself, was the corrective mechanism social or political, that is, through governance? As regards the first, the famous *Purusasukta* of the Rig Veda is often quoted, to establish that the system was fixed and purely hierarchical. A careful reading of the hymn will make it clear that this hymn invokes the image of a Cosmic Man, a paradigmatic model of the universe. All aspects are taken into account. No doubt that the Brahmins are compared to the head, the limbs to the kshatriyas and the stomach to the vaishyas and feet to the shudras – but is it not true that a human being cannot be complete without each of these parts of the body? Can one live without the stomach, that is food and all materiality, can anyone be mobile without limbs, walk without feet and have direction without a mind? If we take the original hymn in its entirety into consideration, and not insulate the parts, then it is clear that the hymn sets up a model of inter-dependence of the parts and the whole. It alludes to an interdependent structure and not to either aggregating or insulating any part. It is a metaphor of an inter-connected structure. Indeed, one commentary asks the question, whether a society can walk without feet, can man live without food?

While this is not the occasion to dwell on the original conception, it is necessary to mention that no culture venerates feet as much as the Indian culture. Also as and when transgressions took place, there were systems of legitimisation or the recognition of excellence. Valmiki, the author of the *Ramayana*, was a shudra, and Satyakema the thinker was born of doubtful parenthood. More, while brainpower did assume hierarchical power, it was not absolute. As and when hierarchy was imposed, invariably there were powerful social movements of dissent and protest. There was a call for the establishment of a new social order. The history of the pervasive bhakti movement in medieval India from the south to the north, east to the west, speaks of the voices of ironsmiths, cobblers and weavers who raised their voice against inequalities. We read and venerate a Kabir, Rahim, and Manivachanar.

Much later in the nineteenth century when oppression and hierarchy again surfaced, there were the social reform movements which eschewed caste distinctions: the Arya Samaj, Brahmo Samaj and many others. These facts are so well known that they need no recounting. Nevertheless, it is necessary to point out that these were social reform movements of the people, what we would call civil society today. These were not acts of governance by the political state. The reform movements aimed at breaking insulation, facilitating movement with an insistence on equalisation of social status and not a mechanical representation of numbers in power structure. This distinction is fine, but real and meaningful. Gandhiji's movement of the removal of untouchability also aimed at social equality, not the representation through numbers.

While the number of castes, jatis, categories of Brahmins, Kshatriyas, Vaishya and Shudras were and are innumerable, there was a measure of plurality and social intercourse. The colonial state, by recognising these social structure identities for administrative purposes and privileging and under-privileging others, gave fixity to a flexible network. Alas, the nation-state of political free India, instead of fostering the idea of nationalism by eschewing these identities for political purposes [and fostering social reform movements] has used, almost exploited, these identities for purposes of political mobilisation. A sphere of life which was best left to the inner dynamism of its self-organising system of complex social structures has been made the vehicle of empowerment, in a system which should have eschewed these identities. It is not necessary for me to mention that over these decades, these identities have been exploited ruthlessly in a race for numerical strength, and power. As a result, the social structure originally envisaged as an interconnected integral system itself split. There is irreversible fragmentation.

What is true of the constituents of what is called caste-society is even more true of that category of the population whom we have by consensus called Scheduled Castes, Scheduled Tribes and the OBC. The history of the nomenclature of SC, ST is revealing and educative. Yes, there were groups of people who were considered low and were disempowered. However, were the groups or their identities fixed and never changing, was there no overlap? It is well known that some were considered Scheduled Caste in one region but were part of the general caste structure in another region. Different configurations could be formed. It was an act of governance of the raja which notified these identities, these 'fixed' identities forever.

Thus, there was the category not only of the martial races in the caste system, but a category called criminal tribes. Now, could there be such a caste as being criminal from birth? The ridiculousness of some of these classifications has alas been perpetuated by changing the nomenclature of criminal tribes to 'denotified' tribes. No more needs to be added. It would appear that with good intentions but not sufficient thought and perceptions, the fluid and changing overlapping identities of societal structures were given permanent fixed single identities – for purposes of administration and governance, and not greater social interaction and mobility. There was no recognition of optimum skills and the special creative faculties of some of these communities.

In the context of the SC/ST/OBC, perhaps only one aspect may be highlighted. It is accepted that the crafts sector of India is a foreign exchange earner, with everyday reports of the increase in exports. The creators and makers of these crafts are mostly, if not all, either SC or ST or OBC. In statistical terms nearly 15 to 20 per cent from amongst the SC/ST are hereditary craftsmen, called workers of the craft sector. We do not call them 'artists' because they do not give individual signatures. They are not industrial workers because they are not mechanical replicators. They are the highly creative skilled givers of an Indian identity in which we all take pride. We export this creativity and display it on our person as clothes, jewellery and decoration in homes. We also use this creativity by recycling the forms and techniques at sophisticated levels in the urban milieu. However, by adopting another set of criteria of literacy or economic status, we classify them as 'backward'.

Besides the crafts sector, there is the section of Indian population we call traditional and folk artists. These are the Bhavais of Gujarat, the Langas and Manganers of Rajasthan, the Theyyam dancers of Kerala, the Terukuthu dancers of Tamil Nadu, the Tolapavakoothu puppet artists of Kerala, the Marias of Madhya Pradesh, the Ho's and Oraons of Bihar, the Bodos of Assam, the several groups of Nagas of Arunachal Pradesh, Mizoram, the Riangas of Tripura, to mention only a few. In addition there are the Purulia, Seraikala and Mayurbhanja dancers of Bengal, Bihar and Orissa, and the traditional musicians and dancers and puppeteers. In socio-economic classification, they are labelled as Scheduled Tribes and Scheduled Tribes and backward. In cultural terms, they are the highly gifted artists of India – the givers of an Indian identity. Any sensitive appraisal of their creativity and the cultural context of their social status, reveals that they were given a higher social status on certain occasions. In short, social identity was not static or fixed. The case of Seraikala dancers becoming Brahmins for the month of Vaisakh is an outstanding example. There are many others.

By recognising only a single identity of caste or SC/ST, there has been disempowerment. This is a very complex issue of plural identities and one-dimensional classification systems. They can hope to have social status and empowerment and if they were to enter the single monolithic structure of standardised education and employment in bureaucratic jobs. Is this not a paradox?

IV

Let me introduce another paradox. Indians sometimes are apologetic about the multilingual Indian state; at other times they take pride in the plurality of languages and literature. Also, sometimes an inflexible one to one correspondence is established between race and language, or place and language. Do all Aryans speak Sanskrit or the Indo-European/Indo-Aryan languages? Do all living in Tamil Nadu speak only Tamil, or those in Kerala speak Malayalam? In short, while the plurality of linguistic families is a self-evident fact and the contours/development of languages can be generally identified, no categorical statement can be made on the absolute purity of a language, its insularity and lack of interaction, and the exact geographical space which it now occupies.

Languages like the river systems flowed and also co-mingled. Sometimes large lakes were formed, and at other times, single streams. This is the history of languages, and what we term as dialects. Plurality comprised language families, but multiplicity of expression existed within a family, of Hindi/Maithili/Kaithi/Rajasthani, as also mutual interaction in Hindi-Urdu, Telugu-Tamil, Sanskrit-Malayalam. Recognition of this plurality and multiplicity was logical. However, as in the case of castes and the SC/ST, the succeeding Census reports and the initial survey of 1908 by Grierson, in the very nature and criteria adopted for languages, speakers and dialects resulted in giving a fixity to a changing fluid phenomena. Also it gave absolute priority to the written over the oral.

In the formation of states, a territory was identified with a single language, and the population was considered to be the speakers of a single language. Now each of these is a partial truth, and not the whole truth. The written and oral were two strong parallel streams in the Indian tradition, whether the *sruti* of the Vedas, which by purpose was not written or the rich corpus of Santhali, Mundari, etc. While most people used a language in an area, there were strong pockets of other languages: Telugu speakers in Tamil Nadu, Tamil speakers in Kerala, Konkani speakers in Maharashtra. Finally many, if not most people were not monolingual but bi-lingual. Even these simplistic examples make clear that language and race, language and religion, and language and territory could not be set up in a frozen one-to-one equivalence.

Any discerning person realises sooner or later that India is not an aggregation of linguistic groups as in Europe. At all times it is a multiplication of several socio-cultural historical factors; resultantly there is the co-existence of plural language identities in an individual or group. You speak one language at home, another in the courtyard, a third in the street and a fourth in office. Each of these co-exists with ease. There is an overlap of a partial universe in a single person or group. The plurality has given richness, vibrancy and a continued potential for creativity. However, with the ever-increasing pressure of legitimisation and prioritisation of language as an instrument of upward mobility in white collared jobs, it has also led to the shrinking of differences in languages, as also an inability to cross boundaries effectively. The plurality of languages, our classification systems, and the boundaries of geographical/ political states have led to the complex and almost unresolvable issues of mother tongue, national language and foreign languages in the educational system.

In our categories, we have to touch upon the most obvious and much discussed reality of India as a multi-religious country. Religion is, however, defined and identified as institutional religion. The entire division of the population into Hindus, Muslims, Sikhs, Parsis, Jews, Christians and majority-minority is on the premise that all those who are not Muslims, Sikhs, Parsis, Jews, and Christians are Hindus. And yet in anthropology and philosophy we speak of a category of people who are 'animists' and atheists. Also we have categories of the Wahabee Sikhs, Sufis and a host of others – not to speak of Buddhists, Jains and others. As in other spheres, while there was distinctiveness and some exclusivity, there were many overlaps of identities. Whether in Indonesia or India there was no contradiction in being a devout Muslim and equally dedicated to the story of *Ramayana* as the Wayang Ustads of Java; or to be a Muslim musician and sing of Hari Om as Bade Gulam Ali did; or to play the Naubat before the temple of Shiva. Besides, the history of Indian temple building and mosque architecture clearly manifests cooperation and reciprocity; the Govind-Deva temple of Vrindavana is an example of such cooperation and fusion of styles. There are countless other examples. Treatises of music in Persian speak of both distinctive identities as also overlayerings and assimilation.

The *Risale-Raga darpana* is one example. The transmission system through the *Daggar bani* is indicative of the overlapping of religions and cultural identity.

These multiple identities were scattered throughout India. Although there were dogmatic tendencies, they were contained by as also contested by the inclusive open movements. Also there was reciprocity in social conduct. Regional or local identity took precedence. By essentialising these identities into fixed identities and juxtaposing them against each other, the foundations of conflict were laid. The Indian character of religious identities gradually began to give place only to the fundamentalism of dogma and doctrine.

V

I turn now to the area of education and the parameters of making a division between the literate and illiterate. Although abject poverty and deprivation is certainly related to illiteracy and illiteracy has to be eliminated, not all illiterates are uneducated and uncultured. The craftsmen, traditional artists and artisans have already been mentioned. In our demographic profiles we took no note of the oral system of transmission of knowledge still prevalent, not only in India but also in many parts of Asia and Africa. By not taking cognizance of this system or the variety of knowledge systems still extant, the educational system was restricted to the teaching of the 3Rs and only minimal cerebral skills. It is not necessary to delineate upon the history of the foundation of the present system of education as a consequent upon the debate between the Anglicans and the Orientalists. The educational system was to prepare Indians for white collared jobs, to put it gently.

Over these decades, we have certainly educated a large number of people, and have achieved great heights in some domains; but the process of education at the primary and secondary level has become a tool of alienation and uprooting from local cultural contexts. Also there is the largest percentage of the educated unemployed, while at the same time there is a dearth of teacher at the primary and elementary level. The prophetic but demonic minutes of the Hunter and Wood report have become a reality. The report had said: "By not recognizing the indigenous system of education for jobs, we shall have shrunk the system, so that it will shed of its own accord, without our being held responsible". Our parameters of quantifying the illiterate and literate, the educated in the 'modern system of education' and others in the traditional or non-formal system has marginalised the illiterate but educated through the oral system, and those others in specialized disciplines of the earlier knowledge systems. Here also the plurality of educational systems and pedagogical tools has been assessed by the application of a single monolithic yardstick. Plurality of approaches in their cultural context had characterized the earlier systems. A single model has more or less replaced these.

We must also remember that plurality and flexibility was solidly grounded in speculative thought and theoretical models of Indian civilization. From earliest times there was an unequivocal commitment to plurality of paths: from the first articulations of the Vedas to the medieval poets and thinkers, the varied schools of philosophy, the mathematical systems. There was differentiation and plurality, but with interconnections in the pursuit of knowledge. Different configurations could be formed in space and time, and there was room for exceptions, as also transgression. At the level of social organization, the plurality could be regulated through a variety of strategies. This was the theoretical level. At the operational level there were rigidities and distortions; but correctives came from the civil society, not the state.

It was into this situation of long continues and changes that India, like some other countries, experienced as a civilization the impact of another worldview, which came with the era of enlightenment, political colonization, and intellectual transformation. Newtonian mechanistic determinism, Cartesian dualism, as also the entire baggage of positivism. This was internalized by the many, in a slow but a sure process. They largely accepted the categories evolved in the West at a particular moment in history. While this is not the occasion to dwell on the evolution of categories and acceptance of derived models, it has to be recognized that these schools of thought greatly influenced the development of structures of governance, administration, and the education of nation-states.

In addition there was the concomitant counterpart of the Orientalist discourse. We also viewed ourselves in terms of the categories evolved in the construct of the Orient. Thus, although we struggled for political independence and attained it, when it came to governance we accepted – by compulsion or volition – the left-hind baggage of the intellectual discourse, as also the linear single monolithic models. Resultantly, the alternate or indigenous knowledge systems were devalued, and their plural institutional systems marginalized. A holistic tradition began to fragment.

Mahatma Gandhi, more than anyone else, was acutely conscious of the fact that *selfhood*, that is, *swarajya* could be gained only by a self-cleansing system and a discarding of previous structures. He advocated a system of self-governance at locals' levels. We have today after decades recognized it in the model of alternate modernity. The educational programme was the pivot of local self-governance and micro-level village economies. He envisaged an equalization of potentials of each constituent. Boundaries of caste, religion, class, and language could be broken in ways other than through a single linear model of economic development. However, his vision was not realized. The history is too well known. Others, even those who shared this vision, were compelled to accept the structures left behind. Thus, while the goals were new and idealistic, the vehicles were not only old but also inappropriate and ill suited for the vast majority of the people inhabiting a subcontinent of plural cultures.

This was the case not only for India but other erstwhile colonies with plural cultures. Resultantly, the mismatch between the generic or the genetic self-nature of plural cultures and monolithic single models (called 'universal'), at the level of intellection, education and governance led to conflict and tension between and amongst groups and levels of society. We recognized it sometimes as the voice of the disempowered, at other times as ethnicity, and at other times as economic disparities. However, few nation-states preserved with the objective of evolving appropriate and more suitable models of development for plural culture societies. The rhetoric of distinctiveness and uniqueness was matched by an over-riding compulsion to become equal members of a global society – that was fast becoming a homogenized mass of a unipolar model called a universal model for development. We opt by choice or compulsion to assess and evaluate ourselves on the basis of the dominant discourse of other lands. Indeed the choices were difficult and the paths tortuous. The eco-cultural balance was disturbed. The more we tried to put fluid living cultures into monolithic homogenized structures, the greater the tensions, and violence.

VI

The subject is vast and complex. In the modern context, at this end, let me restrict myself only to a few examples of how the fluidity and plurality was replaced by a 'fixity' and contrived uniformity which gave rise to disjunctions. One amongst them was the use of common land and water resources and was a well-known fluid structure. The pattern of the Bengal Land Settlement Act, and others in the pre-independent era has been followed uniformly in many parts of India by Acts and Ordinance. The history of settlements in and around the Jagannath Temple and others in Tamil Nadu is revealing. The notion of 'sacredness' was a strategy for conservation and societal responsibility. The moment both became the property of the state or individuals there was trouble and turmoil. The balance of eco-zones and human habitation could not be maintained through single uniform models of state action, without involving and empowering those who both communicated with and were the users and beneficiaries of these primary resources.

Let me now briefly turn to the subject of education and the structures of the educational system. Education is crucial for a democracy, but what kind of education? Can a single monolithic model either in structure or curriculum meet the needs of societies of plural cultures of long communities? Again, it was Gandhiji who spoke as early as 1908 about a new and more appropriate system of education. *Hind Swarajya* articulated his total philosophy. Education, *Bunyadi Talim* was a central pivot. From a different but related point of view, Tagore formulated a policy of Lokashiksha in 1930. He modified it sometime during his last days in 1941. Both advocated and stressed the need for the natural integration of the 'head' and the 'hand', and the cultural specific of the plural educational models. Distant but also relevant was Aurobindo's call for the integrated self of the physical, mental and spiritual faculties. Gandhi's Wardha scheme was part of his larger economic model. Tagore called for the inculcation of a total being, and he did not envisage a divide between Sriniketan and Shantiniketan.

Independent India in the first decade adopted *Bunyadi Talim*, Basic Education. It was discarded or rejected, as was bound to happen in the absence of the economic and social underpinnings. A number of commissions were set up for educational reforms, as for example, the Mudaliar Commission, the Radhakrishnan Commission, the Kothari Commission. Each of them made valuable suggestions including diversification of structures and curricula. However, at the implementation stage, there was the outmoded top-down approach. While the Constitution of India provides for free and compulsory elementary education, we are far from the goal; what is more, the content of the education with an emphasis on only the 3 Rs. and cerebral skills dissociated the learner from his/her cultural roots.

Many years ago a blue print was made to make the single teacher schools into two-teacher schools. It was recommended that the second teacher may be from the traditional craftsmen – the potter, the ironsmith, the cobbler, etc., literate or illiterate. The recommendations were not accepted, nor modifications made in the nature of planning at the micro-level with an integrated approach. Even this brief narration makes it clear that primary and elementary education in a vast country with plural geo-physical environment and cultures has to be matched with plural structures and diversity of approaches for different situations. The replication of a single model for all parts of India, from the Himalayas to the Arabian Sea, deserts to marshlands, with differentiation in societal structures, could not be viable, as it has not been. There are other instances within polytechnic and university systems where there is a disjunction between the vibrant creativity and productivity of the sector, called non-formal or traditional, and the institutional structures established by the state. Through this system white collared jobs naturally became the only aspiration.

Finally, the issue of structure, content and pedagogical methods of education cannot be dissociated from the administrative system that a country adopts for governance. As mentioned before, Gandhiji wished to completely re-haul if not reject the system. Jawaharlal Nehru wanted to reform the system. Morarji Desai headed an Administrative Reforms Commission. Smt. Indira Gandhi had a love-hate relationship with it and, therefore, often bypassed the system. Rajiv Gandhi wanted radical changes. And yet the strongest monolithic structure is the administrative system, with or without the rusted iron frame of the administrative services. The fundamental question is, does the uniform administrative system for the take into account plurality, and is there space to administrative system take into account plurality, and is there space and place for flexibility and initiative? The answers to both questions are unfortunately in the negative. However, the tripartite balance of the administrative, executive, judiciary and legislative cannot be ignored in any discussion on plural cultures and monolithic structures.

Pertinently many analysts and observers have spoken about these issues and challenges, More than ever before there is a sizeable body of opinion which recommends a plurality of models for organizing and governing plural societies. A different intellectual framework emanating from within South Asian

(Indian) methods, cultures and knowledge systems must be used, both for analyzing the complex realities and the processes of change. In this exercise, it is evident that many conventional or derived notions will have to be given up. It is possible to do so, and the time is ripe for it. India has the great potential and human resource for it. The challenge is of a sensitive comprehension and a skillful harnessing of these multifaceted energies, of plural sources of creativity.

3

The Homogenised Other: Cultural Diversity and Social Inequality

Alan Mayne

Difference and disagreement, mediated by inclusiveness and respect for others, are essential elements in the ongoing social well-being and political stability of nation states. However in policy debate today, adjustments to the effects of globalisation[1] since the late twentieth century have downplayed these elements and entrenched a spurious consensus about the supposedly homogenising effects around the world of free market democracy.

Homogenisation, it seems, is breeding dangerous polarities within and across societies and nation states. On the one hand, conservative commentators in the developed world imply that the uneven effects of economic globalisation mirror deep-seated cultural and political differences between advanced and dysfunctional cultures and nation states. The invasion of Iraq, the war in Afghanistan, and the pressures for acculturation by Islamic communities within European nations (British Prime Minister Tony Blair, for example, recently told British Muslims that they had a 'duty to integrate' into British society[2]), are linked to such thinking. On the other hand, critics of globalisation in the developing world and policy makers in international agencies such as the United Nations and the World Bank contrast the lifestyles enjoyed by a handful of the super-rich with the poverty and oppression endured by the majority of the world's population. Mike Davis's recent book Planet of Slums, for example, argues that as a result of the neoliberal restructuring of third world economies since the late 1970s, the majority of the world's population now live in poverty, oppressed, dispossessed and starving in city slums.[3] Such unequal relationships create conditions for conflict by eroding life chances, and feeding mistrust and hatred.

Homogenising stereotypes about insiders and outsiders command public attention, but by polarising opinion they are unhelpful to policy debate and programme delivery that advance social well-being, political cohesion, and conflict resolution. By universalising disadvantage into an homogenised and downtrodden Other, they marginalise and disempower the diverse communities that hitherto have been hurt by globalisation under neo-liberalism, and whose active and constructive participation is now needed in order to build a global alliance of sustainable democratic societies.

In this paper, I will discuss how two homogenising stereotypes about entrenched economic disadvantage and cultural dysfunctionality are skewing effective policy making in Australia and India. In Australia, sensationalism about the supposed unsustainablility of remote Aboriginal communities and outstations is poisoning public knowledge about Aboriginal inequality and is narrowing public policy choices. In India, well-meaning public policy analysis that begins with the premise that one third of Indians are trapped in appalling slum conditions leads inevitably to policy choices that are just as circumscribed as those facing legislators who simplify Indigenous issues in Australia. Homogenised stereotypes of Australian desert communities and Indian slums obscure the wide diversity of experiences and of scenarios for grassroots change, and they fly in the face of clear evidence of resilience and capacity building at the local level. There are historical as well as social justice parallels between these two examples. The stereotyping of remote Aboriginal communities today echoes the 'slum stigma' that attached to poor immigrant districts in Australia's cities during the nineteenth and much of the twentieth century. It was easier then to homogenise and condemn these places as slums than it was to address the diverse causes and consequences of urban poverty. This history of social reform failure in Australia should be heeded by those who currently shape federal and state policy on Indigenous affairs and sustainable desert communities. It is a history that also has relevance for policy makers in Indian cities today, because it demonstrates how homogenised stereotypes of marginality and dysfunctionality – when applied either to city slums or rural outstations – frustrate progressive social reform.

Poverty, inadequate services and rudimentary infrastructure are real impediments to social wellbeing in India and Australia. Solutions to these problems are to be found by first acknowledging the diversity of local conditions and the multiplicity of common-sense grassroots responses to them, rather than by universalising the issues and imposing ill-considered and ill-fitting policies. Lasting solutions are to be found by setting aside homogenisations of difference and inadequacy so as to work in partnership with disadvantaged communities in order to identify real needs and lasting solutions.

These are global issues. Although in relative terms the percentage of people living in poverty around the world is falling, the absolute number of people in poverty is rising. Moreover the gap between rich and poor is widening. As Joseph Stiglitz (the former World Bank chief economist and Nobel-prize winning author of Globalisation and its Discontents, and Making Globalisation Work: The Next Steps to Global Justice) points out, notwithstanding the paper benefits of globalisation for the world economy as a whole, and the personal fortunes it has made for a few, it has made many people poorer.[4] The Guardian Weekly newspaper recently highlighted this disjunction. On the one hand, it said, 'Developing countries are experiencing a rapid emergence of a new elite of super-rich individuals as their economies expand and mature.' In India, for example, the number of 'super rich' has increased by 19 per cent over the past year. However facilities for healthcare and primary education have simultaneously deteriorated. Up to a third of Indians now live in extreme poverty and deprivation.[5] The World Bank defines extreme poverty as living on less than $US1 a day, and poverty as living on under $US2 a day. In the developing world as a whole – where some 80 per cent of the world's population lives – poverty has actually increased over the past two decades as a result of economic globalisation. Some 40 per cent of the world's population live in poverty.[6]

The United Nations General Assembly, in adopting the Millennium Declaration in September 2000, identified poverty abatement as the essential central plank of its vision for a new global order.[7] Neslon Mandela recently provided an eloquent justification for this global push to reduce poverty. 'Like slavery and apartheid', he said, 'poverty is not natural':

It is people who have made poverty and tolerate poverty, and it is people who will overcome it.

Overcoming poverty is not a gesture of charity. It is an act of justice. It is the protection of fundamental human rights. Everyone everywhere has the right to live with dignity, free from fear and oppression, free from hunger, and free to express himself or herself and associate at will.

Yet in this new century millions of people remain imprisoned, enslaved and in chains. Poverty and inequality are terrible scourges of our times – times in which the world also boasts breathtaking advances in science, technology, and wealth.

While poverty persists, there is no true freedom.[8]

The first target of the UN's Millennium Development Goals is to halve global poverty by 2015.[9] This objective is being actively pursued by the United Nations Human Settlements Programme (UN-HABITAT). The preamble to the UN-HABITAT Agenda begins:

We recognize the imperative need to improve the quality of human settlements, which profoundly affects the daily lives and well-being of our peoples. There is a sense of great opportunity and hope that a new world can be built, in which economic development, social development and environmental protection as interdependent and mutually reinforcing components of sustainable development can be realized through solidarity and cooperation within and between countries and through effective partnerships at all levels. International cooperation and universal solidarity, guided by the purposes and principles of the Charter of the United Nations, and in a spirit of partnership, are crucial to improving the quality of life of the peoples of the world.[10]

Poverty eradication on the scale envisioned by UN-HABITAT – spanning all human settlement types from tiny rural villages to large cities – is a huge undertaking. It requires the global mobilisation of will and resources. Oxfam calculated that to meet the health, education and sanitation targets of the UN Millennium Development Goals would require an extra $US48 Billion in aid a year.[11]

Much of this programme delivery must be channelled into disadvantaged rural communities. In Africa, for example, which Stiglitz calls the region most exploited by globalisation, the per cent age of people living in extreme poverty increased from 42 per cent in 1981 to 47 per cent in 2001.[12] In rural Bangladesh BRAC (the Bangladesh Rural Advancement Committee) and Muhammed Yunus' Grameen Bank have shown how local interventions in community health and education, and the provision of micro-credit facilities, can turn the tide of rural poverty. Later in this conference Dr. Priti Singh will highlight the socio-economic inequality experienced by tribal communities in India.

In Australia today public attention focuses on homogenised representations of outback Aboriginal communities. The best known is Wadeye (formerly known as Port Keats), a remote Aboriginal community of some 2,500 people located on the western edge of the Daly River reserve. It is the largest Aboriginal community in the Northern Territory. Last year the Age newspaper likened it to 'a Third World refugee camp', characterised by minimal education, an acute housing shortage, and gang violence that had turned the community into a 'war zone'.[13] The Sunday programme on national Australian television featured a sensationalist report by journalist Sarah Ferguson, who lived for two weeks 'among the gangs of Wadeye' to provide a supposedly 'unique insight into a community with third world living standards, in a first world country'. Ferguson focused selectively on 'the gang leaders, filming them in their homes, witnessing the aimless lives of young Aboriginal men obsessed with marijuana and the surprising influence of heavy metal music.'[14]

Another such place is Borroloola in the Northern Territory. The town is located almost 1,000 kilometres southeast of the capital city, Darwin. Borroloola and some 30 surrounding outstations comprise approximately 600 Aboriginal people and 200 Europeans. It has been called the remotest place in Australia. Borroloola services the big cattle stations, and a huge zinc mine that is owned by the global mining giant Xstrata. But there is little work on offer there for the local Aboriginal population.

Gordon Lansden is a leading elder at Borroloola. In frail health and with limited means, he currently lives in the town's health clinic. Gordon's outstation, the Yunnggurrie Outstation, is located about half an hour by car away from the town. Gordon is a talented Aboriginal artist. Two Qantas jumbo jets are vividly decorated with designs that are based upon Gordon's work. Yet he lives in relative poverty, bitter that others have profited from his talents. He has worked hard to establish a sustainable business enterprise for local artists.

Nancy McDinny and Stuart Hoosan are two other local artists in the Waralungku Arts Centre. Here they stand in the studio of their outstation, called Sandridge Outstation. Some of Stuart's paintings are on sale in city art galleries for $AUS20,000. But Stuart and Nancy both still qualify for income support through the CDP (Community Development Programme), which provides the financial backbone for most Aboriginal outstations. The Australian Government is currently tightening the eligibility requirements for receiving CDP in such remote Aboriginal communities. They claim it saps self-reliance, and that such settlements are too small and remote to be sustainable in the long term.

Notwithstanding the scale of entrenched inequality in rural communities in Outback Australia and around the world, the success or failure of the global War On Poverty will in very large part be determined in the world's cities. Urbanisation is accelerating, and today half the world lives in urban areas. Policy makers concede a paradox in this global urbanisation process. On the one hand, as the UN-HABITAT agenda recognises, 'During the course of history, urbanization has been associated with economic and social progress.... Cities and towns have been engines of growth and incubators of civilization'.[15] But on the other hand, policy makers identify social inequality within today's cities as the greatest impediment to poverty reduction. They identify city slums – which today comprise almost 900 million people – as the most visible and challenging outcome of urban growth. Jeffrey D. Sachs, Director of the UN Millennium Project, contends that 'The world's slums, arguably, constitute the greatest concentration of development deficits that cut across the Millennium Development Goals: poverty, education, gender inequality, child mortality, disease, degraded environments, and so on.'[16]

Several months ago Professor Gopal showed me one of these slums. It is close to IGNOU, and is bordered by a busy city highway. The men in this second settlement, Professor Gopal explained, were construction workers. They did not want their photographs taken because, they said – sternly but without personal animosity – others had taken them before but nothing for the good had resulted. This young woman reacted differently. 'Take my photograph' she said proudly, 'because I am young and beautiful'. Her child, however, hides his head in fear.

The problem with my description of this New Delhi slum and of the Borroloola outstations is that what I saw and how I reacted were shaped and constrained by the distorting lens of the homogenising stereotypes through which we recognise city 'slum' and rural 'outstation', and upon which we base our conclusions and recipes for social action.

Borroloola, notwithstanding most Australians' disdain for this remote and apparently ill-fated rural community, is a complex cultural crossing point where four Aboriginal language groups intersect and where the cultures of the interior dry lands overlap with those of the coastal lands and islands of the Gulf of

Carpentaria. The people of Borroloola are centred in a long established and multi-layered local cultural landscape. In Delhi, the complex social factors that have created the shanty camps are obscured by similar outside stereotypes, but in this large metropolis these stereotypes are expressed through the metaphor of the slum.

The Cities Alliance (launched in May 1999 by the World Bank and UN-HABITAT) argues that:

Hundreds of millions of urban poor in the developing and transitional world have few options but to live in squalid, unsafe environments where they face multiple threats to their health and security. Slums and squatter settlements lack the most basic infrastructure and services. Their populations are marginalised and largely disenfranchised. They are exposed to disease, crime and [are] vulnerable to natural disasters. Slums and squatter settlements are growing at alarming rates, projected to double in 25 years.

Slums are the products of failed policies, bad governance, corruption, inappropriate regulation, dysfunctional land markets, unresponsive financial systems, and a fundamental lack of political will. Each of these failures adds to the toll on people already deeply burdened by poverty and constrains the enormous opportunity for human development that urban life offers.[17]

The Cities Alliance, looking back at the history of urban growth, and looking forwards at the accumulating social costs of ongoing urban development, concludes that 'unless the squalid legacy of past neglect is rapidly addressed, the slums and squatter settlements in cities of the developing world are set to proliferate over the next 25 years in staggering dimensions – doubling in population by the year 2025.'[18] The Alliance has proposed an action plan that is designed to improve the lives of 100 million slum dwellers by 2020. This plan closely corresponds with UN goals. UN-HABITAT, for example, argues that 'The eradication of poverty is essential for sustainable human settlements.... particularly in the developing countries where poverty is acute, as well as the objective of enabling all women and men to attain secure and sustainable livelihoods through freely chosen and productive employment and work.'[19]

These are laudable objectives. They address acute social needs. But if the 'slum' is to be taken as the core element in this global plan for social action, what exactly do we mean by this term? City slums are often referred to as a measuring stick of the social imbalances that have been caused by globalisation. For example, Davis argues in Planet of Slums that residents of slums comprise only six per cent of city populations in developed countries, but that as a result of globalisation they comprise a staggering 78 per cent of city populations in the least developed countries of the world.[20]

A slum is defined in the Oxford English Dictionary as 'a thickly populated neighbourhood or district where the houses and the conditions of life are of a squalid and wretched character'.[21] According to the City Alliance, 'Slums are neglected parts of cities where housing and living conditions are appallingly poor. Slums range from high density, squalid central city tenements to spontaneous squatter settlements without legal recognition or rights, sprawling at the edge of cities. Some are more than fifty years old, some are land invasions just underway.'[22] The term 'slum' is today usually associated with the developing world, but the word originated in Britain during the early nineteenth century, and was used until the middle of the twentieth century to describe socially disadvantaged districts in the cities of the developed world.

When urbanisation began to transform British and North American society during the nineteenth century, policy debate about urban poverty in the core economies of the English-speaking world during this first wave of globalisation denied the need for fundamental social reform by inventing the slum and then blaming city problems on it and its inhabitants. Although the urban inequality that was produced by the global spread of capitalism during the nineteenth and twentieth centuries was of course real, the slum stigma that was attached to poor neighbourhoods was not, and impeded poverty eradication in Britain, North America, and my homeland, Australia. I elaborated upon this point in my 1993 book *The Imagined Slum*.[23]

In history, slums and 'slum-minded' people were not products of city growth. However concentrations of capital-starved people and capital-starved neighbourhoods were, and they posed fundamental social and ethical dilemmas for the hierarchy of class groupings that benefited from the urban transformation of society. Slums were therefore fashioned by a nineteenth-century narrative and visual genre which, triggered by the cleavages created by capitalist-influenced and urban-expressed global change, constructed slums as an outsider's prism for visualising people, places, and behaviours in terms of their apparent distance from the essentials of modernising cities and mainstream city culture. These homogenised slum depictions of a demonised Other bore little resemblance to the people and places they purported to describe.

The slum was created as a universalising caricature which masked the diverse outcomes of urban inequality by reducing them in the public's mind to a simple image of dysfunctionality and inappropriateness. The slum was necessarily represented as an abhorrent and dysfunctional realm, because it was fashioned as the antithesis of common sense understandings of decency, harmony, and utility in the modern city. It was fashioned thus because the slum genre sought to contain the diverse social contradictions and tensions that were created by urbanisation, by mobilising public opinion around core principles about individual and collective behaviour which purported to identify and explain the causes and effects of urban poverty, and which offered straightforward solutions for these social ills. Slums are thus representations of actuality, created by words and images, and achieved a spurious imaginary reality in the realms of public opinion and public policy. In so doing, they also achieved tangible (and deplorable) expression in heavy-handed slum-clearance, city 'improvement,' and 'renewal' projects which tore apart working-class neighbourhoods rather than empowering residents to improve them. Preventive and ameliorative poverty eradication measures were long delayed by this punitive obsession with slums.[24]

The history of slums is therefore to be traced through language and the inappropriate public policies that language shaped, rather than through the social geography of cities. The noun 'slum' originated as a slag term derived from 'slumber' in early nineteenth-century London, J.H. Vaux's Flash Dictionary (1812) defining it as an unsavoury back room, or a sleepy and unknown back alley. The word's meaning subsequently broadened, and during the second quarter of the century the word (often incorporated into the phrase 'back slum') became widely used to characterize entire London neighbourhoods of back streets and lanes. By mid century the term was being applied not only in London but in other British cities, in North America, and Australia. Charles Dickens, who visited the United States in 1841, compared New York's Five Points with London's notorious St Giles. The adjective 'slummy' also derived from nineteenth-century British usage, and referred both to slum conditions and to the narrative forms which sensationalised them. The noun 'slummer' (and hence the verb 'slumming') gained currency in both Britain and the United States during the 1880s and 1890s to describe slum tours by middle class reformers and (increasingly) tourists.

H.J. Dyos (the founder of modern urban history) sought to overcome the epistemological contradiction of applying this slum construct to the actual social geography of cities when, in his widely influential 'The Slums of Victorian London,' he sought to differentiate between factual accounts of slums (which he said were grounded in serious-minded reform), and fictitious accounts (which he dismissed as being grounded in frivolous entertainment).[25] But as Anthony Wohl noted perceptively in a later appraisal of London's slums, the fictions and the descriptions were all woven into the same slum genre of theatrical performance.[26] The essence of all slum performances – from reform polemic to melodramatic novel – is the homogenising theatricality with which they were presented, rather than the spurious 'factual' content which they contained. Theatricality commanded attention and thereby sought to shape public opinion. A master of the genre, Charles Dickens, called this power 'the attraction of repulsion.'[27]

'Slummy' performances such as Dickens' simplified social tensions and their supposed remedies and mobilised public opinion in response to these issues. They entertained, and in entertaining they simultaneously provided a recipe to guide individual and collective behaviour. Dickens applied this recipe well when he theatrically depicted New York's Five Points as a moral abyss in 1842.[28] So too did Jacob Riis half a century later, when he combined words and images to represent Five Points as a slumland blot, and invited his audiences to imagine thereby 'how the other half lives.'[29] Reformers and entertainers around the world echoed and standardized this approach until its potency in the 'advanced world' – the credibility gap between assertions of slumland reality and independent public knowledge of urban actualities stretched impossibly wide – began to erode during the middle of the twentieth century. It was replaced by other theatrical tropes which sought more effectively to modulate opinion.[30]

In Australia, Britain, and North America, 'slum' was replaced by other homogenising stereotypes of marginality. In the cities this became the immigrant ghetto or enclave (which in Australia during the 1980s was used by Prime Minister Howard, then in Opposition, as the basis on which to attack multiculturalism). In the countryside (or rather, in urban Australia's imaginings of rural society) the stereotype became that of the dying country town and increasingly the desert outstation.

In the developed world today 'slum' is applied only to the so-called 'third world', and to a bygone era in their own history. Tellingly Davis drew upon that era in his reformist polemic Planet of Slums, explicitly echoing the great nineteenth-century slum entertainer Dickens. Davis argued that 'neoliberal capitalism since 1970 has multiplied Dickens's notorious slum of Tom-all-Alone's in Bleak House by exponential powers.'[31] But Dickens' slum, as we have seen, was not an accurate description of urban poverty; it was an homogenised caricature of it. Davis in not alone in his misunderstanding of Dickens' representations of slums. Historians have perpetuated the slum myth, notwithstanding its disappearance from domestic policy debate and from popular entertainment. Mesmerised by the dramatic intensity of the caricatures that remain embedded in the documentary record from the past, historians insisted that 'the essence of slums was their "environmental reality".'[32] They have confused and thereby inadequately conflated the imagined reality of slums with the actualities of working class neighbourhoods that were labelled in this way. These histories underpin a positivist viewpoint that champions the progressive development of democratic free enterprise societies. Such societies, it is asserted, matured from hard times in the past to an across-the-board sharing of wealth in the present. By highlighting the early social costs of industrialisation and urbanisation during the 'take-off' phase of a developing society, these histories emphasise the longer-term ameliorating effects of modernisation, integration, and increasing affluence upon society.

This viewpoint is anchored in the 1920s perspectives of University of Chicago sociologists, who argued that cities comprise a system of ecological areas that include a central slumland 'zone of deterioration' comprising 'submerged regions of poverty, degradation, and disease, and their underworlds of crime and vice,' within which the more resourceful of recent migrants to the city shed the inappropriate cultural residues of the societies they had come from, adjusted to American life, assimilated, and moved from the unstable slumland zone into the metropolitan mainstream.[33] Other sociologists in the middle of the twentieth century gave this deviant way of life an evocative name: the culture of poverty.[34] These characterisations of slum culture not only homogenise social life into a universal stereotype of deviant 'slum-minded' behaviour; in doing so they also preclude recognition of non-pathological energy and strategy among the inhabitants of the supposed slums. The effect of present-day histories that perpetuate these older academic mindsets is to suspend critical judgment today about the uneven consequences of globalisation by implying that 'Third World' slums will also wither if benign 'First World' trading cartels and democratic 'coalitions of the willing' hold sway.

These histories have done a huge disservice to efforts more fully to understand the urban past. They have perpetuated a set of clichés which homogenise and trivialise the diversity and fluidity of city neighbourhoods. They subsume the particularities (and the underlying human scale) of actual places within an abstraction of urban disequilibrium and menace. They drain the savviness and adroitness from working-class culture, and marginalise the neighbourhoods within which these robust cultures thrived as supposedly aberrant and destabilising elements within modern cities. These characterizations are deceits. It is poor history to conflate 'slum' (an imaginary overlay which is properly studied in relation to urban popular culture) and the actual social geography of urban disadvantage. To study the first is to study the bourgeois imagination, and the complicated control and reform agendas pursued in order to comprehend and regulate an urbanising world. To study the second requires us to set aside these agendas and frameworks, because otherwise this cultural overlay obscures our vision of actual people and places.[35]

Recent collaborations between historians and archaeologists have begun to puncture outside stereotypes about slums in order to investigate the obscured inside world of poor neighbourhoods that existed during the nineteenth and early twentieth centuries. With my colleague Tim Murray, professor of historical archaeology at La Trobe University in Melbourne, Australia, I published the results of such studies in The Archaeology of Urban Landscapes: Explorations in Slumland, which contains case studies from Britain, the US, Canada, South Africa, and Australia.[36] These reveal poor but diverse and resilient communities that suffered from official neglect or coercive over-regulation and 'renewal'.

One of these case studies is that of the central-city district once known as 'Little Lon' in Melbourne, Australia. This neighbourhood had been notorious since the nineteenth century and was called Melbourne's most infamous slum. The Age newspaper characterised it in 1931 as 'the heart of slumdom'.[37] The

Little Lon precinct was compulsorily resumed by the Australian Federal Government in 1948 in order to undertake what the Sun newspaper had advocated since the early 1940s as a 'slum penetrating' scheme of city redevelopment.[38] Two thirds of the resumed area was rebuilt during the next half century. In 2002, with redevelopment of the remaining portion pending, an opportunity was offered to examine the archaeological imprint of this last fragment of Little Lon. The resulting project showcased the interweaving of archaeological and historical analysis in order to provide a subtle ethnographic interpretation of a long-vanished working-class community.[39]

No historical attention had previously been paid to this micro-area. It seemed an unlikely site for historical research because almost nothing remained of the built environment to trigger historical questions. Most of the study area had been levelled long ago to make a car park. What buildings once stood here? What sorts of people had lived and worked in them?

The first of these questions was relatively easy to answer by delving into land title records, rate books, post office directories, and allotment plans. During the third quarter of the nineteenth century the study area was transformed from a city-edge community into a densely built inner-city precinct. During the first half of the twentieth century the district gradually unravelled as a residential district as homes were replaced by factories and offices.

The second question was much harder to answer. In order to tease out the details of a social landscape that had effectively vanished by the late 1930s it was necessary to integrate historical and archaeological data. This was no easy task. The excavations uncovered many domestic artefacts that subsequent analysis was unable to locate within a clear explanatory historical context. On the other hand, there were cases where individual and family lives could be traced in documentary records but could not be correlated with archaeological evidence from the sites where they had once lived.

As excavation and analysis proceeded the old slum myths unravelled. Informed by our findings, today's newspapers ran very different story lines to those that they had published about Little Lon during the early twentieth century. The Herald Sun commented: 'History books show that the area known as "Little Lon" was once Melbourne's sleazy red-light district. But physical evidence uncovered during a six-week archaeological dig shows a vibrant ethnic community where families shared the dark laneways with prostitutes'.[40] The Age concurred, noting that the investigators had found 'a past far richer than the designation "slum" suggests'.[41] Richer, that is, in its social complexity than had previously been imagined. Little Lon was no workers' paradise, but neither was it a changeless and marginalized place of social outcasts.

Slum myth notwithstanding, Little Lon had not been a socially homogenous place of universal and grinding poverty. A diversity of manual occupations were represented, skilled and unskilled, manual and small-scale entrepreneurial.

Children from labouring families – if they survived childhood in this insanitary place – often moved into skilled trades and the professions. Tenants lived alongside owner-occupiers, and landlords often lived close at hand.

This is not to downplay disadvantage. The homes in Little Lon were humble: two main rooms was typical. The houses were valued low by municipal rate assessors. They formed the bottom of the city's rental housing market. Many of their occupants knew economic hardship. In 1905 Elizabeth Booth, who operated a brothel in neighbourhood, explained to police that she did so because of 'having a large family to support and my Husband lying in a dying state in the Hospital'.[42] These small houses were crammed with people. In 1892 the principal tenant of one such house was fined 'for allowing twelve people to sleep in one room, seven in each bedroom, and three or four in two other rooms'.[43] The occupants were Indians. Facilities for hygiene – running water, waste removal – were basic. Rear yards held over-flowing cesspits, and rubbish was disposed beneath the floors.

Although Little Lon was a poor neighbourhood, it was not an unstable community. It did not correspond with slummer stereotypes. Rapid changeover of tenants in some properties was balanced by long sequences of continuity in others. Many of the owner-occupiers who settled here during the third quarter of the nineteenth century remained here until their deaths. Although there was a continual flow of people through the houses, movement was often between houses in the same street and within the local neighbourhood. Long-term residents maintained neighbourhood continuity and cohesion. They represented the community in times of distress (serving as jurors, for example, in local inquests). Local support networks were based in part upon kin. These networks were sustained as well by neighbourliness. When one long-term resident, David Cunningham, wrote his will in 1879, he knocked on the nearby doors of friends to have the document witnessed.[44]

Neither did Little Lon comprise a distinct and deviant subculture of poverty. There is no evidence to support outsiders' slummer allegations of endemic violence and criminality, although it was certainly – in part – a noisy, rowdy, and rule-breaking community. Police Commissioner John Sadleir commented in 1874 that the area 'always has been a low neighbourhood', and Senior Constable Patrick Drum noted in 1882 that the local inhabitants were 'a low rough lot of people'.[45] But these are outsiders' characterisations. Little Lon was equally a place where young immigrant couples settled and raised families. Mary Toomey and her husband Daniel, a labourer, emigrants from Ireland, rented a small wooden house in the neighbourhood between 1864 and 1867. They squeezed into its two main rooms with their four small children. When they moved, the house was occupied by William Pugh, a painter from Londonderry, newly married to Jane Donaghy. They lived here until 1871, by which time they too had four small children. William Jobb, a blacksmith, rented the house during the early 1870s. He and his wife Eliza, from Londonderry, had lived just around the corner during the late 1860s, and in 1876 moved into another nearby house before moving out of the neighbourhood to settle in the suburbs with their three young sons. These family micro-histories encapsulate the actualities of daily neighbourhood life.

Little Lon was not a slum. Yes, it was poor. It was also resilient and resourceful. This was a community constrained by economic disadvantage, but its residents were not passive victims of poverty. They devised strategies to survive within those constraints, and – by maximising their meagre assets – in some measure to subvert them.

This revisionist historical critique of slums, which is highlighted using the example of Melbourne's Little Lon, is beginning to reformulate historical understanding of urban poverty and social policy during the first wave of globalisation in the nineteenth and twentieth centuries. It has had no impact at all upon policy debate about poverty and poverty abatement during the second wave of globalisation in the late-twentieth and early twenty-first centuries. The homogenous slum concept continues to dominate UN poverty abatement strategies. This is highlighted by the global Cities Alliance that was developed by the World Bank and UN-HABITAT in order to realise the Millennium Development Goals. The Alliance's reform programme is called 'Cities Without Slums'.

It could be argued that the new historical perspective needs to be applied to present-day policy debate about poverty eradication in order to counteract negative and disempowering slum stereotypes, and thus assist in developing poverty eradication programmes that engage with, rather than impose upon, disadvantaged city neighbourhoods and rural communities. According to this line of argument, the inadequacies inherent in conventional characterisations of slums necessitates that understanding of the term be radically reformulated. The word 'slum' was coined and has been so heavily used in order to condemn, to marginalize, to ridicule, to rebuke, and thereby to avoid fundamental reform, that these purposes are perhaps irreversibly embedded in the word's essence. They cannot easily be stripped away in order to use the word as a neutral scientific term with which to describe the actual social geography of urban disadvantage, and with which to pursue an effective reform agenda.

This line of argument is given strength by recent events in Mumbai, where in 2005 the Government of Maharashtra – in an apparent carbon copy of urban 'renewal' schemes during the nineteenth and twentieth centuries – embarked upon a slum clearance programme that destroyed some 30,000 homes before the programme stalled in the face of mounting protests. The Cities Alliance concluded that this slum clearance programme had badly compromised Mumbai's hitherto good reputation for 'its flexible, pro-poor approach', and threatened to withdraw its support in Mumbai if the scheme is resumed.[46]

Anna Tibaijuka, the Executive Director of UN-HABITAT, suggests that the Cities Alliance's Cities without Slums initiative has 'enhanced the visibility of slum dwellers' in present day poverty eradication programmes.[47] However the mixed messages that come from events in Mumbai require us to consider carefully whether the visibility of the 'slum' in today's reform agendas has a progressive or a regressive influence upon reform efforts to build sustainable human settlements.

It is encouraging that core principles in today's poverty programmes do explicitly reject concepts that in the past formed the basis of thinking about slum problems and slum reform. The complicated diversity of conditions within poor neighbourhoods, for example, is starting to receive attention.[48] The Cities without Slums action plan calls for 'Reversing slum eradication and "urban renewal" policies'. In their place it advocates the 'Central commitment, role, ownership and responsibility and commitment of the slum residents and community' in the upgrading of disadvantaged neighbourhoods.[49] This upgrading is to be achieved by installing or upgrading basic community infrastructure; by improving health, education, and security; and by providing micro credit – as BRAC and Muhammed Yunus' Grameen Bank are doing in Bangladesh – in order to build up depleted social capital at the community grassroots. The action plan insists that these initiatives must be 'undertaken cooperatively and locally among citizens, community groups, businesses and local authorities.'[50] The Cities Alliance cautions that the harnessing of local grassroots initiatives to the achievement of the UN's Millennium Development Goals 'is only possible when local governments are empowered with the necessary policy responsibility, authority and resources within a clear and supportive national framework.'[51] Ethical and effective governance is clearly a crucial mechanism for fundamental social reform. However the key question to be resolved in the Cities without Slums approach – and more broadly in the War on Poverty – is whether highly visible but homogenising and disempowering concepts such as slum help or hinder positive engagement between local community groups, local and national governments, and non-government agencies.

In my opinion they do not. This is in part because they cannot usefully engage with the diversity of local conditions in which rural and urban poverty is expressed. Still more so, it is because they disregard the energy of local people and the efficacy of local knowledge systems. They are deaf to the voices of the poor. Overturning this denial of grassroots agency was recently identified by Stiglitz as a key strategy for making globalisation really work. He cites a World Bank survey Voices of the Poor, which emphasised the sense of powerlessness that was felt by the 60,000 people who were interviewed. This powerlessness resulted not from their passivity, but from disregard of their voices and actions. Stiglitz says of these people: 'Unsurprisingly, they stressed not just their inadequate income but their feelings of insecurity and powerlessness. Those without jobs, especially, felt marginalized, shunted aside by their societies.'[52] Stiglitz applauds interventions at a local level by agencies such as BRAC, the Grameen Bank, and the World Bank's programme for local communities, because they acknowledge grassroots resourcefulness and empower local people to act. They harness local knowledge and local energy. 'What makes their programs so successful', Stiglitz reflects, 'is that they come out of the communities that they service and address the needs of the people in those communities.'[53]

In India the voices of the poor are being asserted by organizations such as the National Slum Dwellers' Federation (established 1974), the Society for the Promotion of Area Resource Centres (established 1984), and Mahila Milan (established 1986). All of these organizations emerged as the result of mobilisation within poor communities in Mumbai in reaction to inappropriate slum programmes. These Indian organizations now play an important part in Slum/Shack Dwellers International, a global network of people's organizations.

In Australia Aboriginal voices are likewise asserting local identity in reaction to the homogenising stereotypes about Outback marginality and despair. The Waralungku Arts Centre is a good example. The Centre is housed in a recycled doctor's clinic. It is an unremarkable building in a supposedly remote and blighted town. The remarkability of this place derives from the diverse local story lines that are being translated here into paint. The Waralungku art movement style accelerated during the 1990s after artists such as Gordon Lansden abandoned the European town of Borroloola and established their own outstations in their traditional homelands. One of the characteristics of the Waralungku art style is its eclectic quality. Nancy McDinny's paintings, for example, range from stylised representations of traditional Aboriginal food gathering to historical snapshots of the Macassan trade and European settlement that tap into family memory. Another characteristic of Waralungku art is its self-belief, its pride in place. A pioneer of the Waralungku art style, the late Dinny McDinny, commented just before his death in 2002 that 'These are paintings of the country where we live'.[54] Gordon calls this approach 'telling about the country'. He means 'our country', and he is confident that the world is paying attention. By telling these stories the artists centre the marginalised Other.

The UN-HABITAT agenda advises correctly that:

Sustainable human settlements development requires the active engagement of civil society organizations, as well as the broad-based participation of all people. It equally requires responsive, transparent and accountable government at the local level. Civic engagement and responsible government both necessitate the establishment and strengthening of participatory mechanisms, including access to justice and community-based action planning, which will ensure that all voices are heard in identifying problems and priorities, setting goals, exercising legal rights, determining service standards, mobilizing resources and implementing policies, programmes and projects.[55]

Historically throughout both the first and second waves of globalisation, the homogenisation of social disadvantage in public understanding has stood in the way of achieving these mechanisms for fundamental and enduring social reform both in rural and urban societies. This is evident both in Australia and India. The challenge for us today is to avoid the mistakes of the past.

Endnotes

1. Joseph Stiglitz writes: 'Globalization encompasses many things: the international flow of ideas and knowledge, the sharing of cultures, global civil society, and the global environmental movement. This book, however, is mostly about economic globalization, which entails the closer economic integration of the countries of the world through the increased flow of goods and services, capital, and even labour.' Joseph Stiglitz, *Making Globalisation Work: The Next Steps to Global Justice* (London: Allen Lane, 2006), p. 4.
2. *Guardian Weekly*, 15–21 December 2006, p. 10.
3. Mike Davis, *Planet of Slums* (London and New York: Verso, 2006); see review in *Guardian Weekly*, 1–7 September 2006, p. 25.
4. See Ibid, 15–21 September 2006; also 29 September-5 October 2006.
5. Ibid, 16–22 June 2006.
6. Stiglitz, *Making Globalisation Work*, pp. 10–11.
7. United Nations General Assembly, 55th session, 55/2 (18 September 2000). See also Asian Development Bank, *Poverty and Environment Fund* (June 2003).
8. *Guardian Weekly*, 10–16 November 2006, 'While poverty persists, there is no freedom' p. 17.
9. *UN Millennium Development Goals* (http://www.un.org/millenniumgoals).
10. UN-HABITAT, *The Habitat Agenda Goals and Principles, Commitments and the Global Plan of Action* (http://www.unhabitat.org/declarations/habitat_agenda.htm), clause 1.
11. *Guardian Weekly*, 8–14 September 2006.
12. Stiglitz, *Making Globalisation Work*, p. 11.
13. *Age*, 23 May 2006, 'Hate stalks a community where gangs rule roost'.
14. 'Inside the gangs of Wadeye', *Sunday*, 30 July 2006, available at http://sunday.ninemsn.com.au/sunday/cover_stories/article_2034.asp.
15. UN-HABITAT, *The Habitat Agenda*, clause 7.
16. Cities Alliance: Cities Without Slums, *2005 Annual Report*, p. 14.
17. World Bank and UN-HABITAT, *Cities Alliance for Cities Without Slums*, p. 1.
18. Ibid, p. 5.
19. UN-HABITAT, *The Habitat Agenda*, clauses 2, 28.
20. See review in *Guardian Weekly*, 1–7 September 2006, p. 25.
21. *The Oxford English Dictionary*, s.v. slum.
22. World Bank and UN-HABITAT, *Cities Alliance for Cities Without Slums*, p. 1.
23. Alan Mayne, *The Imagined Slum: Newspaper Representation in Three Cities, 1870–1914* (Leicester: University of Leicester Press, 1993).

24. See Alan Mayne, 'A Just War: The Language of Slum Representation in Twentieth-Century Australia', *Journal of Urban History*, vol. 22, no. 1, 1995, pp. 75–107.
25. H.J. Dyos, 'The Slums of Victorian London', *Victorian Studies*, vol. 11, 1967, pp. 5–40.
26. Anthony S. Wohl, 'Social Explorations Among the London Poor: Theatre or Laboratory?' *Revue Francaise de Civilisation Britannique*, vol. 6, 1991, pp. 76–97.
27. Ibid, p. 89.
28. Charles Dickens, *The Works of Charles Dickens*. Volume 1: *American Notes*. London: Chapman & Hale; and Henry Frowde. (New York: Oxford University Press, n.d. [first published 1842]).
29. Jacob A. Riis, *How the Other Half Lives: Studies among the Tenements of New York* (New York: Dover, 1971 [first published 1890]).
30. See Sam Bass Warner Jr's overlooked piece 'The Management of Multiple Urban Images' in Derek Fraser and Anthony Sutcliffe, eds., *The Pursuit of Urban History* (London: Edward Arnold,, 1983), pp. 383–394.
31. Davis, *Planet of Slums*, p. 23.
32. S. Martin Gaskell, *Slums* (Leicester: Leicester University Press, 1990), p. 1.
33. See Robert E. Park, Ernest W. Burgess and Roderick D. McKenzie, *The City* (Chicago: University of Chicago Press, 1967 [first published 1925]), 54–55). See also Robert E. Park and Herbert A. Miller, *Old World Traits Transplanted* (New York: Arno Press and New York Times, 1969 [first published 1921]).
34. See Oscar Lewis' seminal works *Five Families* (1959), *The Children of Sanchez* (1961), and *La Vida* (1966).
35. See Mayne, *The Imagined Slum*; also Alan Mayne, 'A barefoot childhood: so what? Imagining slums and reading neighbourhoods', *Urban History*, vol. 22, no. 3, 1995, pp. 404–413; Alan Mayne, 'On the Edge of History', *Journal of Urban History*, vol. 26, no. 2, 2000, pp. 249–258; Alan Mayne, 'Tall tales but True? New York's "Five Points" Slum, *Journal of Urban History*, vol. 33, no. 2, January 2007, pp. 320–331.
36. Alan Mayne and Tim Murray (eds.), *The Archaeology of Urban Landscapes: Explorations in Slumland* (Cambridge: Cambridge University Press, 2001).
37. *The Age*, 3 January 1931, quoted in Alan Mayne and Tim Murray, '"In Little Lon … Wiv Ginger Mick": Telling the Forgotten History of a Vanished Community', *Journal of Popular Culture*, vol. 33, no. 1, Summer 1999, pp. 49–60.
38. *Sun*, 12 March 1943, quoted in Ibid.
39. Tim Murray and Alan Mayne, 'Casselden Place Development Archaeological Works, Final Interpretative Report'. Prepared for Godden Mackay Logan Pty Ltd in association with Archaeology Program La Trobe University and Austral Archaeology Pty Ltd (December 2004). See also Alan Mayne and Susan Lawrence, 'Ethnographies of Place: A New Urban History Research Agenda', *Urban History*, vol. 26, part 3, 1999, pp. 325–348; Alan Mayne, Tim Murray and Susan Lawrence, 'Historic Sites: Melbourne's "Little Lon"', *Australian Historical Studies*, vol. 31, no. 113, 2000, pp. 131–151.
40. *Herald Sun*, 6 July 2002.
41. *Age*, 2 June 2002.

42. Letter by Elizabeth Booth, 30 March 1905, Police Files, VPRS 807, Bundle 2, Unit 1198, Public Record Office Victoria.
43. Town Clerk's files, quoted in Justin McCarthy, *Archaeological Investigation: Commonwealth Offices and Telecom Corporate Building Sites. The Commonwealth Block, Melbourne, Victoria*, volume 1 (Melbourne: Commonwealth Department of Administrative Services and Telecom Australia, 1989), p. 80.
44. Will and probate papers for David Cunningham, VPRS 7591/P2, unit 49; VPRS 28/P0, unit 224, Public Record Office Victoria.
45. Memo by Police Commissioner John Sadleir, 19 August 1874, Inward Correspondence to the Chief Commissioner of Police, VPRS 937, Unit 296, Bundle 1; Report by Senior Constable Patrick Drum, 12 April 1882, Inward Correspondence to the Chief Commissioner of Police, VPRS 937, Unit 306, Bundle 3, Public Record Office Victoria.
46. Cities Alliance: Cities Without Slums, *2005 Annual Report*, pp. 36–37. An alternative resettlement approach is described in Sheela Patel, Celine d'Cruz and Sundar Burra, 'Beyond evictions in a global city: people-managed resettlement in Mumbai', *Environment & Urbanization*, vol. 14 no. 1, April 2002, pp. 159–172.
47. Cities Alliance: Cities Without Slums, *2005 Annual Report*, p. 67.
48. See Robert Neuwirth, *Shadow Cities: A Billion Squatters, a New Urban World* (New York: Routledge, 2005).
49. World Bank and UN-HABITAT, *Cities Alliance for Cities Without Slums*, p. 8.
50. Ibid, p. 2.
51. Cities Alliance: Cities Without Slums, *2005 Annual Report*, p. 14.
52. Stiglitz, *Making Globalisation Work*, p. 11.
53. Ibid, p. 52.
54. *Northern Territory News*, 10 August 2002, 'Artists capture images of home'.
55. UN-HABITAT, *The Habitat Agenda*, clause 181.

4

Deliberative Democracy and Modern Pluralism

Subrata Mukherjee

Theories of deliberative democracy are about a democratic system that deliberates to the extent 'that the decisions it reaches reflect open discussion among the participants, with people ready to listen to the views and consider the interests of others, and modify their own opinions accordingly' (Miller 2000:3). The thrust is on will of the people and human rationality. Accepting the societal character of human beings in the Aristotelian sense it emphasises on commonality transcending narrow selfish individualism culminating in a loosely defined aspiration of common good. Putting a high premium on public deliberation it enlarges the public domain of democracy by highlighting virtues of active participation leading to proper filtering of rational legislation, an increased arena of self governance, a large legitimisation process in the context of indirect mass democracies of today and in emphasizing the need of a larger consensual framework of policy framework and execution in the context of public apathy and alienation that exists in all mature democracies, without disturbing plurality and divergence. In deliberative democracy decisions are taken wholly by consensus. It accepts the premise that there would be conflict regarding political preferences, which the democratic institutions have to resolve through an open and un-coerced discussion. Unlike liberal democracy that gives importance to individuals' distinct preferences, deliberative democracy maintains that a person is rational enough to set aside particular interests and opinions to aspire for fairness and the common interests of the collectivity. It values the manner of open discussion that hears all points of view and reaches a decision, which differs from the procedure of majority rule of liberal democracy. For deliberative democracy to work well, people must exercise democratic self-restraint and "must think it very important that the decision reached should be genuinely democratic one than that it is the decision that they themselves favour" (Miller 2000:22).

The umbrella ideology of deliberative democracy, as there are many differences amongst its chief protagonists, reflects an important component of modern liberal theorising since the 1980s. It is a theory that concentrates on refining the familiar framework of liberal democracy. Deliberative democracy is a normative theory with an intention to influence the actual political process by improving the popular input into policy by making it as broad based as possible. However, about its popular appeal, feasibility or desirability there are a very large number of unanswered questions. What constitutes public deliberation and how it is to be carried out? The pluralists are clear about a rough parity of groups leading to a large degree of competition between groups, which ultimately leads to a filtering of policy in which all the major groups participate, deliberate, bargain and compromise leading to some kind of a consensual policy framework. But the deliberative democratic theory is silent about the nature and content of public participation in the context of mass democracies of today with all their complexities, diversities, inequalities and technical details, for which an average citizen neither has the inclination, time or expertise to deliberate carefully and judiciously. It is also not very clear about the process of arriving at a consensus in a situation of heterogeneity of interests in the contemporary world. Deliberative democracy has no clear-cut answer to a proper framework of power sharing or to provide a framework to deal with the problem of a permanent majority and a permanent minority in the political order with deep cleavages.

One very important ingredient of a new political theory is rejection of the older theories and dissatisfaction triggered by a crisis. Both these dimensions are there in the origin of deliberative democratic theory. Till the 1970s in the US, the liberal democratic theory emerged out of sociological and economic dimensions. Because of the domination of Dahl's polyarchy and Schumpeter's democratic elitism, under the overall sway of the behavioural revolution, the applied side of democratic theory flourished with emphasis on the nature of the political parties; interest group politics, the role of the media and voting behaviour were the important subject matters of democratic theory.

Development being relegated as a Third world problem, with projections of an affluent society, or a post industrial society, the idea of common good or republican virtue remained confined to the writings of Dewey and Arendt rather than dominating a large segment to be termed as a school of thought. But the Vietnam War, the 1968 student revolt, and the impact of civil rights movement signalled a shift in the academic perception leading to the rise of the neo-conservatism, which slowly consolidates as the left of centre perception. They focus not only on the actual political functioning but also raise normative questions of participation, quality of life, post materialist values, a resurrection of Jeffersonian brand of idealised self-governing democracy and the desire for a consensual form of democracy inspired by the Swedish model. Rawls' seminal work *A Theory of Justice* (1971) revives interest in the older form of grand theorising by raising normative questions. The critical literature that emerges out of Rawls' work and the subsequent Rawls' approval for deliberative democracy led to its formulation.

It is Joseph Basette (1994) who coins the phrase 'deliberative democracy' to provide a critique to the elitist or aristocratic interpretation of the US constitution by questioning endemic conflict and competing interests and bargaining, the basis for the popular rational choice theory and the institutional arrangement of a minimal state as articulated by Nozick in the *Anarchy, State and Utopia* (1974) and the New Right economists like Friedman and Hayek. In addition, the emphasis on negative liberty of atomised individuals, the civil culture projection of dangers of enthusiastic participation and the need for control and balance with dangers of overload also led to the discovery of the virtues of direct democracy like small group initiative, new social movements[1], democracy at work place, reviving the spirit of the guild socialists like G.D.H. Cole. The unity of the deliberative democratic theorists lie in a belief that the political process has an autonomy of its own and has to be analysed much beyond the competitive bargaining of Hobbesian individuals. The rejection of the rational choice paradigm[2] inevitably leads to the key question of the demarcation between the political behaviour of the political man from the economic man of the market. A derivative of the rational choice theory is Social Choice Theory, which postulates that a rational individual with a desire of collective decision chooses that course of action that is most likely to realise one's goals. Rationality is about the means employed for one's preferred ends. It is the individual who is taken as the basic unit of analysis so even when the focus is on a group. Social Choice Theory like classic pluralism accepts conflicts as inevitable among self-interested political actors and democracy with electoral competition but do not share with the pluralist stress on group. Mancur Olson sees a serious flaw in pluralist approach: "groups are supposed to act to advance the common interests of the individual who compose them but among these interest is the economic one to minimise costs required to provide resources for the group as a whole, so that each individual will try to avoid incurring these costs and will not voluntarily make any sacrifices to help them attain its political (public or collective) objectives" (1971:126).

The general framework of deliberative theory emphasizes on civic virtue, which means that political activity is a public act beyond the category of private preferences and gains. The deliberative democratic theorists emphasize on the market (the private sphere) and politics (the public arena) and refer to the ideals of J.S. Mill and Arendt. Elster focuses on two aspects: (a) the capacity and motivation to go beyond one's own market or economic interest and (b) from this civic standpoint deliberation is defensible only if political decision-making helps to achieve common ends. The first pre-requisite is validated by the second proposition that an act of this kind can be propagated and defended only if it helps in achieving common purposes.

Harbermas desires to combine the spirit of civic republicanism with liberalism emphasizing the participatory characteristics of democracy with due emphasis on institutions and legality. He tries to link political power with the rule of law. In an attempt to incorporate the radical democratic ideals of the French Revolution with the mass democracies of today he resurrects the notion of popular sovereignty by a network of broad and widely dispersed 'subject-less communication' which would reflect an autonomous public sphere with the constitutional decision-making process. Joshua Cohen links political legitimacy to an ideal consensus that would emerge out of free and reasoned deliberation and agreement among equals centring around common good within the specificity of procedural standards like freedom and lack of coercion, both formal and substantive equality of participants with preservation of individual autonomy but with enough safeguards against objectionable outcomes. This suitable procedure will lead to outcomes, which will be broadly acceptable, enduring, just and feasible, institutionally with mediating offshoots of a constitutional democracy like voting and a competitive party system. Procedure is of great importance as it standardises the nature and content of deliberation, eliminating the possibility of a realistic or metaphysical notion of common good dominating the discourse. A decision-making process for Cohen must exhibit sufficient evidence for ensuring correct political judgement and the need for a proper co-ordinated machinery to synchronise deliberation and democratic decision-making. However, there is considerable disagreement among the theorists of deliberative democracy about the ideal procedure. Some emphasise linkage between deliberative democratic theory and rational choice theory whereas others resurrect Condercet's jury theorem[3] , which coordinates voting analysis with deliberative theory.

Rawls dissects the relationship between deliberation and common good, which subordinates individual preferences and proposals. For Rawls the major obstacle to deliberation does not lie in pursuance of private interest but in the wide divergence between what constitutes common good and a just world. Relying on plain truth and 'duty of civility' Rawls emphasizes consensus based on shared values, which in spite of alternative views will be acceptable to all. He also emphasises the formal democratic mechanism. Public reason depends on mutual reciprocity in a pluralistic world. In response to his communitarian and republican critics he wrestles with the problem of cultural heterogeneity within liberal states in *Political Liberalism* (1993). Despite variances in their personal views and in accepting the public-private divide that is crucial to the liberal theory, Rawls formulates the political as latent in the public culture of a democratic and plural society and applies the conception to the basic structure. He stresses the variety, diversity and unending competition of ideals and languages in human societies and believes with help of reason one could reach an overlapping consensus both with regard to the diverse views and also about the political conception. Political conception is different from comprehensive religious, philosophical or moral doctrines and the latter are excluded from public deliberations on justice given the pluralistic nature and the presence of incommensurable version of human good in modern societies. He considers reason as an attribute of all free and autonomous citizens. Contending parties would sort out rival claims on the basis of certain neutral values likes impartiality, consistency and equal opportunity. Justice as fairness remains the main procedural value in an adversarial process where neither side debates and is in a position to impose its moral convictions on the rest of society by force. In the *Law of Peoples: The Idea of Public Reason Revisited* (1999) he extends the argument to the global society with the intention of working out principles of justice that liberal and non-liberal people can agree upon to govern their international relations and are tolerant of people with different moral and political traditions. In *Political Liberalism* he had already emphasised toleration as the key to stability in a well-ordered society. He focuses on what he calls decent hierarchical societies where a particular religious outlook dominates but is governed by a 'common good idea of justice' lending legitimacy to the political regime as it is widely shared. Critics chasten Rawls for considering these as decent even though they place limitations on the rights of other religions and also of women.

The main thrust of deliberative democratic theory is an emphasis on reason and equal citizens his in an ideal order. The emphasis is on public deliberation even when the non-deliberative order may be both fair and democratic. Deliberative democracy emphasises four essential attributes: (i) aim full deliberation with a specified target of consensus and to a lesser degree co-operation and compromise, (ii) the process of deliberation is of vital importance and will consist of three aspects – forums of public discussion, formal institutional structure and the process of decision-making, (iii) the essential conditions for deliberation is freedom and equality of citizens, (iv) the framework of deliberation must include cultural plurality and social complexities of modern mass democracies (Bohman and Rehg 1997: xviii).

Some deliberative theorists accept that procedural equality, which ensures equality of opportunity and participation in political decision-making are of crucial significance for legitimising democracy. But they equally emphasise substantive aspects of political equality. For instance Knight and Johnson emphasise the need for equity of opportunity in accessing political influence. Bohman's equality demands an assurance for equal opportunity in speaking. Both these theories derive their inspiration from Amartya Sen's theory of 'capability equality', better known than the Rawlsian approach as a resource based formulation for it is practically relevant since uncertainties and inequalities restrict political participation and deliberation. However, Bohman and Rehg comment that Sen's theory not only highlights "the weaknesses of procedural equality of opportunity and equality of resources, but also the possible elitism of deliberative theories" (Ibid: xxiv). This elitism springs from the fact that deliberative democratic theorists demand political equality as a pre-condition so that the better educated, the more virtuous or just the better off do not get favoured. It must ensure all citizens have equal opportunity to influence political decisions. Richardson and Young try to bridge the gulf between epistemic and fair proceduralism by emphasizing on truth or fairness as the result of deliberation by arriving at 'partially joint intentions'. Cohen argues that reasonable pluralism concretises the deliberative mechanism of free and equal citizens. It is based both on a procedural and a substantive conception of politics elucidating equalitarian and liberal values of rights and liberties. Reasonable pluralism ensures that none would be excluded because of practicing a particular religion or moral doctrine. Equality envisages capacity to participate in a process, which authorises the exercise of power. Like Rawls, Cohen claims that public reasonableness and consensus is possible in spite of wide disagreements in moral and political belief structure. Cohen is categorical that reasonable pluralism and deliberative democracy guarantees religious, moral and other liberties. The purpose is to provide genuine membership to all citizens in ensuring participation in the filtering and exercise of power. Freedom and equality are intrinsic to such an order and since the process accepts disagreement as part of democracy liberties of conscience, religion and expression are the essential requirements coupled with the idea of reasonableness. He considers the notion of deliberative democracy as "rooted in the intuitive ideal of a democratic association in which the justification of the terms and conditions of association proceeds through public argument and reasoning among equal citizens" (1997:72).

Benhabib another exponent of deliberative democracy points out that conflicts over values and visions of good cannot be resolved 'by establishing a strong unified moral and religious code without forsaking fundamental values thus distinguishing the conception from civic republicanism'. She points out that agreement has to be reached not over substantive beliefs but on procedures, processes and practices that attain and revise these beliefs (1996:73). Habermas (1996 & 1998) too insists that institutionalising conditions for deliberative communication is the crux of the matter. It differs from liberalism that sees politics as the administration of competing private interests among citizens and considers democracy as legitimising the exercise of political power, and from republicanism that structures law and government to reach positive consensus on moral values and creates solidarity among citizens. For a republican, democracy is supposed to constitute a society as a political community. Unlike the liberals who see popular sovereignty as the exercise of duly authorised state authority and the republicans for whom popular sovereignty resides in a popular general will, the deliberative approach sees sovereignty as an ongoing process of "interaction between legally institutionalised will formation and culturally mobilised publics" (Habermas 1998:295–302).

Pluralism

The Pluralists accept diversity and contend that the modern liberal state is too complex for any single group, class or organisation to dominate society. Pluralism affirms the separation of state and civil society and distinguish economic from political power. It considers the political system to be all-inclusive operating on the basis of consensus by taking into account everyone's interests and ensuring satisfaction of everyone as a part of a larger group or association. It differs from the elite theory that establishes a dichotomy between the ruler and the ruled. The classical theory posits the existence of common good that the democratic system throws up, while the pluralists accept that the existence of groups of particular interests does not necessarily indicate the absence of general interest. The classical theory perceives individuals as isolated and discrete persons and not as members of a group(s) that overlap. This is unrealistic in view of the multiple identities of a person in modern society. Pluralism, like Madison's theory is preoccupied with factions and pressure groups, for it considers society to be essentially heterogeneous and pluralistic with diverse aspirations, interests and wills. It accepts Madison's concern for factions and its modern counterpart – interest groups and pressure groups – as a natural counterpart of free association in a world where most desired goods are scarce and where the complex industrial system fragments social interests and creates a multiplicity of demands. Like Madison, the pluralists accept that the basic function of government is to protect the freedom of factions to advance their political interests, while preventing any individual faction from encroaching on the freedom of others. However, they differ from Madison in not regarding factions as a major threat to democratic associations or as a source of instability or as undemocratic in nature. They consider the existence of diverse competitive interests as the basis of democratic equilibrium and for a favourable development of public policy. The pluralists combine Locke's individualism, Dewey's participatory ethic with Burke's concern for continuity and stability.

The pluralists view politics as an arena of resolving conflict between different groups who represent all the dominant interests of society. They see conflict as 'democracy's lifeblood' (Lipset 1960:83) as "whatever the explanation for conflict may be its existence is one of the prime facts of all community life" (Dahl 1967:6). By accepting conflict as given they prescribe democratic forums to accommodate it. They concede that some marginal groups might be left out, but assert that all the major streams get usually represented.

They also argue that certain groups try to establish close links with particular departments in the government and that may lead to a neglect of other interests.

Truman (1951:10) acknowledges that institutionalised relationships between an agency and its attendant interest groups could develop and this could lead to other interests getting ignored. However, Wilson (1977:45) points out to the existence of Whitehall pluralism, meaning that even if one department ignores the interest of a particular group, it is not necessary that others ignore them as well. Their views could be taken up 'by the fact that other departments have checks and have different departmental views accordingly'. The pluralists perceive the state as a balancing factor between departments that represent a range of interest groups. Thus interest groups are accepted as the basic building blocks of the theory. Interest for the pluralists means 'subjective interests' or what Truman called 'attitudes'. Authority is distributed within government (Eckstein 1963:392), meaning that the state is not controlled and dominated by any single interest. Yet the state is seldom neutral but mirrors the range of group pressures it faces as 'policy arises from the interaction of various social elements' (Easton 1965:172). The state attempts to make policy by bargaining between a range of conflicting interests and the government takes into consideration the interests of 'unorganized and potential groups' and, therefore, they do not need 'organized expression except when these needs are flagrantly violated' (Truman 1951:448).

Politics is a constant process of negotiation with new issues emerging all the time that ensures resolution of conflicts peacefully (Dahl 1967:24). It is thus contended that an explanation of the actual process of politics is an analysis of groups. Policy emerges as a result of constant method of conflict and exchange between different groups with the government being regarded as just another group. Only by organizing themselves into groups could individuals get their interests represented in government. The state is a distinct organization that makes policies in response to the innumerable groups exerting pressure on the government. It is accepted that conflict between groups is persuasive within liberal democracy and this conflict rarely threatens the stability of the system. Consensus defining the limits of political action and the framework of policy outcomes ensures political stability.

The pluralists understand power as the capacity to achieve one's aims despite opposition from others. They concede that there are many dimensions of inequalities in society and that not all the groups have equal access to all types of resources, let alone equal resources. However, nearly every group has some advantage that could be utilized in the democratic process to make an impact. Since different groups have access to different kinds of resources, the influence of any particular group would generally depend on the issue at hand. The pluralists perceive power as non-hierarchical and competitively arranged and embroiled in 'endless process of bargaining' between many groups representing different interests. These groups in the long run change their concerns and shift their positions. Both at the local and at the national level political decisions are not a reflection of a unified public opinion on basic issues that Locke, Rousseau and Bentham have presumed. The details of policy-making in the complex world of today emerge out of intense lobbying of different interest groups and ultimately the policy reflects the inputs of all such divergent groups. Political outcomes are the consequence of mediation and adjudication between competing demands of groups. There is no powerful decision-making centre in the pluralist model. Since power is dispersed throughout society there is plurality of pressure points, a variety of competing policy-formulating and decision-making centres. Equilibrium in society is achieved, according to Truman (1951:503–516), because of the existence of diversity of interests and overlapping memberships, which unleash competing forces without any one force wielding excessive influence. The existence of these varied groups sustains democratic goals and helps citizens to advance their own interests.

The key questions for the pluralists are: who are involved in the decision-making process; and who is it that could be seen to influence outcomes? Polsby advises that a researcher has to study actual behaviour first hand or from documents, informants, newspapers and other appropriate sources. The pluralists stress on the actual process of decision-making: and by ignoring untested concepts like false consciousness, hegemony and dominant ideology they have been able to develop a theory of power that is empirically verifiable. Their notion of 'modern society and polity as fragmented, diverse and democratic' is 'more accurate about the distribution of power than found in monolithic Marxist and elitist theories' (Smith 1995:214). Owing to their equal emphasis on both democracy and pluralism it is called democratic pluralist view. Modern Pluralism has some similarities with the early pluralist view expressed at the beginning of the twentieth century by Barker, Follet, Laski, Lindsay and MacIver as the associational nature of modern society and acceptance of authority as federal in character. However, the major difference between the two emerges from the fact that while the essential focus of early pluralism is more Aristotelian in the sense of their emphasis on all kinds of different associations, modern pluralists' emphasise is on interest and pressure groups.

Polyarchy

Dahl specifies the exact nature of pluralist democracies and argues (a) that if competitive electoral systems is characterised by a multiplicity of groups who have strong views on different subjects, then democratic rights will be protected and extreme political inequalities other than those guaranteed by law and constitution would be certainly avoided. (b) There is empirical evidence to suggest that at least certain policies, for example, Those of the USA and Britain, fulfil these conditions. Dahl is convinced that power is distributed and shared by many groups in society representing diverse interests and they defend their particular interests through government, creating a proclivity towards 'competitive equilibrium' that benefits the citizens in the long run. At the minimum 'democratic theory is concerned with processes by which ordinary citizens exert a relatively high degree of control over leaders' (1965:3). This control is maintained by two methods: regular elections and political competition among parties, groups and individuals. He dismisses the concerns of Madison, Mill and Tocqueville about the tyranny of the majority as misplaced, for a tyrannous majority is impossible because elections express the preferences of divergent competitive groups rather than the wishes of a strong majority. He agrees with Madison about the existence of factions and feels that it is possible to deal with its effects rather than eliminate them. Madison's justification for not attacking factionalism is that it would be improper and wicked and that government's first object is the protection of human diversity which makes possible different kinds and degrees of property, as property is a fundamental right.

Polyarchy or pluralist democracy is a rule by a series of minorities – some self-interested and others disinterested – within the boundaries stipulated by consensus with none being able to dominate but all having a space for their manoeuvre and bargaining. This emphasis on consensus is in contrast to Schumpeter's view of democratic politics as managed ultimately by competing elites. The pluralist system is a decentralised one aiming to arrive at compromise rather than truth. The competition among groups is a safeguard of democracy. Democracy does not establish the sovereignty of the majority but a rule by 'multiple minority oppositions'. The competition among groups establishes the democratic nature of the system. The difference between dictatorship and democracy for Dahl is the difference between 'government by a minority' and 'government by minorities'. The more the presence of competing interest groups the more secure is democracy. Furthermore, he points out that the change in size from the city-states to modern nation-states inevitably moves from monist to a pluralist democracy. This change in scale is crucial to understanding present-day democracies. In the modern context, the very essence of democracy is realised by polyarchy that stipulates the presence of a large number of organizations and associations, which enjoy relative autonomy both in relationship to one another as also with regard to governmental power and jurisdiction. The institution of polyarchy distinguishes a democratic regime from an authoritarian one.

The preconditions for a functioning polyarchy are consensus on the rules of procedure, consensus on the range of policy options and consensus on the legitimate scope of political activity, which act as a buffer against oppressive rule. The greater the level of consensus the more secure is democracy. A society enjoys protection from tyranny in non-constitutional provisions. It is not as if Dahl does not accord importance to principles like separation of powers and system of checks and balances, for it is pivotal in deciding the importance of benefits and burdens that groups face in a political system, which is why they are so bitterly fought over. However, the importance of constitutional rules to the successful development of democracy is less compared to non-constitutional ones. Dahl is convinced that democracy is safe for it brings about moderation and agreement and maintains social peace if the social preconditions are secure (Ibid: 134–135, 151). He does not consider equal distribution of control over political decisions or that all individuals and groups to have an equal political weight as necessary for a successful working of democracy (Ibid: 145–146).

In *A Preface to Economic Democracy* (1985:54–55), in a departure from his earlier works, Dahl addresses economic sources of inequalities in political resources, mainly 'ownership and control of firms' which contribute to the creation of great differences among citizens in wealth, income, status, skills, information, control over information and propaganda, access to political leaders' among other things. These differences help in the generation of significant inequalities among citizens in their capacities and opportunities for participating as political equal in governing the state. Contrary to Madison he argues against the view that property is a fundamental right and devotes half the book to describing a 'self-governing equal order', a kind of workers self-management and defends it realistically to achieve economic egalitarianism that would be conducive to democracy.

In *Democracy and its Critics* (1989:333) Dahl once again cites the problems that economic inequalities pose for democracy, but maintains that its prospects are 'more seriously endangered' by political inequalities 'derived not from wealth or economic position but from special knowledge'. He contends that common goods are the informed interests that individuals share and that 'the rights and opportunities of the democratic process are elements of the common good' because informed people would realise that these are necessary, among other things, for them to gain the enlightenment required to know what is in their interests (Ibid:306–308). He points to the conflicting visions of what American society is and ought to be, 'where one is of the world's first and grandest attempt to realise democracy, political equality and political liberty' while the other is of 'a country where unrestricted liberty to acquire unlimited wealth would produce the world's most prosperous society' (Ibid:162). He proposes a system of self-governing firms partly to expand the number of people who can be politically active, both within their workplace and in broader political arena due to the resources and experiences gained in the firms. This is one way that he addresses the criticism of pluralism that it sanctions narrowing access to democratic politics to those who have the time and resources to be parts of interest groups.

The deliberative democratic theory tries to resurrect the Periclean principles of popular participation and refines it with the Jeffersonian ideal of harmony by making a balance between liberty, equality and democracy in the modern mass democracies. However it wants to re-inculcate the spirit of Jeffersonian radical individualism without his commitment to rough parity and equality, an integral part of the libertarian tradition of liberalism. But in resurrecting these ideals any democratic theory for our times is to take note of Dahl's (1986) four-fold categorisation: (1) what constitutes people in democracy, (2) problem of size or scale, (3) problem of pluralism and (4) consequences for democracy, liberty and equality in the context of an alternative scheme of change or scale in economy. The theorists of deliberative democracy do not deliberate on any of these issues at length and that makes their account sketchy and impractical. Even what constitutes the procedural and substantive is not clear in the deliberative theory of democracy. Any critical alternative model to indirect polyarchy in the contemporary world has to provide a coherent and practical primer to aforesaid four-fold categorisation of Dahl. As long as it is unable to do this, the theory will merely remain a abroad critic without emerging as an alternative.

References

Bessette, J.M. (1994): *The Mid Voice of Reason: Deliberative Democracy and American National Government,* Chicago, University of Chicago Press.

Benhabib, S. (1996): Democracy and Difference: Contesting the Boundaries of the Political, Princeton NJ, Princeton University Press.

Bohman, J. and Rehg, W. (1997): *Deliberative Democracy: Essays on Reason and Politics*, Massachusettes, London, The MIT Press.

Cohen, (1997): 'Procedure and Substance in Deliberative Democracy' and 'Deliberation and Democratic Legitimacy' in *Deliberative Democracy: Essays on Reason and Politics* (eds.), J. Bohman and W. Rehg, Cambridge MA, The MIT Press.

Cunningham, F. (2000): *Theories of Democracy: A Critical Introduction*, London, Routledge.

Dahl, R.A. (1965): *A Preface to Democratic Theory*, Chicago, University of Chicago Press.

—— (1967): *Pluralist Democracy in the United States,* Chicago, Rand McNally.

—— (1985): *A Preface to Economic Democracy*, Berkeley, University of California Press.

—— (1986): *Democracy, Liberty and Equality*, Oslo, Norwegian University Press.

—— (1989): *Democracy and its Critics*, New Haven, Connecticut, Yale University Press.

Dryzek, J.S. (2000): *Deliberative Democracy and Beyond*, Oxford, Oxford University Press.

Easton, D. (1965): *A Systems Analysis of Political Life*, Englewood Cliffs, NJ. Prentice Hall.

Eckstein, H. (1963): 'A Perspective on Comparative Politics, Past and Present' in *Comparative Politics: A Reader*, (eds.), H. Eckstein and D.E. Apter, London, Free Press.
Habermas, J. (1996): 'Three Normative Models of Democracy' in *Democracy and Difference: Contesting the Boundaries of the Political*, (ed.) S. Benhabib, Princeton NJ, Princeton University Press.
—— (1998): *Between Facts and Norms: Contributions to a Discourse Theory of Law and Democracy*, Cambridge MA, MIT Press.
Lipset, S.M. (1960): *Political Man*, New York, Doubleday.
Olson, M (1971): *The Logic of Collective Action: Public Goods and the Theory of Groups*, Cambridge MA, Harvard University Press.
Rawls, J. (1993): *Political Liberalism*, New York, Columbia University Press.
—— (1997): *The Law of Peoples: The Idea of Public Reason Revisited*, Cambridge Mass, Harvard University Press.
Smith, M. (1995): 'Pluralism' in *Theory and Methods in Political Science*, (eds.), D. Marsh and G. Stoker, Basingstoke, Macmillan.
Truman, D. (1951): *The Governmental Process*, New York, Alfred A. Knopf.
Wilson, G. (1977): *Special Interests and Policy Making*, Chilcester, John Wiley.

Endnotes

1. New social movements are loosely organised popular protest groups, which thrive at a time when conventional political participation as measured by membership in political parties and trade unions and even voting is on the decline in most Western democracies. Social movements have always existed and have been the source for many political parties and trade unions but in its new incarnation it displays some key differences. The new social movements enlist predominantly those from the educated and affluent segments, the middle class, who are expressly disenchanted with ordinary politics and aspire for more participatory activities, wanting to get rid of bureaucratic elites within their own organisations and espouse radical actions with preference for street demonstrations, sit-ins and some degree of violence rather than the routine pressure group tactics for realising their aims. They try to pressurise the state to adopt their specific policies rather than assume power, reinforcing the perception that there is a link between the new social movement and post materialist culture of the West. Their aim is usually to promote and achieve one single specific issue rather than elaborate an overall ideology or programme.
2. Rational choice theory maintains that the primary explanation for an action is that the actor has calculated the said action to be the most efficient way of acquiring a desired goal. Voting behaviour is the first area in which political scientists have applied rational choice theory, as it is relatively easy to see the act of voting as akin to making a purchase.
3. The Condercet jury theorem, in its standard form, says this: suppose each member of a jury is more likely to be right than wrong, then the majority of the jury too, is more likely to be right than wrong. Furthermore, the probability that the majority of the jury might support the right outcome is a rapidly increasing function of the size of the jury, converging to one as the size of the jury tends to infinity.

Extrapolating from juries to electorate more generally, that result constitutes the jewel in the crown of epistemic democrats, many of whom offer it as powerful evidence of the truth-tracking merits of majority rule. What drives the Condercet jury theorem is just the 'law of large numbers'. As the number of voters increases the actual proportion of the votes won by the correct opinion comes increasingly to approximate the antecedent possibility of each individual's voting for the correct opinion. Within a small group of 100, the actual distribution of votes might turn out to be 48:52 and the correct option might therefore be lost. But the larger the group, the more likely it will be that the proportion of people voting correctly approximates the same 51% as the probability of each individual voter's voting correctly. And that of course is just to say that it is more likely among a large number of voters that the correct option will win the election (and indeed, will do so by the same majority as represented by the individual's probability of voting correctly in the first place). Hence, if each individual is more likely to be right than wrong- and increasingly so, thanks to the law of large numbers as the number of voters increases.

5

'A long and winding road'. From Cultural Homogeneity to a Multicultural Society: An Analysis of Inclusion and Exclusion in Australia

David Roberts

The contemporary impact of globalization has led to the proposition that a 'global village' is emerging, that the pace of cultural homogenization globally is increasing and that there is a concomitant weakening of ethnic ties and points of differentiation.[1] The emergence over recent decades of ethno-nationalist movements based on the politics of racial, ethnic, and religious identity, however, has confounded predictions that cultural diversity will become less relevant. Most modern nation-states are characterized by ethnic diversity and in many of them the politics of identity has come to pose a significant challenge as they endeavour to manage sectional interests in ways that are inclusive and which strengthen the fabric and unity of society.[2]

While the patterns of ethnic relations vary from state to state and are constantly evolving, inter ethnic tension and conflict prevail in many of them. These tensions frequently reflect direct or indirect exclusion where ethnic identity determines access to resources and power. Some societies have attempted to manage ethnic diversity by following policies that are based on assimilation where ethnic minorities are required to abandon their points of difference and fully adopt the culture of the dominant society. Others pursue policies based on integration where ethnic identity and its maintenance is respected and supported within a framework where the dominant culture and its institutional practices are maintained. In others policy frameworks are based on separation and forms of communitarianism which can lead to indirect or direct exclusion of those who belong to minority ethnic communities. In some states ethnic tensions have erupted into sustained conflict and violence and, in extreme forms, to "ethnic cleansing" and genocide. Since the beginning of the 1970s some states, primarily liberal democracies, have developed policies and strategies designed to manage ethnic diversity under the rubric of multiculturalism. While there are multiple uses of the term multiculturalism, ranging from the simply demograghically descriptive, to policy and program initiatives, and to ideological and theoretical frameworks for political action, it is characterized by state recognition and support of the rights of ethnic communities, the removal of barriers to inclusivity and the promotion of values and norms that are universally shared.[3]

In 1995 UNESCO undertook a study to explore the potential of multiculturalism to enable social and cultural diversity to be managed successfully.[4] The study examined the implementation of multiculturalism and its effectiveness in managing cultural diversity in three countries where it had been in place for some time – Australia, Canada and Sweden. Despite differences in approach and factors unique to each of them, each was found to have developed a comprehensive policy framework together with strategic action that was inclusive of "difference" and provided an effective response to the challenges of managing social and cultural diversity. The analysis found that the strength of multiculturalism as implemented in the three countries was founded on respect of individual rights and a civic and contractual definition of citizenship.[5]

Australia's inclusion as one of three effective and successful exemplars of multiculturalism is an unlikely one given its history since British colonization in 1788. It reflects a remarkable journey away from earlier policies and practices designed to replicate the "British nation" and which focussed on the assimilation, separation or exclusion of those who were defined as culturally or racially different and "other". It suggests that in a little over two generations Australia has achieved a dramatic social transformation from what was essentially a culturally homogeneous society in 1947 to a multicultural society today. What was exclusionary was the exclusionary nature of Australia's past and has this been changed fundamentally over the last sixty years? Is Australia now a fairer, more open and culturally diverse and inclusive society? Has the Anglo Celtic hegemony of the past ended or at least diminished?

Australia has a long history of cultural diversity. The Indigenous peoples who had lived on the continent for at least 50,000 years before its colonization had their own distinct cultures and territories with five different language groups and more than 250 languages spoken, each with its own dialects. While territorial boundaries were not tightly defined the map below provides some sense of the linguistic and cultural diversity of Indigenous Australians.[6]

In the early years of colonization attempts were made to assimilate the Indigenous population into colonial life as 'brown Englishmen'. These attempts were largely unsuccessful. Indigenous people found little in the way of life of colonial society that attracted them to it until the impact of violence, dispossession and introduced disease led to the collapse of their societies. The survivors were left destitute and forced to eke out a living as fringe dwellers. The rapid decline in the size of the Australian Indigenous population following colonisation demonstrates its catastrophic impact on Indigenous societies. The

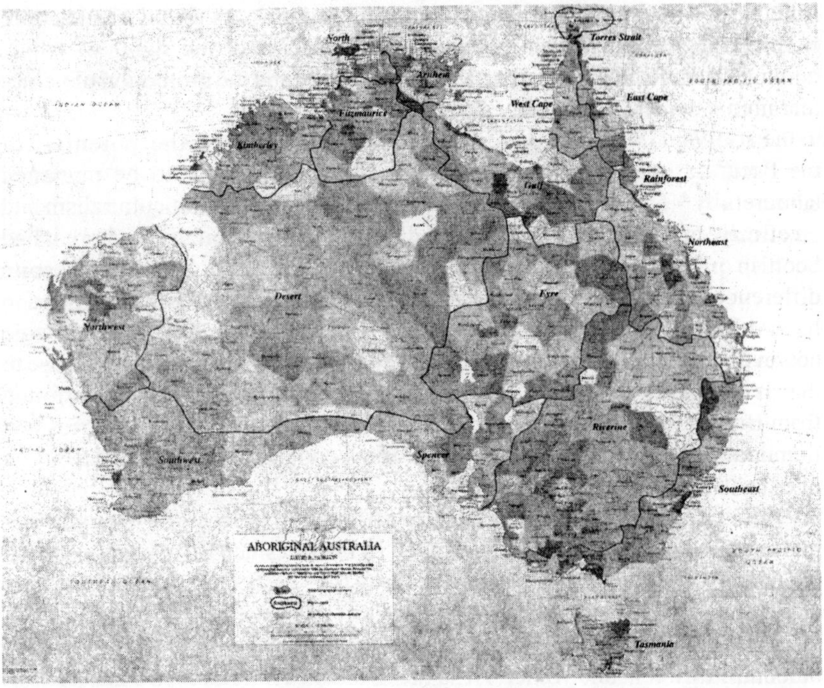

population, estimated by Butlin to have numbered between 1 and 1.5 million in 1788, was decimated over successive generations to fall to 67,140 in 1933.[7] Indigenous Australians lost more than 90 per cent of their population as well as their land, their capacity to maintain their traditional ways of life, much of their cultural heritage and most of their languages.

In the latter part of the nineteenth century with the emergence of Social Darwinism and the widely held belief that the Indigenous population constituted a "dying race", assimilation was replaced by the introduction of a policy of separation and the segregation of most of the survivors onto reserves and missions for their "protection". While this policy was to revert back in 1950 to assimilation for those of mixed descent, in most states the dismantlement of reserves and the repeal of segregation legislation did not commence until the mid 1960s while in Queensland it remained in force for a further decade.

While Indigenous Australians comprise nearly 3 per cent of the Australian population in 2007 the remaining ninety seven per cent of Australians are either immigrants or their descendants. Early colonial settlement was dominated by people from the British Isles – English, Scottish, Welsh and Irish – but they also included small numbers of people from a wide range of cultural backgrounds including other Europeans, West Indians and Maori. With the gold rushes of the 1850s large numbers of immigrants from Europe, North

America and China were attracted to Australia. Later in the nineteenth century people from other European countries migrated to Australia, many to escape religious persecution. In the same period Malays, Filipinos and Japanese were recruited to work in the pearling industry, Afghans were encouraged to settle in the arid regions of Australia to help open up the interior and Kanakas from the Pacific Islands were brought into Queensland to work as indentured labourers in the sugar industry. While by the end of the nineteenth century the great majority of immigrants and their descendants were of English, Irish, Scottish or Welsh descent there were also a significant number of people from different ethnic backgrounds, including 47,000 non Europeans.[8]

Attitudes towards people from non-English speaking backgrounds, however, were at best ambivalent even in the early colonial days. It is evident that as early as the 1820s there was a clear preference for immigrants to come from Britain with leading colonial figures demanding the introduction of an immigration policy that would reproduce the blend of peoples from the British Isles.[9] As aspirations to build an "Antipodean Britain" in Australia began to crystallize the colonies sought to attract immigrants only from Britain and to this end from 1835 they established schemes of assisted passage for "suitable applicants". Differentiation between desirable and undesirable immigrants based on race and ethnicity emerged clearly in the late 1830s when, despite an acute labour shortage, colonists campaigned against the introduction of indentured Indian workers who they argued would depress wages and form a separate class, distinct in colour, language and religion. The British Government established a Select Committee to enquire into the proposal. While the scheme was found to be financially viable the Select Committee rejected it as "Whatever defects may be chargeable upon the state of society here, it is at present so unmixed in its composition as to promise to supply material for the fabrication of a social and political state corresponding with that of the country from which it derives its origin."[10]

In the 1850s, in response to a large influx of Chinese attracted to the goldfields in Victoria and New South Wales, colonists again moved to exclude people deemed as "Other" from Australia. While the campaign to restrict their entry was strongly influenced by fears of economic competition, it also reflected and drew upon community opposition to the entry of people who were considered as being unable to assimilate. The arrival of 40,000 Chinese in just five years in Victoria led to claims that the colony was being "overrun" by a "swarm of human locusts"[11] and dire warnings were sounded about the dangers of the development of "a nation within a nation".[12] In the 1870s, with the discovery of the Palmer goldfields in Queensland, the influx of a new wave of Chinese immigration stimulated an upsurge in anti-Chinese sentiment leading to the passing of legislation to prevent their entry. While the British Government disallowed the Queensland legislation fears that the entry of the Chinese would lower wages, working conditions and living standards intersected with a growth of working class solidarity and the trade union movement, the rise of Australian nationalism and the federation of the colonies into the Commonwealth of Australia.

Between 1880 and 1888 the political leaders of the Australian colonies held three Inter-Colonial Conferences at which one of the main issues of discussion was Chinese immigration and the need to put in place a strategy that would preserve the unity and homogeneity of the Australian people. The delegates at the conferences came to a general agreement that "…it is our duty to preserve the type of British nation and we ought not, for any consideration whatever, to admit any element that would detract from or in any appreciable degree lower that admirable type of nationality."[13] To preserve the unity of national life it was argued that a people could only admit immigrants from foreign nations who could be assimilated.[14] The agitation against the Chinese was strongly laced with claims that they were racially inferior and incapable of assimilating. The campaign drew heavily on racist ideologies that were popularized in the late nineteenth century. Accompanying the doctrines of European racial superiority was a related upsurge in pride at being British in origin and part of a greater empire in which "Australia is the front buckle in the white girdle of power and progress encircling the globe".[15] Despite tensions between colonists of English and Irish descent the vision of an Australian identity as the "new Britannia in the southern hemisphere"[16] was articulated well into the first half of the twentieth century and in 1938, in the official documentary made in celebration of the sesquicentenary of New South Wales, Sydney was described as "the second white city of the Empire" and Australia as a new "Anglo Saxon empire under the Southern Cross".[17] Racism had become so entrenched and normalized by the end of the nineteenth century that the introduction of the White Australian Policy to exclude all non-European immigration to Australia was among the settled principles underlying federation.

The importance of racial homogeneity in the newly formed Commonwealth of Australia was stressed by its Attorney General, and later Prime Minister, Alfred Deakin, who, in introducing the Immigration Bill to Parliament, commented,

> A united race means not only that its members can intermarry and associate without degradation on either side, but implies one inspired by the same ideals, of a people possessing the same general cast of character, tone of thought, the same constitutional training and tradition – a people qualified to live under this constitution, the broadest and most liberal perhaps the world has yet seen reduced to writing; a people qualified to use without abusing it, and to develop themselves under it to the full height and extent of their capacity.[18]

The benefits of preserving a racially and culturally homogeneous society were argued to be seen also in its capacity to assist in the development of an equitable and socially just society. Indeed as Deakin was to tell the House of Representatives in 1903,

> … the White Australia policy covers much more than the preservation of our own people here. It means the multiplication of our own people so that we may defend our country and our policy. It means the maintenance of social conditions under which men and women live decently. It means equal laws and opportunities for all … it means social justice and fair wages. The White Australia policy goes down to the roots of our natural existence, the roots from which the British social system has sprung.[19]

While exclusion based on race was designed to keep Australia white it was also aimed at keeping Australia British. Not all Europeans were welcome. Any groups that established ethnic communities and maintained their ethnic identity were subject to resentment and antagonism. The agitation against German settlers in rural parts of South Australia and Queensland is the case in point, although it did not reach the level of continuous violence that was carried out in the early decades of the twentieth century against southern European immigrants on the Western Australian goldfields and in Melbourne. As the number of southern European immigrants increased so did the campaign against them. The Australian Government responded initially by placing ad hoc bans on the entry of Greek and Maltese immigrants in 1916 and eight years later it introduced a strict quota system to curtail immigration from southern Europe.[20]

Even the British immigrants who were encouraged to settle in Australia were frequently singled out as "different" and came to be described over the course of the nineteenth century as "New Chums" and in the twentieth century, as "Poms" and, more derogatorily, as "whingeing Poms". Immigrants who were perceived to be unassimilable were excluded, while those that remained of the Indigenous population, who were deemed unable to assimilate, were segregated onto reserves where they were expected to eventually 'die out'. By the time of the second world war a high degree of cultural homogeneity had been achieved with over ninety per cent of Australians being of British or Irish descent.

The Pacific War had a profound affect on Australians, their sense of vulnerability. "Populate or perish" became the catch cry, and in 1947 the Australian Government commenced an ambitious immigration program. Initially it focused on attracting people who had been displaced during the war in Europe. In order to allay public fears about bringing large numbers of continental Europeans to Australia the then Minister of Immigration, Arthur Calwell, provided assurances that British immigration would remain the principal target and would be facilitated by a scheme of subsidised passages to Australia, that most immigrants would be British and that all new migrants would be expected to assimilate. While the British continued to be the single largest source of immigrants, large numbers of migrants from across Europe came to Australia under the Displaced Persons program. They were followed in the 1950s and 1960s by new waves of migrants from southern Europe, particularly Italy and Greece.

Ethnic diversity in Australia increased even more rapidly following the gradual relaxing of the exclusionary provisions of the White Australia Policy from mid 1960s and particularly after its replacement in 1973 with a non discriminatory immigration policy. While British immigrants have continued to be the largest single source of permanent settlers in Australia, with 12.5 per cent of the immigration intake in the period 1990 to 2000, this percentage has been trending down significantly.[21] The 2003–04 permanent settler data in Table 1 illustrates that Asia has passed Europe, including Great Britain, as Australia's major source of immigrants by a considerable margin, with Africa an emerging significant new source.

Table 1: Permanent additions by country of birth 2003–04[22]

Region of origin	*Percentage of permanent settlers*
Europe (including UK)	23
South-east Asia	15
North-east Asia	14
Oceania	13
Southern Asia	11
Sub-Saharan Africa	9
North Africa and the Middle East	8
Northern America	3
Central Asia	1
Central and Southern America	1.4

Since World War II Australia's population has increased from seven to over twenty million people with more than six million people having settled permanently, of whom over 600,000 have entered under humanitarian, displaced persons or refugee programs. The 2001 Census reveals that almost one quarter of the population was born overseas and that 43 per cent were either born overseas or had at least one parent born overseas, a marked change from the early 1940s when 90 per cent of the population was Australian born.

Immigrants from over two hundred countries now live in Australia and more than two hundred languages are spoken. The 2001 Census showed that 2.8 million people, 16 per cent of the population, spoke a language other than English at home with the five most commonly spoken languages other than English being Italian, Greek, Cantonese, Arabic (including Lebanese) and Vietnamese. While Christianity remains the predominant religion with over twelve million followers. Buddhism (357,814) and Islam (281,586) are the religions whose numbers are increasing most rapidly.

As the number of ethnic communities and their numbers increased, their capacity to maintain their cultural identities strengthened, and they gradually gained political and economic leverage. The Government found that its Assimilation Policy was not effectively incorporating migrants into Australian society[23] and in 1961 it was replaced with a policy based on integration. Under the Integration Policy it was no longer expected that immigrants should assimilate and relinquish their cultures. In addition measures were introduced to provide more support for the settlement and integration of new immigrants and their communities.

The shift from assimilation to integration was also applied to Indigenous Australians and marked the beginning of an era of major change which included the ending of the reserve system and the gaining of constitutional authority for the Commonwealth Government to legislate in the field of Indigenous affairs, establish services and provide funding direct to communities. The right to choose became an underlying principle of Government policy in Indigenous affairs and in 1973 it acknowledged the right of self determination for Indigenous communities.

During the Whitlam Government the concept multiculturalism was introduced as a way of more effectively incorporating new migrants into Australian society by actively promoting their rights and supporting them in the retention of their ethnic identities. 1978 marked the formal adoption by the Fraser Government of multiculturalism as the policy framework within which migrant settlement and ethnic diversity would be managed. Fraser was highly critical of assimilation, and the monoculturalism which it engendered, for the high costs it exacted on individuals, their families and communities, and society, arguing that:

> It denies people their identity and self-esteem. It drives a wedge between children and their parents. Ultimately it poses a real threat of alienation and division. We cannot demand of people that they renounce the heritage they value, and yet expect them to feel welcome as full members of our society. Realism alone demands that cultural differences must be responded to in a positive way.[24]

Building on the initiatives commenced under the Whitlam Government, Fraser attempted to completely reverse those long established policies and ideologies which had been designed to create and maintain a monocultural society which was deeply embedded in British origins. Instead, diversity was now portrayed as a virtue and of benefit to all Australians. The focus of the new policy was on inclusion, choice, tolerance and respect for difference within the broader framework of adherence to some core Australian values and institutions. Under Fraser's Government and those of his immediate successors the normalization of cultural diversity was promoted as a characteristic that was a quintessential part of modern Australia, one that fitted in well with the easy going "live and let live" approach with which most Australians characterize themselves.

To Fraser and the Hawke and Keating governments that succeeded him the adoption of multiculturalism reflected the reality of the rapidly expanding ethnic heterogeneity of the Australian population, provided a more equitable and just means of managing the multiplicity of ethnic minorities and incorporating them into the Australian polity, and presented an opportunity to capitalise on the wealth of resources offered through this diversity to enrich Australian culture and contribute to Australian economic development and progress. The policy had three main foci:

- the right to maintain culture,
- the right to social justice, and
- the obligation to develop and employ the skills of all Australians for economic progress and an increased standard of living for all.

Since the 1970s Australian Governments, particularly since the introduction of multiculturalism, have adopted a strong institutional approach to the management of cultural diversity, the recognition and protection of ethnic rights and the provision of support for the settlement of migrants. They have introduced a wide range of programs and policies which include specific purpose funding for welfare, housing, health, education and other services to migrants, translation and interpreting services, teaching English as a second language and adult education services, support for the teaching of migrant languages, support for the conduct of cultural events and festivals, the establishment of migrant resource centres, and the establishment of the multi-lingual Special Broadcasting System (SBS) in radio and television. State based Ethnic Community Councils have been established along with a coordinating Federation of Ethnic Communities Council which provides national support. In addition the Australian Government has established the Australian Institute of Multicultural Affairs to provide advice to governments, conduct research and inform and educate the public. More recently there has been increased emphasis on removing barriers to the access of services by ensuring that they are culturally and language sensitive. A *Charter of Public Service in a Culturally Diverse Society* supported by performance management frameworks and reporting and accountability requirements has been introduced to improve services. The Government has undertaken a wide range of strategies, including the running of a website at www.diversityaustralia.gov.au/, to encourage the private sector to embrace multiculturalism. It assiduously promotes the benefits to be gained for their businesses and the broader economy by employing a culturally diverse workforce. Indeed, the Australian Government has been unashamedly pragmatic in its promotion of the economic benefits of immigration and multiculturalism, the opportunities they provide to strengthen the skill base of the workforce, to expand and assist in the restructuring of the economy, and to open up new markets overseas. The Government has also placed considerable emphasis on citizenship as a means of including and embracing immigrants. It liberalized the requirements for Australian citizenship making it open to all legal entry immigrants with a minimum of two years residence. It encourages migrants to apply for citizenship, showcases naturalization ceremonies and allows dual citizenship. Citizenship ceremonies are conducted at regular intervals across the year and over 10,000 people from 111 different countries became Australian citizens at the most recent ceremonies held across the country on Australia Day 2007.

In its policy documents the Government claims that "Australians have embraced respect for cultural diversity, making our nation one of the most harmonious societies in the world."[25] Certainly contemporary public opinion polls indicate strong support for multiculturalism with a December 2005 poll conducted by the Bulletin finding that eighty per cent of those surveyed supported multiculturalism. A study conducted by SBS of first, second and third generation Australians aged sixteen to forty found that "multiculturalism is perceived as a long-term investment in a more vibrant, tolerant and cosmopolitan nation."[26] The study found that older generations, however, were not as comfortable with cultural difference as younger generations.

Inglis's evaluation of the implementation of multiculturalism in Australia provided a strong endorsement of its success. She found that racism and discrimination were not marked, even in periods of economic downturn and recession where scapegoating of minorities could be more likely to occur, that the dominant group exhibited a high level of acceptance of ethnic difference, that ethnic minorities were able to participate in and influence political decision making, and that there was "extremely limited evidence of either inter-ethnic violence or conflict."[27] She found that while support for the maintenance of ethnic minorities remained an important component of multiculturalism in Australia the focus of policy under the administration of the Hawke and Keating governments had shifted increasingly towards equality, the removal of structural disadvantage and the improvement of the status of minorities. She attributed the success of multiculturalism in Australia to the cumulative effect of strong government leadership and the introduction of a range of policy initiatives and programs. These initiatives included educational support to ethnic minorities, community education and cross cultural training programs, language programs, the provision of translating and interpreter services as well as multilingual radio and television stations, the introduction of anti-discrimination legislation to target institutional and individual racism, employment initiatives in both the private and public sectors and the provision of affordable and suitable housing. She observed that strong federal government leadership had been successful in encouraging state and local governments to embrace and implement multiculturalism in their respective jurisdictions. Inglis found that Australian policies were not aimed solely to maintain cultural diversity but to manage it in a way that provided individuals with "meaningful" choices that ensured that they were not excluded nor forced to assimilate and abandon their own cultures.

There are a number of indicators including employment statistics, the rate of intermarriage, the taking up of citizenship, population dispersion and crime rates which all suggest that Government policies have had a large measure of success in managing cultural diversity and achieving equitable outcomes for migrants and ethnic communities. The unemployment rate for all people born overseas in August 2004, for example, was less than that of those born in Australia at 5.3 per cent compared to 5.5 per cent.[28] While migrants who have been in Australia a short time have a higher unemployment rate than the Australian average it falls significantly the longer they have lived in the country. Those who are classified as "long-established" (23 years or more) had an unemployment rate 30 per cent lower than the Australian born in August 2004.[29] In respect to intermarriage, a key indicator of the degree to which cultural difference is accepted, over the past two decades the percentage of people marrying out of their own ethnicity has increased between the first and third generations of every ethnic group except the English, and Australia has "the highest level of second generation intermarriage of any society".[30] The taking of Australian citizenship is one way migrants can publicly demonstrate their identification with the country and their interest in being involved in its democratic processes and governance. Based on 2001 Census data the Australian Bureau of Statistics estimates that 74 per cent of all migrants take up citizenship and in the case of some ethnic communities including the Greeks, Vietnamese and Filipinos, 90 per cent or more have taken up citizenship.[31] A study of a sample of statistical local areas conducted by the Australian Bureau of Statistics (ABS) found that ethnic enclaves are uncommon in Australia. Of the 61 local areas sampled only 13 had more than 10 per cent of any single ethnic group.[32] Crime rates can serve as an indicator of exclusion and alienation however ABS data analysis has found no causal relationship between crime and ethnicity. While there are variations in crime rates between ethnic groups the ABS found that overall crime rates of the overseas born are lower than those for those of the Australian born and that the latter had a higher rate of imprisonment. [33]

While there is considerable data suggesting that ethnic communities are receiving a much better deal than they were 30 and more years ago this data can, and does, mask the situation of some minority groups. At the risk of generalizing, given the diverse range of different communities of which it is comprised, one of these groups is Australia's Indigenous population. The marginalisation of its Indigenous population for most of Australia's history since 1788 has already been noted. In the early 1990s they too were brought under the umbrella of multiculturalism. The decision to do so was contentious as their status as the original occupants of the country is unique. As "just another ethnic group" they expressed fears that their status would be further compromised. Table 2 below provides some comparative data between Indigenous and other Australians.

Table 2: Australia: Comparison of selected demographic and socio-economic characteristics of the indigenous and total population, 2001

Characteristics	*Indigenous Population*	*Total Population*
Expectation of life at birth (years) – male	55.1	77.4
Expectation of life at birth (years) – female	61.0	82.6
Infant mortality rate	9.8	4.6
Unemployment rate	20.0	7.2
Percentage of deaths due to cardiovascular disease	28.0	14.0
Percentage of adults suffering obesity	61%	48%
Completed year 12 (15 years+)	16.8	39.5
Percentage of persons aged 18 to 24 attending university	5.2	23.5
Mean equivalised household weekly income	$364	$585
%age in lowest household income quintile in 2001	45.9	22.4
Percentage of home ownership/purchasing	32.0	67.4
Percentage of households in rental accommodation	63.5	26.6
Percentage in prisons, corrective and detention institutions – adults	1.0	0.1

Source: ABS 2001 Census.

Table 2 clearly demonstrates that Indigenous Australians are significantly disadvantaged compared to other Australians on a wide range of socio economic characteristics despite the introduction of policies of self determination and multiculturalism.

The data shows that Indigenous Australians have a much shorter life expectancy than the rest of the population – at birth for Indigenous boys it is 22.3 years less than for all boys and in the case of girls the gap is 21.6 years. Infant mortality is more than double that of other Australians. Their unemployment rate is almost three times higher than that of other Australians. Their health status is significantly worse than that of other Australians. Overall they have a much higher rate of infectious diseases, obesity, heart disease, kidney disease, diabetes and cancer than other Australians. In the case of diabetes Indigenous males are six times as likely to be hospitalized for care involving dialysis than other Australian men. In the case of Indigenous women compared to other women the multiple for care involving dialysis increases to fourteen.[34]

In respect to educational attainment, critical because of its effect on earning capacity, only 16.8 per cent of the Indigenous population had completed year 12 compared to 39.5 per cent of the non Indigenous population. The discrepancy between the two groups in respect to progressing to university is even more marked with almost five times as many non-Indigenous persons aged 18 to 24 studying at university compared to Indigenous persons.

The extent of disadvantage of Indigenous Australians is further illustrated when contrasting mean equivalised household incomes. Nearly half of all Indigenous families fall in the lowest household income quintile, more than double the rate of other Australian households. Weekly median income levels for Indigenous households stand at slightly over 60 per cent compared to those of non Indigenous households.

The level of Indigenous disadvantage is also reflected in their high dependency on rental housing. Home ownership/home purchase rates are less than half of the rest of the population while Indigenous households are heavily over represented in the rental market. Indigenous households are highly concentrated in poorer quality low cost rental housing and Indigenous tenanted houses on average have less rooms and have more residents. The rate of overcrowding in houses among the Indigenous population is six times that of other Australians. Compounding this sorry trail of data Indigenous adults have a rate of imprisonment which is ten times that of other Australians.

The data provides little evidence that multiculturalism has benefited Indigenous Australians. Indeed, when considering income levels for example, the opposite appears to be the case. The ABS found that average equivalised gross household income for Indigenous persons had decreased from 64 per cent to 62 per cent of that of non-Indigenous persons between the 1996 census and the 2001 Census.[35] The same file noted that 72 per cent (an increase from 70 per cent in 1996) of Indigenous income earners were in the lowest two income quintiles and that this increased to 91 per cent in very remote areas. Such data suggests that the situation for Indigenous Australians is not improving but going backwards. Multiculturalism does not appear to have had a marked impact on assisting Indigenous Australians to enjoy:

- their right to maintain culture,
- their right to social justice, and
- the development and employment of their skills for economic progress and increased standard of living.

In its 2003–06 updating of the 1999 New Agenda for Multicultural Australia the Government identified three strategic directions:

- access and equity in the provision of government services,
- productive diversity, and
- community harmony for all Australians.

It is in the third area of strategic action, the strengthening of community harmony, that other cracks underlying multiculturalism in Australia become apparent.

While Australia is now one of the most culturally diverse nations in the world the adoption of multiculturalism has been contested on a number of grounds including arguments that it fosters divisiveness, that it denies and undermines Australian culture and that it is extremely expensive. In particular it has been attacked for threatening social cohesion and promoting divisions based on ethnicity that could lead to conflict and violence. This first came into the public arena as a major issue in the early 1980s when highly distinguished historian, Professor Geoffrey Blainey, criticised the increased intakes of Asian immigration and claimed that multiculturalism was creating a "nation of tribes".[36] In 1988 sociologist Kathleen Betts found that there was little public support for immigration and multiculturalism, a position that was also reflected in public opinion polls of the time. In the same year a Government commissioned inquiry into immigration reported that it had found considerable confusion and negativity among the public in respect to Asian immigration and multiculturalism with many describing the latter as a form of "social engineering which actually invites injustice, inequality and divisiveness".[37] Public concerns and confusion in respect to immigration policy and multiculturalism continued into the 1990s and were successfully exploited by Pauline Hanson in the 1996 Federal election and by her One Nation party at the following Queensland election.

While the Hawke and Keating Governments maintained a strong commitment to cultural diversity and multiculturalism they responded to the public disquiet by tightening immigration policy, increasing the number of skilled migrants, and taking a tougher approach to asylum seekers. In 1989 multicultural policy underwent a significant change with the introduction of the *National Agenda for a Multicultural Society* which shifted the emphasis from the needs and rights of migrants to those of all Australians. Alongside these rights was a strengthened focus on the civic responsibilities of all citizens and their obligation to commit to Australia and its core values. These changes marked the beginning of a shift from a focus on ethnic rights to citizenship and its obligations as the basis for multiculturalism.

The emphasis on citizenship rather than ethnic rights as the basis for policy became the prevailing theme under the Howard Government. Following its election in 1996 expenditure on multicultural programs was reduced and some areas of activity, including the Office of Multicultural Affairs, were closed. The Prime Minister, never comfortable with the use of multiculturalism, made his opposition to it evident from the mid 1980s when he described it as divisive, claiming it "ensnares individuals in ethnic communities, denying them the opportunity to fully participate in Australian society".[38] In 1997 he stated that "multiculturalism is in effect saying that it is impossible to have an Australian ethos, that it is impossible to have an Australian culture"[39] a position he has continued to hold. While Howard has been a strong advocate for immigration from as many different countries as possible, and immigration intakes under his administration have reflected this, he holds that migrants have a responsibility to adapt to and embrace their new home. In his view multiculturalism does not secure a cohesive, integrated society. The initial success of Hanson and her One Nation Party suggested that a significant proportion of the Australian public held similar views. In 1998 his Government had the National Multicultural Advisory Council distribute an issues paper, *Multicultural Australia: The Way Forward*, which questioned the appropriateness of the use of the term multiculturalism to encapsulate the intent of Government policy.

While the Howard Government affirmed its commitment to a multicultural Australia, though not the ideology of multiculturalism, in policy documents in 1999 and again in 2002, it has continued to move away from an ethnic rights model to a citizenship model for all Australians. The title of the 2002 policy document, *Multicultural Australia: United in Diversity: Updating the 1999 New National Agenda for a Multicultural Australia* (Commonwealth Government of Australia, 2002), with its subtitle of *United in Diversity* and its strategic focus on promoting harmony illustrates the impact of terrorism on the Government's approach to domestic security and the management of cultural diversity. The document reflected the Government's view that:

> Australians now see themselves as directly threatened by terrorism. In this context, community harmony and social cohesion are pivotal elements in enabling Australia to contribute effectively to the international effort to combat terrorism, and in safeguarding Australians domestically. The Government believes firmly that Australian multicultural policy provides a framework of national unity and coherent ethos for a diverse Australia at a time of conflict, as well as in times of peace. National security begins with domestic community harmony.[40]

The London bombings in July 2005 caused considerable concern in Australia, particularly as the perpetrators, while of immigrant families, had been born in Britain. It raised concerns that there were similar ethnic communities in Australia and similar potential for "home grown" terrorist attacks. Australian Muslims became the target of keen scrutiny and of abuse. Muslim leaders were called on to condemn the bombings and for the several months the media, talk back radio especially, was bombarded with attacks on Muslims, with callers demanding that they should be "sent back to where they came from", that immigration should be stopped and that the mosques should be closed down. The hysteria was not limited to the public and the radio jockeys but also included political leaders including the Treasurer, Peter Costello, and the Education Minister, Dr. Brendan Nelson, calling for Muslims to be "thrown out" of Australia if they did not respect and adhere to Australian values.[41]

Muslim clerics were regarded with considerable suspicion as reports circulated in the press that some were preaching support for jihad. Fatih Shahin, a business leader, told a journalist that "what we have here [Australia] is a society and system of justice that is 500 per cent better than that offered in any Arab Muslim country. We must protect that for Islam and for Australia" and added that he advised "the imam to report anything to them [the Australian Security Intelligence Organisation] that does not promote harmonious living and the assimilation of Muslims into Australian society".[42] Joining the fray in questioning the role being played by overseas clerics, Dr. Nelson stated his concern that many Muslims were not integrating into Australian society or understanding and respecting its values and suggested that the Australian Islamic community might benefit from some assistance in their training. Some Government Members of Parliament called for a ban to be placed on Muslim girls in state schools from wearing the hijab. Supporting the call from fellow Member of Parliament Sophie Panapolous to ban the hijab, Bronwyn Bishop declared that "in an ideal society you don't ban anything. But this has really been forced on us because what we're seeing in our country is a clash of cultures and the head scarf is being used as a sort of iconic item of defiance".[43] The Opposition joined in and demanded that the Government force the 29 Islamic schools in Australia to enshrine Australian values such as respect, tolerance, diversity and mateship in their teachings and put in place strategies to "stamp out any extremism in schools".[44] Other civic leaders described the crisis they saw emerging in Australia as the consequence of multiculturalism "coming home to roost".

The tolerance and respect for cultural diversity which had been lauded by the Government in its policy documents was appearing increasingly fragile. Muslims have continued to be the subject of abuse and the South Australian Equal Opportunity Commissioner Linda Matthews warned that racism was increasing and that "recent attention on terrorism and Islam has seen local Muslims singled out more than ever before".[45] The Federal Police Commissioner, Mick Keelty, warned that rising levels of racism and hatred towards Muslims might incite terrorism.[46] Increasing levels of racism also were reported against other groups with the Executive Council of Australian Jewry finding that the number of physical attacks against Jews had reached an "all time high".[47] Ethnic violence between Croats and Serbs erupted at the Melbourne Open in January 2007 while the organisers of the Big Day Out, a concert to be conducted in Sydney on the eve of Australia Day, banned the crowd from bringing the Australian flag which they described as "gang colours". Justifying the ban they explained how patrons at the 2006 event had been threatened and intimidated by "xenophobic racists" who demanded they kiss the Australian flag and swear allegiance to it. The ban provoked an outcry led by the Prime Minister, the Leader of the Opposition and the Premier of New South Wales. While the ban was dropped the following day a large number of people responded to it by asserting their identity as Australians through taking flags or wearing items with replicas of the flag to the concert.

The riots in Sydney in December 2005, initiated by a crowd of about 5,000 young "Anglo Australians", many brandishing Australian flags, to "reclaim" Cronulla beach from the "lebs" and "wogs" who they alleged had been harassing young women and attacking some life savers, is the most serious example of ethnic violence that Australia has experienced for many years. The ensuing violence that followed a day later when Muslim Lebanese youth went on a rampage in Cronulla serves to provide some sense of their feeling of alienation from Australian society. The events brought to the surface deep seated and long term tensions that challenge views that multiculturalism has made the level of progress in achieving respect for and tolerance of cultural diversity that has been claimed. However, that the riots did not escalate to other parts of Australia or develop into a series of ongoing clashes, along with the speed with which community leaders moved to defuse the situation and enter into constructive dialogue and action, suggests that there is a widespread endorsement and commitment in Australia to the principles underlying multiculturalism.

The posting of a video on the Youtube website glorifying gang rapist Bilal Skaf and boasting of a Lebanese takeover of Australia in western Sydney in January 2007, however, indicates that the tensions that surfaced at Cronulla continue to persist. While the video was removed from the website The Australian reported that "more race hate videos that threaten 'war at its best' between Lebanese and white Australians and glorify gang rape have surfaced online... Warning 'Aussies' to stay out of Bankstown and Punchbowl, the video is a montage of young Lebanes males with guns. ...it features a burning Australian flag and a map filled with bullet holes." [48] Such events, along with statements by controversial mufti Sheik Taj Aldin Alhilali that Australian women were like "uncovered meat" inviting rape, suggest that there is still some distance to travel in order to achieve a culturally diverse society based on mutual respect, tolerance and shared universal values.

Multiculturalism as policy, however, is in the process of being jettisoned as the Government returns to the use of the term "integration" to describe its future vision of Australia and tightens citizenship provisions. The parliamentary secretary to the Immigration Minister, Andrew Robb, advised the Government appointed Council of Multicultural Australia in November 2006 that the term multiculturalism was not particularly meaningful and that he wanted it dropped in the forthcoming redrafting of policy.

In the shift away from multiculturalism towards integration and citizenship the process to become a citizen has been made more demanding by increasing the residential requirements for eligibility from two to four years. In addition applicants will be required to pass a citizenship test in English based on a set of questions that probe their knowledge about Australia and their understanding of its core values. While speculation has abounded as to what these values might be Prime Minister Howard nominated democracy, freedom of the media, gender equality, mateship, the idea of "having a go" and caring for the vulnerable in society. He believed that four years should be an adequate amount of time to have lived in Australia and have gained a working knowledge of English, Australian society and its core values. He said "I couch it in a positive way of ensuring that newcomers are more fully integrated into Australian society. This should not be looked at in negative terms".[49] The public appear to be in strong agreement with him as 85 per cent supported the introduction of a citizenship test in a Newspoll in December 2006.[50] In his reshuffle of Cabinet at the beginning of 2007 John Howard symbolically closed the door on multiculturalism as he dropped the "Multicultural Affairs" from the Department of Immigration and renamed it the Department of Immigration and Citizenship. Multiculturalism as a philosophy within which cultural diversity is managed is being replaced by a policy based on integration and the pursuit of a "shared national identity", although the use of "multicultural" as an adjective to describe Australian society and policy initiatives designed to support migrants to integrate can be expected to continue. It is unlikely that the Opposition, should it win government, will reverse this policy shift as it too has supported the tightening of the criteria for citizenship and in its policy statements has increasingly focussed on the need to ensure the integration of migrants and ethnic communities into Australian society.

Rob Brookman, a prominent identity in Australian arts and one of the recipients of 2007 Australia Day honours, reflected the concerns of the champions of multiculturalism when suggesting that the change of the name of the Ministry of Immigration and Multicultural Affairs to the Ministry of Immigration and Citizenship masked a more sinister shift away from cultural diversity. He expressed his fear that "the cultural clock is being turned back" and warned that "the progressive notion of a rich, diverse and tolerant society is being replaced by an implicit ideal of monoculturalism – the 'White Australia' policy in more sophisticated sheep's clothing".[51]

Is Australia about to slide back into monoculturalism and the hegemony of the dominant group in society – those of Anglo Celtic descent?

Certainly those of Anglo Celtic descent continue to constitute the largest ethnic group by a significant margin. The three most common ancestries identified in the 2001 Census returns were Australian (35.9%), most of whom are of Anglo Celtic descent, English (33.9%) and Irish (10.2%) and illustrates the extent to which those of British and Irish descent remain collectively the dominant cultural group in Australia, constituting perhaps as much as 75 per cent of the population.[52] When the next most common identified ancestries, Italian (4.3%), German (4.0%), Chinese (3.0%) and Greek (2.0%), are considered it is doubtful that the dominance of those of Anglo Celtic heritage has ever been seriously threatened, even when multiculturalism policy was at its zenith in the 1970s and 1980s. Indeed, multiculturalism, while it has improved access to services in Australia for ethnic minorities and supported language and cultural maintenance, has not altered Australia's fundamental political, economic and legal institutions and their processes. They remain firmly rooted in their British origins. Similarly no other language remotely challenges English as its *lingua franca*.

With the demise of multiculturalism the government will continue to proclaim and laud the benefits of Australia's cultural diversity, but ethnic rights will be subordinate to those of citizenship and nation. However the likelihood that Australia will return to an assimilationist approach that attempts to turn the clock back to the point feared by Brookman is extremely small. Australian society has changed dramatically from the kind of society that existed in the first half of the twentieth century. The impact of the immigration of over six million people into Australia from more than two hundred countries has changed the country irrevocably. Australians belong to an increasingly cosmopolitan society and they no longer see themselves as a British bastion in the southern hemisphere. The kind of identification that flourished with Britain and "things British" in the first half of the twentieth century has gradually dissipated to the point that has little current purchase either politically or emotionally. As has been increasingly evident in recent decades, through their participation, support and celebration of national events such as the commemoration of ANZAC, Australia and Remembrance Days as well as sporting events and other forms of achievement Australians are taking pride in their own history and sense of identity. While there are examples among some extremist fringe groups of this erupting into xenophobia and jingoism the abandonment of multiculturalism does not in itself predicate increasing support for such groups or the death knell of cultural diversity in Australia. Integration, based on principles of respect, tolerance, compromise and accommodation provides a continuity that can enable cultural diversity to thrive. A policy of integration has the capacity to continue the strengths that have been associated with multiculturalism along with a much stronger emphasis on identification with the nation and core values including the rule of law, equality and freedom of speech, association and religion. It is difficult to see how the return to integration could be a code for return to assimilation as this implies that there is an homogenous identity with which all, or at least nearly all, Australians identify. Australians are no more alike than any Muslim or other ethnic community members are, nor are they defined only by their nationality or religion. They have multiple and over lapping identities which are maintained and enjoyed because of the underlying liberal values that define Australian society. Any attempt to return to some form of xenophobic nationalism based on a constructed concept of an idealized and homogenized Anglo-Australian identity would be futile in a society where diversity and multiple identities have become the norm.

Endnotes

1. M. McLuhan, *Understanding Media*, (London: Routledge, 1964), A. Giddens, *The Consequences of Modernity*, (Cambridge: polity press, 1990), R. Robertson, *Globalisation*, (London: Sage, 1992), M. Waters, *Globalisation*, (London; Routledge, 1997).
2. A. Smith, "The Problem of National identity: Ancient, Medieval and Modern?", *Ethnic and Racial Studies* vol. 17, No. 3, 1994, p. 382.
3. C. Inglis, *Multiculturalism: New Policy Perspectives to Diversity,* Management of Social Transformations (MOST) – UNESCO, Policy Paper No. 4, 1995, p. 7 at www.unesco.org/most/pp4.htm, 20 December 2006.
4. Inglis, *Multiculturalism: New Policy Perspectives to Diversity.*
5. Inglis, *Multiculturalism: New Policy Perspectives to Diversity.*
6. A. Schmidt, *The Loss of Australia's Aboriginal Language Heritage*, (Canberra: Aboriginal Studies Press, 1990), p. 1.
7. N.G. Butlin, *Economics and the Dreamtime*, (Melbourne: Cambridge University Press, 1993), p. 139.
8. A.T. Yarwood, *Attitudes to Non-European Immigration*, (Australia: Cassell, 1968), p. 80.
9. W. Hancock, *Australia*, (London: Ernest Benn, 1930), pp. 59–60.
10. M. Willard, *History of the White Australia Policy to 1920*, (Melbourne: Frank Cass and Co., 2nd ed., 1967), p. 5.
11. Willard, *History of the White Australia Policy to 1920*, p. 15.
12. C.A. Price, *The Great White Walls are Built*, (Canberra: ANU Press, 1974), p. 76.
13. C.A. Price, *The Great White Walls are Built*, p. 256.
14. Yarwood, *Attitudes to Non-European Immigration*, p. 94.
15. F.S. Stevens, ed., *Racism: The Australian Experience*, (New York: Taplinger Publishing Company, 1972, vol. 1), p. 116.
16. H. McQueen, *A New Britannia*, (Melbourne: Penguin, 1971), p. 16.
17. Stevens, *Racism: The Australian Experience*, p. 138.
18. Willard, *History of the White Australia Policy to 1920*, p. 189.
19. Willard, *History of the White Australia Policy to 1920*, p. 204.
20. C.A. Price, *Southern Europeans in Australia*, (Melbourne: OUP, 1963).
21. DIMIA, *Immigration – Federation to Century's End, 1901–2000*, (Canberra: Commonwealth of Australia, October 2001), Table 5.
22. DIMIA, *Immigration Update 2003–04*, (Canberra: Commonwealth of Australia, January 2005), p. 10.

23. M. Lopez, *The Origins of Multiculturalism in Australia*, (Melbourne: Melbourne University Press, 2000).
24. P. Georgiou, *Multiculturalism does not breed terrorism*, Speech to the Castan Centre for Human Rights Law, 18 October 2005 at www.safecom.org.au/georgiou-multiculturalism.htm 18 December 2006.
25. Commonwealth of Australia, *Multicultural Australia: United in Diversity. Updating the 1999 New Agenda for Multicultural Australia: strategic directions for 2003–2006*, (Canberra: AGPS, 2003), p. 7.
26. *Connecting Diversity: Paradoxes of Multicultural Australia* at http://diversityatwork.com.au/node/115 17 December 2006.
27. Inglis, *Multiculturalism: New Policy Perspectives to Diversity*, p. 32.
28. DIMIA, *Population Flows: Immigration aspects, 2003–04 edition*, (Canberra: Commonwealth of Australia, January 2005), p. 81.
29. DIMIA, *Population Flows: Immigration aspects, 2003–04 edition*, pp. 84–85.
30. Helen Hughes, *Difference of Opinion*, (ABC TV, 9:30 pm, 12/2/07).
31. *Face the Facts – Some Questions and Answers about Refugees, Migrants and Indigenous People* at www.humanrights.gov.au/racial_discrimination/face_facts/migrants.html, 18 December 2006.
32. *Face the Facts – Some Questions and Answers about Refugees, Migrants and Indigenous People.*
33. Australian Bureau of Statistics, *Prisoners in Australia*, Catalogue No. 4517.0, (Canberra: ABS, 22 January 2004).
34. Australian Bureau of Statistics, *National Health Survey: Aboriginal and Torres Strait Islander Results*, Catalogue No. 4438.0, (Canberra: ABS, 2002).
35. Australian Bureau of Statistics, *Population Characteristics, Aboriginal and Torres Strait Islander Australians, 2001*, Catalogue No. 4713.0, (Canberra: ABS, October 2003).
36. G. Blainey, *All for Australia,* (Sydney: Methuen Hayes), 1984.
37. Committee to Advise on Australian Immigration Policy, *Immigration: A Commitment to Australia* (Canberra: AGPS, 1988).
38. J. Brett, *Relaxed and Comfortable: The Liberal Party's Australia,* Quarterly Essay, No. 19, (Black Inc, Melbourne, 2005), p. 25.
39. Brett, *Relaxed and Comfortable: The Liberal Party's Australia*, p. 37.
40. Commonwealth of Australia, *Multicultural Australia: United in Diversity: Updating the 1999 New National Agenda for a Multicultural Australia*, p. 7.
41. Phillip Coorey, "Treasured thoughts", *The Advertiser*, (Adelaide), 30 August 2005, p. 19.
42. Peter Goers, "A Muslim – and a proud Aussie", *The Advertiser*, (Adelaide), 14 August 2005, p. 32.
43. No author, "Push for headscarf school ban divisive", *Sunday Mail*, (Adelaide), 29 August 2005, p. 6.
44. Sean Fewster and Ian McPhedran, "We are Australian through and through", *The Advertiser*, (Adelaide), 12 August 2005, p. 7.
45. Kara Phillips, "Disturbing rise in race complaints", *The Advertiser*, (Adelaide), 17 November 2006, p. 9.
46. Michael Owen, "Racial abuse in SA on rise", *The Advertiser*, (Adelaide), 1 January 2007, p. 15.

47. Jessica Leo, "Anti-Jew site defying court", *The Advertiser* (Adelaide), December 3, 2006, p. 32.
48. Imre Salusinszky and Simon Hayes, 'Sickening' video puts race back on election agenda", *The Australian* (Sydney), 25 January 2007, p. 4.
49. Maria Moscaritolo, "Making model citizens", *The Advertiser* (Adelaide), 13 December 2006, p. 21.
50. Mark Lopez, "Multicultural spirit lives on", *The Australian* (Sydney), 25 January 2007, p. 12.
51. Patrick McDonald, "Warning of slide into xenophobia", *The Advertiser* (Adelaide), 26 January 2007, p. 16.
52. DIMIA, The People of Australia: Statistics from the 2001 Census, 2003, Table 11, Ancestry, (Canberra: Commonwealth of Australia), p. 54.

6

Limits of Multiculturalism in a Liberal Polity: Need for a Shared Identity

Sushila Ramaswamy

Multiculturalism inquires into the ways of accommodating cultural diversity of different groups rather than uniformity in a mass democracy. The term was first used in Canada in 1971 and then Australia in 1978 to describe a new public policy that moved away from assimilation of ethnic minorities, and immigrants in particular, towards policies of acceptance and integration of diverse cultures (Lopez, 2000:2–3). It entered the American and British political lexicon in the 1980s (Glazer, 1997:8). In the US, when it entered the public debate in the first instance, it was about the need for reform of public school curriculum in disciplines like history, literature and social sciences as its contents reflected a Eurocentric bias. Glazer observes that initially it was about 'how American society, particularly American education, should respond to diversity' (1997:8). Since then, multiculturalism questions the traditional conception of America as a 'melting pot' of diverse people bonded in a common culture of the New World. Multiculturalism considers the metaphor 'melting pot' a cover for oppressive assimilation to the dominant or hegemonic white culture. It insists that American society has in fact always been multiracial and diverse and therefore, there is a need to underline the separate characteristics and virtues of particular cultural groups. Instead of 'melting pot', terms such as 'salad bowl' and 'glorious mosaic' is preferred as it conveys more a sense of separateness and distinctiveness in describing a nation of immigrants (Ibid:10).

What is Multiculturalism?

Like many other concepts in political theory, there is no unanimity about what constitutes multiculturalism. It remains a contested concept. For some, multiculturalism requires reasonable changes in social and political institutions to enable cultural minorities to preserve their language and their distinctive customs. For others, multiculturalism is about eliminating racism and nurturing rather than repudiating or tolerating 'difference' and, this implies greater social transformation. A unifying theme amongst the multiculturalists is their resistance to homogenization or assimilation which is evident in the conception of citizenship implicit in the contemporary theories of justice that conceptualizes justice as equal rights for all citizens irrespective of their gender, religion and ethnicity. Kymlicka points out that the logical conclusion of liberal principles of justice "seems to be a 'colour-blind' constitution – the removal of all legislation differentiating people in terms of their race or ethnicity (except for temporary measures, like affirmative action, which are believed necessary to reach a 'colour blind' society" (1989:141). Multiculturalists see this attempt towards a 'colour blind' society as ill founded, for it is not possible to separate the state and ethnicity and when the liberal state attempts to do this, it unfairly privileges certain ways of life over others. They allege that liberals do not take diversity seriously. This is despite the fact that liberals value pluralism, with Rawls stressing on 'reasonable pluralism', which is why liberals defend a neutral public philosophy that entails equal rights for all citizens. Kymlicka argues that liberals, like Rawls and Dworkin, have falsely assumed that members of a political community are members of the same cultural community. Bikku Parekh observes that Rawls, like many liberals, "is sensitive to moral but not cultural plurality, and thus takes little account of the cultural aspirations of such communities as the indigenous peoples, national minorities, sub national groups, and the immigrants" (2000:89).

Multiculturalism is not merely "about difference and identity per se but about those that are embedded in and sustained by culture, that is, a body of beliefs and practices in terms of which a group of people understand themselves and the world and organize their individual and collective lives" (Parekh, Ibid:2–3). The issue of cultural diversity and dominance is also integral to the politics of recognition of difference and notion of differentiated citizenship and group rights. Like multiculturalism, it challenges the traditional notions of citizenship, which define citizenship in terms of regarding people as individuals with equal rights under the law. This is how democratic citizenship is normally distinguished from feudal and pre-modern views that decided people's political status by their group identity of guilds. When this well established social practice of group identity, behaviour and social balancing was challenged by the theory of Divine Rights of King, then the present form of natural rights theory that provides the individualist basis to liberalism emerged. However, cultural pluralists deny this very basis of liberal individualism and argue that citizenship must reflect the distinct socio-cultural identity of groups like African American, indigenous peoples, ethnic and religious minorities, gays and lesbians, who feel excluded and marginalized because of their 'difference' from the mainstream of society.

There are two broad types of differentiated citizenship. For some groups – the poor, women, ethnic minorities and immigrants, the demand for group rights is a demand for greater inclusion and participation in the mainstream society, as they feel excluded, under-represented or un-represented. Or, they might seek exemption from laws that disadvantage them economically or they want school curriculum to recognise their contributions to society's culture and history. These groups accept the goal of national integration, for they desire to be part of mainstream society as full and equal members but only insist that recognition and accommodation of their 'difference' is needed to bring about national integration. The other group demanding differentiated citizenship reject the goal of national integration and wish to be self-governing, to freely develop their culture and are usually national minorities or distinct historical communities occupying their own territory with a distinct language and history. They do not want greater representation in the central government but transfer of power from the central government to their communities, often through some kind of federalism or local autonomy. They do not desire greater inclusion into the larger society but autonomy from it.

Multiculturalism and its Defenders

It was in the 1990s, political theorists began to furnish the theoretical basis of a multicultural society. The first systematic theory of multiculturalism was elaborated by Will Kymlicka in his two major works: *Liberalism, Community and Culture* (1989) and *Multicultural Citizenship* (1995). Kymlicka criticizes the earlier models of unitary republican citizenship in which all the citizens enjoy common citizenship rights on the grounds, that in its assumption of a more homogenous political community, it ignores cultural and ethnic diversity. He observes that liberalism with its stress on individual rights has not paid adequate attention to group rights. He argues that in a multicultural state, a comprehensive theory of justice would have to include both universal rights and certain group differentiated rights or special status for minority cultures (1995:6). He observes that the individual's ability to choose the good life necessarily takes place within a cultural context. One's ethnic or national culture constitutes a condition of autonomy and it is for this reason that group rights and differentiated citizenship needs to be guaranteed.

Kymlicka is dissatisfied with post-war liberal political theory, which in his view, wrongly assumes that provision of basic individual rights could resolve the problem of national minorities. He contends that minority rights could not be subsumed under human rights because "human rights standards are simply unable to resolve some of the most important and controversial questions relating to cultural minorities" (Ibid:4). These included questions about which languages should be recognized in parliaments, bureaucracies and courts; whether any ethnic or national groups should have publicly funded education in their mother tongues; whether internal boundaries should be drawn so that cultural minorities form majorities in local regions; whether traditional homelands of indigenous people should be reserved for their benefit; and to what degree of cultural integration might be required of immigrants seeking citizenship (Ibid:4-5). As traditional human rights doctrines offer no guidance on these questions, Kymlicka recommends the need for a theory of minority rights to supplement human rights theory. This would enable us to confront burning issues that raged in places like Eastern Europe which was mired in disputes over local autonomy, language and naturalisation. He proposes to develop a liberal theory of minority rights which would explain "how minority rights could coexist with human rights and how minority rights are limited by principles of individual liberty, democracy and social justice" (Ibid:6).

Kymlicka, in course of elaborating his theory, distinguishes three kinds of minority or group differentiated rights that are to be assured to ethnic and national groups: self government rights, polyethnic rights and special representation rights. Self-government rights require the delegation of powers to national minorities, such as indigenous peoples, but are not available to other cultural minorities who had immigrated into the country. Polyethnic rights are for cultural minorities as it guarantees financial support and legal and political protection from the state for certain practices associated with particular ethnic or religious groups and in particular to aboriginal people as to enable them to maintain their culture and autonomy. Polyethnic rights might include legislation to prevent suppression or marginalisation of cultural and identity concern of minority ethnic groups by the deliberate, or unthinking, discrimination of the majority ethnic population within a country. Special state support for media policies and funding to address the media interests of minority ethnic groups are one particular expression of polyethnic rights. Both indigenous peoples and immigrant minorities might also be eligible for special representation rights which guarantee places for minority representatives on state bodies or institutions.

Of pivotal importance in Kymlicka's account of group-differentiated citizenship is the distinction that he makes between two kinds of minorities: national minorities and ethnic minorities. The former are peoples whose previously self-governing, territorially concentrated cultures have been incorporated into a large state. These are 'American Indians', Puerto Ricans, Chicanos and native Hawaiians in the United States; the Quebecois and various aboriginal communities in Canada and the Aborigines in Australia. Ethnic minorities are peoples who have immigrated to a new society and do not wish to govern themselves, but nonetheless wish to retain their ethnic identities and traditions. A modern state might be 'multicultural' in one (or both) of two senses: either because it is 'multinational' since its members belong to different nations; or it is polyethnic, since its members emigrated from different countries (Ibid:18). The two groups have very different legitimate claims to make: the national minorities need not fear a reduction to the status of migrants as a result of the policies of multiculturalism just as other citizens need not fear that multiculturalism means immigrants have a legitimate claim to self government.

But Kymlicka also strongly believes that group-based protection should not violate rights fundamental to individual well being. He acknowledges the fact that individuals might need protection from the abusive power of their own ethnic communities. He endorses group-differentiated rights which provide for external protection for groups, but does not permit 'internal restrictions' except in cases of systematic and gross human violations like slavery or genocide, in which case state intervention is warranted. For Kymlicka, culture is important because it is the context within which individuals learn how to choose, but its value reduces when it disallows individuals to choose their lives for themselves, thus retaining the overall spirit of liberalism that it permits individual's capacity for autonomous choice.

Charles Taylor has offered an alternative theory in his *The Politics of Recognition* (1994) by rejecting as inadequate the liberal theory of multiculturalism. Liberalism, in his view, is incapable of giving culture the recognition it requires. Liberalism emphasizes sameness, viewing individuals as bearers of rights and possessors of dignity as equal citizens but cultural groups desire recognition of their distinctness and not sameness. He rejects Kymlicka's efforts to develop a liberalism that might accommodate difference by granting individuals differentiated rights to enable them to pursue their particular ends. According to Taylor, this solution works only 'for existing people who find themselves trapped within a culture under pressure, and can flourish within it or not at all. But it does justify measures designed to ensure survival through indefinite future generations" (1994:62). In this context, he cites the example of Quebecois whose aim is the long term survival of the French speaking community in Canada.

Defenders of the politics of difference desire an extension of the democratic processes to give greater scope to the participation of cultural minorities in the shaping and governing of the polity (Young 1990, 2000; Phillips 1995; Williams 1995; Tully 2003). In *Strange Multiplicity* (1995), Tully recommends a reconstruction of modern constitutionalism as to accommodate the wide variety of cultural traditions to enhance the quality of liberal constitutional arrangements. Williams (1998) proposes measures like proportional representation, holding reserved seats in legislative bodies for members of under-represented marginalized groups, redrawing of electoral boundaries when under-represented groups are concentrated in geographically determined ridings or providing for multi-member districts when appropriate and providing for quotas for under-represented groups in political party candidate lists.

Young demands guaranteed representation only of oppressed disadvantaged groups and veto power over policies that affect them. These groups can only be fully integrated through what she calls differentiated citizenship. It means that members of certain groups should be incorporated into the political community, not only as individuals, but also through their group, and their rights should depend in part on their group membership.

A democratic public should provide mechanisms for the effective recognition and representation of the distinct voices and perspectives of those of its constituent groups that are oppressed or disadvantaged. Such group representation implies institutional mechanisms and public resources supporting (i) self organisation of group members so that they achieve collective empowerment and a reflective understanding of their collective experience and interests in the context of the society; (ii) group analysis and group generation of policy proposals in institutionalized contexts where decision makers are obliged to show that their deliberations have taken group perspectives into consideration; and (iii) group veto power regarding specific policies that affect a group directly, such as reproductive rights policy for women, or land use policy for Indian reservations (1990:184).

Young does not consider protection of minority cultures as a state responsibility, a notion advanced by some liberal multiculturalists like Kymlicka and Raz (1986; 1994), as adequate, as this is tantamount to confining groups to the private sphere. It fails to give public endorsement to their distinct identities. The public sphere is dominated by norms which appear to be universal and culturally neutral but in reality reflect cultural values of the dominant social categories – middle class white males.

The standpoint of the privileged, their particular experience and standards is constructed as normal and neutral. If some groups' experience differs from this neutral experience, or they do not measure up to those standards, their difference is constructed as deviance and inferiority. Not only are the experience and values of the oppressed thereby ignored and silenced but they become disadvantaged by their situated identities (Ibid:116).

Young (1992), picking up on the model of 'associative democracy' that Cohen and Rogers (1992) proposes that the state ought to be an organization of oppressed minorities with the view that they could exercise real power. Arguing within the US context she (2000) also points out that exclusive emphasis on rational argument further disadvantages minorities who are well versed in its niceties. She supports forms of communication like rhetoric, story telling (or testimony, or narrative) and an oral tradition argument, which are more accessible to disadvantaged minorities.

Phillips (1995) puts forward an essentialist assumption of what she calls 'the politics of presence' namely representation for the under-represented (in her example – women) by reserving places in governmental bodies for people from marginalized groups or 'the politics of ideas' of ensuring that at least some political party platforms feature marginalized group interests. The second one is complementary to the first one and that will ensure representation of the un-represented segments in government. But it is possible that the representatives would not pursue the specific interest of the group that they represent. Party discipline may lead to some accountability but even proportional representation may not lead to electoral success. One solution is by including group list in the list of political party candidates ensuring representation of marginalized groups.

Phillips (1991) conceptualizes the public and private spheres as interdependent but distinct. She thinks it is necessary to integrate the private sphere into analysis and focus on gendered nature of power relations within the family, and not ignore it as traditional political science has done. The inequities within the family are as relevant to issues of social justice as inequalities in the public sphere. Democratization of the public sphere understood in terms of higher participation of women is possible only if there is prior democratisation of the private sphere. This, she desires by maintaining the public-private distinction, like Okin (1991) and Young (1987), so as to preserve areas for individual decision and privacy. In this context, she mentions the right of abortion. She also argues for the need to detach the two spheres of gender differences and base it instead on the criterion of right to privacy.

Multiculturalism and its Critics

Critics of multiculturalism have raised a number of objections to its basic formulations. For some, it is simple that only individuals, not groups, have rights (Narveson 1991; Hartney 1991). Graf (1994:194) observes that groups are fictitious entities and fictitious entities could not be right bearers. The idea of differentiated citizenship is a contradiction in terms. If groups are encouraged to focus on their 'difference' then how citizenship can be a shared identity, a source of commonality and solidarity among the various groups in society.

Aboriginal peoples, on whose behalf multiculturalists speak, see multiculturalism as facilitating further marginalisation of their communities and culture in a modern state which is more attuned to the needs of migrants than to the aborigines. Many press for the rights of indigenous minorities and insist that unlike immigrants, what they need is not only recognition of their independent status but also rectification of past injustice.

Kukathas (2003:185) wonders about the utility of Kymlicka's liberal principles emphasizing the importance of individual autonomy, as he refuses to grant the liberal state the right to intervene in illiberal groups. A severe objection to multiculturalism is that in pleading for special rights for cultural groups or religious communities, it may permit these groups to continue with practices that are sexist and highly disadvantageous, if not harmful to women. Okin (1998; 1999a; 1999b; 2002) finds among most exponents of multiculturalism a weak commitment to women's rights and interests.

The non-liberal critics contend that the prevailing theories of liberal multiculturalism are essentially arguments for homogeneity, since the idea is that one will support cultural diversity as long as the cultures are liberal. They observe that liberal multiculturalism is narrow: since its base is in a liberal theory of autonomy, it does not give enough support to non-liberal cultures (Deveaux 2000, Parekh 2000). The non-liberal multiculturalists stress on the intrinsic worth of culture.

Mouffe (1992) in response to group-differentiated citizenship points out that the solution is not to make gender or other group characteristics important to the concept of citizenship but to reduce their significance. She proposes a conception of citizenship which is neither gendered nor gender neutral but one based on real equality and liberty for all citizens. She stresses political issues and claims, and observes that the public-private distinction needs to be re-defined from case to case, according to the type of political demands, and not in a fixed and permanent way.

Miller (2000) criticizes the advocates like Young of what he calls 'politics of recognition', those who argue that the 'primary aim of democratic politics shall be to endorse and promote, both symbolically and materially the group identities of historical disadvantaged groups, such as women and ethnic minorities' (Ibid:4). He observes that this perspective is dangerous to the groups as well, which it is supposed to serve. The identities of these groups are much more open and fluid than recognised by the advocates of group identity. He writes:

"Identity politics is self-defeating, for it looks to politics to provide a confirmation of identities that the political sphere by its very nature cannot provide; and in encouraging groups to affirm their singular identities at the expense of shared national identities, it undermines the very conditions in which minority groups, especially disadvantaged groups, can hope to achieve some measure of justice for their demands" (Ibid:79).

Criticizing the theorists of group rights, Miller argues that politics of recognition by its emphasis on separateness creates a barrier to the politics of inclusion. This political mechanism of inclusion is important to reshape the public space, as an expression of shared national identity in a manner that, it is 'more hospitable to women, ethnic minorities and other groups without emptying them of content and destroying the underpinnings of democratic politics'(Ibid:80).

Miller mentions J.S. Mill who, despite lending support to the independence movements in Poland, Hungary and Italy, is appreciative of the role that national identities play in supporting liberal institutions (2006:534). In the *Considerations on Representative Government* (1861), Mill argues that unless the several groups, which compose a society, have mutual sympathy and trust that is derived from a common nationality, it would be difficult to have free institutions. There would be no common interest to prevent government excesses and politics would become a zero-sum game, in which each group could only hope to profit by the exploitation of the others. Rule of law in such a situation usually becomes the first casualty. Miller also cites the example of

Mazzini who argued passionately for Italian unity and independence while defending individual rights and republican government. He observes that liberal thinkers by the mid-nineteenth century "forged links between individual freedom, national independence, and representative government in opposing the imperial powers of Europe" (Ibid:534). Miller (1995; 2000; 2001) states that nationality is important and its recognition need not mean suppression of other sources of ethnicity. One major reason as to why nationality is important is because it is the precondition for the pursuit of social justice, which cannot be pursued globally (1999). The pursuit of social justice requires a measure of social solidarity and that would mean that citizens go along with the institutions which perform a redistributive function.

Barry argues that multiculturalism is a fog that blots out recognition of class inequalities and human rights abuses. It is inconsistent with liberalism and disrespectful of liberal values and should be rejected. By replacing the idea of equal citizenship based on equal rights with culturally differentially rights, and in modifying the doctrine of equal citizenship, the multiculturalists are insensitive to the abuse of power which is inevitable in such a policy. Barry considers the concept of uniform citizenship and individual autonomy as an achievement of the Enlightenment. By criticising the Enlightenment and in advocating culturally differentiated rights, these theorists overlook the gross irregularities and inequities that existed prior to the era of Enlightenment. Barry finds an affinity between the Right and the Left in their anti-liberal rhetoric as emphasis on special interests is an old policy of divide and rule beneficial to those who gain from the status-quo. Such an emphasis denies any unified struggle for the common demand of the disadvantaged. There is a larger arena at the shared disadvantages of all like unemployment, poverty, low quality housing and inadequate public housing which can be tackled only from the point of view of the larger category of the disadvantaged. Particularity of group politics dissipates the political effort for mobilising people on the basis of a broad shared interest. Emphasis on cultural heterogeneity does not lead to either promotion of liberty or equality. Such policies are policies of retreat as group differentiated politics is inimical to the pursuit of a programme of universal material benefit to which all must have access. He insists that politics of multiculturalism undermines the politics of redistribution.

The consequence of this 'culturalization' of group identities is the systematic neglect of alternative causes of group disadvantage. Thus, the members of a group may suffer not because they have distinctive culturally derived goals but because they do poorly in achieving generally shared objectives such as a good education, desirable and well-paid jobs (or perhaps any job at all), a safe and salubrious neighbourhood in which to live and enough income to enable them to be adequately housed, clothed and fed and to participate in the social, economic and political life of their society (2001:305–306).

Barry is clear that the conflict between culture and law is over-emphasized as exemptions in the name of culture normally lead to sidetracking or breaking the law in the context of denial of individual rights within the group. He additionally regards multiculturalism and group rights discourses as endangering protections hard won over the centuries, in now liberal polities for individuals' religious and family autonomy. Arguing within the framework provided by J.S. Mill, Barry writes:

"The defining feature of a liberal is, I suggest, that it is someone who holds that there are certain rights against oppression, exploitation and injury to which every single human being is entitled to lay claim, and that appeals to cultural diversity and pluralism under no circumstances trump the value of basic human rights. For [the multiculturalists] a society is to be conceived as a fictitious body whose real constituents are communities" (Ibid:132–133, 300).

Contrary to 'Enlightenment liberalism' which Barry defends is 'Reformation Liberalism' propounded by Galston (1995) one which takes into account diversity and underlines the importance of "differences among individuals and groups over such matters as the nature of the good life, sources of moral authority, reason versus faith, and the like" (1995:521). Barry rejects Reformation Liberalism on three grounds: (i) Liberal theory is based on the primacy of respect for individuals which included the culture as well provided culture is not illiberal by itself and does not violate equal respect to other cultures. (ii) On the question of liberalism's commitment to diversity as enhancing the range of choice, Barry argues that for liberals, individualism is more important than diversity. (iii) Regarding the question of public-private divide and the liberal commitment to non-intervention in the private sphere, Barry points out that throughout the process of history, liberalism has challenged both parental and paternal authority while protecting the individual from the group to which he belongs. On the question of every group having to conform to liberalism, Barry points that it is a free choice of the individuals to join any group or association with a rider that such groups are to be consistent with the legal protection that exists for all those outside the group. There are, however, two important preconditions: (a) all participants in the group are sane adults and (b) and participation should be voluntary (Ibid:148). Groups may then do as they please, provided those who do not like the way the group functions can exit without facing undue costs (Ibid:150).

Conclusion

Liberal individualism accepts the multiple identities of persons but restricts it to the private sphere. Like radical feminism of the 1960s which proclaimed 'personal is political', multiculturalists grossly exaggerate the notion of cultural exclusivity and differentiations. They ought to take note of Rorty's (1994) warning of the dangers of cultural essentialism. Rorty points out that within the parameter of the sanctity of individual rights overemphasis on culture can be both coercive and oppressive. One-person-one-vote achieved after years of long and protracted struggle, constitutional guarantees of individual rights to all, without which no other right is meaningful, and the notion of public-private divide are the time tested mechanisms of a well governed and effective state. The procedural framework emphasised both by Schumpeter and Rawls is to be the basis of a substantive theory of accommodation and redress of grievances and injustice. Multiculturalism with its zeal to stress on difference and cultural exclusivity underestimates the safety values that exist within liberal political theory for answering satisfactorily its concerns.

References

Barry, B. (2001): Culture and Equality: An Egalitarian Critique of Multiculturalism, Oxford, Polity.

Cohen, J. and Rogers, J. (1992): 'Secondary associations and democratic governance', *Politics and Society*, 20, 393–472.

Deveaux, M. (2000): *Cultural Pluralism and Dilemmas of Justice*, Ithaca, NY: Cornell University Press.

Galston, W. (1995): 'Two Concepts of Liberalism', *Ethics* 105 (3), pp. 516–534.

Glazer, N. (1997): *We Are All Multiculturalists Now*, Cambridge, MA: Harvard University Press.

Graf, James A. (1994): 'Human rights, peoples, and the right of self determination' in J. Baker, (ed.), *Group Rights*, Toronto, University of Toronto Press.

Hartney, M. (1991): 'Some Confusions concerning collective rights', *Canadian Journal of Law and Jurisprudence*, 4, pp. 293–314.

Kukathas, C. (2003): *The Liberal Archipelago: A Theory of Diversity and Freedom,* Oxford, Oxford University Press.

Kymlicka, W. (1989): *Liberalism, Community and Culture*, Oxford, Oxford University Press.

—— (1995): *Multicultural Citizenship: A Liberal Theory of Minority Rights*, Oxford, Oxford University Press.

Lopez, M. (2000): *The Origins of Multiculturalism in Australian Politics*, Melbourne, Melbourne University Press.

Miller, D. (1999): *On Nationality*, Oxford, Clarendon.

—— (1999): 'Justice and Global Inequality' in A. Hurrell and N. Woods, (ed.), *Inequality, Globalization and World Politics*, Oxford, Oxford University Press.

—— (2000): *Citizenship and National Identity*, Oxford, Polity.

—— (2001): 'Nationality in Divided Societies' in A.G. Gagnon and J. Tully, (eds.), *Multinational Democracies*, Cambridge, Cambridge University Press.

Narveson, J. (1991): 'Collective Rights?' *Canadian Journal of Law and Jurisprudence*, 4, pp. 329–345.

—— (2006): 'Nationalism in J.S. Dryzek, B. Honig and A. Phillips, (eds.), *The Oxford Handbook of Political Theory*, Oxford, Oxford University Press.

Mouffe, C. (1992): 'Feminism, Citizenship and radical democratic politics', in J. Butler and J. Scott, (eds.), *Feminists Theorise the Political*, New York, Routledge.

Okin, S.M. (1991): 'Gender, the public, the private' in D. Held, (ed.), *Political Theory Today*, Cambridge, Polity.

—— (1998): 'Feminism and Multiculturalism: some tensions', *Ethics*, 108, pp. 661–684.

—— (1999a): 'Is Multiculturalism bad for women?' in J. Cohen, M. Howard and M. Nussbaum, (eds.), *Is Multiculturalism bad for Women*? Princeton, NJ: Princeton University Press.

—— (1999b) 'Reply' in J. Cohen, M. Howard and M. Nussbaum, (eds.), *Is Multiculturalism bad for Women*? Princeton, NJ: Princeton University Press.

—— (2002): 'Mistresses of their own destiny: group rights, gender and realistic rights of exit', *Ethics*, 112, pp. 205–230.

Parekh, B. (2000): *Rethinking Multiculturalism: Cultural Diversity and Political Theory*, London, Macmillan.

Phillips, A. (1991): *Engendering Democracy*, Cambridge, Polity.

—— (1995): *The Politics of Presence*, Oxford, Clarendon.

Raz, J. (1986): *The Morality of Freedom*, Oxford, Clarendon.

—— (1994) 'Multiculturalism: a liberal perspective' in his *Ethics in the Public Domain*, Oxford, Clarendon.

Rorty, R. (1994): 'Strangers and Liberals', Political Theory, 22, February, pp. 167–175.

Taylor, C. (1994): 'The Politics of Recognition' in A. Gutman, (ed.), *Multiculturalism: Examining the Politics of Recognition*, Princeton, NJ: Princeton University Press.

Tully, J. (1995): *Strange Multiplicity: Constitutionalism in an Age of Diversity*, Cambridge, Cambridge University Press.

—— (2003): 'Ethical Pluralism and Classical Liberalism' in R. Madsen and T.B. Strong, (eds.), *The Many and the One: Religious and Secular Perspectives on Ethical Pluralism in the Modern World,* Princeton, NJ: Princeton University Press.

Williams, M. (1998): *Voice, Trust and Memory: Marginalized Groups and the Failings of Liberal Representation*, Princeton, NJ: Princeton University Press.

Young, I.M. (1987): 'Impartiality and the civic public' in S. Benhabib and D. Cornell, (eds.), *Feminism as Critique*, Cambridge, Polity.

—— (1990): *Justice and the Politics of Difference*, Princeton, NJ: Princeton University Press.

—— (1992): 'Social Groups in associative democracy', *Politics and Society*, 20, p. 529–534.

—— (2000): *Inclusion and Democracy*, Oxford, Oxford University Press.

7

"Australia is a Multicultural Community – you'll feel at home": Cultural Diversity and the Promotion of Australia Internationally

Andrew Hassam

The internationally successful Yash Raj production, *Salaam Namaste*,[1] which was set in Melbourne, Victoria, explores how various Australian government agencies have attempted to project Australia overseas as a culturally diverse nation.

Government Agencies

Film Agencies

Australian State film agencies, such as Film Victoria and the New South Wales Film and Television Office, are able to offer cash production incentives to overseas film-makers, but these typically require a minimum spend in Australia of A$3.5 million, and Indian productions spend in the region of only A$1 million.[2] *Salaam Namaste* had a reported budget of A$3.3 million ($US2.5 million),[3] but that was still not enough to qualify for State film production incentives. And it is nowhere near the size of spend required to qualify for Australian Federal Government tax offsets, for which qualifying productions need to have a minimum Australian expenditure of A$15 million.

The film agencies put most of their effort into attracting big budget US productions, with budgets ranging from A$30 million to A$100 million or more for blockbusters like the Mission Impossible and Superman movies. On the whole, film agencies do not think of Bollywood as a future major contributor to the local film industry, and Film Victoria was unable to support *Salaam Namaste*, instead referring the producers to the State tourism commission, Tourism Victoria.[4]

Tourism Agencies

Salaam Namaste has been described as "the first Indian film to be fully shot in Australia",[5] and like other countries, Australia has openly courted Indian film-makers. Yash Chopra, who produced *Salaam Namaste*, has himself spoken of the ways in which government agencies can ease the task of filming abroad.

Yash Chopra says the governments of Singapore, Malaysia, Australia, New Zealand, Mauritius, Canada, Germany and Italy are approaching Indian film-makers to shoot there. "The tourism departments show you around, recommend good locations, and are very enterprising when it comes to providing infrastructure for the shoot. They help with everything right from cooking and cleaning facilities to arranging for dollies and cranes. If I had to shoot in India, I would have to lug all that heavy equipment when I went location hunting or on a shoot. So shooting abroad works out much easier," he recommends.[6]

Salaam Namaste features many iconic shots of Melbourne and Victoria, and because Tourism Victoria saw the film as a way of pushing their "brand strengths" in India, they contributed A$10,000. Tourism Victoria also provided assistance with location permits, which can be difficult to obtain, though the most iconic location in Melbourne for the Indian market, the Melbourne Cricket Ground, proved too expensive to use.[7]

Tourism Australia, the Australian Federal tourism commission, has reported that "The average annual growth rate for visitors from India over the decade from 1996 to 2005 was 15 per cent."[8] The total for visitors from India is expected to rise to 85,000 in 2006. The figures, however, are modest when compared with the 300,000 visitors from China in 2006, and India is therefore categorised as an emerging market rather than a developed market. As a result there are only limited resources available for promotion, making collaboration with film and television producers the most cost effective way of showcasing Australia in India.[9]

The international success of *Dil Chahta Hai* and *Salaam Namaste* has demonstrated how useful Bollywood films can be to promoting Australia in India, and both *Salaam Namaste* and *Dil Chahta Hai*[10] have been used by Tourism Australia to showcase Australia in India.[11] Melbourne's success with *Salaam Namaste* is the kind of success that the South Australian Government is hoping for with their recent support of Love Story 2050[12] which was filmed mainly in Adelaide and country South Australia. The film was going to be filmed in Scotland but the production was attracted to South Australia by a reported "$150,000 cash grant and a number of incentives such as assistance with road closures."[13] A press release by the South Australian Premier, Mike Rann, was, not surprisingly, upbeat about its potential in putting South Australia on the map: "Placement of our State in mainstream entertainment, such as this movie, is a great way of increasing our profile among an increasingly affluent and mobile audience of many millions of people."[14]

Australian Trade Commission

Of course, Premier Mike Rann is hoping that increasing South Australia's profile "among an increasingly affluent and mobile audience of many millions of people" will benefit more than tourism: "South Australia's relationship with

India is increasingly important – trade between us is growing and there is an increasing awareness of Adelaide as an education destination."[15]

India's strong and growing economy is hugely attractive to Australia in terms of trade, and while on a Trade Mission to India in 2006, Australia's Prime Minister, John Howard, made time in his tight schedule to take a photo opportunity with Yash Chopra and to meet some of the cast and crew of *Salaam Namaste*:

Austrade officials in Mumbai – India's film capital – are working hard to promote Australia as a film location. On a four-day visit to boost trade with India, Prime Minister John Howard met some of the cast and crew of the hit musical [*Salaam Namaste*]. Despite previously confessing to a soft spot for British crime drama Midsomer Murders,[16] Mr Howard showed himself to be a man of varied tastes, proclaiming he and his wife, Janette, had "enjoyed immensely" a viewing of the movie.[17]

John Howard was clearly persuaded by Austrade, the Australian Federal trade commission, that associating himself with Bollywood was a good way of publicising his presence in India, and Austrade officials play a role in channelling Bollywood production towards Australia. But the presence of Austrade officials demonstrated not so much the Prime Minister's interest in cinema, either Indian or Australian, as an interest in promoting tourism and trading links generally between Australia and India.

What Images of Australia Do Government Agencies Wish to Promote?

Any discussion of the desire by Australian film, tourism and trade commissions for Indian film-makers to shoot in Australia needs to consider the images of Australia being projected onto cinema screens in India. An indication of what Indian film producers are looking for was given in an interview in *The Age* by Mitu Bhowmick Lange, a director of Melbourne-based Black Cat Films, the company which brought *Salaam Namaste* to Victoria.

Anand [Siddarth Anand, the director] had been preparing to film *Salaam Namaste* in San Francisco when he visited Melbourne last year on the recommendation of a friend who had been one of eight up-and-coming directors invited to the Victorian capital for a Bollywood festival. Anand was blown away by the city's architecture, variety of settings and clear light for filming. "They wanted a place that was very multicultural and cosmopolitan," says Mitu Bhowmick Lange, an expatriate Indian who is the film's line producer. "But they also wanted a quaintness and charm to it (just like) Melbourne."[18]

Melbourne seems to appeal to Indian film-makers because, on the one hand, it is "multicultural and cosmopolitan" while, on the other, it has "a quaintness and charm to it". In other words, it is both modern and old. This combination of modernity and heritage is consistent with the kind of cosmopolitanism that both Film Victoria and Tourism Victoria project as a feature of Melbourne. In its promotional literature, Film Victoria links Melbourne's multiculturalism with its cosmopolitanism: "With a population of 3.4 million people descended from a multitude of continents around the globe, Melbourne is alive with cosmopolitan energy that offers up countless experiences and attractions to thrill its visitors."[19] However, there is no necessary link between multiculturalism and cosmopolitanism and it is not specified how Melbourne's "cosmopolitan energy" derives from a population "descended from a multitude of continents around the globe."

Melbourne's "cosmopolitan energy" appears to be related to middle-class affluence and a transnational consumerism: "Melbourne is an exciting, modern metropolis, bustling with award-winning restaurants, hip music venues, cool bars and sensational shopping".[20] Yet the diversity of cultures in Melbourne, which has significant migrant communities from, for example, Italy, Greece, China, Vietnam and the South Asian subcontinent, has been largely the result of unskilled and semi-skilled migration rather than the skilled migration of middle-class professionals, and the diversity of restaurants or the diversity of national dress displayed at Melbourne's multicultural festivals is not the same as the cosmopolitanism of global consumerism, with its chic and expensive "ethnic" cuisines and clothing.

According to the Australian anthropologist, Ghassan Hage, this linking of cosmopolitanism and multiculturalism has produced what he refers to as "cosmo-multiculturalism", an appropriation of cultural diversity by a white Eurocentric Australia:

> Following the colonial "We are here as British" and the Australo-British "We are British Europeans who have been changed by the Australian Environment", we now have "We are cosmopolitan Europeans who have been changed by migration, have become multicultural and are turning to Asia." The crucial difference, however, is that the dominant White cosmo-multiculturalist type is no longer simply any White person, but necessarily a classy one.[21]

From this perspective, it is this new class of Australians, a cosmopolitan elite within which Hage places the former Prime Minister Paul Keating,[22] that frequent Australia's "award-winning" restaurants and the "cool" bars. It is, in Hage's words, "a specific cosmopolitan capital accumulated through exposure to a certain 'sophisticated internationalism' which gives the cosmopolitans a global consciousness of the field in which they are operating."[23]

Turning to the other quality which reportedly attracted the producers of *Salaam Namaste* to Melbourne, its "quaintness and charm", this relates more to Melbourne's architecture than its inhabitants, and the city is presented as enjoying a diverse built and natural environment: "The city is blessed with many beautiful parks and gardens as well as great beaches just moments from downtown. The city's busy tree-lined streets are shadowed by towering modern skyscrapers interspersed with stately European architecture giving the sense of a truly international city."[24] "Quaintness and charm" can be linked to the projection of Melbourne as "European", and architecturally the city has many fine colonial buildings dating from the period of its economic boom in the 1880s, and its laneways and alleys now accommodate European-style street cafés and bars where once they accommodated warehouses and workshops. The term "European" is intended to evoke stylish and sophisticated European cities, such as Paris, Berlin or Rome, the kind of European cosmopolitanism that appeals to the Asian honeymoon market.[25]

It needs to be admitted that the modernity of both Sydney and Melbourne, their "towering modern skyscrapers", also evokes images of US cities like New York and San Francisco, and indeed the ability of Australian cities to stand in for US cities is, paradoxically, one of their attractions for Indian film-makers; part of Kitne Door Kitne Paas, for example, is set in the USA but it was filmed in Brisbane.[26] And it also needs to be admitted that towering modern skyscrapers are equally a feature of the Asian cities which are increasingly appearing in Bollywood, such as Bangkok, Seoul and Singapore. Nonetheless, the degree to which such cities also contain "award-winning restaurants, hip music venues, cool bars and sensational shopping" indicates the extent of a fascination with a Western consumer cosmopolitanism by what Sudhanva Deshpande calls "hyper-consumerist" Indian audiences, both within India and abroad, those Bollywood audiences comprising the rich who fund "big-budget, high-profile, large revenue films".[27]

Links between Tourism Promotion and Education Agencies

In *Salaam Namaste*, Preity Zinta plays Ambar, a medical student studying in Melbourne at La Trobe University, and the film apparently generated a huge demand by Indian students wanting to study medicine at La Trobe, a demonstration of not only the power of Bollywood in creating particular images of a country, but also the desire by Australian universities to attract students from India. On one estimate, the growth rate of Indian students studying in Australia is around twelve per cent, with the overall number projected to reach 50,000 in 2007.[28]

Education is linked to tourism by the flow-on of friends and relatives visiting the overseas students while they are in Australia. But tourism and education are also linked through the kinds of images of Australia they project overseas, and when, in 2004, Australian Tourist Commission (ATC),[29] launched Brand Australia, it was keen to ensure that the images of Australia being projected by tourism and education were compatible: "The ATC's brand personality of 'infectious candour and optimism' and emphasis on 'difference' complements Study in Australia's differentiator of 'freedom' as keys to Australia's unique identity and credible positioning in the eyes of the world."[30]

"Freedom" had been identified as a differentiator of Australia in the education market in a report published in 2001 by Australian Education International (AEI), the Education and Training Network of the Australian Department of Education, Science and Training (DEST). The report, Positioning Australian Education and Training for the Future, aimed to identify the most effective brand position for Australian education and training "that is attractive to students and differentiates Australian education and training from its major competitors, the United States of America (USA) and United Kingdom (UK)".[31] According to the report, a key feature that differentiated Australia from the USA and the UK was "freedom", and in this regard, Australia's multiculturalism was thought to provide the friendly environment that enabled young overseas students to enjoy the freedom of an Australian lifestyle:

Australia also benefits from being perceived as multicultural – a particular advantage for Asian students. One of the strongest elements of Freedom is interacting with other young people. A multicultural community makes this more likely. Only the USA and Canada were seen to be on par with Australia for this attribute.[32]

As a result of its research, the report identified a number of key brand messages of Australian education and training, including the message: "Australia is a multicultural community – you'll feel at home." It is not clear how far evidence of the perception of Australia as multicultural is taken by the report as an indication that Australia is multicultural in reality. In addition, the report does not define what is meant by the term multicultural, and one is left to infer from the message "you'll feel at home" that it could mean either that cultural difference is respected or that the presence of Asian migrant communities means that Asian students will see and hear people like themselves. Or it could mean both of these. Neither does it allow for those students whose experience of multiculturalism "at home", might not be positive, such as those in India who have experienced communal friction, and the conclusion of the report clearly views multiculturalism as a positive element in the image of Australia it wishes to promote: "Australia is seen favourably as a Western culture where it is possible to immerse oneself in the English Language; where students know they will be welcome and where they can experience a truly multicultural society."[33] But there is a fuzziness about the meaning of "multiculturalism" as it is being used here and this fuzziness is shared by the statements of other Australian government agencies.

Salaam Namaste presents Melbourne as a modern, Western and cosmopolitan city, a representation consistent with the brand messages of Tourism Australia, Tourism Victoria, Film Victoria, Australian Education International and, presumably, also Austrade. But this is not a multicultural city, except in so far as it is inhabited by South Asia taxi drivers, and the nearest *Salaam Namaste* gets to portraying Melbourne's multiculturalism is in the figure of Jaggu Yadav, played by Javed Jaffrey; in the words of the film's English sub-titles: "Someone suggested going abroad and driving a cab. And so he arrived in Melbourne." Following the death of Rajneesh Joga, an Indian student killed while working as a part-time taxi driver in Melbourne, the Indian Voice, a community newspaper, commented:

Indian Voice believes more than 7,000 (about 85%) taxi drivers in Victoria are from the Indian subcontinent and most of them are overseas students. The irony is that this large influx of workforce is often unrepresented and unheard within the taxi industry, Victorian Government and the wider community. These students often live under a lot of pressure of earning for living and tuition expenses; meeting deadlines of school assignments; living under the constant fear of being deported in case of lack of attendance in the class; being caught by the Immigration Department officials for working more than 20 hours a week; lack of support and of course home sickness.[34]

Whatever the accuracy of the figures, there are certainly a number of Indian students driving taxis in order to earn the international student fees they are being charged for studying in Australia, and Melbourne's taxi driving Indian students would generally not earn the kind of income to allow them to enjoy the chic and expensive "ethnic" cuisines and clothing of Melbourne's cosmopolitan consumerism. Instead, they, like other disadvantaged groups, service it.

Conclusion

In conclusion, it seems that while Australian government agencies are keen to promote Australia overseas as a multicultural nation, the view of multiculturalism projected not only equates it with cosmopolitanism, but with a particular type of stylish European cosmopolitanism. The images associated with a "sophisticated internationalism", to use Ghassan Hage's term, are restaurants, bars and expensive shopping malls.

The most obvious omission from the discourse of cultural diversity employed by these government agencies is an acknowledgement of indigenous Australia. In a forum on multiculturalism broadcast on Australian radio in March 2006, Marcia Langton, Professor of Indigenous Studies at the University of Melbourne and a distinguished aboriginal rights advocate, commented on an address given by the Australian High Commissioner at a conference on globalisation and postcolonial writing in Kolkata in February 2006.

The High Commissioner reported that Australia is an Anglo-Saxon country. Ninety-six per cent of Australians are Anglo-Saxon and four per cent are from Asia, he said. As I listened to this extraordinary demographic and ethnic analysis, schadenfreude welled up inside me as I peered around the room at various Australians, my Irish Australian colleagues, Scottish Australian, Polish Australians, Jewish Australians, and many others from the great fruit salad of Australian ethnicity had been obliterated along with almost half a million

Indigenous Australians, the Aborigines and Torres Strait Islanders, of which, obviously, I am one.[35]

Langton was justifiably exasperated about the High Commissioner's poorly expressed account of Australia's ethnic composition, especially the lack of any reference to indigenous Australia. The official projection of a multicultural Australia aimed at attracting tourists, students and Bollywood producers from India so often leaves out the everyday lives of migrants in Melbourne, those, like Indian student taxi drivers, who service but do not enjoy Melbourne's cosmopolitanism. Of course, there will be a few who make their fortune, such as Jaggu Yadav in *Salaam Namaste* who wins the lottery and invests in property. But Jaggu Yadav as a naturalised Australian becomes a parody of Crocodile Dundee and this suggests that, in the absence of images of Australia's everyday cultural diversity, pressure on migrants to assimilate to an image of a White Australia will produce a shrinking of cosmopolitanism rather than its further development. Rather than feeling at home, the Indian student in *Salaam Namaste* is confronted by a landlord reluctant to lease his property to students from India because, as he puts it: "I hate Indians."

Endnotes

1. *Salaam Namaste* (Siddharth Anand, 2005).
2. At the time of writing, January 2007, A$1.00 = US$ 0.80 or Rs. 33.
3. Daniel Ziffer, "Bollywood makes a Comeback," *The Age* (Melbourne), 28 September 2006.
4. Interview with Freya Campbell, Marketing Manager Asia, Tourism Victoria, 20 December 2006.
5. Mark Phillips, "Bollywood on Bourke Street," *The Age* (Melbourne), 13 May 2005, Metro p. 4.
6. Bella Jaisinghani, "Shooting with a Business Angle," *Financial Express* (Mumbai) 13 June 2004, http://www.financialexpress.com/fe_full_story.php?content_id=61229, 11 June 2005.
7. Interview with Freya Campbell.
8. "India: Visitor Profile," *Tourism Australia*, 16 June 2006, p. 2.
9. Interview with Maggie White, Regional Manager, South and South East Asia, Tourism Australia, 7 December 2006.
10. *Dil Chahta Hai* (Farhan Akhtar, 2002).
11. Interview with Maggie White.
12. *Love Story 2050* (Harry Baweja, 2007).
13. "Bonanza for Tourism," *Sunday Mail* (Adelaide), 24 September 2006.
14. Press release by South Australia Premier Mike Rann, 6 September 2006.
15. Press release by South Australia Premier Mike Rann, 6 September 2006.
16. *Midsomer Murders* is a British detective drama series which began broadcasting on television in 1997.
17. "Aussies Lure Bollywood Bigwigs in Mumbai," http://news.ninemsn.com.au/article.aspx?id=9048, 9 March 2006.
18. Mark Phillips, "Bollywood on Bourke Street," *The Age* (Melbourne), 13 May

2005, Metro p. 4.
19. "Film Melbourne Now – About Melbourne," http://www.film.vic.gov.au/fmn/aboutmelb.shtml, 10 December 2006.
20. "Film Melbourne Now – The Melbourne Lifestyle," http://www.film.vic.gov.au/fmn/aboutmelb_life.shtml, 10 December 2006.
21. Ghassan Hage, *White Nation: Fantasies of White Supremacy in a Multicultural Society* (Sydney: Pluto, 1998), p. 201.
22. Ghassan Hage, *White Nation*, p. 203.
23. Ghassan Hage, *White Nation*, pp. 204–205.
24. "Film Melbourne Now – The Melbourne Lifestyle."
25. Interview with Freya Campbell.
26. *Kitne Door Kitne Paas* (Mehul Kumar, 2002).
27. Sudhanva Deshpande, "The Consumable Hero of Globalised India," in Raminder Kaur and Ajay J. Sinha, eds., *Bollyworld: Popular Indian Cinema through a Transnational Lens* (New Delhi: Sage, 2005), pp. 186–203.
28. *Hansard*, Joint Standing Committee on Foreign Affairs, Defence and Trade, Australia's Relationship with India as an Emerging World Power, Dr. Som Majumdar, 20 September 2006, p. 21.
29. The Australian Tourist Commission has itself now been re-branded as Tourism Australia.
30. "Launch of refreshed brand Australia 7 June 2004," http://aei.dest.gov.au:80/AEI/MIP/ItemsOfInterest/04Interest15.htm, 25 July 2004.
31. "Brand research," http://aei.dest.gov.au/AEI/OffshoreSupport/StudyInAustraliaBrand/BrandResearch/, 4 January 2005.
32. *Positioning Australian Education and Training for the Future: A report on the findings of Australian Education International's research into the branding of Australian education and training offshore* (Canberra: Commonwealth of Australia, 2001), pp. 19 and 114.
33. *Positioning Australian Education and Training for the Future*, p. 126.
34. "Loss of Another Precious Life," *Indian Voice*, August 2006, http://indianvoice.com.au/newsarticle649.aspx, 10 December 2006.
35. *World View: Forum on Multiculturalism 3*, SBS Radio, 23 March 2006.

8

Accommodation of Cultural Diversity in India: Reflections on Past and Present

Abdulrahim P. Vijapur

India's manifold socio-cultural, linguistic and religious diversity is unparalleled in the world. It is a mosaic of religious pluralism and linguistic variety. People belonging to all the major religions of the world and speaking more than one thousand languages and having divergent cultural values and practices have been living in peace, harmony and with the spirit of accommodation and with the understanding of each others identity for thousands of years. This unique experience of socio-cultural interactions has produced remarkable moorings for India's stability and dynamism, which other societies and countries can emulate. Since the colonial engagement with India the process of communalization of polity and society has begun and now India is at the cross-roads. Its stability and prosperity will depend to the extent India learns and emulates its own past before it expects other societies to emulate its traditions of cultural accommodation.

The purpose of this paper is to study the process of accommodation of cultural diversities in India with a specific focus of India's three "Golden Traditions" – (i) Religious freedom/tolerance; (ii) Inclusive policies and empowerment of the "other"; and (iii) education and language problems. It also discusses the way these traditions are being constantly eroded by communal politics of contemporary India. An attempt is made to situate these three golden traditions in contemporary socio-political contexts to stress the point that India and the Indians need to emulate their own traditions and values of cultural and religious accommodation more than anyone else.

Religious Freedom and Tolerance

The early Hindu teachings, as reflected in *Bhagvad-Gita* and *Upanishads*, propounded certain universal principles which represent human rights and values. An important axiom of Hinduism states that God is omnipresent and immanent in all that exists in the universe.[1] Thus, according to Hinduism, this universal spirit or soul (i.e., God) manifests itself in all human beings and indeed pervades all creation, as the very first verse of the *Isa Upanishad* declares: "God covers all that moves in the Universe".[2]

What follows from this fundamental belief in the omnipotent presence of God in every being? Since God permeates every being, there is unity and equality in diversity. The early Hindu teachings (before the introduction of stratified caste system, which institutionalizes inequality) reiterate the human goal of the realization of the Divine in everything, which means unity of all faiths. This means not only freedom from any hatred or malice to other human beings, but also an affirmative duty and obligation to serve God's creation if one is to reach the highest level of spiritual attainment in being identified with the Divinity. The well-known Hindu saying: "*Vasudaiva Kutumbakam* (All humanity is one family)", aptly captures this sentiment.[3]

The onset of Muslim rule in India during the medieval period led to a greater degree of socio-cultural interactions between the Hindu majority and the ruling Muslim minority. Freedom of religion or belief of Hindus was ensured. The general policy and attitude of Muslim polity was one of accommodation, religious tolerance and respect to the religions and cultures of the Hindus. This policy continued from the times of early sultans of Delhi till Mughal rule. Quoting a contemporary chronicler (Farishta) R.C. Majumdar writes that the early Sultanate of Delhi gave full religious liberty to their non-Muslim subjects. Even in the imperial city of Delhi they bowed before their idols, blew their conches, bathed in the river Jamuna and took out their religious processions without hindrance.[4]

There is archaeological evidence to show that the construction of new temples, during the 13th century, was not checked or stopped. Thakur Phero's work on medieval temple architecture, *Vastusara,* written during Ala-u'ddin Khilji's reign, does not make any reference to state interference in the construction of temples. There is, on the contrary, definite evidence, according to Prof. K.A. Nizami, that temples were constructed during this period. Three images of the Jain sect, discovered in Etah (UP), contain dated records of their installation in the year 1278 AD. A fragment of a bilingual inscription, in Persian and Sanskrit, found in the Purana Qila of Delhi records the endowment of 12 *bighas* of land to a temple dedicated to Sri Krishna. Feroz Shah's protest that the "Hindus and idol-worshippers had built new temples in the city and the environs", should be read in this perspective.[5]

The Mughal rulers not only followed these liberal/secular policies of the Delhi sultans but also went much further ahead. Among the Mughals, Akbar's record surpasses those of his predecessors as well as successors. His reign marks a new beginning in evolving a model government based on religious tolerance and broad humanism. He reconciled his Hindu and Muslim subjects by his policy of *Sulh Kul* or peace towards all. Though unsuccessful, he tried to bring about a synthesis of the two religions – Islam and Hinduism, which provoked vehement opposition from the theologians of both communities. Akbar's decisions to abolish *jazia,* the pilgrimage tax, and lift the ban on conversions to Islam of the prisoners of war, allowing his Hindu wives to perform religious practices of Hindu worship, establishing new courts under Brahmin judges to decide cases between Hindus; prohibiting cow slaughter; himself abstaining from eating beef, garlic and onion; participating in Hindu festivals like Rakhi, Dipavali, Sivaratri, engaging in religious discourse with many *yogis* on their beliefs; and getting translated many Hindu religious books into Persian – such as *Atharva Veda, Mahabharata, Ramayana*, etc. speak for themselves.[6]

Jahangir tried to follow his father's policy of liberalism and religious tolerance. He prohibited the slaughter of animals twice a week – on Sundays and Thursdays. This was strictly enforced. Once when he discovered that his orders were flouted and meat was sold on one of these days, he flogged the *Kotwal* of the area. It is gratifying to note that once when '*Id*' fell on a Thursday, he ordered the postponement of sacrificing of animals to the following Friday.[7] Shahjahan too continued to have liberal policies towards Hindus.

While there are cases on record of some temples having been demolished for one reason or another during Aurangzeb's reign, recent research has shown that many generous grants were given by him for the maintenance of temples. B.N. Pandey, in his book on the role of Islam in Indian culture, documents the examples of more than 30 temples (including those of Abu, Ujjain, Chitrakoot, Guwahati, Gimar) which have even today copies of *farmans* (decrees) issued by Aurangzeb granting them land and protection! Sikh gurudwaras (temples) also got handsome grants from him.[8]

Thus the Mughal rulers followed the policy of religious tolerance and accommodation. They treated Hindus as people of the book, i.e., *Dhimmis* (protected minorities). Dara Shikhoh translated the *Upanishads* and declared them to be heavenly books referred to in the *Quran*. In fact, only Torah and Bible are explicitly mentioned in the *Quran*, though it indicates that prophets/messengers of God and Holy books have been sent in every community and nation in the world. It should be acknowledged that Hindu law was applied to Hindus and *Shariah* to Muslims. In fact, in civil cases, arising out of the personal laws of the Hindus which came before the Mughal court, the Law was explained by a Brahmin lawyer, i.e., Pandit, whose status was equivalent to that of a Mufti. It may be noted that oaths were administered to witnesses according to their religions. The Muslim said "by God", the Hindus swore on the Cow and the Christians on the Bible.[9] Each religious group was governed by their personal laws. *Shariah* was not imposed on non-Muslim subjects. Babur in his will to his son, Humayun had asked his son not to destroy temples or impose restrictions on the constructions of new temples.

Against this background it is apposite to note here the observation of C.H. Alexanderowicz, who writes: "[T]he European agencies in the East learned the lesson of co-existence of Hinduism, Islam and Christianity in India (particularly on the West coast) and transplanted their experience to the West, which had been so long incapable of extricating itself from the obsession of religious wars".[10] Prof. S.R. Sharma, a noted historian of medieval India, also has commented on the religious policy of Mughals saying that "the position of Hindus in India was generally much better than those of many communities in Europe whose faith differed from that of their rulers" during medieval times.[11]

Inclusive Policies and Empowerment of the Other (Hindus)

Like the policies on religious tolerance and freedom, Muslim rulers did not practice discrimination against Hindus for appointment to important imperial posts. S.R. Sharma has all praise for Akbar in this regard. He writes that the percentage of Hindu officers in Akbar's army was higher than the percentage of Indian officers holding the King's commission in the army in India before World War II. Against four Hindu governors in Akbar's reign of half a century, there was only one Indian governor in India during a century and a half of British rule till 1937. No one in British India ever rose to the high rank, which Todar Mal held as the Finance Minister. Of the 12 provincial finance ministers, appointed in 1594–95, eight were Hindus.[12] During the Sultnate and the Mughal period many Hindus were commanders in the army too. There was no discrimination against them for appointment to important political offices.

Prejudices and Discrimination against Minorities in Contemporary India

The past legacy of accommodating socio-cultural diversities is not reflected in contemporary India. The level of socio-political and cultural interactions between Hindus and Muslims in today's India does not correspond to the one that prevailed in medieval India. There are many reasons for this state of affairs. The British policy of "Divide and Rule" during colonial period, the partition of Bengal in 1905, introduction of separate communal electorates for Muslims and Untouchables in the 1930s and the partition of India are some of the significant factors which have affected the process of accommodation of cultural diversity in contemporary India. Moreover, in the 20th century many communal organizations were established such as the Muslim League (1906), the Hindu Mahasabha (1907), Rashtriya Swamsevak Sangh (RSS) (1925), Jamat-e-Islami (1941), Bhartiya Jan Sangh (1951), the Bhartiya Janta Party (1979), the Vishva Hindu Parishad (1964) and Bajrang Dal (in the 1980s). These socio-political organizations are mainly responsible for communalizing and dividing society on the ground of religion and culture. The discussion in the following pages reflects on the present policies and practices of the government and certain organizations which not only adopt policies of discrimination towards minorities, specially the Muslims but also weaken the very foundations of India's unity, secularism and legacy of co-existence, tolerance and accommodation of diversities.[13]

Before we discuss the marginalization of Muslims in the political and decision making process, it is pertinent to quote here the ideological statement made by M.S. Golwalkar, the prominent and articulate Sar Sanghchalak of the RSS, who wrote in 1939 in a Pamphlet, *We or Our Nation Defined* that:

> The non-Hindu people in Hindustan must learn to either adopt the Hindu culture and language, must learn to respect and hold in reverence Hindu religion, must entertain no idea but those of glorification of the Hindu race, and culture... may stay in the country, wholly subordinated to the Hindu nation, claiming nothing, deserving no privileges, *not even citizens rights. In this country, Hindus alone are national, and Muslims and others, if not actually anti-national, are at least outside the body of the nation*" [italics added]".[14]

The writings and speeches of V.D. Savarkar and M.S. Golwalkar contributed greatly to the rise of *Hindutva* ideology. In the ideological framework of *Hindutva* and Hindu *Rashtra*, the people of semitic religions – Muslims, Christians and Jews – are considered to be hostile "other", whose loyalty to India is considered to be doubtful. They have been kept outside the purview of the Hindu *Rashtra* (Nation). Thus, the ideology of *Hindutva* is antithetical to the concepts of pluralism, secularism and the accommodation of cultural diversities.

Under-representation of Muslims in Governance

Many studies have been conducted on the plight of minorities especially dealing with the questions of their security, educational backwardness, religious and cultural rights, representation in political bodies, opportunities for employment and economic development. Let us elaborate some aspects of these issues. Among the various minorities the plight of Muslims is very deplorable as far as their representation in Parliament/State Assemblies and government jobs is concerned. According to one study their members in Lok Sabha were around 5 per cent (average). For instance, in 1952 they constituted 4.4 per cent; in 1962, 4.7 per cent; in 1967, 5.5 per cent; in 1977, 6.2 per cent; 1980, 9.2 per cent (it was highest number so far); in 1984, 8.7 per cent; in 1989, 5.4 per cent and in 1996, 4.9 per cent. In some state assemblies there was not a single member from their community. For instance, under this category were following states: Madhya Pradesh (1993), Orissa (1961), Pondicherry (1977), Goa, Daman & Diu (1972 & 1974) and Nagaland (1974 & 1987).[15]

The problem of Muslim representation in civil services is far more deplorable than their representation in legislative bodies. Their share in government jobs is far less compared to other minorities like Christians and Sikhs. The Gopal Singh Panel report provides many tables on minorities' representation in Indian Administrative Service (IAS), Indian Police Service (IPS), and other central services and state government services etc. These tables disclose startling facts. Between 1971 and 1980 the representation of Muslims in IAS was 2.86 per cent, which was extremely low compared to their population proportion of 11.20 per cent. The share of Christians was 5.64 per cent (their population proportion was 2.60%) and of Sikhs was 4.71 per cent (their population proportion was 1.89%). In IPS the representation of Muslims, Christians and Sikhs was 2 per cent, 2.27 per cent and 5.34 per cent respectively.[16]

The same trend of under-representation has continued till this day. Justice Rajendra Sachar Committee Report, *Social, Economic and Educational Status of the Muslim Community in India* confirms this. The report states that "in a pluralistic society, a reasonable representation of various communities in government sector employment is necessary to enhance participatory governance". The report reveals that though Muslims have a share of 13.4 per cent in the country's population, their representation in government jobs is a mere 4.9 per cent. In the elite civil services like the IAS (3%), IFS (1.8%) and IPS (4%) their representation is as low as 3.2 per cent.[17] Their representation in different government sectors is as follows:[18]

Public Sector Units	4.9 per cent
Railways	4.5 per cent
Judiciary	7.8 per cent
Health	4.4 per cent
Transport	6.5 per cent
Home Affairs	7.3 per cent
Education	6.5 per cent

There is more to it. The report reveals that under representation is acute in States in which Muslims constitute large minorities. In West Bengal, Uttar Pradesh, and Assam, where Muslims form 25.2 per cent, 18.5 per cent and 30.9 per cent of the population respectively, the representation of the community in government jobs is as low as 4.7 per cent, 7.5 per cent and 10.2 per cent respectively.[19] The share of Muslims in all recruitments by State Public Service Commissions is about 2.1 per cent whereas their share in the population is about 12.4 per cent in the States that provided the Committee with data. This shows a deficit of about 83 per cent in recruitment.[20]

The Sachar Committee further reveals that Muslim representation is very low in the universities. Among the teaching faculty, Other Backward Classes (OBCs) have a good representation, more than their population share. Only Muslims and Scheduled Castes (SCs) and Scheduled Tribes (STs) are under-represented in university employment. Muslims are just 3.7 per cent in the teaching faculty and 5.4 per cent in non-teaching staff and SCs and STs are 7.4 per cent in teaching and 16.9 per cent in non-teaching staff; the population share of the two SRC's are 13.4 and 25.2 per cent respectively.[21]

Many Muslim scholars and political leaders are demanding preferential policies for Muslims to improve their participation in national and state civil services. Such affirmative action programmes already exist for ex-untouchables, tribals and backward classes, but are not extended to Muslims. There are many reasons for the under-representation of Muslims in civil services. One reason is the widespread abandonment of Urdu in Northern Indian states. This has made it difficult for a great many Muslim candidates whose mother tongue is Urdu to take competitive examinations for government jobs. This accounts for the fact that very few Muslims take the examination at all; another reason, of course, is a constant fear of discrimination if they do.[22] Moreover, the denial of an opportunity to Muslim children by government schools to study in Urdu violates the constitutional mandate under Article 350A, which obligates the State to provide primary education in mother tongue.

The Muslim minority experienced discrimination in availing the benefits from various government schemes aimed at improving the conditions of disadvantaged sections of society. Of the houses allotted by the State governments to lower and middle-income groups, until 1985 only 2.86 per cent went to Muslims. Of the licenses issued for fair price shops only 6.9 per cent were awarded to them. Their share in availing benefits extended to artisans by the Khadi and Village Industries Commission was a mere 0.25 per cent. Finally, only four units were owned by Muslim industrialists, in a group of large corporate units, each with a minimum annual turnover of Rupees 50,000,000. The cooperative sectors fared no better. Of the loans advanced by financial institutions, only 3 per cent of those between Rupees 50,000 and 100,000 went to Muslims. Of those between Rupees 100,000 and 200,000, less than 2 per cent was received by Muslim, and of loan between Rupees 200,000 and 1,000,000 the figure was under 1 per cent.[23]

Discrimination Based on Religion

Discrimination based on religion is perpetrated or religious hatred is practiced not only by various religious communities against each other but also by the State itself through its executive agencies like the police[24] or sometimes in subtle ways through legislative Acts. The report of the Special Rapporteur of the United Nations on the Elimination of Religious Discrimination provides a broad overview of the pattern of incidents revealing communal tensions/riots following the demolition of Babri Mosque on 6 December 1992.[25]

The Rapporteur had sought comments by the Indian Government on some of these incidents: that more than 1200 people died or were killed by the police in Hindu-Muslim riots after the mosque demolition, that in Bombay at least 200 people died in inter-community clashes, where police sided with the Hindus and fired upon the Muslims; the more than 2,50,000 Kashmiri Hindus have left their homes and sought refugee status in their own country; that between

40,000 and 50,000 Sikhs – men, women and children – have fallen victim to the Indian forces in Punjab (many have just disappeared); that in November 1992, 2000 Christians demonstrated in Ahmad Nagar to protest against the Shiva Sena's attempt to convert hundreds of Christians to Hinduism, etc. With a few exceptions, the Government confirmed many of these incidents.[26]

Almost all religious minorities have experienced discrimination, in various manifestations, from certain sections of the Hindu majority. The report of the Special Rapporteur only provides a sample of these cases. Though communal riots have occurred sporadically since independence, what is of grave concern is the alarming increase in their number and intensity in the 1980s and 1990s.

Laws Affecting Conversions

From time to time unsuccessful attempts were made to introduce in the Parliament restricting conversions of untouchable and tribal Hindus to other religions specially Christianity and Islam. In 1950 the Presidential Order on positive discrimination for SCs and STs stated that reservation benefits are available only to those SCs and STs who are within the fold of Hinduism. On conversion to Islam or Christianity – the religions of non-Indian origin – these SCs and STs become disqualified to get the benefit of affirmative action. This executive order directly violates Article 25 of the Indian constitution which guarantees freedom of religion, which includes freedom to profess any religion, practice and propagate any religion, including freedom to change one's own religion.

In 1954 the Indian Converts (Regulation and Registration) Bill was introduced and was rejected, as it proposed to give power to the Deputy Commissioner to issue a license for converting people. In 1960 the Lok Sabha rejected the Backward Communities (Religious Protection) Bill. Again in 1978, the Freedom of Religion Bill was introduced in the Lok Sabha and was withdrawn subsequently. However, in some States such bills have been passed. For example, Orissa State Assembly passed the Freedom of Religion Act in 1969. Similarly, in 1978, Arunachal Pradesh passed the Freedom of Religion Act. Christians and Muslims perceived the Arunachal Act as directed specifically against them, as it ruled against converting but not against "reconversion" (to Hinduism). An ominous feature of the times was the absence of public opposition to such erosion of tolerance. Moreover, these Bills are not intended to prevent conversion per se but are geared to prevent the use of force, inducement or fraud means in conversion. It is paradoxical to note that intentionally or unintentionally, the government policy of protective discrimination law (reservation of jobs and seats in educational places and legislatures) for ex-untouchables and tribals has tended to perpetuate the solidarity of the Hindu community and to prevent their conversion to other religions. The Tamil Nadu government of Jayalalitha had enacted anti-conversion bill, which she repealed after loosing 2004 parliamentary election. The governments of Gujarat and Rajasthan have also adopted anti-conversion laws in recent years. Moreover, during the last decade many Christian missionaries have been murdered, their properties have been destroyed and nuns have been raped or beaten.

Legislative enactments and policies such as these are aimed at putting restrictions on the constitutionally guaranteed right to propagate religion. Most of these treated conversions merely as law and order problem by the State. The selective approach of these restrictions was only for Islam and Christianity as these religions are projected by the Hindus as products of conquest and colonization. The acceptance of Islam by 200 ex-untouchables in 1981 in Meenakshipuram village (Tamil Nadu) sent shock waves among Hindu religious organizations, which raised slogans of "Hinduism in danger". In contrast, one does not come across such a response/concern when a large number of people embrace one of the religions of Indian origin – Buddhism, Jainism and Sikhism. For instance, between February and August 1981, soon after stopping the Meenakshipuram conversions, the VHP 'reconverted' 50,000 Christians and 4,000 Muslims into Hinduism and in October under the leadership of R.S. Gavai, some 1,50,000 to 3,00,000 untouchables embraced Buddhism to celebrate the 25th anniversary of B.R. Ambedkar's conversion from Hinduism. These two events of mass conversion did not move the conscience of the Indian State to intervene, partly because no organized pressure was put on it and presumably because the public order was intact. Thus, the freedom of religion operates only in one direction. While widespread public remorse was expressed on Meenakshipuram episode in the Indian Press, the VHP reconversions to Hinduism and the conversions to Buddhism evoked no strong reactions. Therefore, it is clear that State intervention is selective. Such a response erodes the meaning of secularism. A major shock came to these minority religions of non-Indian origin when the Supreme Court decided in 1977 that there can be no such thing as a fundamental right to convert any person to one's own religion (*Rev. Stanislaus* v. *State of Madhya Pradesh*).

There is more to it. Three Acts concerning Hindu Code Bill (governing personal law), as our analysis reveals, have also touched upon the question of conversion indirectly.

1. The Hindu Marriage Act of 1955 lists as one of the nine grounds for divorce if the other party's ceases to be a Hindu by conversion to another religion. S. Natarajan commented that this provision is understandable from the viewpoint of Hindu marriage as a religious sacrament, but added: "It is strange that a secular State should not insist on further proof to establish that the conversion interferes with the religious life and practice of other party".[27]

2. Under the Hindu Adoptions and Maintenance Act of 1956, a Hindu wife is entitled to live separately from her husband with maintenance if he is converted to other religion. Further, the Act includes a discriminatory clause which reads: "A Hindu wife shall not be entitled to separate residence from her husband if she is unchaste or *ceases to be Hindu* by conversion to another religion" (italics added). In other words, unchastity and conversion must be penalized! Thus, even if the husband treated her with cruelty, was a leper, or kept a concubine in the same house in which the wife was living (all grounds for separate maintenance under the Act); she would still not be entitled to separate maintenance if she ceased to be a Hindu. The principle is broadened further; the Act gives an elaborate definition of the relatives deemed to be dependents but then states that no person shall be entitled to claim maintenance under these provisions upon conversion to another religion.

The Hindu Succession Act of 1956 also follows the same spirit. This Act made sure that none of the converts' children or their descendants would be entitled to inherit the property of any of their Hindu relatives, unless such children or descendants are Hindus at the time when the succession opens. An American scholar commented that intentionally or unintentionally, this Act could in some cases constitute a powerful financial inducement for the children or descendants to be converted to Hinduism. He further adds that the net effect of these provisions in the Hindu Code Bill is to discourage conversion from Hinduism and to reinforce the religious status quo. However progressive, even radical, these laws are in terms of the Hindu social system (the introduction of divorce, inheritance by daughters, etc.); they actively discourage change in religious affiliation. There are definite penalties to be borne if the exercise of freedom of conscience leads the Hindu outside the fold.[28] Thus, the *Shuddhi* (purification) movement, which started in the 1930s, and is quite active even now, can be seen in this perspective. Through *Shuddhi* people from Islamic or Christian faith are reconverted to Hinduism.

Biased Text Books and Denial of Education in Mother Tongue

The BJP Governments, both at the Centre (during 1999–2004) and the states have been continuously engaged in revising history books to project a distorted view of minorities' role in the past. The National Democratic Alliance Government led by Prime Minister Atal Bihari Vajpai carried out systematically its project of safronising the contents of textbooks. As a result; many books produced by National Council of Educational Research and Training (NCERT) have been changed.[29] Let us elaborate this aspect further.

Former BJP government in north Indian State of Uttar Pradesh has made a concerted attempt to change the contents of the school textbooks of history to give a communal projection/interpretation of certain historical developments in medieval India. Among many changes that are incorporated in these books, two are most striking. First, the revised text inserts a three-page narration on Keshavarao Hedgewar, the founder of RSS, while making no mention of other leaders of freedom struggle. What is more objectionable is that the one-page narrative which the older text had, made no mention of Mahatma Gandhi, father of the Nation. Second addition pertains to the controversy of Ayodhya mosque/temple. The revised text says: "Babur's local official Mirwaqui (sic) got a mosque built in place of the temple demolished at Ayodhya. Although this building is controversial, nevertheless the Hindu public believes it to be a temple." [30]

A noted historian, R. Nath, recently discovered that original will of Emperor Babur, to his son, which was preserved in the Madhya Pradesh State Library, is missing. In this will he had laid down the policy for the governance of the country. He warned his son not to meddle in the religious affairs of the people and leave them free to practice their religion in accordance with their own faiths and beliefs. He warned against the demolition of temples. He advised that religious bigotry should be shed and the King should live with his subjects in the spirit of peaceful coexistence, tolerance and non-interference in their religious matters. However, a photographed copy of the will (taken on 11 December 1921) and duly certified by the curator of the library is available with H.K. Sherwani of Hyderabad. The mystery of the lost testament casts doubt about the communal role of the then BJP government.[31]

Another form of prejudice experienced by Muslims is the denial of an opportunity by the State-run schools to provide education to their children in mother tongue; in most cases it is Urdu. In most parts of north India, Muslim children are compelled to study in Hindi medium, which of late is becoming, due to State patronage, highly Sanskritized. However, it is encouraging to note that in other linguistic States (especially in South India) the government does not discriminate the Muslims and has established Urdu-medium schools. The attitude of North Indian States violates Article 4, Para 3 of the 1992 UN Declaration on the Rights of Persons Belonging to National or Ethnic, Religious or Linguistic Minorities, which requires the States to take appropriate measures where required and necessary so that, children of minorities may have adequate opportunities to learn their mother tongue or to have instruction in their mother tongue. It is worth recalling here that although in the Constituent Assembly Debates demand for primary education in mother tongue (Article 29) was forcefully advocated by Begam Azaz Rasool, Hasrat Mohani, Z.H. Lari and Pandit Haridaya Nath Kunzru, it was rejected by Govind Ballabh Pant. B.R. Ambedkar accepted its importance but was reluctant to make it a fundamental right enforceable in court because right to education was not made in the constitution a fundamental right. Therefore, the provision to provide instruction in one's mother tongue was included in Article 350A in 1956. Now there is urgent need to shift this provision to the Fundamental Rights Chapter of the constitution in the same way that Article 45 concerning right to compulsory free education up to the age of 14 has been now made a fundamental right under Article 21 A.This amendment was carried out in 2002 by the National Democratic Alliance government led by Atal Behari Vajpai.

Sometimes, the spirit of tolerance towards minorities is being enforced by the Supreme Court, when in one of its judgments it struck down the expulsion from schools of three students belonging to Jehovah's Witnesses faith who refused to sing the national anthem though they respectfully stood up in silence when it was sung.[32]

The Government bias towards minorities is also manifested in its treatment of minority languages, especially while allocating funds for their development. The Government of India allocates funds annually for the development of all Indian languages, including classical, modern and tribal. A careful perusal of the expenditure incurred on this scheme reveals bias against Urdu (though it is not entirely a language of Muslims). For instance, the Lok Sabha was informed on 25 February 1992 that in the year 1990–91 the Government spent Rupees 966.91 lakhs on Hindi, Rupees 829.73 lakhs on Sanskrit and Rupees 79.48 lakhs on Urdu. The allocation of Urdu was made to Tarraqi-e-Urdu Board (which spent most of this money on Gujaral Committee on Urdu). The fact that the Government is spending a meager sum on Urdu, although 5.7 per cent of the population speaks Urdu, whereas it spends huge amount on Sanskrit, which is spoken by less than 1 per cent people and is almost a dead language reveals its step motherly treatment towards minority language, i.e. Urdu.[33]

Concluding Observations

There is urgent need to revive India's golden traditions of accommodative and inclusive policies and practices. To strengthen the traditions of religious liberty and tolerance all laws restricting the freedom of religion should be repealed. Linguistic and religious minorities should be guaranteed the enjoyment of their linguistic and cultural rights. The Constitution of India should be suitably amended to introduce affirmative action programmes for those minorities, which are educationally backward and under-represented in legislative bodies and civil services. Recommendations made by Gopal Singh and Sachar Committees in this regard should be implemented. The concerned governments should take immediate and appropriate steps to implement the right to free and compulsory education up to the age of 14 years which is now a fundamental right. Moreover, the primary education should be imparted to the children in their mother tongue in accordance with Article 350A of the constitution. In fact, by amending the constitution this article should be shifted to Part III of the constitution (dealing with Fundamental Rights), as this part of the constitution is enforceable by the High Courts and the Supreme Court of India.

By way of conclusion it is worth recalling here the words of Mahatma Gandhi, who once said, "A civilization can be judged by the way it treats its minorities."[34] If the Indian Government acts on the policy recommendations suggested above, it would be strengthening the foundations of our civilization that has accommodated diverse religious, cultural and linguistic minorities during the last five millennia.

Endnotes

1. *Bhagavadgita*, Ch. VI, Verse 31; Ch. VII, Verse 19; Ch. VIII, 61; Ch. XI, Verse 38.
2. Cited in Ved P. Nanda, "Hinduism and Human Rights", in Daniel Warner (ed.), *Human Rights and Humanitarian Law* (The Hague: Kluwer Law International, 1997), p. 32.
3. Ibid. pp. 32–33.
4. Quoted in R.C. Majumdar and others, *An Advanced History of India* (Madras: Macmillan, 1985), pp. 298–299.
5. K.A. Nizami, *Some Aspects of Religion and Politics in India During the Thirteenth Century*, 2nd edition (Delhi, 1974), p. 320.
6. For a detailed study see M. Athar Ali, "Translations of Sanskrit Works at Akbar's Court", *Social Scientist*, Vol. 20, Nos. 9–10, 1992, pp. 38–45.
7. Sri Ram Sharma, *The Religious Policy of the Mughal Emperors*, 3rd edition (New Delhi, 1988), p. 73.
8. See for the excerpts of his book, *Role of Islam in Indian Culture, The Sunday Times of India*, 22 August 1993, p. 13.
9. M.B. Ahmad, *The Administration of Justice in Medieval India* (Karachi, 1951), pp. 115 and 221.
10. C.H. Alexanderowicz, "Kautilyan Principles and the Law of Nations", *British Yearbook of International Law,* Vol. 41, 1965, p. 312.
11. Sharma, n. 7, p. 7. On the question of tolerance Rajendra Prasad, the first President of the Indian Republic, made a refreshing observation: "The attitude of the Muslim conquerors had, on the whole, been one of tolerance, and inspite of the fanatical zeal manifested by some of them at times, it may be safely asserted that there had been a continuous effort from the earliest days to deal with the Hindus fairly". Rajendra Prasad, *India Divided* (Bombay, 1964), p. 86.
12. Ibid, p. 73.
13. See Abdulrahim P. Vijapur, "Minorities and Human Rights: A Comparative Perspective of International and Domestic Law", in D.L. Sheth and Gurpreet Mahajan (Ed), *Minority Identities and the Nation State* (New Delhi: Oxford University Press, 1999), pp. 242–267. Also see my other article, "Minorities of India: Manifestation of Prejudices and Discrimination", in Joseph Benjamin (ed.), *Minorities in Indian Social System* (New Delhi: Gyan Publishing House, 2006).
14. Cited in Rasheeduddin Khan, *Bewildered India – Identity, Pluralism, Discord* (New Delhi: Har Anand Publications, 1995), p. 236.
15. Iqbal A.Ansari, "Federal Nation Building : Non-Regional Dimensions of Pluralism and Representation of Muslims in Elected Bodies", in Abdulrahim P. Vijapur (ed.), *Dimensions of Federal Nation Building* (New Delhi: Manak Publications, 1998), pp. 222–223.

16. Gopal Singh, *Report on Minorities*, Vol. I, (New Delhi: Ministry of Home Affairs, Government of India, 1983).
17. *Social, Economic and Educational Status of the Muslim Community of India – A Report by Prime Minister's High Level Committee*, Government of India, November 2006, p. 165.
18. For details see, Ibid, pp. 167–176.
19. Ibid. p. 170.
20. Ibid. p. 175.
21. Ibid. pp. 168–169.
22. Mushirul Hasan, "Muslims and the political Future of Secularism in India", in T.V. Sathyamurthy (ed.), *Region, Religion, Caste, Gender and Culture in Contemporary India*, Vol. 3 (New Delhi: Oxford University Press, 1996), p. 219.
23. Ibid. p. 218. For latest data see Sachar Committee Report on Muslims.
24. See Abdulrahim P. Vijapur and Mohibul Haque, "Endangered Minorities in India: Understanding the Role of Police", in Asghar Ali Engineer and A.S. Narang (ed.), *Minorities and the Police in India* (New Delhi: Manohar, 2006).
25. E.Cn.4/1994/79, dated 20 January 1994.
26. Ibid.
27. S. Natrajan, *A Century of Social Reform in India* (Bombay: Asia Publishing House, 1959), p. 194.
28. Donald Smith, *India as a Secular State* (Princeton, NJ: Princeton University Press, 1963), p. 187.
29. For a detailed discussion on the changes made in history textbooks during the years 1999–2001, see *Communalization of Education – The History Textbooks Controversy* (New Delhi: Delhi Historians' Group, C/o 122 Uttarakhand, Jawaharlal Nehru University, December 2001). This book is a compilation of Articles on the subject by eminent historians such as Romila Thapar, Bipan Chandra, Irfan Habib, R.S. Sharma, Satish Chandra, Arjun Dev, Sumit Sarkar, Mridula Mukherjee and Aditya Mukherjee. It provides an overview of the textbooks controversy.
30. See for a detailed analysis of the changes in history textbooks, Krishna Kumar, "Continued text," *Seminar* (New Delhi). No. 400, December 1992, pp. 16–20. Professor Krishna Kumar, an eminent educationist of Delhi University, and now Director of NCERT, who got an access to these history books with the help of an official of the State Government was informed that an adjective meaning "innumerable" will be inserted before "Hindu Public" and the clause "a temple" will ultimately read as "Ram temple". It is interesting that there is no intention, at least so far, the author was informed, of describing the temple as the birthplace of Lord Ram. Before these additional changes could be incorporated the State government was dismissed on 6 December 1992 following the demolition of Babri Mosque. At another place, Krishna Kumar describes how a newly prepared set of history textbooks (in 1992) by Bhartiya Vidya Bhawan for use in schools of BJP ruled States intends to inform the School children and create bias among them towards Muslims. In their textbooks: the revivalists depict the Mughals as foreigners and oppressors, and interpret Indian achievement of freedom from English rule as but the latest episode in a long ongoing struggle to free India from foreign influences. Muslims are, by this interpretation, the contemporary

incarnation of the Mughal pattern of dominance. Krishna Kumar, "Hindu revivalism in north-central India", in M.E. Murty and R.S. Applebee (eds.), *Fundamentalism and Society* (Chicago, Il: University of Chicago Press, 1993), p. 555. Cited in Jagdish Gundara, "Aspects of Religion in Secular Education" *in Education Rights and Minorities* (London: Minority Rights Group, 1994), p. 26.

31. R. Nath, "The Lost Statement", *Times of India, Sunday Review* (New Delhi), 5 December 1993. This article reproduces the text of Babur's will.
32. Cited in Soli J. Sorabjee, "Spirit of Tolerance – Indian Courts' proud record safeguarding right of dissent", *The Indian Express* (New Delhi), 28 January 1994.
33. Abdulrahim P. Vijapur and others, *Pluralism, Minorities, National Integration – Problems and Prospects* (New Delhi: South Asian Publishers, 1997), p. 46.
34. Cited in John Humphrey, *No distant Millennium – The International Law of Human Rights* (Paris: UNESCO, 1989), p. 46.

9

Gandhian Ideas on Cultural Diversity and Unity in India

Sailaja Gullapalli

> India is by itself almost a continent. It contains one-fifth of the human race. It represents one of the most ancient civilizations. It has traditions handed down from tens of thousands of years, some of which...remain intact.
> (Gandhi's Broadcast to America, September 13, 1931)

> 'To many distant observers, India seems a single geographical peninsula neatly bounded by the high mountains and the deep seas, which must, therefore, have a homogeneous population and culture; and its philosophy must, of course, always have been the world-negating Monistic Vedanta, as so many western scholars of all times have testified. To most foreign travelers, on the other hand, India has appeared as a hopelessly heterogeneous medley of diverse peoples, and creeds that defy consistency and baffle understanding. The truth which can be perceived only by a patient and sympathetic observer, who has the time to study the country closely, lies perhaps in the middle. India is a subtle unity beneath her apparent diversity...the cultures and faiths during the last four thousand years inspired different types of philosophical systems and which present almost all the types of philosophy the world knows of'.[1]

One such philosophy that originated in India in the early 20th century was that of M.K. Gandhi. His philosophy was based on the understanding of the great civilization and culture of the east that imbibed in itself diverse cultures, faiths, religions, languages and people. Amid this diversity, there is a fine synthesis of cultural unity offering varied paths of philosophies and life patterns that could be followed according to one's interest and aptitude. This unity in diversity calls for a great deal of tolerance, love, understanding and sacrifice for the welfare of all. Gandhi stood for these principles all through his life and diligently made efforts to foster a society based on these virtues. It is apt to recollect that 'Gandhi saw, in the whole of geographical India one country, and in her people, one nation. It was his passion to unite all her races and religious communities together, and to secure their independence as a single unit, which could take its proud place among the greatest nations of the world'.[2]

It is rather a marvel that Gandhi foresaw almost a century ago what India was to face in the post independence era-be it the cultural aspects, communal harmony, or assimilation of minorities.

Interestingly, Gandhi himself denied carving a new philosophy. He tried to analyse and apply the simple truths of daily life combining them with the traditional religious teachings and values. Truth and non-violence form the core of his thought. His profound insistence on treading the path of truth, non-violence, morality and spirituality bore fruitful results as was evident in his travails in South Africa and also during the freedom movement. He utilized the new positive ideas of modern India by assimilating them in thought, living them in his life, and giving them social and political shapes.[3] This thought process evolved as a philosophy in itself, thus changing the course of life of millions of Indians and the humanity as a whole. He had an absolute truthful approach be it in the minute aspects of life or complex social problems. Thus his thoughts and ideas were 'not only unbreakable, but also sacrosanct.'[4]

Gandhi's insistence on the merits of Indian civilization, as is evident in his Hind Swaraj, primarily emanates from his conviction that India has much to offer to the world. The materialistic West was merely mechanized and modernized only in terms of technology, lacking human values. But the Indian civilization, on the contrary, provides an ideal solution to the ills that are slowly creeping into the society. It is, as per Gandhi's firm belief, one and held even the uneducated peasants as highly religious and spiritual, full of virtues. This predominance of Sattva in India made it a sattvik civilization.[5] Infact Gandhi, in one of his speeches in Almora (June 18, 1929), referred 'not to regard India's most ancient culture and civilization as a relic of barbarism to be looked down upon and despised but to treasure it as a precious heritage that had to be enriched and enlarged'.[6]

Before taking up the leadership mantle of the Freedom Struggle in India, Gandhi traveled through India extensively and was depressed by what he saw–its division by caste, religion, selfish motives, malicious, unhealthy, unhygienic and thoroughly rustic society. As a part of facilitating its regeneration, an 18-point treatise, the Constructive Programme, was evolved through which he intended to achieve sarvodaya (uplift of all, welfare of all). Most importantly, it was designed with the aim of reviving the sagging village industries and handicrafts that are a prime source of income to the rural folk. It is this acute moral conscience and affirmative faith in the Indian culture that places Gandhi ahead in the league of those who nurtured the idea of an ideal society, based on truthfulness, openness, non-violence and their interdependence.

India, for centuries, came under different rulers – different in the political, cultural and social aspects in many a sphere. It constantly acclimatized itself to these different phases, making itself a seat of confluence of cultures. In the process, a society based on deep-rooted religious traditions, and strong cultural ethos emerged, which, over long centuries, has shaped a tenacious pattern of daily life. All through these variations in the society, the people of India have been advocating peace via the teachings of Hinduism, Buddhism and Jainism and have been highly successful in weaving a peaceful society. Since all these religions had also professed equality of all, the presumption that some are superior to other holds no relevance. It is this aspect of India to which Gandhi was deeply attracted to and based his idea of a peaceful society on the convergence of these different cultures. Gandhi's conception of an ideal society though widely contested and even dismissed as too idealistic, holds much relevance in the contemporary society across the world.

Role of the State: Swaraj or Self-rule

For Gandhi, an ideal society would undeniably mean 'Rama Rajya'. He clarifies thus: "By Rama Rajya, I do not mean Hindu Raj. I mean divine raj, the kingdom of God. I acknowledge no other God but the one God of truth and righteousness. It ensures equal rights alike of prince and pauper... and undoubtedly a true democracy".[7] He reiterated that a society based on love, tolerance and equality irrespective of religion, caste, class and colour would ensure a safe and secure social environment, leading to real Swaraj (self-rule).

The idea of a modern state deeply troubled Gandhi. His search for alternative to the existing form and role of the state in terms of promoting the cultural unity of diverse communities was relentless. He was against any form of organized state that controls and centralizes the authority, bureaucratic, and equipped with violent methods of addressing issues of civil unrest. Since the individual and his freedom remains the supreme consideration in the society, it would be an injustice to curtail the same in the guise of state authority. Gandhi questions, 'if the individual ceases to count, what is left of society? Individual freedom alone can make a man voluntarily surrender himself completely to the service of society. If it is wrested from him, he becomes an automaton and society is ruined'.[8]

To begin with, individual freedom as propounded by Gandhi cannot be taken as an absolute constituent in society. For an individual's goodness greatly determines the existence of goodwill and sacrifice in a society. An ideal society is the end product of an individual's respect and tolerance towards each other, which is crucial for peaceful co-existence. Much of the responsibility lies in the hands of the individual to foster a society based on the spirit of wisdom and faith. It is to be remembered that the virtues of personal space, integrity, and spirit of charity in an individual constitute the deciding factors of unity in a society. Another deciding facet is the courage to condemn an intimidating approach in an individual's conduct toward his or her society. A free society, therefore, connotes a society enriched with moral and spiritual values. A society, based on immoral values, on the other hand, constantly endangers the individual freedom and liberty. In such a case, the liberty is subjected to constant misuse, consequences of which will be harmful requiring an increasingly powerful state to deal with these, thus ultimately negating the concept of a liberal society.[9] This, undoubtedly, was considered as the first step towards an ideal Swaraj.

The concept of Swaraj (self-rule) represents true democracy. In this scheme, people's empowerment and the reduction to the minimum the interference of the state in conducting people's affairs was of much significance. The state is envisioned as an entity that does not represent the exercize of political power but the one that promotes exercize of power by people through communities. These communities that were all-inclusive, well-organized and self-governing ruled out any sectarian elements based purely on a particular religion or culture.

Further, true democracy cannot be imposed by the state but has to evolve from within. People are the prime and direct agents in the process of decision-making related to governance. As Gandhi believed, democracy disciplined and enlightened is the finest thing in the world.[10] Therefore, the role of the state was limited to enhancing the empowerment of the people to manage their own affairs, settle their disputes by mutual consent and respect, decide their own economic priorities and constitute a body to ensure the enforcement of their decisions. The foundation of this form of government is laid in villages. This would promote, as Gandhi asserted, a sense of sacrifice for each other's welfare, along with 'a strong sense of solidarity, genuine sense of community, and act as nurseries of civic virtues'.[11]

Precisely put, the role of the state's authority, in this set up, should be only to the extent that it keeps the various institutions together. In the process, the state should take care not to get obsessed with homogenizing the society, for the diversity enables a spirit of oneness and sacrifice for the welfare of all. Any attempt towards homogenization not only destroys the culture of the land but also creates divisions among the diverse communities, which, any state can ill afford to do. The state should take enough care not to patronize or act as a custodian of any one particular religious community. To bring all the communities under a uniform civil code would mean:

Undermining the unity of the state
Divesting the sense of deep cultural roots
Intolerance towards the inter-religious practices
Provocation of communities involving violent resistance.

As observed by Bhikhu Parekh, Gandhi reiterated that these practices were best left to the reformist campaigns of the enlightened members of the society who are best equipped to discredit them.[12] Even the system of justice should be based on goodwill and should be entrusted to a small body comprising all communities. This ensures an evenhanded approach in dispensing justice. In this structure too, the role of the state should be minimal. The underlying component is that the state, given a dominant role, not only mars the collective trust of individuals as such but also raises the possibilities of adopting a biased approach in conducting the day to day affairs of the communities.

Therefore, the principal object of the state lies in maintaining the secular structure of the society; promote spirit of veneration and tolerance, harmony and peace. Any disturbances may be solved through non-violent means assisted by enlightened public. To relish the cultural confluence of the society, Gandhi stressed the importance of respect and forbearance towards others' religious and cultural practices, languages, and educational institutions.[13] The imparting of education should facilitate the upkeep of diverse cultural traditions and harmony and the state should be vigilant not to divert itself from its assigned role of being a custodian of its diverse society.

Sarvodaya or Welfare of All

Closely linked to the above concept of Swaraj is Sarvodaya. Sarvodaya literally means the welfare of all, meaning a social uplift. Through sarvodaya, Gandhi visualized the establishment of a welfare state where all are equal in a society. Deeply disturbed by the prevalence of divisions—casteist, religious, malicious and rustic society–Gandhi enunciated his views on sarvodaya as essential to unity in society. This social philosophy of his has its roots in the 'positive freedom as self-determination (Swaraj), meaning the affirmation of the uniqueness of individual. This should be deeply rooted in man's sense of relatedness to his community of fellowmen.[14] Alienation or exclusion of some sections will invariably lead to an individual's sense of rootlessness, and loss of identity[15], thereby creating cultural barriers and disharmony.

Deeply inspired by John Ruskin's Unto This Last, which glorified the simple life based on manual labour, Gandhi himself observed that its reading was a turning point in his life. The result was Sarvodaya that he had insisted on:

- the good of all (not the good of the greatest number). The good of the individual is contained in the good of all
- all have the same right of earning from their occupation/work.
- life of labour, the life of the tiller of the soil and the handicraftsmen is the life worth living.

Gandhi skillfully interconnected the attainment of Swaraj and Sarvodaya. The realization of Swaraj seemed to be almost an impossibility without achieving sarvodaya. 'However important political freedom was, its justification lay in making possible the fulfillment of this vision. The essential platforms, therefore, are the home-spun cloth, khadi, Hindu-Muslim unity and anti-untouchability'.[16] Gandhi interrelated these factors and visualized their implementation towards creating a society based on equality. Firstly, with the removal of Untouchability, comes the broader inclusion of downtrodden societies. This would not only elevate the social status of the individual but also make him contribute positively to society, thus realizing the good of the individual. Secondly, the unity between varied communities is also an inclusion-oriented dimension that leads to harmonious relations between individuals. The inclusion of the deprived into the mainstream society underlines this principle. Thirdly, the home-spun khadi not only symbolizes the self-sufficiency but also improves the economic status of the individual, thus justifying Swadeshi. Swadeshi, for Gandhi, means the use of home produced goods or products that came from one's own culture and one's immediate surroundings.[17] It proves the third dictum of his sarvodaya, that the life of labour is the life worth living. The successful combination of Swadeshi and Sarvodaya is possible only under Swaraj. It is rather futile to debate the relevance of such a beautiful synthesis of welfare and governance aspects, which many of the contemporary welfare and development experts are trying to put forward in a different tone and language today.

Gandhi scores above the rest with a humane touch to the entire concept. While the integration of these radically moral and economic aspects is in itself an amazing phenomenon, the addition of an element of service adds further credibility to this concept, for the simple reason that service represents 'true humility, which means most strenuous and constant endeavours entirely directed to the service of humanity.'[18]

Another important facet which Gandhi diligently stressed upon was the compatibility between the ends and means. Gandhi's insistence that morality be the base of this dichotomy underlines his firm conviction that only the rightful means need to be adopted to achieve a noble end. Deviation from this not only leads to resorting to violent 'means' but also strips the 'end' of its profound sanctity. And with a noble end like sarvodaya that aims at the welfare of all, it would be an injustice with the absence of compatibility between the means and ends.

Gram Swaraj or Village Upliftment

Unity in society also depends on how the concept of equality works. It not only encompasses social but also economic equality. Gandhi argued that a materialist and consumerist approach in economics contradicts the values of a higher civilization. The establishment of Gram Swaraj was evolved with the aim of making the villages and subsequently, the nation, self-sufficient. Secondly, it aimed at forging a society based on not just equality in abstract terms but to realise it socially and economically too.

The best way to put forward Gandhi's ideas on Village upliftment or Gram Swaraj is to quote what he said, that deserves to be quoted in full:

> 'My idea of village Swaraj is that it is a complete republic, independent of its neighbours for its own vital wants. Thus every village's first concern will be

> to grow its own food crops, and cotton for its cloth. It should have a reserve for its cattle, recreation and playground for adults and children. The village will maintain a village theatre, school and public hall. It will have its own waterworks ensuring clean water supply. Education will be compulsory; every activity will be conducted on cooperative basis. There will be no castes such as we have today with their graded untouchability'.[19]

It is important to note that Gandhi provided an alternative strategy that encompasses a comprehensive worldview of not only the human welfare but also the environment which is being much talked about today.

Gandhi's economic philosophy thoroughly emphasised on 'decentralisation' through sustained agro-industrial units reconstructed on a permanent basis that would meet the local, rural and national requirements to a large extent. Devoid of exploitative motives, these village units provided a source of income for the rural habitants thereby arresting their migration to the cities in search of their livelihood means. The stress on promotion of Khadi connotes that the production and distribution of the home-spun cloth, can solve a number of economic problems, if implemented appropriately. The following five points need to be gauged keeping in view their beneficial aspects.

- Under khadi economy, the capital is under the control of the labour.
- Each village can be self-sufficient thereby strengthening the concept of Gram Swaraj.
- Earning bread labour through weaving of cloth via spinning wheel involves a great deal of labour.
- It also provides employment opportunity to all sections of society.[20]
- Most importantly, the 18 point Constructive Programme depicting the welfare measures is much easier to adopt, with no other capital except the human labour.

The use of spinning wheel denotes no outlay of capital; moreover, it affords relief in times of famine, provides livelihood to the poor and is the most potent instrument of securing cooperation of all without any discrimination.[21] Gandhi reiterated that in the middle ages, economics was subordinate to ethics. What needs to be done is the amalgamation of the two; but for this to materialize, it requires enormous human solidarity. Unless we restrict our wants, no materialistic race can be regulated. Thus the socio-economic dimension is predominantly based on the standard of life rather than standard of living.

Gandhi envisaged the village reconstruction on the above-mentioned pattern. As he said, craft, art, health and education should all be integrated into one scheme.[22] The Constructive Programme was definitely a direction towards this end. It involves the communities to participate in this village reconstruction programmes irrespective of their religion or caste. Gandhi likened the process to an oceanic circle, where the outermost circumference will not wield power to crush the inner circle but give strength to all within and derive its strength from the centre in this picture, every religion has its full and equal place. There is no room for machines that would displace human labour and concentrate power in few hands'.[23]

Village reconstruction meant a great deal for Gandhi. For him, it not only meant self-rule, self-sufficiency, and unity of different communities, but also a way of resisting the domination of the powerful be it the foreign, or societal. Exploiting villages meant a form of organized violence that goes against the spirit of Swaraj. Therefore, Swaraj has to be built on non-violence, giving the villagers their due.[24] It would be no exaggeration to say that it was Gandhi's dream to make possible the creation of a non-violent society with emphasis on the 'moral and cultural dimensions of the economic system, humane process of production, sustainable development, right to gainful employment, and decentralized production'.[25]

The following reasons justify Gandhi's vision of evolving Gram Swaraj. Gandhi detested both capitalism and communism for he opined that they catered to the elite section of the society. While capitalism is hypothesized on the 'survival of the fittest', communism introduced an element of force or coercion and vested the state with absolute political and economic powers. Secondly, it is also bereft of an inclusive dimension. While some are automatically benefited by virtue of their status, the majority, comprising the poor, are continually exploited. In Gandhi's vision, private ownership was replaced with trusteeship to ensure equality. Trusteeship requires the rich to allocate a portion of their wealth for the welfare of the society, through formation of trusts. Voluntary reduction of wants effectively complements this doctrine. Gandhi asserted, 'without moral discipline, moral persuasion and voluntary control of greed for wealth and power, neither the individual nor the society can prosper'.[26] Gandhi was mistaken for disseminating voluntary and absolute poverty. It would be unjust not to recall that he abhorred the extreme levels of poverty or affluence. What he visualized was a marginal gap between the two; he often made an effort to relate that a 'society's wealth consisted in the character of its members, not in the quantity of its material objects, and the purpose of its economic arrangements should be to create the necessary economic basis of the good life. This ensured a sense of limit built into it and remained subject to collective human control'.[27]

Communal Unity and Removal of Untouchability

Gandhi incessantly worked towards Hindu-Muslim unity. No other leader in the history of India so diligently pursued the Hindu-Muslim unity as Gandhi did. He did it even to the extent of antagonizing the people who were considered as his close associates, held captive by their extreme views regarding the religion. Gandhi had undertaken countless number of fasts to bring about unity between these two groups. It needs to be clarified that this equally applies to the broader context of majority-minority relations and not confined only to the Hindus and Muslims. He remarked that 'everybody is agreed about the necessity of this unity. But everybody des not know that unity does not mean mere political unity which may be imposed. It does, however, mean an unbreakable heart-unity'.[28] All religions taught the vast humanity to be true, and promote universal brotherhood and goodwill, while at the same time no man expounded religion could claim perfection, which was the attribute of God alone. Gandhi constantly pleaded 'to cultivate an attitude of sympathy and broad tolerance towards each other to understand and appreciate their viewpoint and to help them not by proselytizing them but by making Hindus better Hindus, Mussalmans better Mussalmans, and all of them better Indians'.[29]

There are enough strong reasons as to why Gandhi vehemently espoused the Hindu-Muslim unity to a great extent. His enormous faith in the Hindu-Muslim unity was shaken soon after his return from South Africa. He was aghast at the vast divisions that characterised the relations between the two communities. During the Satyagraha struggle in South Africa, 'he had little difficulty uniting Hindu and Muslim traders, many of whom shared a common language and culture. He generalized this experience and both underestimated the distance between the two communities in India and exaggerated his own ability to bridge it'.[30] With the same exaggerated faith, he denounced the two-nation theory of Jinnah, his colleague in the Congress, who was a staunch advocate of the partition. Gandhi argued that 'Hindus and Muslims shared a common culture and since even their religions had deeply influenced each other, they could not possibly be called separate nations... the very idea that each nation should have its own state was preposterous and impractical. Since both the states were bound to be multi-religious and had to find ways of accommodating minorities, there was no reason why the united India could not do the same..'.[31] As one of his close associates recollects, 'Gandhi's work had been devoted to securing the independence of a united country, and now that it was so near fruition, he was not prepared to contemplate seeing it undone'.[32]

Gandhi believed in religious pluralism though he himself was a pious Hindu but with a difference. He did not worship in temples; his prayer meetings in the ashrams owed more to Christian practice. His subsequent prayer meetings consisted of the recital of verses from all religious texts. The Gita served as a source of his moral conscience and he relied more on his inner voice. As far as religion per se is concerned, Gandhi said: I do not believe in people telling others about their faith, especially with a view to conversion. Faith does not admit of telling. It has to be lived and then it becomes self-propogating.[33] He also persistently reminded people about the one-ness of all the religions, though the rituals are in contrast. His disinclination towards the rituals converted into a call for a heart-unity, and a united humanity. He was highly critical of those who did not comply with these norms. To revile one another's religion, to make reckless statements, to utter untruth, to break the heads of innocent men, to desecrate temples or mosques, as he said, is the denial of God.[34]

Equally important on Gandhi's agenda was the removal of Untouchability and caste discrimination. In this aspect too, Gandhi did not de-link the religion as he believed that Untouchability has no religious sanction: 'I regard untouchability as the greatest blot on Hinduism… it is a sin to regard anyone born in Hinduism as polluted or untouchable—it is satanic to do so'.[35] He also reiterated that 'Hindus will never deserve freedom, nor get it if they allow their noble religion to be disgraced by the retention of the taint of Untouchability…let us not deny God by denying to a fifth of our race the right of association on the equal footing'.[36] He believed that Hinduism would destroy itself if the community does not take effective remedial measures. According to him, Untouchability based on an individual's birth in lower strata of society can be removed by acknowledging that they too are the children of God. If the distinctions are based on the job they perform, 'the Bhangis are entitled to our highest reverence for the sanitary service they perform for society'.[37] Gandhi practiced what he taught. His acceptance of an untouchable family into his Ashram, against the will of other inmates, amply demonstrates his sincerity for living up his principles. Since he believed in the Hindu philosophy of rebirth, he even preferred to be born as an untouchable so as to experience and also alleviate their constant sufferings. According to him, it is the touch of sin that pollutes us and not the sinner. Therefore, the discrimination on the basis of high and low caste is a scar on Hinduism, which all devout Hindus must annihilate.

Cultural Pluralism

How did Gandhi correlate swaraj, swadeshi, sarvodaya, gram swaraj and village upliftment? How was it possible to achieve cultural pluralism through these methods? The first inherent component, which was put forward by Gandhi, was the synthesis of different cultures. As he saw it, 'India stands for synthesis of the different cultures that have come to stay in India, that have influenced Indian life, and that, in their turn, have themselves been influenced by the spirit of the soil. This synthesis will naturally be of the Swadeshi type, where each culture is assured its legitimate place, and not of the American pattern, where one dominant culture absorbs the rest, and where the aim is not towards harmony, but towards an artificial and forced unity'.[38] Gandhi's ideas had an inclusive aspect. What he spoke for a Hindu applied equally to a Muslim. What he preached a high caste Hindu applied in the same measure to an untouchable or any other person.

Gandhi's concept of cultural pluralism is inseparable from religion but is devoid of rigidity. A religiously plural society contained enormous resources as long as religion was not regarded as the primary marker of identity. Social order, in a way, is also an extension of cultural plurality. He was against isolating any singular cultural trait and identifying with identity of a community in his broader vision of a society. While identifying it with specific cultural traits is good for revealing one's identity, on the negative it warns of an individual sinking in the rigid extremities of one's culture. Gandhi's faith in the Indian cultural plurality was undiminished; this plurality, he perceived, existed even in undivided India. This plurality is especially necessary in addressing the common grievances, which he termed as matters of 'all-India concern'.[39]

Plurality is a must for a healthy society for it is a source of enrichment, as it enables a spirit of mutual accommodation, signifies manifold evidences of common insight and provides multiple paths to truth. Truth and non-violence thus help in establishing harmony between one community and other, and also build up collective action across all divisions of religion and caste. Apart from enabling a 'dialogue' and 'exchange of ideas', it is the working together of people that enables better understanding and a sense of affinity. As Margaret Chatterjee points out, it also enables the setting of a remarkable example of pooling of talents in society. Three most outstanding requirements for forging unity include:

1. Dealing with one's own imperfections or what Gandhi says 'put your own house in order first', to realise the flaws in society and how difficult it is to assimilate.
2. Bringing about a change in one's outdated or rigid perceptions, going beyond the confines of tradition and convention. Gandhi himself initiated a change in his perception if an alternative thought was found to be more relevant and logical and one, which serves the good of all.
3. Getting rid of one's bigotry to bring about sahishnuta (tolerance), peaceful and harmonious co-existence, while retaining one's diverse legacies.

One of the most interesting expressions of Gandhi's conception of a peaceful society can be attributed to the eminent social scientist, B.N. Ganguli. He interprets that Gandhi had an artistic view of society, for it is open to the eyes of the rich mind to see in the same colours a subtle meaning (like in an art piece). The unity lies in the diversity of colours. Any incompatibility suggests an erroneous combination of colours, composition, and plan, distorting the unity of the design. Similarly, in a society, which is compared to an art piece, the distortions are symbolic of the prevalence of inequality, untouchability and absence of communal harmony. Cultural pluralism permits an enormous scope for enhancing the spirit of tolerance and non-violence. The unity based on these two not only minimizes the chances of a social conflict but also provide a non-violent means of resolving differences, if any. The conflicting socio-economic forces need not act in such a way that one eliminated the other, but that both might merge in a unity to move on to a new path traced by the resultant of both the forces.[40] A society based on the principles of Swaraj, Sarvodaya and Gramswaraj can make it possible to merge the diverse aspects in a single thread of unity.

In a society, the conduct of an individual is as important as individual freedom. Gandhi was of the firm opinion that an individual capable of making good use of his freedom for the service of society is the one capable of contributing towards an ideal society. Since the human relations are basically interdependent, the individuals in a society are independently and collectively responsible for their actions. For their decisions affect the others, good or bad – a single family or collective community, men and women, old and young. It is all-inclusive. In this context, it is necessary to be cautious not to interpret the 'all-inclusive' aspect as a way of homogenizing but to synthesize the diverse communities with a sense of moral responsibility.

Conclusion

Today different nations are articulating the significance of removing disparities and ensuring equality of all. Almost a century ago, Gandhi, through his *Constructive Programme* articulated the same. It included those aspects of human development which are relevant even till today. Some of these include Hindu-Muslim Unity (today likened to affable majority-minority relations), removal of untouchability, ban on alcohol, the use of khadi (hand-spun cloth), the development of village industries, and craft-based education, equality of women, health education, the use of indigenous languages, the adoption of a common national language, economic equality, building up peasants' and workers' organizations, integration of the tribal people into mainstream political and economic life, a detailed code of conduct for students, helping lepers and beggars, and cultivating respect for animals.[41] As Dr. Rajendra Prasad, the first President of the independent India, remarked, 'a substantial part of Gandhi's writing relates to political, social, religious, educational, economic and linguistic problems; there was hardly any aspect of life in India which he did not influence and fashion according to his own pattern'.[42]

Gandhi's intense moralistic stand was termed utopianism and his methods constantly cast doubts in others' minds. Yet, he emerged victorious, though his thoughts came under intense censure. His conception of a unified society amid diversity is yet to come true. What we see today is in contradiction to what he visualized for the future of India. Fanaticism, inter-community violence, inequality, materialism and mindless consumerism, gender disparity, hunger, poverty and so on still exist and act as impediments to our peaceful coexistence. Infact, the coercive methods by some of the states are even justified as essential conditions for maintaining peace and order around the world. It is rather apt to quote what George S. Arundale (President, Theosophical Society, Adyar,

Madras) once said: 'we cannot have peace until all the nations treat with each other in a mood of freedom and friendliness until we develop a new conception of the integrated social life. The fate of civilization and humanity on this planet is bound up with that deep instinct for the universal values of spirit, freedom, justice and love of man which form the breath of Gandhi's being. In this distracted world, Gandhi's non-violence seems to be a dream too beautiful to be true'.[43]

Gandhi's philosophy evolved more or less at the same time as did other theories pertaining to world peace and order. His idealism stems from his strong fervour that the world is one and peace is a prerequisite for it. Having been a votary of truth and non-violence all through his life, he despised the idea of using violent and coercive methods. For him, coercion is highly in contradiction with the spirit and dignity of an individual and directly affects the peaceful coexistence of diverse communities in a society. Therefore the concept of 'unity' highly encompasses the convergence of goodness, honesty, morality and non-violence and this leads to the creation of a just and harmonious society. Gandhi aimed at achieving this through truthful means for the means are as important as the end. He was very much opposed to the Machiavellian concept of absolute ruthlessness as the means and end in this concept are highly inconsistent. Gandhi likened the means to a seed, the end to a tree; and there is just the same inviolable connection between the means and the end as there is between the seed and the tree.[44] According to him, peace cannot be achieved by waging wars or suppressing morally superior civilization. Even in evolving these ideas, Gandhi did not tread the same path as others did. His path was less taken or followed; in his time, he sounded more like a radical questioning the rationality of a particular action (when he felt it was rather unjust).

Gandhi was neither a prophet, though he foresaw the ills of today long ago nor a perfect being, who was absolutely free of blemish. His experiments and calculations regarding his methods failed at times. But he made himself great by being a consistent adherent to non-violent and moral approach. His experiments in this approach through truth and love of fellow beings and success thereof endeared him to all. He set an example, which every one of us can emulate. Dhirendra Datta rightly observes that 'Gandhi's life shows that even an ordinary person has within him a capacity for increasing perfection that can work miracles, that is, things which would ordinarily be regarded as impossible. Gandhi can be model and hope for all. The modern generation can hasten this process if it will, and enjoy and create greater peace and happiness, for itself and the future generations'.[45] That would ideally mark a tribute to his vision of an ideal society, living in unity amidst diversity.

On a concluding note, it is apt to quote what Gandhi once said which holds relevance to this day:

> 'The Indian culture of our times is in the making. Many of us are striving to produce a blend of all the cultures, which seem today to be in clash with one another. No culture can live, if it attempts to be exclusive...our remote ancestors blended with one another with the utmost freedom and we of the present generation are a result of that blend. Whether we are doing any good to the country of our birth and the tiny globe which sustains us or whether we are a burden, the future alone will show'.[46]

References

1. Chatterjee, Margaret, (2005) *Gandhi and the challenge of Religious Diversity, Religious Pluralism Revisited*, Promilla & Co. Publishers, New Delhi. (Introduction, pp. 11–38).
2. *Collected Works of Mahatma Gandhi.*
3. Copley, Antony, (1987) *Gandhi*, Basil Blackwell, Oxford.
4. Datta, Dhirendra Mohan, (1953) *The Philosophy of Mahatma Gandhi*, The University of Wisconsin Press, Madison, USA.
5. Ganguli, B.N., (2000) *Gandhi's Social Philosophy: Perspective and Relevance*, National Gandhi Museum, New Delhi (2nd edition) (pp. 435–444, chapter. 21).
6. Kurup, G. Radhkrishna., (2005) *Gandhian Alternative to Globalisation*, ISDA Journal, vol. 16, no. 1& 2, pp. 157–179.
7. M.K. Gandhi, (1961) *My Philosophy of Life*, Earl Publications, Bombay.
8. Parekh, Bhikhu, (1997) *Gandhi*, Oxford University Press, Oxford.
9. Radhakrishnan, S., (ed.) (1956) *Mahatma Gandhi, Reflections on his life and work*, Jaico Publishing House, Bombay.

Endnotes

1. Datta, D.M., The Philosophy of Mahatma Gandhi, The University of Wisconsin Press, 1953, p. 3.
2. H.S.L. Polak, Mahatma Gandhi, Bombay, Jaico, 1962, p. 352.
3. Datta, p. 70.
4. Dr. Rajendra Prasad, the First President of India, in his homage to Gandhiji. January 16th, 1958, Rashtrapati Bhavan, New Delhi.
5. Collected Works, vol. 41, pp. 356–357.
6. *Young India*, 27-6-1929. Also see Collected Works of Mahatma Gandhi, vol. 41, p. 62–63.
7. *Young India*, 19-9-1929.
8. *Harijan*, 1st February 1942.
9. Bhikhu Parekh, *Gandhi*, Oxford University Press, Oxford, 1997, p. 76.
10. *Young India*, 30th July, 1931.
11. Parekh, p. 81.
12. Parekh, p. 82.
13. Ibid.
14. Ganguli, B.N., *Gandhi's Social Philosophy, Perspective and Relevance*, National Gandhi Museum, New Delhi, 2000, p. 12.

15. Ibid, p. 13.
16. Antony Copley, Gandhi, Basil Blackwell, Oxford, 1987, p. 51.
17. Ibid, p. 50.
18. *Yervada Mandir*, Chapter, 12.
19. *India of My Dreams*, p. 96 .
20. Kurup, G.R., *Gandhian Alternative to Globalisation*, ISDA Journal, vol. 16, no. 1 & 2, 2005, p. 176.
21. *Young India*, 21st August, 1924.
22. *Harijan*, 10th November, 1946.
23. *Harijan*, 28th July, 1946.
24. *Harijan*, 20th January, 1940.
25. Parekh, p. 89.
26. Datta, p. 139.
27. Parekh, p. 79.
28. Constructive Programme, December, 1941.
29. *Young India*, 27-6-1929. Also see Collected Works of Mahatma Gandhi, vol. 41, pp. 62–63.
30. Parekh, p. 6.
31. Ibid, p. 20.
32. H.S.L. Polak, pp. 352–353.
33. Margaret Chatterjee, p. 112.
34. Rev. Foss Westcott, Gandhi's Fast for Hindu-Muslim Unity, in S. Radhakrishnan (ed.) Mahatma Gandhi, Reflections on his Life and Work, Jaico, Bombay, 1956, p. 250.
35. M.K. Gandhi, My Philosophy of Life, (ed.) by Anand T. Hingorani, 1961, pp. 150–151.
36. Ibid, p. 157.
37. Ibid, p. 159.
38. *Young India*, 17th November, 1920.
39. Margaret Chatterjee, p. 20.
40. Ganguli, p. 437.
41. Parekh, p. 7. Also see Constructive Programme, Navajivan Publications.
42. January 16th, 1958, Homage to Gandhiji.
43. George S. Arundale, *The Essence of Gandhiji*, in S. Radhakrishnan (ed), Mahatma Gandhi, p. 37.
44. *Hindswaraj*, 1909, CWMG, vol. 10.
45. Datta, p. 20. See also p. 154.
46. *Harijan*, 9th May, 1936.

10

Multiculturalism: Australian and Indian Approach

Sonu Trivedi

In many countries, multiculturalism has been taken as a corrective to the excesses of the one-sided nation-building process that has tended to privilege the majority and to marginalize the minorities. A successful management of multiculturalism and multi-ethnic societies requires not only a democratic polity, but the struggle against social inequalities and exclusion. Thus, any effort to formulate policies of managing ethnically and culturally diverse societies needs to consider not only the specific programs and practices but also the social context and the objectives of the State and its citizens. Given the convergences and divergences in the Australia-India relationship both these countries may complement each other in coping with the management of ethnic and cultural diversity through policies which promote ethnic and cultural minority groups' participation in, and access to the resources of society, while maintaining the unity of the country. In this background, the present paper provides an insight into the concept of multiculturalism with the perspectives from Australia and India. The paper has been divided into three sections. Section I offers a glance into the concept of multiculturalism. Section II provides a perspective into the evolution and development of multiculturalism in Australia. And the last section discusses the Indian example of multiculturalism and the lessons that can be learnt from it by other multi-ethnic societies. It is concluded that the Australian case resembles India's evolution as a multicultural society assimilating diversity and grasping opportunities. However, in both cases there are bumps ahead on the road, but the journey remains worth pursuing. The partnership can enable both to overcome the difficulties and play a constructive role in international affairs in solving the multi-ethnic conflicts.

Multiculturalism is based on the fundamental belief that all citizens are equal. It ensures that all citizens can keep their identities, can take pride in their ancestry and have a sense of belonging. Multiculturalism particularly implies people are included into the nation – state as members of diverse but equal ethnic groups. And the state recognizes that the dignity of individuals is linked to the collective dignity of the community to which they belong. It encourages citizens to integrate into their society and take an active part in its social, cultural, economic and political affairs. Multiculturalism is a distinctive model for the management of ethnic diversity in the public domain. It emphasizes the public recognition of ethnic diversity, especially the recognition and accommodation of minority cultures, identities and sensibilities. By and large, multiethnic societies are faced with two formidable challenges: reconciling the compulsions of ethnic diversity and the imperative of societal cohesion, and integrating immigrants and minorities into mainstream society.

No single theory exists of what multiculturalism is or how it should be applicable at all times and places. A perusal of literatures on 'multiculturalism' shows that it is best understood neither as a political doctrine with a programmatic content nor a philosophical school with a distinct theory of man's place in the world but as a perspective on or a way of viewing human life. Multiculturalism promises a deeper understanding of equality and self-determination on the one hand to that which had earlier prevailed in liberal theory. But on the other, it opens up the possibility for conservative interpretations of ascriptive identities and identitarian politics (Joseph, 1999). Its central insights are three, each of which is sometimes misinterpreted by its advocates and needs to be carefully reformulated if it is to carry conviction (Parekh, 1999).

- First, human beings are culturally embedded in the sense that they grow up and live within a culturally structured world and organize their lives and social relations in terms of a culturally derived system of meaning and significance.
- Second, different cultures represent different systems of meaning and visions of the good life. Since each realises a limited range of human capacities and emotions and grasps only a part of the totality of human existence, it needs other cultures to help it understand itself better, expand its intellectual and moral horizon, stretch its imagination, save it from narcissism to guard it against the obvious temptation to absolutise itself, and so on.
- Third, every culture is internally plural and reflects a continuing conversation between its different traditions and strands of thought.

The early 1970s marked the emergence of the multicultural movement at first in Canada and Australia and then in the USA, UK, Germany and elsewhere. It has now begun to dominate the political agenda and debate of most of the industrially advanced as well as developing countries like India. During recent years, the policy of multiculturalism in various countries has received both appreciation as mechanism to respect pluralism as well as severe criticism for eroding the ideology of nationalism (which claims that a given human population has a natural solidarity based on shared history and a common destiny). Since the 'nation-state' implies a culturally homogeneous society, the rise of multiculturalism has meant the end of the "grand vision" of the culturally homogeneous nation-state, or of national integration (Chandhoke, 1999). However, in many countries, multiculturalism has been taken as a corrective to the excesses of the one-sided nation-building process that has tended to privilege the majority and to marginalise the minorities. Hence, successful management of multiculturalism and multiethnic societies requires not only a democratic polity, but the struggle against social inequalities and exclusion.

The critics of multiculturalism point out that it views cultures and ethnic groups in essentialized and static terms, strengthens ethnic cleavages and thereby breeds separatism and ghettoization. Multiculturalism is also assailed for its failure to provide a viable and sustainable sense of national unity and cohesion in multiethnic societies. However, certain developments at the turn of the century, including the attack on the United States on September 11, 2001, the Madrid train bombing in 2004, the murder of the Dutch film maker Theo van Gogh in November 2004, and the terrorist attack on London in July 2005, have accelerated the rethinking on multiculturalism as a viable model of societal integration. Thus, any effort to formulate policies of managing ethnically and culturally diverse societies needs to consider not only the specific programs and practices but also the social context and the objectives of the State and its citizens.

Every multicultural society needs to devise its own appropriate political structure to suit its history, cultural traditions, and range and depth of diversity (Parekh, 2000). Multiculturalism helps in a complex way since it involves a set of issues "relating to the need for community, a sense of belonging to it, the importance of a secure identity, of status and recognition, of particularity, and the need to recognize and maintain difference with others" (Bhargava et al., 1999). In this milieu, my paper focuses on the Australian and Indian approach to multiculturalism. Australia has adopted a multicultural response to its immigration issue for accommodating ethnically diverse population. For countries like India, multiculturalism was adopted with a view to respect the cultural and religious diversity of the minorities on the one hand and on the other to assuage the fear of Hindu rule.

II
Australian Approach

The nature of any country's culture and identity is a complicated entity and a contested subject. Since centuries, the Australians have forged their own identity in the world. Adaptability has invariably enriched the changing mix of Australian culture and identity resulting from immigration mostly after 1947. Over the past sixty years, Australian society has become much more complex and diverse. Governments and policy makers also generally accept that the imposition of cultural uniformity is undesirable and impossible in Australia. In this background the present section looks into the evolution and development of multiculturalism in Australia.

Early Australians maintained that a society of mixed race would benefit neither dominant nor inferior group and would have profound effect on the economic order, on the moral-social order, and on the political order. However, the international events arising out of the Second World War and its aftermath induced an often reluctant government to look fresh into its policies[1].

Fear about Australia's vulnerability and physical isolation, highlighted during the Second World War, led to the "Great post-war immigration programme" that began in 1947 as a part of post-war reconstruction. For the first time it involved attracting non-English speaking immigrants and substantial numbers were recruited from refugee and displacement camps across mainland Europe. In the late 1950s, attention moved to Southern Europe, particularly Italy, Greece and certain middle Eastern countries such as Lebanon. In the recent past, Australia's major source of immigrants have been from Southeast and East Asia, notably, Vietnam, Cambodia and Hong Kong. In recent years, immigration from South Asia has also increased. Thus since, 1945, Australian social policy structures have had to come to terms with a world in which international movement of capital and labour has dramatically reframed old assumptions and values.

Australia's Multicultural Policy

From Monoculturalism to Multiculturalism

Prior to Second World War, the Australian national identity was identified in terms of 'White Australia policy' which included both, racial and cultural elements. These characteristics were result of British inheritance and its adoption to new social and geographic environment. The 'White Australians' considered themselves naturally endowed with virtuous qualities which were significantly absent in other races. As inheritors of British political traditions, they felt themselves possessed of certain ingrained capacities for living under a liberal democratic constitution.

The arrival of non-European immigrants in Australia in the post World War II period emphasized the need to accommodate plurality of ethnic cultures. The Australian experience of immigration has often been analysed in terms of epochs of settlement policies pursued by successive central governments. Usually these epochs have been identified as assimilation; integration; and multiculturalism (Jacubowicz, 1989).

Australia adopted the policy of assimilation from 1947 to 1964. This involved the development and implementation of policies which assumed the natural superiority of the dominant cultural practices of Anglo-Australian society. They presumed that immigrants would become Anglo-Australians overtime. The policy of integration was followed from 1964 to 1973. According to this policy Government came to see it, both formaly and informaly, as a means of supporting the individual through the settlement process. The end point of such a policy was still assimilation. In fact, the racist policy of assimilation reinforced non-assimilation and thus, constituted the problem of the migrants to be addressed by multiculturalism. Thus, in 1973 the Government declared Australia as a multi-cultural society. Along with this, the Government also conceded the irrelevance of 'White Australia' policy in order to meet the exigencies of the time and changing architecture of the world affairs.

Although immigration program began in Australia since 1947 for attracting non-English speaking immigrants, a paradigm shift was brought about in 1978[2]. From the mono-cultural emphasis of the post war era, the shift was towards recognition of cultural pluralism and sympathetic understanding of many ethnic experiences that were now legitimately seen to constitute contemporary Australian society. The reasons for official shift in the policy are as follows:

- Within Australia, both due to ideological and economic reasons it was becoming apparent that the simplifying strategy of homogeneity could not, given demographic and geographic realities, be maintained forever.
- With the end of the Vietnam War and other developments in the world, the refugees problem had assumed serious proportions. The countries were now looking at Australia for help.
- The decade of 1970s had also marked the rise of economic multi-polarity. Rise of Japan and other Asian tigers forced Australia to take a serious view at the region in terms of economic development.
- Rise of the third world and their voices against colonialism, neo-colonialism, apartheid and racism helped in building the Australian perspective on multiculturalism.
- Finally, Australia's increasing trade with countries also provoked a re-appraisal of its cultural, economic and political identities.

The Australian multicultural policy is given special attention here for two reasons: firstly, it constitutes an extensive effort to cope democratically with diversity, developed in the very short time-span of two decades, against the earlier, long-standing assimiliationist, and later integrationist, tradition. Secondly, this policy is founded on a civic and contractual definition of citizenship, rather than on ethnic and cultural communitarianism, a feature which is crucial for avoiding conflicts and reconciling diversity with societal cohesion.

Australia's non-discriminatory immigration policy has resulted in a diverse society in which people of different ethnic and racial origins live together sharing a commitment to the language, laws, institutions and interests of

Australia. The Government's policies on multiculturalism are founded on three principles (as laid down by the National Agenda of 1989):

- *Cultural identity*: the right of all Australians, within carefully defined limits such as the rule of law and parliamentary democracy, to express and share their individual cultural heritage, including their language and religion;
- *Social justice*: the right of all Australians to equality of treatment and opportunity, and the removal of barriers of race, ethnicity, culture, religion, language, gender or place of birth;
- *Economic efficiency*: the need to maintain, develop and utilize effectively the skills and talents of all Australians, regardless of background.

Multiculturalism accepts the contribution of all cultures to Australia but it is not a policy to encourage ethnic or cultural separatism. Rather, it is a policy to provide all Australians, including the original inhabitants, the Aboriginal and Torres Strait Islander peoples, and the descendants of all later immigrants, with the opportunity to participate fully in and contribute to Australian society.

Multiculturalism in Australia has evolved through two major phases, in the short period of three decades. A characteristic of all the phases was that it necessitated a far more pro-active governmental response than required by earlier policies where it was assumed that, while there might be a few delays and disruptions along the way, ultimately, ethnic homogeneity would ensue so that no specific institutional change was required. A major impetus for the changes in policy was the emergence of an ethnic rights movement including articulate and politically active immigrants from non-English speaking backgrounds and grass roots workers in a range of welfare areas, education, health and social services, concerned about the disadvantages faced by many non-English speaking background immigrants. The 1972 elections of a non-conservative reformist government committed to social welfare provisions and overcoming social disadvantage was responsive to changes addressing class related disadvantage and the potential contribution of ethnicity.

In the first major phase of Australian policy, when the target groups were newly arrived immigrants of non-English speaking background, the main focus was on the provision of linguistically and culturally appropriate services with the long term acceptance that cultural maintenance, especially involving language diversity, should be supported. Funding of the nationwide Telephone Interpreter Service, and of welfare and health services for specific ethnic groups were major initiatives. Other major initiatives in this period included the development of "community" language programs and, to a much lesser extent, bilingual education in schools as well as government funding of after-hours ethnic community language schools and the setting up of government radio and television networks broadcasting in languages other than English.

In the second phase of the policy the focus of concern shifted from cultural maintenance to concerns about inequity and social disadvantage and, subsequently, to community relations and racism. Contributing to this shift was the perception that cultural maintenance and cultural pluralism were insufficient to overcome structural inequities confronting many communities of non-English speaking backgrounds, even if not themselves immigrants. The response was not, however, to set up parallel institutional structures but to move towards deep change in the major institutions, especially those bureaucratic institutions associated with the delivery of government services. The term "mainstreaming" was used to refer to the strategies involved in changing the essentially mono cultural bureaucracies. Programmatic political multiculturalism had already resulted in a variety of Federal and State agencies to oversee policy development and implementation, but the shift now was towards changing the way general government agencies operated. These changes intended to remove structural barriers to social participation and were enunciated in the 1989 National Agenda for a Multicultural Australia[3]. They were part of the government's broader agenda for promoting social justice and ensuring equitable access to government programmes and services for a range of groups perceived as disadvantaged, including Aborigines and Torres Strait Islanders, the disabled and women as well as those of non-English speaking background.

The Australian National Agenda is significant for the way in which it heralded the shift from multiculturalism as a policy for specific targeted groups to being a broader policy for "all Australians". In this way, the programmatic political definition of multiculturalism shifted from an "ethnic group" model to what has been described as a "social-democratic concept of citizenship for an ethnically diverse nation" (Castles, 1991).

The changes in Australian multiculturalism policy over the last two decades are the outcome of a variety of factors, including:

- changing awareness of the limitations and outcomes of earlier stages of the policy (as with supplementing cultural pluralism and maintenance initiatives with efforts to reduce disadvantage by removing structural barriers);
- changes in the policy objectives of different elected governments and the changing outcome of the interplay of interest groups affected by multicultural policies; and
- emergence of a generation of Australians who have grown up under the policy of multiculturalism and accept the changes it has produced in Australian society.

These include a much more inclusive approach to the attributes of Australian identity and a remarkably high level of tolerance. This is indicated by an absence of extensive inter-group conflict involving either those from the Anglo-Celtic majority as well as that between groups such as those from the former Yugoslavia who outside Australia have become embroiled in extensive and violent conflict. High levels of inter-generational mobility have also contributed to acceptance of the policy among those of non-English speaking background.

As public policy multiculturalism encompasses those government measures designed to respond to the cultural and ethnic diversity of contemporary Australia. The Federal Government and some of the State governments have adopted access and equity policies aimed at ensuring that all residents of Australia enjoy equal access to the resources managed by the Government on behalf of the community. The object of the access and equity strategy is to remove the barriers of race, language, religion or culture in policy formulation, programme design and service delivery. Measures now in place to help achieve this aim include the provision of information in languages other than English, access to the telephone interpreter service, cross-cultural training of public servants and community consultations. This strategy also contributes to the Government's focus on strengthening social cohesion between various elements of the Australian community and fostering good community relations. There are measures in place to enhance communication and cooperation between the Government and the community to this end. The Government is also known for having established the EA ethnic radio in June 1975. The Fraser Liberal Government (1975–1983) continued promoting Australia as a multicultural society through a number of policy initiatives, including the establishment of the Special Broadcasting Service in 1978, designed to oversee EA ethnic radio and later multicultural television introduced in 1980.

While it is true that in Australia, some of the state and national ethnic organizations are still based on ethnic group model and managed mostly by first generation patriarchs, the move away from ethnic identity politics as the sole basis for struggle and change has been happening for quite sometime now. Of late, a great deal of work on multiculturalism is being carried out by immigrant women and by the second generation, often women, working in bureaucracies, community services, as volunteers and in academia. These workers have much broader political commitments which include gender, class, ethnic, local and environmental politics (Vassta, 1993). The ideology and policies of multiculturalism have created a public space for cultural diversity in official conceptions of Australian identity and it has made efforts to manage the plurality accepting pluralism through multiculturalism (Narang and Gopal, 2002)

Appraisal of Australian Policy on Multiculturalism

Multiculturalism, as Australia's official policy towards ethnic diversity is only three decades old. It replaced earlier policies of assimilation and, briefly, integration. The latter beckoned a policy which envisaged that while individuals might retain cultural traditions in their private lives, they would in other respects accommodate to the national culture and public institutions of Australia. The Anglo-centric assimilation policies of the 1940s, 50s and 60s were first criticized and government adopted a multicultural approach since 70s onwards. The first official national multicultural policies were implemented by Malcom Fraser's Liberal Government in 1978. The Labour Government of Bob Hawke continued with these policies. While Paul Keating's Labour Government was an advocate of multiculturalism in the early 1990s, the current Prime Minister of Australia, John Howard himself is a critic of multiculturalism, preferring instead a "shared national identity". Under the leadership of Prime Minister John Howard, Australia evolved from a "tolerant", forward-looking society into one of the most intolerant and conservative societies in the Western world. Today, Australia's multiculturalism is only useful as political rhetoric and an instrument of marginalization (Hassan, 2005). Nevertheless, the policy of multiculturalism has remained largely intact. John Howard seems to favour the policy of social integration because according to him 'integration was under-done in Australia'. To Quote him, "Migrants are obliged to "be Australian" and social integration must be pushed harder" (As he spoke in an interview marking his 10th anniversary as Prime Minister) (Humphries, 2006).

While Multiculturalism, as a policy was adopted in Australia as safeguard against the immigration policies, which were threatening the social homogeneity considered vital for maintaining a stable social and political order, it has been criticized from several opposing quarters. There are differences of opinion with regard to its acceptability. Deployment of public funds so that migrants can retain there own culture, often has been criticized, for perpetuating intolerance between ethnic communities and promoting favouritism and discrimination. Such consequence would also be offensive to the liberal and egalitarian elements of our culture.

According to the critics, multiculturalism as conceived at present has no place in a democratic society. The democratic society is characterised by the absence of discrimination and the presence of individual freedom. In such a society there is cultural freedom and the freedom of conscience. An individual is free to engage in cultural activity by himself or in association with others. If one wishes to live in isolation, he may do so. But he also has the freedom to intermingle and interact. What is not permissible in a truly free society is the imposition of rules of behaviour or the state sponsorship of culture. Culture belongs to the people and its destiny must remain in their hands.

Multiculturalism, with its stress on social cohesion mystifies and obscures the underlying structural features of social and economic inequality, and class exploitation at work. Although in public sphere, multiculturalism celebrates diversity and toleration, it disguises the fact that most migrants remain a lower paid under-class, performing menial labour at lower rates of pay than the rest of Australian society. According to its later critics, by co-opting ethnic elites multiculturalism has become a 'necessary ideology', which has created its own constituency and institutional basis (Jupp, 1997). Right from its inception in 1973, 'separatist multiculturalism' has been slammed for threatening national identity and denying superior legitimacy to the host culture.

However, this situation which critics claim is the result of somewhat different strategies of managing ethnic diversity, which focus on cultural pluralism while ignoring its structural elements, especially as these involve social inequalities. In the Australian case the earlier formulation of the Australian identity was partially developed as a reaction against the perceived inadequacies of the European societies from which the settlers came (albeit located on a dominant British linguistic and institutional foundation which also had a strong pro-European racist element). The most recent reconsideration of national identity has been the consequence of earlier initiatives in programmatic political multiculturalism. The task of changing the national identity is certainly contested, but, at a level very different from that encountered elsewhere. This in part is because of the relatively weak form of Australian nationalism (Castles et al., 1988) which had as one of its institutional elements a rejection of the strong nationalism evident in 19th century Europe, a society which many early settlers had left to seek a better life.

Multiculturalism enjoys a high level of support in Australia. While the extremely diverse and relatively small individual ethnic groups in Australia have clearly set the parameters within which policies are developed, it must also be acknowledge that Australia has managed and implemented programmatic political multiculturalism in a manner which has produced considerable cohesion, rather than opposition. Those of non-English speaking background have not been fused into a unified opposition such as happened with the very diverse groups comprising Aboriginal Australian society. Even the latter are now considering their place within a multicultural Australia within the framework of specific policies of self-determination and self-management, attests to a growing acceptance of the potentially more diverse model of Australian national identity.

III
Indian Approach

In India multiculturalism came along with the inauguration of democracy. While our Constitution, with great foresight, allowed for universal adult franchise, minority protection and positive discrimination for the historically deprived, India still has a long way to go (Mahajan, 1999). Unlike Australia, India has not adopted multiculturalism as an official policy, still in a disguised form; we find it reflected in the constitution and other political arrangements.

Furthermore, the fortuitous presence of pre-independent liberal institutions and their post-independence broadening and deepening as a consequence of assertive political transaction have produced a thriving multicultural society (Bhattacharya, 2003; Mitra 2001). In this respect India is quite unique. The issue of multiculturalism and secularism, which is used as its surrogate concept in Indian political discourse, have been taken from the early years following independence. In this perspective, the present section discusses the Indian example of multiculturalism and the lessons that can be learnt from it by other multi-ethnic societies.

In the euphoria of independence, with fresh memories of the Hindu-Muslim riots and the partition of India, the post-colonial state in India considered its solution in the 'fuzzy multiculturalism' to be an optimal solution for the political conditions that surrounded its inception (Mitra, 1999). The post-colonial state, thus, made attempts to accommodate both the fact of the existence of several religions which played a salient role in the social life of her citizens and to assuage the apprehension of non-Hindus of a possible Hindu majoritarian dominance (Parekh, 1999).

The Indian Constitution can be said to be a multi-cultural document in the sense of providing for political and institutional measures for the recognition and accommodation of the country's diversity. The composition of the Constituent Assembly, which was entrusted with the onerous responsibility of drafting the country's constitution after independence, represented the plural character of Indian society. It spent several years deliberating over a central issue: how to transform a heterogeneous, hierarchical and fragmented society into a unified, egalitarian, modern and forward-looking nation. In this effort in the past fifty years, it has been pulled this way and that, tossed about in the rough and tumbles of parliament-judiciary tussle, and frequently stretched beyond recognition to fit the demands of whichever political party happened to be currently in power[4].

The process of search for the identification of the core values of the state was effected by a constitutional provision of equality of all faiths and the commitment of the post-independence regime to this principle. The constitution of India lays down that the conduct of the state shall be governed by the principle of secularism, that state action must be determined by fairness, non-partisanship and impartiality. The principle of secularism, which is defined as a matter of state policy, stipulates that the state shall treat all religions in the country with equal respect, that it shall not privilege one religion or community over others, that it shall provide equal opportunities to the followers of all religions (Right to Freedom of Religion, Articles 25–28). The institutions of the state are expected to ensure that the principle of secularism is observed in letter and spirit in public life.

The Indian Constitution provides for the conservation and cultivation of the rights of minorities as the fundamental rights of every citizen of India. Article 29(1) says that any section of the citizens of India having a distinct language, script or culture of its own shall have the fundamental right to conserve the same. Further Article 30(1) stipulates that minorities can establish and administer educational institutions of their own choice, and the state cannot compel them to attend institutions not of their liking. It not only provides for the protection of minority interests, but seeks to ensure that individuals belonging to minorities do not suffer from discrimination. Thus Article 29(2) forbids any discrimination against any citizen on the basis of religion, race, caste or language in the matter of admission into educational institutions maintained or aided by the state. This means that if a cultural minority wants to preserve its own language and culture, the state cannot by law impose on it any other culture belonging to the local majority. Both religious and linguistic minorities are protected by this provision. The constitution also defines a positive, directional role for the state in this respect. It directs every state (federal unit) to provide adequate facilities for instruction in the mother-tongue at the primary stage of education of children belonging to linguistic minority groups, and empowers the President to issue proper direction to any state (Article 350A). The Supreme Court, in a series of judgments over the years, has expanded the scope of these provisions.

The federal debate since independence has emphasized the multi-cultural underpinnings of political institutional arrangements. Thus, Article 370 of Indian Constitution gave Kashmir powers and protection not available to other states. This asymmetry extends to the Northeast region too, where the culturally distinct and economically backward tribal communities are anxious to preserve their ways of life (Parekh, 1999). Furthermore, the story of statehood within the Indian federation since 1950 is the story of acceding to ethnic identity demands for political recognition, for autonomous powers within the federation, and for a more secure environment for the protection and maintenance of identity. The major re-organization of States in India in the 1950s and the 1960s on the basis of dominant ethno-linguistic and ethno-religious group is a witness to the fact that multiculturalism is given due respect in a heterogeneous country like India[5]. The strength and viability of the Indian federation in accommodating diversity is illustrated by the creation of three new states in 2000[6]. Thus, the ongoing federalising process which politically accommodates ethnic identity, has remained the most effective method of management and resolution of conflicts (Bhattacharya, 2003).

In the light of the aforesaid facts, we can say that although multiculturalism was visualized in various constitutional and political processes (federalism) in India, but the origin of multiculturalism in academic literatures is of very recent origin. It was only in the late 90s that Indian scholars joined the 'global debate' on multiculturalism (Seminar, 1999; Deb, 2002; Bhargava et al., 1999).

The constitution of India as well as the dominant political discourse in the country define India's national identity in terms of its inclusive and interactive openness[7] (Sen, 2005), its composite legacy, and a set of political principles including equality, citizenship, fundamental rights and secularism. The constitution explicitly outlaws all forms of discrimination based on caste, religion, birth and ethnicity. India's national emblems – the country's flag and the national anthem – reflect its motto of unity-in-diversity. The constitution of India recognizes a system of legal pluralism whereby it guarantees to Muslims and other minorities not only fundamental rights available to all citizens of the country but also community-specific religious and cultural rights, including the right to maintain their family laws, religious schools and other educational institutions. This can be best described in the words of Bhikhu Parekh as follows:

> "In India, we have a common criminal law but no unified civil law. It was hoped that the latter would be developed overtime. The constitution also exempted minority educational institution from the policy of affirmative action. The Indian Parliament or State legislatures have passed laws banning bigamy among Hindus, but not among some minority communities. The state exercises greater administrative control over the Hindu religious institutions than over the non-Hindu. The reason for such differential treatment is that the state hopes that by starting with them, it will set an appropriate example for minority communities."

Lessons Learnt: Forging a Common Partnership

According to our ex-Prime Minister Rajiv Gandhi, "Australia's policies and influence are now centre stage in international affairs. We see that the destinies of our countries are tied with the Indian Ocean, which laps both our shores. Arising out of our shared democratic values, we have a common interest in justice, fair play and human rights" (Dobell, 2006). As noted in the forgoing, India's strength lies in its inclusive openness and its accommodative ethos. Other countries may learn out of modern India by defining their national identities in an inclusive, accommodative, multicultural and communitarian framework.

Multi-ethnic societies can gain much from the constitution of India, especially in respect of the principle of secularism which enjoins strict impartiality and non-discrimination on the state, and the explicit recognition of a universal, comprehensive regime of fundamental rights, including the cultural, religious and linguistic rights of the minorities (Momin, 2006). Contrary to the spectre of the rise of Hindu 'fundamentalism', India presents a relatively successful case of the growth of a multicultural nation, ensconced within a post-colonial, democratic state (Mitra, 2001). However, while presenting India as a model for multiethnic societies, one should guard against complacency and cultural solipsism.

India and Australia both can also learn from the contemporary European societies which have much to offer, especially in respect of anti-discrimination laws and institutions aimed at combating discrimination and exclusion on grounds of religion, gender or ethnicity, viable democratic institutions, efficient governance, an uncompromising commitment to the rule of law, and a relentless striving for collective self-introspection and self-correction. Autonomous watch-dog institutions (such as the European Monitoring Centre on Racism and Xenophobia) that act as guardians of human rights need to be replicated in all countries, including India. The constitution of the European Union, which includes a Charter of Fundamental Rights as well as the Race Directive (200/43/EC), which ensures non-discrimination on grounds of race and ethnicity in areas such as employment and training, the Commission for Racial Equality in Britain and the Committee for Equal Treatment in the Netherlands offer valuable guidelines to multiethnic societies, including India (Momin, 2006).

Given the convergences and divergences in the Australia-India relationship[8] both these countries may complement each other in coping with the management of ethnic and cultural diversity through policies which promote ethnic and cultural minority group participation in, and access to the resources of society, while maintaining the unity of the country. The Australian case resembles India's evolution as a multicultural society assimilating diversity and grasping opportunities. However, in both cases there are bumps ahead on the road, but the journey remains worth pursuing. The partnership can enable both to overcome the difficulties and play a constructive role in international affairs in solving the multi-ethnic conflicts.

References

Bhargava, R., Bagchi, A. and Sudarshan, R. eds. (1999). *Multiculturalism, Liberalism and Democracy*. Delhi: Oxford University Press.

Bhattacharya, Harihar. (2003). "Multiculturalism in contemporary India" *International Journal on Multicultural Societies (IJMS)*. Vol. 5, No. 2. pp. 148–161. Retrieved from http://www.unesco.org/shs/ijms/vol5/issue2/art4

Castles, S. (1992). "*Australian Multiculturalism: Social Policy and Identity in a Changing Society*" pp. 184–201 in G. Freeman & J. Jupp (eds), Nations of Immigrants: Australia, The United States and International Migration. Melbourne: Oxford University Press.

Castles, S. et al. (1988). *Mistaken Identity*, Sydney: Pluto Press.

Chandhoke, Neera. (1999). "The logic of recognition". Seminar. No. 484. Online Edition. Retrieved from http://www.india-seminar.com/1999/484/484%20problem.htm

Deb, Kushal. (ed.) (2002). *Mapping Multiculturalism.* Rawat Publishers. New Delhi.

Dobell, Graeme. (2006). "*Australia-India Relations Through History*" Correspondents Report. March 5. Online Edition. Retrieved from http://www.abc.net.au/correspondents/content/2006/s1583823.htm

Gurry, Meg. (1995). "*Australian views of India: From Evatt to Evans*" in Dipankar Banerjee (ed.). Towards an era of Cooperation: An Indo-Australian Dialogue. IDSA. New Delhi. p. 388.

Hassan, Ghali. (2005). "*Rising Tide of Xenophobia: Australia's Shallow Multiculturalism*". Global Research. Online Edition. Retrieved from http://www.globalresearch.ca/index.php?context=viewArticle&code=HAS20050927&articleId=1011

Humphries, David. (2006). "Live here and be Australian". *The Sydney Morning Herald.* February 25. Online Edition. Retrieved from http://www.smh.com.au/articles/2006/02/24/1140670269194.html

Jakubowicz, Andrew. (1989). "The State and Welfare of Immigrants in Australia". *Ethnic and Racial Studies*. Vol. 12. No. 1. p. 1.

Jha, Ganganath (2007). "Australia as a factor in India-ASEAN Relations" in Dennis Rummley and D. Gopal (eds.). *Globalisation and Regional Security: India and Australia*. Shipra Publication. New Delhi. p. 195.

Joseph, Sara. (1999). "*On Minorities and Majorities*" Seminar. No. 484. Online Edition. Retrieved from http://www.india-seminar.com/1999/484/484%20joseph.htm

Jupp, James (1997). "Immigration and National Identity: Multiculturalism" in Geoferry Stokes (ed). *The Politics of Identity in Australia*. Cambridge University Press. p. 133.

Kaul, Man Mohini (2002). "Australia-India Relations: A Critical Survey" in D. Gopal (ed). *Australia in the Emerging Global Order*. Shipra Publications: New Delhi. pp. 220–232.

Mahajan, Gurpreet. (1999). "*The Problem*". Seminar. No. 484. Online Edition. Retrieved from http://www.india-seminar.com/1999/484/484%20problem.htm

Mitra, Subrata K. (2001). "*Constitutional Design, Democratic Vote Counting and India's Fortuitous Multiculturalism*". Heidelberg Papers in South Asian and Comparative Politics. Working Paper No. 1. November. p. 2.

Momin, A.R. (2006). "India as a model for multiethnic Europe". *Asia Europe Journal*. Volume 4, Number 4.

Narang, A.S. and Gopal, D. (2002). "Multiculturalism in Australia: Perspectives and Problems" in D. Gopal (ed). *Australia in the Emerging Global Order*. Shipra Publications: New Delhi. p. 54.

Parekh, Bhikhu. (2000). *Rethinking Multiculturalism: Cultural Diversity and Political Theory*. New York: Palgrave Macmillan.

Parekh, Bhikhu. (1999). "*What is Multiculturalism*?" Seminar. No. 484. Online Edition. Retrieved from http://www.india-seminar.com/1999/484/484%20problem.htm

Sen, A. (2005). *The Argumentative Indian: Writings on Indian Culture, History and Identity*. London: Penguin.

Taylor, Charles. (1992). *Multiculturalism and the Politics of Recognition*, Princeton, Princeton University Press.

Vasta, Ellie. (1993). "Multiculturalism and ethnic identity: The relationship between Racism and Resistance". *The Australian and New Zealand Journal of Sociology*. Vol. 29, No. 2. p. 210.

Endnotes

1. Until the First World War the founding fathers of Australia continued strengthening monoculturalism.
2. The Galbally Report reviewed the post arrival services and the programs in 1978. It laid down that all members of our society must have equal opportunity to realize their full potential and must have equal access to programs and services and every person should be able to maintain his or her culture without prejudice or disadvantage and should be encouraged to understand and embrace other cultures.
3. Practical outcomes of the National Agenda included improvement of the procedures for recognising overseas qualifications; a campaign to improve community relations; a strengthening of the government's access and equity strategy; extension and improvement of multicultural broadcasting; extension of English language teaching programs and support programs; a commitment for continued support for second language learning and reviews of law and administrative decision-making.
4. It is primarily for this reason that Granville Austin regards it as an intensely contested document.
5. The first state created in recognition of the linguistic principle in the post-independence period was Andhra Pradesh (Telegu language, 1953).This prompted the Government of India to form the States Reorganization Commission in 1953 and, on the basis of its recommendations, to pass the famous States Reorganization Act of 1956. The basis in the first major reorganisation of states in 1956 was strongly linguistic: federal units were created to corresponded largely with linguistic boundaries. Since 1956, the formation of new federal units in India has remained more or less a continuous process. The basis for state creation has been ethno-regional or linguistic. In the 1950s and 1960s, the linguistic factor played the most determining role with the sole exception of the creation of Punjab (1966) in which it was combined with religion. In the 1970s, India's north-east (now comprising seven federal units) became the area of major state reorganisation, giving birth to three new states as political recognition of tribal identity. In the 1980s, another three states were created (two in the north-east provinces, and Goa in the southwest). The essence of the statehood demand has always been the congruence between federal political boundaries and the ethno-linguistic boundaries of the people. In the formation of the three states – Chhattisgarh, Jharkhand and Uttaranchal – language as a symbol of identity has however played a very minor role.
6. Chhattisgarh (carved out of Madhya Pradesh), Jharkhand (carved out of Bihar), and Uttaranchal (carved out of Uttar Pradesh).
7. The processes of extensive migration, indigenization, interaction and cultural hybridization contributed to the evolution of India's composite, syncretistic civilizational legacy. The fabric of Indian civilization has been woven from strands of varied textures and hues drawn from a variety of sources. This was made possible by what Amartya Sen has aptly described as India's inclusive, interactive openness, which constitutes one of the most distinctive features of Indian civilization.
8. Both India and Australia were British colonies in the historical past, but there was a sharp divergence in their perception and policies during the cold war years. The

lowest point between the two countries was in 1960 when the first Prime Minister of India, Jawaharlal Nehru stood at the podium at the United Nations to savage a draft resolution on the Cold War put up by Australia. During Menzies rule (his 2nd term-1949–1966) Australia was closer to Pakistan, this was particularly apparent due to their common membership to South East Asian Treaty Organisation (SEATO). However relations between the india and Australia somehow seemed to improve once Mrs. Indira Gandhi came to power. She was the first Indian Prime Minister to visit Australia, which she did in 1968. Inspite of it, closer links could not be forged "as cold war thinking continued to dominate Australia's strategic thinking"(Gurry, 1995).

With the Cold War gone and India and Australia both dismantling the high walls of economic protection, the wind has been blowing fair from the Indian Ocean, but it's been a slow breeze (Dobell, 2006). The Howard Government's first Foreign Affairs White Paper in 1997 did not rank India as one of the states that "most substantially engage Australia". And only six months after India announced itself as a nuclear weapons power with its bomb blasts in 1998, Australia's Foreign Affairs Department scrapped its separate South Asia and Indian Ocean branch as a budget measure.

The change in India's significance is told through two multilateral moments. Back in 1997, Australia was a leading player in shutting the door on India joining the Asia Pacific economic forum when APEC (Asia Pacific Economic Cooperation) imposed a 10–year moratorium on new members. India thought it had been vetoed by a jaundiced Australia. But by the end of 2005, Australia was slipping in to the new East Asia Summit on India's diplomatic coa-ails. The ASEAN (Association of Southeast Asian Nations) hosts could not allow China to veto India attending the first summit. So admitting India – a geopolitical must these days – made it easier to invite two other non-East Asian states, Australia and New Zealand.

In spite of all these, the two countries have remained associated with the Commonwealth and other regional forums. Both are pluralistic democracies and they tend to identify themselves as integral part of the Asia Pacific region (Jha, 2007; Kaul, 2002).

11

Post Colonial Formation, Paradigm Consolidation and Economic Marginalization

S. Ram Vemuri

Post-colonial formations in Australia and India are a result of two major historical narratives. One relates to the periods of contact and the ensuing interactions that occurred amongst and between the colonizers and the colonized. The other relates to the way economic thinking evolved as a result of these interactions. The outcomes of these events are so powerful that in spite of escalating awareness about Indigenous knowledge systems and its significance for addressing issues concerning sustainability, as well as, increases in Indigenous populations, economic marginalization of the Indigenous populations continues to occur producing disastrous results. To achieve better socio-economic successes, paradigms need to be developed that embrace notions of pluralism.

Introduction

Both Australia and India celebrate their colonial links on January 26th each year. Majority of the Indians celebrate the formation of the Republic, while many Australians celebrate the birth of a nation. What we are witnessing today in both these countries are the effects of past discourses which have very powerful bearing on contemporary thinking and invariably involves understanding post-colonial formations.

Post-Colonial Formations

Post-colonial representations are a result of adopting "processes of subjectification made possible (and plausible) through stereotypical discourse"[1] present in populous literature. Examination of populous literature reveals multiple narrations of the colonising experiences. The analysis is based on three periods of time – the contact, the process since the contact and the future, intertwined with four modes of thought – the pre-colonial, colonial, colonised and the contemporary. These narrations reveal commonality of patterns, as well as quite distinct representations, pertaining to Australian and Indian experiences.

Australia

The colonial intentions to occupy the expansive land mass was to populate the barren lands and bring order, structure and build civil society.

> When the white person came he saw the land as virtually uninhabited. In his terms it *was* uninhabited, but he could see wealth, vast expanses there just for the taking, which could be utilized for agriculture, grazing, mineral exploitation and building houses. The white person also brought with him systems of organization which were very different from the Aborigines. Their political system was very different and their social mores poles apart. Whites put a great deal of emphasis on material objects. Most of all, their attitudes showed that they considered us rather primitive beings not capable of abstract thought. All these differences brought us into great conflict, which are well known to us all now.[2]

There is recognition and acknowledgement that Australian interactions between the colonised and the colonialists have been marred by what can best be termed fractured realities of the 'other'. They are fractured, as colonisers adopted diverse and often extreme positions with regards to Indigenous people. As Indigenous people reacted to these diverse positions, their perception of the 'other' was also disrupted.

> Australia's history of indigenous relations consists of a succession of policy phases that included 'elimination' that began with the deliberate killing of entire populations of Indigenous people in conjunction with the possession of their land. This was extended in December 1901 with legislation passed by the new Federal Parliament (Immigration Restriction Act 1901) that established 'White Australia" with a clear intention of excluding all 'coloured people' from Australia.... And, from that policy we can observe subsequent shifts towards 'protection', 'separation', 'assimilation', 'integration' and, most recently, 'multiculturalism'.[3]

Since the period of contact, there have been shifts in perceptions on both sides of the divide – even imaginary ones – ranging from lack of acknowledgement of the significance of the 'other', to the pursuit of sameness[4], to acknowledging and celebrating 'differences'[5].

> In the early days of modern Australian polygenesis, the projected identity of Aborigines that Europeans bestowed had little effect on Aborigines' own primary identity. This was because there was very little embedding of the two societies at that stage. As the embedding grew, however, this projected identity grew; however, this projected identity became devastating. Recovery from that situation has been very slow[6].

Shifts in attitudes did not produce marked deviations from past constructs. New consciously created constructs continued to "operate within policy-making communities which are sustained by theoretical narratives"[7] that relegated socio-economic issues of Indigenous people by and large as "problems" that policies must address. Post colonial constructs pose Indigenous people as a problem. They were considered a problem, have been a problem and continue to be a problem. Very few people take heed of statements such as "(I) if we are to talk in terms of problems, then it is the Gubba, the policy-making and practices of non-indigenous communities that are better understood as the problem."[8]

India

The perception of the 'other' was quite different in the case of India at the time of contact. There has been a much more of structured recognition of the 'other'. The 'other' on both sides of the divide recognised existence of a number of "stencils"[9]. There was recognition and acknowledgement of well established and entrenched structures, recognizable customs, practices and rituals on both sides of the divide at the time of contact. "In many ways British India saw the development of trends already existing in Mughal India and it is certain that British India would have been a very different place had the Mughals never ruled before them."[10]

In spite of such beginnings, post colonial formations in the Indian context were also largely influenced by imaginations of the colonials. For example, historians, such as James Mill[11] "set the tone for many of the discussions on colonial policy including educational arrangements"[12]. Once again the hues for the tone were set at the time of historical narrations of contact. "Even though early colonial administrators in the last eighteenth century – Warren Hastings among them – took a very broad interest in India's intellectual past, the narrowing of the imperial mind was quite rapid once the empire settled in."[13]

While there are inherent difficulties in recognizing the 'origins' of post colonial formations, it is necessary to acknowledge, what currently exists are a result of several sets of interactions and mutations involving forward and backward movements generating several constructs. Post colonial formations of today's Australia and India are neither direct translations of the 'mother country' nor are they extensions of the Indigenous cultural constructs. This is because colonial cultures are "never direct translations of European society planted in the colonies, but unique cultural configurations, homespun creations in which European food, dress, housing, and morality were given new political meanings in the particular social order of colonial rule"[14].

Post colonial formations are therefore considered hybrids. "Hybridity, …exhibits…a space and form of existence which not only is neither 'modern' nor 'traditional', neither 'advanced' nor 'backward' though it is tellingly contemporary –but which also disrupts the historical, and the extra-historical, claims of both (futuristic) modernity and (revivalist) traditionalism."[15] The historical disconnect that eventually creates narratives about post-colonial formations need to be governed through strategic practices rather than extension of space and time analysis.

As post-colonial formations are the result of adopting strategic choices of colonisers, colonial moulds of thinking continue to be used as backdrops for further analysis. Very little, if anything, changes. First impressions linger on and consolidate. In the Australian context, even after tumultuous past, perceptions of the 'other' still linger on and become structural in nature with far reaching implications for policy making. Such thinking permeates many facets of Australian psyche and pervades contemporary thought. "What may well have begun as a simple forgetting of other possible views turned under habit and over time into something like a cult of forgetfulness practised on a national scale".[16] In the case of India, there is seeming acceptance of the 'other'. The brown sahib replaced the white sahib.

European Power dominated the natives of India and Australia through colonial thinking. It persisted and survived in independent India and 'created' Australia, by supporting the native elites. "Colonialism teaches the native elite it creates to admire – all too often to ape – the ways of the foreign rulers."[17] The modus operandi was different. "European power expanded slowly from apparent weakness in the case of India."[18] In the case of Australia, European domination was persistent since settlement. "From the inception of 'white settlement', Australian governments have sought through policy to regulate both lives of Indigenous people as well as the relations between white and Indigenous populations."[19]

The effect of such colonial thinking created a distinct membership of the Australian continent. There are clear signs of contrast in contemporary Australia between two groups in political, historical and socio-economic terms based on ethnicity. Most notable contrasts are in the realms of economic achievements, social disadvantages, business participation and political representation. There are also explicit and noticeable contrasts in education, health and general welfare levels.

In the case of India, an elite class was crafted that ruled the masses whereby "India's elite have never recovered from their colonial hangover, and so they have not developed the ideology, the attitudes and the institutions which would change the poor from subjects to partners in the government of India."[20]

The most noticeable impact of post colonial formations can be witnessed in the treatment of the Indigenous peoples in these two countries.

As Indigenous people were considered "rather primitive beings not capable of abstract thought"[21] they are bombarded with policies to improve their standards of living. At the same time there are evidences that the Indigenous people are at the end of the receiving line of such policies which blatantly attempt to eradicate their cultural underpinnings. As a result, policies become ineffective as Indigenous people continue their resistance to being streamlined.

There are sound strategic reasons for Aborigines to invest in essentialist versions of Aboriginality. "It is heard all the time from Aboriginal people because in some ways Aboriginality is 'all they have', while 'we' have all the material and institutional support. Hence, these people *have* to stick to a kind of essentialism. Once this is abandoned, they could become 'fragmented unknowing subjects' like the rest of us; multicultural in a weak sense, as it were."[22]

In the Indian context, post-colonial formations are engulfed in terms of "the left-behind baggage of the intellectual discourse."[23] This is in spite of forming a new nation. The resultant effect is "Indigenous knowledge systems have been devalued, and their plural institutional systems marginalized. A holistic tradition began to fragment."[24]

One of the major domino effects of post-colonial formations has been the consolidation of paradigms, in particular, the governing economic paradigm.

Paradigm consolidation

Paradigm consolidation is an offshoot of the process of paradigm creation. A paradigm establishes itself in the main as the numbers of its advocates grow and other pre-paradigmatic schools or the previous paradigm fade.

Prior to colonisation, Indigenous people based their decisions on notions of holism. There were meanings attached to individuals being an integral part of the environments they lived in and associated with. Human activity was judged in terms of the impact on the environments and strategies recognized or otherwise, acknowledged or ignored. They were proposed to ensure that humans would act in a sustainable manner. These strategies involved not only understanding rules governing conservation techniques but also appropriating these to a growth context. Techniques cited in the literature included seasonal exploitation[25], limited exploitation[26], and "protection of over-exploitation of resources by developing systems of taboo, enforcing restrictions of diet on certain social groups and on certain age grades"[27]. These were all several ways to "come to terms with their environment and ...establish(ed) a balance on which harmony depended."[28]

If Indigenous people were left to their destinies and adopted an undisturbed evolutionary path, one would have perhaps witnessed an accession of an Indigenous paradigm as "societies evolve by interactions between ideas, economy and power, and in particular (as Habermas would have it) by transformations in the nature of and relations between State and society, public and private."[29] While this is a pure conjecture, one thing is certain that through colonial formations, there was a disruption of such natural processes of evolution. While existence of social relations in India was not only recognized but also acknowledged by early colonisers, they were mostly marginalized for being 'inferior' to those exhibited by 'advanced' societies of the colonizers. There was total rejection in the case of Australian Aborigines. For considerable periods of time, they were considered to be devoid of any norms of civility in the main.

The way societies are constructed affects society itself – its shape and its content – and this in turn affects decisions about society. Explanation of marginalization therefore rests with formations of society and the frameworks used for policy prescriptions. There was conspicuous absence of recognizable Indigenous paradigms that could compete with paradigms based on strategic intentions of the colonizers. What ultimately evolved were disruptions of natural processes of evolution, partly contributing to the power of discipline oriented paradigms. 'Modern' economics consolidated as a paradigm by itself.

Paradigm rarely explains all facts that it confronts. "To be accepted as a paradigm, a theory must seem better than its competitors, but it need not, and in fact never does, explain all the facts with which it can be confronted."[30] Selective use of economic literature occurred. The "literature of economics is extensive; our use of it is highly selective. Each generation of economists perpetuates what it likes and neglects what it does not".[31] Therefore, there is a need to understand the nature and basis of selection. Such selectivity is based on values and convenience commensurate with the decision making fraternity as "acceptance of a paradigm frees the community from the need to constantly re-examine its first principles and foundational assumptions."[32] For example, for a long time, "it was convenient to pretend that the subject had been invented by Adam Smith in 1776, a convention that saved subsequent economists (and their students) a good deal of work."[33]

It is, therefore, of little surprise that the majority of the events that unfolded from such convenient and restrained beginnings of post-colonial formations to such an extent that they became norms.

It is necessary to recognize the downside of such an eventuality. Such conveniences incur opportunity costs resulting from mainstreaming economic thinking. As discipline evolves many 'schools' of thought develop. Economics became a study of method making research possible. "Economics is a method rather than a doctrine, an apparatus of mind, a technique of thinking which helps its possessor to draw correct conclusions."[34]

Development of various schools of thought created a perception that opportunities existed for interpreting economic realities from different perspectives. Unfortunately, it was not recognized that even with the development of many schools of thought, "many interesting and, perhaps, meritorious works have passed out of the literature and remain unknown and unread"[35]. This resulted in paradigm consolidation. "Those that please the orthodox are cited with approval and preserved. It is the ones that neither please nor displease"[36] because they are either spoken or written in a medium that others fail to comprehend or those that cannot readily be incorporated into mainstream thinking that "are least likely to survive"[37].

There are inherent dangers in constructing reality from a well-focused, often narrowly conceptualized, framework[38] as they unfortunately result in restricting domains of influence for achieving economic betterment. It is inconvenient for policy analysts and decision makers involved, who are in influential positions in institutions to promote economic betterment, to recognize and even acknowledge possibilities for pluralistic perceptions and existence of alternative frameworks. Therefore, these realizations seldom translate into formation of alternative frameworks for conducting economic management because managing diversity is perhaps one of the most arduous tasks to perform. It is far easier to limit the voices of concern than address simultaneously several different approaches.

One of the serious ramifications of such occurrences is that, "(T) the ideas of economists and political philosophers, both when they are right and when they are wrong, are more powerful than is commonly understood. Indeed the world is ruled by little else. Practical men, who believe themselves to be quite exempt from any intellectual influences, are usually slaves of some defunct economist."[39] Human capacity to tackle the 'rational' is limited, among other things, by the vocabulary used, the frameworks adopted and the analytical tools that are available. Therefore, the ways in which ideas are generated, narrated and acted upon all become significant issues. This is most noticeable in the way Indigenous knowledge is managed in post-colonial Australia and India.

Importance and Significance of Knowledge

Many notable and influential Economists, including Alfred Marshall, acknowledged the importance of human knowledge.

> Human knowledge, after all, is the crucial factor in production: 'It has been well said that if all the material wealth in the world were destroyed by an earthquake, leaving only the land, knowledge, and food enough to sustain life till the next harvest, mankind would in a generation or two be nearly as prosperous as before; but, if accumulated knowledge were destroyed, while the material wealth remained, several thousand years might be needed to recover lost ground.'[40]

There is increasing recognition of the significance of the knowledge of Indigenous people and the importance of preserving their knowledge base.

> The indigenous people of the world possess an immense knowledge of their environments, based on centuries of living close to nature. Living in and from the richness and variety of complex ecosystems, they have an understanding of the properties of plants and animals; the functioning of ecosystems and the techniques for using and managing them is particular and detailed.[41]

Not only is there recognition and celebration of the significance of the knowledge of Indigenous people, but there is also an awakening, in some quarters, that mainstream knowledge is too limited in scope and content for it to be universally applied at all times, in all spaces and in all cultural contexts.

Knowledge of Indigenous people is proving to be an important analytical base for decisions in some aspects of the modern world. It is therefore not surprising that increasingly more and more scientists, technocrats, policy analysts and decision makers rely and accept the need to dwell into the depths of knowledge of Indigenous people in deciding policies. For example, Indigenous knowledge was accorded a high status in Principle 22 of the Rio Declaration.

> Indigenous people and their communities, and other local communities, have a vital role in environmental management and development because of their knowledge and traditional practices. States should recognize and duly support their identity, culture and interests and enable their effective participation in the achievement of sustainable development.[42]

At a practical level, awareness of significance of knowledge of Indigenous people has led to creation of mechanisms and processes whereby their knowledge could potentially become public knowledge, and can be used in economic policy deliberations. The importance of knowledge of Indigenous people is by no means accepted without questioning. Even today Indigenous knowledge systems are still challenged. Even where it is recognized, its acceptance has met with resistance. Recognizing that the knowledge of Indigenous people is indeed even crucial to complete the missing pieces of the puzzles of sustainability continues to be met with resistance. This is bound to happen if the post-colonial formations and paradigm consolidation are interpreted in terms of narrow confines of 'rational' 'homo-economicus'.

A far deeper influence of colonized thinking relates to the way knowledge is managed. Approaches or conceptual frameworks that would enable people in 'power' to grasp the complexities of economic betterment without assimilation do not exist in abundance. A main reason for not having a comprehensive methodology that simultaneously allows for "individual upward social mobility but still avoids the assumptions of assimilationism"[43] is the Dragon Principle.

"Dragon Principle"[44] has been in vogue whereby the custodians of knowledge become 'guardian-keepers' and 'gate-keepers' who control the ebb and flow of information to and from the society at large. Application of the Dragon Principle also is responsible for unintentionally, at times, equating knowledge of the Indigenous people to what is most commonly considered as Indigenous knowledge. Indigenous knowledge is used as a synonym for the knowledge of Indigenous people. However, it is necessary to distinguish indigenous knowledge and knowledge of Indigenous people. The former depicts what can be comprehended using a particular paradigm, such as the mainstream, while the later is much more disparate, complex and interwoven knowledge base that simultaneously involves many paradigms that often involve other dimensions of knowledge including rituals.

Two stylized reactions to the knowledge of Indigenous people can be observed, in both the literature and the reality. They are all outcomes of post-colonial thinking. They are denial of any difference (the 'denialists'), and those that are committed to redress the 'disadvantage' (the 'minimalists').

Denialists

The fundamental philosophical basis of the 'denialist's' approach to knowledge of the indigenous people, is existence of "non-rational" components which constitute hindrance to progress and betterment. The dominant method of approach of the 'denialists', is to build a rational economic model wherein problems of 'scarcity' are tackled by prescribing policies to make individuals empowered to act as atomic rationalist human beings.

Knowledge of Indigenous people is selectively used to become Indigenous knowledge. Indigenous knowledge once again was used to formulate "objectives of investigation". The fundamental basis upon which the denialists underpin their approach to Indigenous knowledge is that they use the economic framework to provide a logical constructive framework, based and developed on the model frames of Neo-classical synthesis. The role of policy is to change reality to closely fit the model assumptions. "If the theory did not correspond to the reality, so much the worse for reality: it would have to be changed so that it would correspond to the assumptions…of theory."[45]

Search for "best practice" and "bench marking" methods to solve these objects of investigation are made in order to illuminate understanding for initiating further policies. The idea is to work out tried and tested approaches for redressing problems construed by information derived from Indigenous knowledge. This is achieved by understanding proven to be 'successful' practices and keep repeating them until people change their behaviours to suit the model. Examples can be cited from many fields, including education, employment, health, income, housing and general development pursuits, where these concerns are all modelled in a 'rationalistic manner'. Policies are prescribed with little regard to any differences. Indeed, if differences persist they become challenges for policy makers to address. There is a belief that, over the years, continuation of policies will enable differences in levels to disappear. Thus the extent of the success of policies is measured in terms of the extent by which differences are reduced. The overwhelming message is one of repetition and replication. Policies are based on a notion that problems once defined, using logic, produces solutions that need to be relentlessly applied for sufficient period of time to produce the necessary change. The usual management mantra that reverberates policy circles is that 'it takes time' for policies to work. There is a sense of exactness about the concept. The notion that 'one size fits all' is based on an ideology that 'all are born equal' and if they are not, policies are needed so that they can indeed be made equal.

An extrapolation of the economic philosophy underlying such paradigm consolidation is that if Indigenous people do not function in the mainstream it is because they are considered to be too 'backward', too 'disinterested', and above all too 'lazy' to change. Culture stands in the way of progress. Daily observations such as substance abuse activities, of being drunk, and people becoming itinerants that throng the urban centres, are considered symptomatic of problems encountered with adjusting to new and unfamiliar systems.

Policies are prescribed and money is further allocated to address these symptoms. Financial and non-monetary expenditures are incurred for adjustments to take place. Indigenous knowledge is sought after to improve insights about how to define symptoms better but also to understand who should be approached in order to effectively implement solutions to these symptoms.

Indigenous people are recognized for their leadership qualities who can promote the best of both world views and they can effectively manage the model frames of the mainstream. They become the contemporary elites of the consolidated paradigms.

Minimalists

The minimalists approach and dwell into knowledge of the Indigenous people in order to bring about change in a practical sense. They attempt to re-specify behavioural equations and hence become active participants in reconstructing rational models of economic behaviour.

Their philosophy is based on reasoning that "(K) knowledge is sought and acquired by individuals for some purpose or another."[46] An underlying assumption of the minimalists is that there is a common and shared purpose among all members of the society. The specification of what constitutes economic problems fundamentally remains the same.

The way to address these problems, and therefore prescription of alternative solutions, differ. There is cultural sensitivity whenever there is recognition that a single model is inadequate to address different narratives of the same problem. There is recognition for developing appropriate models.

It is suggested that the problem, once defined, needs to be solved by producing culturally appropriate solutions. Indigenous people become 'informants and assistants' and their knowledge is valued for producing local solutions to problems. Two reasons are accorded for celebrating the significance of indigenous knowledge. They are (a) for "its long and deep roots, and origin in a specific culture and a local ecological system"[47] and, (b) for its ability to adjust and 'not be static' in nature. It is felt that much can be gained by dwelling into the treasure trove of Indigenous knowledge where "tradition is still usually unwritten and based not only on what each generation learns from the elders, but also on what it adds to that knowledge."[48]

It is suggested that cross-cultural contextualisation of the challenges to development pursuits will yield practical solutions in a modern world and provide 'win-win scenarios'. Such hybridization of knowledge bases – between the 'scientific' and the 'traditional' – is sought after that will result in a workable compromise whereby appropriate cultural adaptation of the mainstream thinking in education, employment, health, income, housing and other developmental pursuits will provide better results than before, and at the same time, preserve the culture of the Indigenous people.

A significant caveat for adopting such an arrangement must be recognized here. Once Indigenous knowledge is collected, mainstream paradigm requires this to be "verified and blended with more technical forms of research, before it can be put to best use."[49] Because of the potential advantage in dealing with Indigenous people and their knowledge bases, the minimalists heed to a simple message, "Don't do anything for us, without us"[50]. This view reverberates throughout in their paradigm consolidations. Often this is translated as providing a bottom up approach to decision making.

Following on from such thinking, there is belief that if Indigenous people do not function in the mainstream there is a need to address the criteria underlying policy prescriptions. For example, if there are not enough Indigenous applicants for a job, then either job advertisements must be made culturally appropriate, or there must be reservations in place to fill these jobs with Indigenous persons. Similarly, calls are made for educational curriculums to identify and conform to community needs. Explanations for why people participate in substance abuse activities, including being drunk, petrol sniffing and exhibit itinerant behaviours, are made on the grounds that people are displaced and alienated from their cultural roots and these behaviours are manifested as Indigenous persons become marginalized from the mainstream.

Suggested policies include addressing issues of land alienation, building bridges across the cultural continuums, promoting cross cultural communication and taking part in capacity building exercises, etc.

Both the 'denialists' and 'minimalists' contribute unwittingly to consolidation of the paradigms which increasingly results in creating a divide between Indigenous and non-Indigenous populations. Nowhere is this more conspicuous than in the labour market where people's characteristics are necessarily matched with job requirements before people are employed.

Economic Marginalization

Marginalization of Indigenous people is a public concern as policy makers contend with the sheer volume and diversity of explicit involvement of policies related with redressing the imbalances and inequities created as by-products of adopting specific paradigms There have been, and in many respects there still are, many policies and institutions involved with the affairs and conduct of Indigenous people. Direct allocation of almost $2.5 billion was made in 2002–2003 for matters related to Aboriginal affairs in the Australian context.[51] Comparable figures exist in India, Canada, USA and New Zealand. These figures are on the increase as there is positive growth in populations. The extent of involvement of concerns with Indigenous peoples in these countries is so overwhelming that it has led to the formation of an "Indigenous sector"[52].

> The indigenous sector consists of thousands of publicly funded organizations. Some are statutory authorities (for example, the Land councils in the new South Wales and in the Northern Territory, and the Aboriginal and Torres Strait Islander Commission – ATSIC), some are incorporated 'councils' performing the functions of local governments in remote parts of the continent, some are employers and job placement agencies (the Community Development Employment schemes), and there are Indigenous health services, legal services, housing associations, schools and sporting clubs.[53]

Growth in the Indigenous sector applies equally in the case of India as much as in the Australian context.

Issues confronting Indigenous people in contemporary societies of Australia and India are complex. Attempts are being made to come to grips with these complexities by examining problems related to economic specification, and by recognizing the myriad number of measures of indicators which have resulted in prescribing a number of solutions that one is confronted with while dealing simultaneously and individually with issues of identity, assimilation and reconciliation. Frameworks that are locked into paradigms, because of their consolidations, are unable to deal with these complexities adequately. The rise in the economically marginalized populations is a result of adopting such inadequate frameworks.

Part of the dilemma faced in the labour markets of both India and Australia, namely, the rise in economic marginalization accompanied by skills shortages are the legitimizing exercises due to paradigm consolidations. Significant differences between choice and deficits are being overlooked when policies are based with a narrow focus of mainstreaming individuals in the societies. Economics, however fabricated, was primarily concerned with scarcity, which at a later stage shifted to evaluation of choices. By recognizing the treatment of such differences in dealing with scarcity, and enabling choices to be made freely, there is every opportunity for 'choices' not to be terminally buried beneath 'deficits'. Potential exists for current and future policy debates to occur concerning appropriateness of policies for actively engaging and involving Indigenous people. Paradigms will be required for providing the necessary focus for persistent and organized articulation so that suitable models can be selected that are so badly needed for offering appropriate policies.

Economic marginalization can be better addressed by examining viable alternative choice sets among decision making units – individuals, institutions, government departments, policymakers – and by building on past experiences of direct and indirect interactions with Indigenous knowledge systems that includes both Indigenous knowledge as well as the knowledge of the Indigenous people.

There is a need for a protagonists approach to economic marginalization. In this approach Indigenous people as well as their thinking is not considered the 'problem' and policies are not prescribed based on post-colonial formations and paradigm consolidations as solutions to the Indigenous problems.

The protagonists approach knowledge of Indigenous people – not Indigenous knowledge per se – from alternative time and space perspectives as well as reference points to that of the mainstream. Indigenous people are considered 'custodians' of their knowledge. In this approach what happens both in time and spaces dictate behaviour. This approach is based on recognition that "economists cannot truly understand social interaction until they incorporate genuinely dynamic elements into their models."[54] These elements refer to Indigenous interactions with time and space as they existed within the basic analytical structure and not enter merely as dimensional adjuncts to the model frame. Protagonists believe that there is a need for modelling decisions that link perceptions, expectations, strategies, interactions and outcomes in a logical loop.

This approach not only recognizes that both Indigenous and non-Indigenous people "accept and believe that each has a valid, civilized structure"[55] but their interactions can lead to achieve appropriate policy outcomes in education, employment, health, income, housing and other developmental issues.

If Indigenous people have not been 'successful' as measured by mainstream indicators, it is because policies have an underlying agenda of assimilation and streamlining. There is a need for adopting more liberating approaches that will provide novel solutions to the contemporary complex problems which are of a multi-dimensional nature. Substance abuse and itinerant behaviour, and the like are an end product that are an outcome of a sense of helplessness emanating from the stifling 'domesticating' nature of policies prescribed. People are driven to such behaviours to escape reality as some regard 'time in the future as being much worse than the time in the present!' Liberating policies must be examined that have potentials to create a sense of hope. This implies a need for policies that will strategically alter perceptions and expectations, on both sides of the divide, to form positive time discounting of the future to occur so that there is a genuine hope in the future that alternative models of development based on this approach can create. If one is to escape the value judgments of post-colonizers and consolidated paradigms, pluralism needs to be managed better to avoid massive marginalization of Indigenous populations.

The policy implications of such attempts are many. I believe through better management of pluralism, there will be extensive spin offs in both the content of policies as well as in the way policies will be implemented. There is every chance that success will follow by managing such a reality in contemporary India and Australia. What is needed is a recollection that British India, before annihilation, recognized pluralism in India. At the same time, there is need to acknowledge existence of economic models of Indigenous people before occupation in Australia. Collaborative research between Indian and Australian academics in areas of model building and testing, concerning economic pluralism, will benefit economic betterment without assimilation. By allowing pluralism to flourish, we may be on the path towards sustainable futures.

References

1. H. Bhabha, "The Other Question", *Screen*, Vol. 24, no. 6, 1983, pp. 18–19.
2. D.H. Penney and John Moriarty, "North-South in Australia: Aborigines in the Australian economy" in John Langmore and David Peetz, ed., *Wealth, poverty and Survival: Australia in the World.* (Sydney: Allen & Unwin, 1983), pp. 110–111.
3. Judith Besant and Amanda Watkinson, "Principles for Developing Indigenous Policy-making", *Australian Journal of Public Administration*, (Australia) Vol. 65, No. 1, March 2006, p. 110.
4. During the period of Assimilation.
5. This corresponds to the era following multiculturalism.
6. Eric Willmot, "The Dragon Principle", in Isabel McBryde, ed., *Who Owns the Past?* (Melbourne: Oxford university Press, 1985), p. 45. The dragon principle is "the gathering and keeping of the information which is bestowed only on to elite..." p. 45.
7. Judith Besant and Amanda Watkinson, p. 102.
8. Judith Besant and Amanda Watkinson, p. 102.
9. Livio Dobrez, "Post-modernity in the post-modern present" in Debajani Ganguly & Kavita Nandan (ed.), *Unfinished Journeys: India file from Canberra*, Centre for Research in the New Literatures in English, (South Australia: Flinders University, 1998), p. 278.
10. Percival Spear, *A History of India Vol . 2*, (Middlesex: Pelican, 1965), p. 13.
11. Whom Amartya Sen described in *The Argumentative Indian: Writing of Indian History, Culture and Identity*, (London: Penguin, 2005), p. 78 as the "most influential colonial historian of British India."
12. Amartya Sen, p. 79.
13. Amartya Sen, p. 77.
14. Ann Laura Stoler, "Rethinking Colonial Categories: European Communities and the Boundaries of Rule", *Society for Comparative Study of Society and History*, 1989, 31(1), pp. 136–137.

15. Prathama Banerjee Reviewed. Gautam Bhadra, Gyan Prakash and Susie Tharu (ed.) "The subaltern-effect: negation to deconstruction hybridity? Oxford University Press, New Delhi, http://www.lib.Virginia.edu/area-studies/SothAsia/SA Serials/Biblio/bss10.html 8 October 2004.
16. W.E.H. Stanner, after the Dreaming.
17. Stanner, p. 3.
18. Peter Robb, *A History of India*, (New York: Palgrave, 2002), p. 116.
19. Judith Besant and Amanda Watkinson, p. 100.
20. Mark Tully, *No Full Stops in India*, (New Delhi: Penguin, 1991), p. 3.
21. D.H. Penney and John Moriarty, p. 111.
22. Stephen Muecke, "Lonely Representations: Aboriginality and Cultural Studies", Bain Attwood and John Arnold (ed.), *Power Knowledge and Aborigines, Special edition of Journal of Australian Studies*, (Victoria: Latrobe University, 1992) p. 42.
23. Kapila Vatsyayan, "Plural Cultures, Monolithic Structures", *India International Centre Quarterly*, Winter 2002, Spring 2003, Vol. 29, No. 3 & 4, p. 109.
24. Kapila Vatsyayan, p. 109.
25. N.B. Tindale. 'Ecology of primitive man in Australia', in A. Keast et al. eds., Biogeography and ecology in Australia, (Den Haag: W. Junk, 1959), p. 40.
26. R.M. and C.H. Berndt, *The World of the first Australians,* (Sydney: Ure Smith, 1964), p. 93.
27. N.B. Tindale, p. 40.
28. Coombs, N., *Kulinma: Listening to Aboriginal Australians*, (Canberra: ACT, Australian National University Press, 1978), p. 28.
29. Peter Robb, p. 296.
30. "Thomas Kuhn's Structure of Scientific Revolutions", http://www.des.emory.edu/mfp/kuhnsyn.html, p. 1 16 January 2007.
31. Guy Roth, *The Origin of Economic Ideas*, (London: McMillan 1989), p. 2.
32. Thomas Kuhn's Structure of Scientific Revolutions, p. 1.
33. Guy Roth, p. 2.
34. J.M. Keynes, 1936, *The General Theory of Employment, Interest and Money*, (London, McMillan, 1936), p. 35.
35. Guy Roth, p. 2.
36. Guy Roth, p. 2.
37. Guy Roth, p. 2.
38. It is in the interest of schools of thought in the mainstream to support exclusivity.
39. J.M. Keynes, ch. 24.
40. Cited in David Riesman, *Alfred Marshall: Progress and Politics*, (London: McMillan, 1987) p. 91, quoting Alfred Marshall, 1923, *Industry and Trade*, (London: McMillan, 1923), p. 466.
41. Federico Mayor, Foreword, *Nature and Resources*, Vol. 30, No. 1, 1994, p. 2.
42. Julian T. Inglis, Introduction, *Nature and Resources*, Vol. 30, No. 2, 1994, p. 3.
43. William Tyler, "Aboriginality and Socioeconomic Attainment in Australia's Northern Territory", *The Australian and New Zealand Journal of Sociology*, Vol. 26, No. 1, 1990, p. 71.
44. Eric Willmot, p. 45.

45. Osvaldo Sunkel, "The Development of Development Thinking" in Jose J. Villamil (ed.) *Transnational Capitalism and National Development: New Perspectives on Dependence*, (New Jersey: Institute of Development Studies, Humanities Press, 1979), p. 22.
46. Bain Attwood, "Introduction", Bain Attwood and John Arnold, eds., *Power, Knowledge and Aborigines, Special edition of Journal of Australian Studies*, No. 35, 1992, p. i.
47. Kenneth Ruddle, "Local Knowledge in the future management of inshore tropical marine resources and environments", *Nature and Resources*, Vol. 30, No. 1, 1994, p. 34.
48. Kenneth Ruddle, p. 34.
49. Kenneth Ruddle, p. 35.
50. ATSIC Commissioner Alison Anderson from central Australia.
51. http://www.atsic.gov.au
52. Tim Rowse, *Indigenous Futures*, (Sydney: UNSW Press, 2002), p. 1.
53. Tim Rowse, p. 1.
54. Randall Bausor, "Toward a historically dynamic economics: examples and illustrations", *Journal of Post Keynesian Economics*, Vol. VI, No. 1, 1984, p. 360.
55. John Djatamirrilli, as cited in Richard Ian Trudgen, *Aboriginal Traditional Economic System in central and East Arnhemland*, (Northern Territory: Northern Regional Council of Congress, 1983), p. 5.

12

Dalits and Indigenous Australians: Affirmative Actions and Existing Realities

Swaraj Basu

Now geographical distance is no longer a deterrent in one's movement from one part to other part of the world. As a result of industrialization, acceptance of democratic institutions and ideologies and lately globalization cultural diversity has become an inseparable fact of modern life. Ideally speaking Cultural diversity provides an opportunity to learn from other and in the process to enrich one's culture. In reality the story is different. In history we have plenty of examples how self-righteous, dominant cultures tried to hegemonize the marginalized cultures. But with de-colonization, democratization and the growing assertion by the marginalized for their democratic rights and own cultural space things have begun to change. While commenting on cultural diversities Bhikhu Parekh has argued that from a multicultural perspective a good society 'should be tolerant, respectful of dissent and disagreement, and allow freedom of expression and religious belief'. In his opinion intra-cultural and inter-cultural dialogue in cultural diversity promotes rationality and provides space and power to challenge conscious and unconscious cultural assumptions.[1] Given this argument on cultural diversity and the need for serious thinking on respecting other's culture, in India and Australia we find that the Dalits and the indigenous Australians strongly feel the pain of denial and deprivation of their legitimate space from the mainstream of the nation-state. Much difference one can find in the origin and manifestation of differences in terms of Dalits and indigenous Australians as distinct cultural groups but much similarity one can find in their sufferings. Commenting on social discrimination in international context it has been observed that Dalit activists have learned from their international experience that 'while oppression can vary in geography, name and degree, the mechanism to ensure the systematic exclusion of entire populations based on their race, ethnicity and caste are largely the same'.[2] Let me begin with the tale of agonies of the Dalits and the indigenous Australians.

'A 50-kilometer journey from the capital of Rajasthan, brings visitors to Chakwara village-and back into the Middle Ages. Here, after all, is a society based on terrible persistent inequalities, servitude and economic bondage.... Oppression of the 160 to 180 million Dalits, who are viewed as being too low to even be part of the caste is one of the most repelling, but enduring, realities of the Indian countryside....Caste-based "tradition" ensures that Dalits are treated worse than the buffaloes, cows and pigs that have virtually unrestrained access to the pond'. The pond of Chakwara village is maintained by raising funds from entire village including Dalits but they are excluded from using the pond.[3]

'Karma in Palamu is a village lacking the most basic facilities. The surveyors were witnesses to quite a degrading practice in many villages in Bihar. When they entered the village and met Santokhi Bhuiya, the leader of the dalit community, a crowd of 50–60 Bhuiya families gathered around and a cot was arranged for surveyors to sit. The surveyors asked Dalit leader to sit with them'. Meanwhile four Rajputs came who were addressed as 'babu saheb' by the Dalits. The Rajputs proudly said that the Dalits would not dare to sit on the cot before us.[4]

'Social justice means being entitled to the same rights and services as other citizens. These rights have been difficult to achieve for Aboriginal and Torres Strait Islander people because of a history of government and colonial racism. Non-Aboriginal Australia has developed on the racist assumption of an ingrained sense of superiority that it knows best what is good for Aboriginal people'.[5]

'The federal government gave the power to Aboriginal people to elect representatives to advise the government on Aboriginal affairs. This advisory called ATSIC, the Aboriginal and Torres Straight Islanders Commission, is continuing to disempower Aboriginal people as far too much money is spent in the administrative arm and very little reaches the grassroots-level.'[6]

References quoted above point to the state of condition in which the Dalits and the Aborigines are living even today. So far as the question of oppression and social justice is concerned a comparative study of the Dalits and the indigenous Australians shows how initiatives taken by respective governments fail to mitigate the miseries of the oppressed. Exploitation of the Dalits began with the development of caste based social hierarchy in India as early as from the later vedic society, i.e. more than three thousand years before. Sufferings of the indigenous Australians started with the European colonization in 1788, they were pushed into the margins. Purpose of this paper is not to look into the question of differentiation between caste based and race based discrimination but to address the broader issue of exploitation and marginalization of the Dalits and the indigenous Australians, affirmative actions taken by the respective governments to bring equity and social justice and to what extent affirmative actions succeeded in bringing the desired justice.

Dalits in India

The term 'Dalit' refers to the oppressed and exploited sections of society; essentially Dalit is used to include those who are at the bottom of the caste based hierarchical social structure. Challenging brahmanical ideology of hierarchy various oppressed social groups have come under the banner of Dalit identity. Caste in India is an age old social institution whose first reference was found in the Rigveda and then more pronouncedly in Manu's dharmashastras. History shows that dissent to the caste system also has a long tradition. Development of Buddhism emphasizing social equality may be considered as the first major challenge to the brahmanical ideology of social hierarchy. Buddhist canonical literature does not attach importance to one's social origin; rather the emphasis is on ethics and pure conduct. Vaishnava religious tradition which developed within Hindu religious philosophy also does not give importance to caste hierarchy. Not only in terms of new ideologies which do not give importance to caste system we find changes in political and economic structures in India over the years which had bearing on its social structure. Mobility within the caste system has been well documented through a number of case studies done on various castes in different parts of India. But mobility within the caste system alongwith development of democratic polity, modernization and urbanization failed to protect the Dalits from caste oppression. Persisting untouchability and poverty are still haunting the Dalits. Recent Dalit killing in Kharlanji in Maharashtra, home state of the most revered Dalit leader Dr. B.R. Ambedkar, is not an isolated incident but such occurrences are not always reported and brought to public notice. In the Annual Report (2005) of the National Crime Records Bureau under the Union Ministry of Home Affairs it is recorded that in every 20-minutes a crime is committed on Scheduled Caste communities in our country.[7] As the focus of the paper is on affirmative actions taken by the state to protect the rights of Dalit communities and to ensure social justice so I would like to confine my discussion to various state initiatives and their impact on the Dalits.

After careful analysis of social dynamics of India during the British rule the colonial government initiated the process of listing those social groups who were placed at the bottom of social hierarchy and were denied benefits of justice. This resulted in the preparation of a list of 'depressed classes' which was later on changed into the list of 'Scheduled Castes' and 'Scheduled Tribes' by the Government of India Act, 1935. This initiative of the colonial government was interpreted by the nationalists as a divisive strategy to check the rising tide of Indian nationalist movement. Whatever may be the political intention based on the list of SC & ST the colonial government made provision for reservation in education, job and representative bodies. Several socially oppressed groups welcomed the government initiative and tried to mobilize them along their caste lines. The upper-caste groups were very much opposed to such affirmative action which had challenged their entrenched status. All these helped in bringing the oppression in the name of caste in the agenda of mainstream politics. In spite of their opposition to the colonial government's policy of protective discrimination the nationalists leaders realized the necessity of accommodating the Dalit representatives within their program. To ensure the confidence of the Dalits in post-independent democratic national polity Dr. B.R. Ambedkar was made the chairman of the committee to draft the constitution of Independent India. The Indian Constitution, taking note of untouchability practiced in India, made a number of provisions under Articles 15(2), 17, 29(2) declaring untouchability as an offence. Untouchability Act was passed in 1955 and to make this Act more effective in the light of discriminations still suffered by Dalits, Scheduled Castes and Scheduled Tribes Prevention of Atrocities Act, 1989 was promulgated to provide more safeguards. Article 46 of the Constitution also stipulates that governments should take special care to promote educational and economic interests of the Dalits. Articles 330, 332, 334, 335, 338, 341 and further amendments including the 93rd Amendment of 2005 provide necessary provisions to ensure economic, educational, social and political justice to the weaker sections. Following this constitutional commitment government has made provision for reservation in education, job and political representation. After all such initiatives one would have expected the end of untouchability and atrocities against the Dalits. But it has not happened.

'Political power in its real sense continues to elude Dalits in Tamil Nadu, notwithstanding the reservation of seats in elected bodies from village panchayats to Parliament. The recent murder of a newly elected *panchayat* president, a Dalit, in Tirunelveli district highlighted this reality once again. Not even the successful conduct of elections in four rebel *panchayat* villages in Madurai and Virudhunagar districts in October is likely to change this situation'.[8] Politicisation of the Dalit masses and Dalit activism more particularly in the last three decades made some progress in Dalit empowerment but majority still are at the receiving end. In a recent study of the present state of condition of the Dalits in various states of India it has been observed that Bihar and Uttar Pradesh, the two large north Indian states, have powerful Dalit-oriented parties and Dalit leaders from these states occupy important positions of power at the national level but still substantial section of Dalit population suffers from acute social and economic backwardness and faces physical atrocities too.[9] This story is not much different from other states of India. G. Shah's study on untouchability in Gujarat shows that Dalits 'are certainly not discriminated in all villages, but as many as 30 per cent of the village *Panchayats* still observe open or subtle discrimination with their elected members belonging to SCs.... They do revolt occasionally. Many of them assert their rights and that is the reason why the cases of atrocities against them are increasing. But at the same time all of them do not confront the dominant castes everyday out of the fear of failure'.[10] In 1990, in Chittoor district of Andhra Pradesh a survey was conducted by the Ambedkar Centenary Celebration Committee to assess the prevalence of untouchability. The findings are as follows:

> 'Throughout the district as a rule, members of SC communities were not allowed into the houses of non-SCs. Even major towns like Chittoor, Tirupathi, etc. are exceptions to the extent that the rule does not apply to unknown persons ....The Padayatra team came across 122 tea shops in 249 villages including 3 mandal headquarters where tea is served in separate glasses for SCs, and in most cases members of SC communities have to wash the tumblers themselves, both before and after drinking tea and hold the glass when the tea shop owner pours tea from a height....Members of SC communities are not allowed entry in as many as 80 temples in 249 villages'.[11] Reports of discrimination, deprivation and atrocities against Dalits from different parts of India are not something new in the domain of public knowledge in spite of having constitutional safeguards and state machinery to protect the Dalits. Dalits in their own way have always tried to put up resistance against discrimination and oppression in the name of caste.

During the colonial rule leaders like Jyotiba Phule, 'Periyar' E.V. Ramasami, M.C. Rajah, Dr. B.R. Ambedkar and other Dalit leaders tried to mobilize Dalit voices against caste discrimination and for equal rights and social justice. In post-independent era the formation of Dalit Panthers in Maharashtra in the early 1970s contributed to the growth of Dalit political activism. This was followed by the rise of political parties of the Dalits and socio-political movements claiming to represent the Dalits, interests. Social and political awareness of Dalits has definitely increased compared to the past. The major shift in agenda of Dalit politics today is from social equality to assertion for sharing of economic and political power. Social awareness and political activism have definitely emboldened Dalits in recent times to stand up to social oppression and to voice for their share in the corridors of power. Recently Dalit activists have taken their struggle to the international forums. In 1993 at the World Conference on Human Rights in Vienna for the first time the caste question was discussed. Then in World Dalit Convention at Kuala Lampur, 1998, International Conference on Dalit Human Rights in London, 2000, Global Conference against Racism in Durban, 2001, caste discrimination was placed on the international human rights agenda.[12] The point I like to make without going into any elaboration of dynamics of the Dalit movements that Dalits starting from challenging the ideological basis of caste-based social hierarchy to mobilization for economic and political rights have succeeded in keeping the story of their plight in public gaze. But the road to social justice and the end of atrocities is still far off.

Aboriginals of Australia

Story of indigenous Australians is little different from the Dalits in India. Numerically indigenous Australians constitute about one per cent of present population of Australia but Australia being their own homeland they should have more meaningful presence in their own country. But reality is different. They narrate their condition as follows:

'Even since the invasion of our country by English soldiers and then colonists in the late eighteenth century, aborigines have endured a history of land theft, attempted racial extermination, oppression, denial of basic human rights, actual and de facto slavery, ridicule, denigration, inequality and paternalism'.[13] With the establishment of penal colony at Sydney Cove on 26 January 1788 the idea was created that the British became sovereign in a legal desert without settled inhabitants, meaning by the complete denial of existence of indigenous peoples in Australia. Thus the British colonization began with the belief that Australia was largely uninhabited. Contrary to this belief writings of early ethnographers, explorers and missionaries refer to the knowledge of land tenure, law and governance of indigenous peoples. Recent debate in Australia concerning historiography of European-Aboriginal contacts and Australian history has broken the silence about indigenous Australians and rescued them from their former status as 'a melancholy footnote'.[14] Particularly Henry Reynolds's works in the field of 'Aboriginal history' have addressed the issues of injustice and oppression faced by indigenous Australians and have tried to situate indigenous Australians in their rightful place in Australia's history.[15] Contrary to the dominant view on the rights of indigenous Australians Reynolds has argued that indigenous Australians were neither nomads nor a people without laws. They were sovereign people having their own laws, customs and rights to land. Bain Attwood in an article has questioned the objectivity of Reynolds's 'The Law of the Land'. Attwood considers 'The Law of the Land' as juridical history rather than a true history with complexities of past. He argues that historian's job is to understand and explain the past rather than judging it.[16] Reviewing Keith Windschuttle's book, 'The Fabrication of Aboriginal History: Volume One, Vand Diemen's Land 1803–1847 (Sydney, 2002)', which focuses on the issue of indigenous Australian's land rights and the place of indigenous people in Australia's history it has been argued that indigenous Australians had the occupancy rights of the land but because of racism many white Australians do not share this perception. 'Windschuttle...wishes to portray Australia as a virtuous, moral, and heroic nation. He does this by denying the existence of Aboriginal massacres, and by implication, that Aborigines had any reason to resist'.[17] All these point to the growing consciousness within Australia of the question of legitimate place of indigenous Australians in Australia's history and to ensure social justice to them.

After prolonged denial of basic rights to indigenous Australians the Australian government came forward with specific legislation having provision for welfare of indigenous Australians. In 1967, a referendum was held where 90 per cent of white Australians voted that indigenous Australians become citizens in their own land. Special fund was allocated for housing, health, education and other welfare projects for indigenous Australians. In the process of recognition of indigenous peoples' rights the greatest landmark development took place in 1992. Since late 1960s there was organized campaign by indigenous Australians for land rights. In 1981 Eddie Mabo and several other Murray Islanders decided to raise their claim to homeland through the courts. In the *Mabo* vs. *Queensland* case the High Court recognized indigenous laws and customs as a source of rights to land. This decision challenged two hundred years of Eurocentric constitutional, legal and political history of Australia although the Court did not come out clearly on the original sovereignty of indigenous Australians. Writing on this judgement Bain Attwood has observed, 'it seems probable that the Court would have ruled in favour of native title in any case. Changing attitudes towards human rights at home and abroad had rendered the conventional story about the colonization of Australia untenable, and so the law needed to re-legitimise itself and the nation by re-aligning its narrative with the new historical truths'.[18] Pressure from within as a result of growing indigenous assertions for fundamental rights of citizenship and social justice and from outside by human rights activists and international human rights organizations resulted in taking various initiatives by Australian government for the rights of indigenous Australians.

In 1991, the Federal Parliament created the Council for Aboriginal Reconciliation with the stated objective of facilitating the process of reconciliation. The government constituted a national committee to inquire into the separation of 'Aboriginal' and Torres Strait Islander children from their families. The National Inquiry Report titled as 'Bringing Them Home', was tabled in the Commonwealth Parliament of Australia in 1997. The National Inquiry Report documents widespread and systematic racial discrimination and ill-treatment of indigenous Australians. The Report made 54 recommendations which included reparations, acknowledgement of truth and an apology, guarantees of non-repetition of violations, rehabilitation, compensation, etc. Australian government also set up a number of commissions like the Aboriginal and Torres Strait Islander Commission and also a separate ministry to address the grievances of indigenous Australians. The commissioner of the Aboriginal and Torres Strait Islander Social Justice Commission is entrusted with the responsibility to monitor the enjoyment and exercise of human rights by indigenous Australians and to submit its findings to the Parliament through the Attorney General. From margins their relentless struggles have succeeded in bringing the indigenous Australians to the centre of government's agenda for affirmative actions. In the light of various initiatives taken by Australian government let us look into the experiences of indigenous Australians.

'We are writing from Ernabella (Pukatja Community), our home on the Anangu Pitjantjatjara Yankunytjatjara lands in northwest South Australia.

We are writing now because we feel that we are being pushed around by the Federal and State Governments. We also have the opinion that our people and our communities are being systematically disempowered.

We want people to know about what is going on here.

For many years, we are suffering the effects of government strategies of extreme delay in service delivery. We are badly affected by the imposition on us of inappropriate and ineffective systems of administration and governance. We are held back by a lack of thoughtful, respectful and culturally aware consultation and planning between us Anangu and governments and their agents – on whom, unavoidably, we depend. All of these things put an almost intolerable burden on our well-being and our capacities.'[19]

This open letter of an indigenous writer speaks of the reality in which indigenous Australians are living despite the affirmative actions initiated by Australian government. On the issue of indigenous stolen wages the Senate Legal and Constitutional Affairs Committee was of the opinion that there was discrimination against indigenous people in the scheme of stolen wages. Gary Highland, National Director, Australians for Native Title and Reconciliation, has said, 'The Senate Committee has confirmed what Indigenous people have been saying for years –that governments around Australia controlled and withheld the wages and savings belonging to Aboriginal people. Much of this money went into public revenue or disappeared through fraud or negligence'.[20] Indigenous peoples are of the opinion that unless their demand for self-determination is accepted and not as tokenism but in real terms and indigenous peoples are involved in decision-making processes there will be no check on the hardships they face. 'If this country is genuinely to move towards a just relationship between its indigenous and non-indigenous peoples, the dynamic of that relationship must shift from patronage, control and interference to support, cooperation and respect. The spirit of reconciliation or self-determination must not be allowed to degenerate into words on placards displayed in celebration of "international years"....When indigenous families can say that we enjoy the security, health and cultural integrity which is our right, this country can move with clear conscience to the next international year'.[21] Through number of initiatives and programs Australian government sought to raise health, education and living standards of indigenous people.

'In 2005–06 the government budgeted approximately $417 million (A$556 million) for the indigenous – specific community housing and infrastructure program; a further $407 million (A$543 million) for indigenous education and training program; $356 million (A$475 million) for indigenous-specific health services; and $607 million (A$809 million) for indigenous employment and economic development programs.... However, indigenous citizens continued to experience significantly higher rates of imprisonment, inferior access to medical and educational institutions, greatly reduced life expectancy rates, higher rates of unemployment, and general discrimination. Poverty and below average educational achievement levels contributed significantly to Aboriginal under-representation in national, territorial, and state political leadership'.[22] This brings us to the question that even after respecting the rights of disadvantaged social groups and initiating affirmative actions by the state to provide justice why the justice is still a distant dream.

Concluding Observations

Promulgation of law and providing institutional mechanism to enforce justice are not enough to bring the desired justice and equality to the deprived sections of the society. Why are the respective state governments in spite of taking number of affirmative actions failing to ensure justice? To my mind the values which people have developed through a process of socialization become major impediment to accept the change. Change is required in the behaviour and attitudes of the dominant groups. Whether it is based on caste or race individuals develop a sense of identity which is further strengthened through rituals, customs and various myths. It provides a sense of oneself as belonging to a historical social group and the groups are measured by a scale of hierarchy. Modern democratic state in spite of its liberal philosophy and commitment to human rights and equality is facing the major challenge to negotiate with the problem of social justice. Responding to the demands of socially marginalized groups the state has initiated measures to do justice but still they are relatively in social isolation and hardship. Modern citizens are aware of immense injustice done towards the underprivileged groups but the way to deliver justice is still a debatable proposition. What Dalits and indigenous Australians demand is not charity but justice. It is not the question of economic emancipation alone but social equality and justice is very crucial. Issues that confront Dalits and indigenous Australians today are how to accept the national identity which has been virtually imposed on them and how their well-being can be decided by 'others' and not by themselves. Patronizing attitude of the dominant groups in the name of welfare is not at all acceptable to those who are at the bottom of hierarchy.

Even after sixty years of Indian independence there is no visible change in the life of Dalits. Rather the welfare of Dalits has become a major instrument of manipulation in today's vote bank politics. Even where Dalits are comparatively better off there is not much change in general attitude towards them. Story of Dalits in Kerala presents a different picture in terms of development. A recent study shows that Dalits in Kerala are not much behind other communities in terms of opportunities for social progress and better living conditions. 'Significantly, among the Dalits in the 18–25 age group, 10.30 per cent and in college, 6.6 per cent are engaged in other studies and 42.2 per cent are employed'.[23] But they too have complaints about social discrimination and lack of representation in government bodies. Dalits in general still have a very small proportion of cultivated land and are tied to the landowners who mostly come from dominant castes. It is known to all that dignity of life, education, economic and political empowerment can only emancipate the Dalits.

The case of indigenous Australians is not much different. The days of repression and denial are over. The task of doing justice to indigenous people is very much on the agenda of the government. In the opinion of Ross Poole 'Justice to indigenous people is a project, not a program. It makes demands on non-indigenous people to come to terms with the past, to acquire some understanding of indigenous cultures and ways of life, to provide the legal, political, social, and cultural space for indigenous people to reproduce their culture; and to transfer the massive resources necessary to make aboriginal self-determination possible'.[24] It is a fact that responsibility lies on the state to ensure justice but the state acts through its machinery which is manned by those who have been conditioned in different value system largely borrowed from the past. Real challenge lies in negotiating with this mindset shaped by the ideology of hierarchy, domination and subordination. Each nation-state is having a cultural past to a great extent constructed by an ideology of domination and subordination, superiority and inferiority. Modern democratic polity, in spite of its strong belief in equality and justice, has failed to protect the rights of the marginalized. As we have seen from the above discussion, even after realizing the need of social equality and justice and taking affirmative actions to address the needs of the aggrieved, Dalits and indigenous Australians are still at the receiving end of oppression and injustice. It has been observed that 'the Prevention of Atrocities Act remains unimplemented with judges, lawyers, prosecutors and policemen hardly interested in the implementation of the statute'.[25] Study done on the participation and intervention of Dalit parliamentarians on Dalit issues shows the failure of Dalit parliamentarians in protecting the Dalits interests.[26] Protective measures taken by the state further consolidated and widened the gaps between the dominant and the oppressed. Both in India and Australia there are strong voices opposing the state initiatives providing reservation and special welfare scheme. Social backlash on such issues in both the countries are also common. There is a strong feeling among the present generations of dominant groups in both the countries against special provisions for the welfare of the oppressed groups. The argument put forward is that they are not responsible for the past injustices so why they should face the brunt of state discrimination today. This kind of thinking generates tension and further consolidates the divides. Therefore, the complexity of problems of the marginalized groups needs to be addressed not by legislation alone but by looking into issue of economic empowerment and effective social mechanism to bridge the socio-cultural gap between 'We' vs 'They'.

Endnotes

1. Bhikhu Parekh, 'Dialogue between cultures', in R. Maiz and F. Requejo (eds.), Democracy, Nationalism and Multiculturalism , Great Britain, 2005, pp. 15–23.
2. Smita Narula, 'Caste Discrimination', in S. Thorat and Umakant (eds.), Caste, Race and Discrimination: Discources in International Context, New Delhi, 2004, p. 284.
3. Source: www.indiatogether.org/dalit/articles
4. Alka Srivastava,'Dalit Identity in Bihar', in Fernando Franco (ed.), Pain and Awakening, Delhi, 2002, p. 128.
5. The Royal Commission on Aboriginal Deaths in Custody, National Report 1992, Source www.hreoc.gov.au/bth/indig-social-justice.
6. Gracelyn Smallwood, The Unrelenting Struggle of Indigenous Australians, Source www.cwo.com/~lucuni/australians
7. *Frontline*, December 29, 2006.
8. *Frontline*, November 3, 2006.
9. *Frontline*, December 29, 2006.
10. G. Shah, 'Untouchability in Rural Gujarat Revisited', in G. Shah (ed.), Dalits and the State, New Delhi, 2002, pp. 144–145.
11. Harsh Mander, 'Status of Dalits and Agenda for State Intervention', in G. Shah (ed.), Dalits and the State, op. cit., pp. 151–152.
12. For details see Debi Chatterjee, Up Against Caste: Comparative Study of Ambedkar and Periyar, New Delhi, 2004.
13. A selected bibliography of the Black Presence in Australia, Source: www.cwo.com/nlucumi/australia-bib
14. W.H. Stanner took the lead in breaking the myth about indigenous Australians. Later, M.C. Hartwig, C.D. Rowley, Sharon Morgan, Henry Reynolds and others have portrayed indigenous Australians as active not passive agents in making Australia's history. Particularly since 1970s because of mobilization of indigenous Australians and civil rights movements at the international level Australian historical narratives began to change acknowledging the dynamism of socio-cultural life of indigenous Australians.
15. Frontier, 1987; The Law of the Land, 1987; Aboriginal Sovereignty, 1996; Why Weren't We Told?, 2000; etc.
16. Bain Attwood, The Law of the Land or the Law of the Land?: History, Law and Narrative in a Settler Society, History Compass 2 (2004), Blackwell Publishing.
17. Gregory D.B. Smithers, 'Reassuring "White Australia": A Review of The Fabrication of Aboriginal History: Volume One, Van Diemen's Land 1803–1847', in Journal of Social History, Winter, 2003.

18. Bain Attwood, The Law of the Land, op. cit.
19. www.antar.org.au
20. www.antar.org.au.
21. Mick Dodson, 'The Rights of Indigenous Peoples in the International Year of the Family', in *Family Matters no. 37, April 1994*, Australian Institute of Family Studies.
22. Source: www.state.gov/g/drl/rls
23. *Frontline*, December 29, 2006.
24. Ross Poole, 'The Nation-state and Aboriginal Self-determination', in Michel Seymour (ed.), The Fate of the Nation-state, Canada, 2004, p. 101.
25. Girish Agrawal and Colin Gonsalves, Dalits and the Law, New Delhi, 2005, p. XII.
26. Narendra Kumar, Dalit Policies, Politics and Parliament, New Delhi, 2004.

13

Exploring a Critical Tradition in Communications Research: A Cultural Discourse

Amita Singh

Even though the status and direction of Indian and Australian traditions in communication technology as it has evolved in the last one and a half decade does not manifest any radical critical discourse, yet University departments of media and cultural studies are brewing up to contest this prevailing status quo. Both in India and Australia communications technology has largely been influenced by the agendas of government and industry thereby betraying a critical impulse in favour of administratively-oriented intellectual pragmatism[1]. The debates and the failings of cultural studies to highlight and question the control of media communications technology upon governance in a manner that the voice of the poor and the oppressed does not get buried under what one refers to as 'consumer sovereignty' demonstrates the influence of neo-liberal economics in technology usages. The potentially powerful scale of this technology and its embedded mass appeal is leading the two nations into a critical cultural discourse about its application.

One may notice that information and communications technology (ICT) infrastructures in the two countries are largely under the control of governments and are therefore vulnerable to global capitalistic economy structured by multinational corporations which for all practical purposes transcend political nation-state boundaries. While socialist tradition has relatively stronger roots in India as compared to Australia and has to some extent played a role in slowing down the rush for an adoption of ICT in governance yet little has emerged in intellectual research to address the veracity of politics in ICT applications. Most studies have ironically been narratives of government programs in which ICT has been given a fluorescent dynamic position as a technology of progress and transformation. Few in cultural studies have been able to rise up to this occasion as dispassionate researchers to investigate many deviations being made in the name of cultural transformations. Australian studies[3] have a far more intense involvement towards this cultural awareness about ICT despite a severe institutional weakness of the left parties as compared to the Indian left. Much of this is also due to the fact that Australian Universities[4] have been quick to start centres for media and cultural studies at the undergraduate level while India has none till today which leaves enormous scope for private institutions to quickly exploit these empty spaces to create nuts and bolts generation to feed the media industry. The University Grants Commission does not have a single Committee to address this gradual nibbling away of Indian socialist tradition and pro-poor agenda of cultural studies through the ICT applications. This poverty and ignorance of Indian cultural studies towards the widening digital divide and emboldening of neo-liberal frameworks in governance has distanced development from its basic concerns of equity and participation in economic decision making.

Technology is 'Change'

History has shown that technology has always arrived with its social and economic ramifications. When electricity reached villages in India, a whole big market of lanterns and candles was gone. People were not bothered about the darkness after dusk and thus their life was freed from the control of the nature clock. Gradually, it seeped into cultural practices such as the festivities on Diwali, one of the biggest festival in India comparable to Christmas in the West, where earthen lanterns coming from the potters wheel gave way to electric lights and decoratives. Thus the familiar sight of the potter and his donkey which reminded the.coming of Diwali disappeared. Similarly a cow is no more a symbol of adulation as she was at one of the post-Holi (a festival of colours) Indian festival of 'govardhan' since the dairy milk replaced her at homes. A large number of tribal and rural communities of India are lost if not become extinct for their inability to participate in the technological changes which gripped their occupations. This loss is a loss of their total ecosystem, their environmental resources, their support animals, indigenous wisdom, native technology and culture. Many fall off the change, many are economically excluded as technology transforms relationships between human beings, nature and the production machines of the State. As these relationships weaken in the course of their transformation it becomes easier for the industry to intrude homes and markets. But never in history has such a potentially powerful engine of change affected human lives as the coming of television, internet and the mobile phone technology. Like every other technological system it has come with a system of both domination and liberation but few in India have raised the question of who dominates and who is liberated while Australian literature has vociferously demarcated the line of class-progress though ICT. This argument remains the core of this discourse.

What Constitutes ICT?

The present study deals with a relatively powerful intrusion of one technology (ICT) into public and private spheres of citizens across the world and which calls for a thorough investigation of theories of deliberative democracy and the new innovations being promoted as forms of good governance practices. ICT (Information and communication technology is commonly used for a combination of IT (information technology), IS (information systems) and CT (communication technology) particularly the internet. It would be interesting to place at this point the concern expressed by Cees Hamelink in his keynote address to the first preparatory meeting for the UN World Summit on Information Society (WSIS) in 2003, "It is disconcerting that in the context of the 'information Society' the notion 'communication' has disappeared. Yet the real core question is how we should shape future 'communication societies'...." However the fact that ICT does not observe geographical and cultural boundaries demands a new form of regulatory system which applies surveillance without dispiriting and monitoring without protectionism.

Internet as a Movement against Centralized Control of Information

Internet has originated out of ARPANET – Advanced Research Projects Agency Net a very small network of computer based network information exchange fashioned by scientists working out of the American Military Industrial Complex in response to perceived cold war threats. (Castells, 2000). The objective of this original internet system was to protect the military industrial data from a nuclear holocaust wipe-out. Thus access to this internet did not allow users from Europe to browse freely into all its spaces. However internet has grown to be very different from what it originally was because it has moved out of a very restricted and closely monitored science based specialized exchange system to a diversified and distributed diffusion of information exchange which defies not only corporate control but also any other form of centralized institutional control as was the case with previous communication and media technologies such as the radio and television. Thus internet and the p2p (peer to peer) exchange has also rendered somewhat more artificial the appearance of 'information scarcity' – the perception that news represents a difficult to obtain resource. This study looks into four key technologies of present times that have potentially transformed the way people live, think and communicate as a result of which much of what traditionally existed in politics and administration is being severely challenged.

Four major technologies have led to a cultural revolution in the world beginning with the USSR split and the fall of the German wall – Microprocessors, wireless networking, artificial intelligence and nano technology. Microprocessors have led to a chain of inventions such as computers, laptops, fax machines, sophisticated automobile technologies, wrist watches and other home and office appliances. It has been estimated that their performance has increased 25,000 times since they were invented in the 1960s. Smart and fast electronics has been the result of an invention in silicon switches called transistors which were much smaller than the vacuum tubes used in early circuitry. Through subsequent sophistication in stored program design and transistor pairing in the same machine that the most epoch making invention of the century Intel 4004 as it was built by putting 2,300 transistors on a single silicon chip which was no larger than a child's finger nail. Wireless technology has revolutionized the metros as well as the countryside by delivering personalized communications to people and basic telephone services to those who never dreamt of having one ever in their lifetime. Invented by Guglielmo Macaroni this experiment of sending radio waves has grown into a wireless network which is becoming digital and more 'intelligent.' It is a technology to locate roaming subscribers and customize the services they receive. An increasing improvement in micro-electronics, digital radio and signal processing has spread the usage with speed and vigor. An interesting example of this is that in USA a 1983 prediction about users in the year 2000 was one million but they were 20 million. Artificial Intelligence or AI has emerged as a storehouse of commonsense knowledge from its first invention in Dartmouth College in 1956. This is being increasingly used in face recognition, medical diagnoses, security devices, airports and customs, automobiles and appliances. It is nevertheless laden with problems which have prevented its growth to the level of its two previously described technologies. While these technological systems reveal their latent might to change the world, there are impending fears to sustain them in a fragile world of growing demands and increasing costs. Thus the change which they bring may turn out to be more virtual than real as in the long run traditional institutions and communication modes may be needed as saviors to aspiring societies. Thus a changing discourse on governance reforms may focus on the sustainability of new technologies in bringing about meaningful transformation in societies. A special issue of a publication by Scientific American in 1996 on 'Key Technologies for the 21st Century' starts with a mild warning from John Rennie about the uncertainties of technical innovations, 'Even the greatest ideas and inventions can flounder, whereas more modest steps forward sometimes change the world.' Thus the technologies mentioned below have a capacity to change the domain of governance but in turn may impose new tensions over it. In terms of their diffusion and use they are described below.

Globalization and Visual Imaging of Human Concerns

In the early years when television arrived, it brought new mobilization amongst women, children and men. People in Indian cities where the TV was first introduced, flocked to see programs in the homes of those more privileged to possess one. Even though it continued to be called an idiot box and produced a much laid back culture through a single government controlled channel yet it produced a common social impact every evening. New relationships were developing through TV in all spheres of life among occupational groups like farmers, doctors, teachers, women and children. Thus if the disappearance of wells and lanterns as community ecosystems and social forces was pushed by the arrival of electricity and tap water then the liberation of women and many aboriginal communities across the world came through their stronger self-imaging in the ICT media such as the television. Rural India which constituted more than 70 per cent of political force and contributed the same in gross development product found a new voice through this media. However, this was a pre-globalization phase. What happened after the coming of globalization provides a different story.

The coming of globalization replaced citizen's choices with consumer sovereignty, consequently breaking down geographical space and occupational links only to be replaced by illusionary bonds created by the transmission of an alien cultural norm within which slowly and gradually the whole society was being sucked into like the black hole in space. The Microsoft, Samsung, google, sapient, verizone, rediff, hotmail and yahoo became household names with computer users in the more privileged regions of the poor country. The companies and many others were quick to expand business on this wave of internet users. Bonds with a far flung imaginary host became stronger than that with next door neighbour. People were gradually becoming less interested in issues in their backyard and more in the politics of hyped passions over the internet and media coverage by big companies. The government of the poor and the oppressed went missing in these flashlights of conversion. The issues of environmental and land degradation, loss of water bodies or famine no more attracted the young as it did in the seventies and the eighties thus major movements and discourses involving poor sections of society and neglected countries like Rwanda and Somalia got reduced time for telecast on television than the fashion bonanzas, bomb blasts and realty shows. Politically powerful presentations pulled mass appeal and thus it became easier to mobilize people's signature campaigns for a whale being slaughtered off Canadian and Norwegian coast than with the poor farmer's stolen cows being butchered illegally for leather by leather industry or the non-procurement of wheat and sugarcane by government leading to an intensification of poverty in rural areas. It became easier for the dam protagonists to label eco-warriors as freaks, anti-development and anti-poor. Internet has replaced natural linkages with problems and made political support and mobilization a matter of signature campaigns over the net. Visual imaging of problems and their transmission has created a cyber world of knowledge. This acquiescence to global imaging at the cost of local disconnections has enabled globalization to penetrate deep fringes of human lives without making any sensitive issue about its invasion either in local politics or economy. This is an allegory of globalization in which Indians as well as Australians are getting increasingly disconnected with their own land, politics and culture to play illusionary active roles in seemingly global missions to save humanity, democracy and development. The world is becoming a 'global village' without any local roots and yet this hollow at the roots is growing unnoticed in great complicity with decisions which are perpetuating the expanse of ICT in human lives. Langdon Winner laments that 'such a world, in which unconscious collective actions govern waking reality, is the world that now exists.' Media was out for sale and thus one of the most reliable tool in the hands of the rich to promote their policies. The question is not of preventing the technological advance but to make it meaningfully beneficial in transforming and strengthening local bonds so that growth and development is not distanced from issues of equity, justice and environmental sustainability.

Technology and Social Structures

Technology has always been used as a magic tool for overcoming an intractable problem overnight. While sociology and political science has to some extent followed the critical tradition of resisting its blind acceptance, public administration has helped to facilitate its intrusion into public life uncritically. While the first has prevented its rightful share to people, the latter has promoted government programs as 'nuts and bolts' of implementation. The failings of both sides to make technology relevant by removing it from its captivity and confinement to either the micro-sphere or the macro-sphere of public policy has only helped the cause of the big market. Technology, as ignored condescendingly as 'nuts and bolts' disciplines in social sciences helped class cleavages and class deprivations in the era of global economic integration.

A more thorough unraveling of the mysteries of technological advance suggests issues which are placed at the core of democracy and equality. If we accept that technology is 'a species of social structure' then it would be easier for us to proceed with its implication on poor in society. It also becomes easier for us to explain the skeptical note saying that the more the world changes the more it remains the same. In *Principles of Social Reconstruction* Bertrand Russell had suggested what the world of technology in the late twentieth century would be. However, the subjugation of women to kitchen and cooking did reduce in proportion yet the issue is still a major debate of civilized countries and real emancipation is nowhere in sight. If left untreated and undebated technology perpetuates a social structure which it is meant to eradicate. This it does by creating political values and social choices which help promote markets for some, and as this grows such norms in public lives take the shape of public laws and regulations. For example, the unregulated promotion of credit facilities and loan markets on cell phones and internet has trapped a large number of citizens from less developed nations under unaccountable exploitation of big corporations like CitiBank, ANZ, ABN Amro, American Express, HDFC and ICICI. In the absence of consumer protection regulations and much of their business gauged under cyber dealings and faceless service providers, big corporations continue to create a regime of new exploitation which government supports by creating efficiency laws in business. Thus what is the role that this technology would play in lives of ordinary human beings especially those in poverty, unemployment, homelessness and starvation. Most conceptions about self and moral reasoning emerge through the way one envisions and understands the world.[5] What has been happening in a world shaped with modern information technology is that there has been a rise in electoral fallacies in which substantive democracy and political equality involving a discourse on citizen's rights and deliberative institutions are clouded through concerns for representative democracy, periodic elections and corporate competition as a panacea for free and customer friendly markets. Unless these issues are resolved through technology its growth may be like the story of four blind men who knew the parts of the animal but could not image them for an elephant and thus their findings were without any meaning and relevance.

At least one system of interrogation in social sciences 'Critical Theory' has in some way initiated a discourse in techno-determinism and econo-determinism. It claims that the socio-historical context is crucial in determining which questions a theory poses, how it formulates and answers them and what are the limitations, grounds and insights of the theory[6]. Three incidents, the First World War, Russian Revolution of 1917 and the abortive German Revolution of 1918 created a strong critique of bourgeoisie capitalism with the handmaiden support from prevalent Marxian philosophy. Marcuse, Horkheimer, Pollock and Fromm spearheaded the movement for critical interrogations into State systems such as war, imperialism and economic domination. The failure of young radicals in establishing left control over social democrats sent them back to their universities where they re-investigated Marxism as a theory of scientific socialism. George Lukas's *History and Class Consciousness* and Karl Korsch's *Marxism and Philosophy* launched what came to be known as Critical Theory. It was later fed by Freud, Heidegger and Habermas in the Frankfurt Institute of Social Research. Their approach to media and mass culture which forms an important component of media research in ICT was first visible in Adorno's writings on music but it was much later during and after the Second World War that critical theorists were able to visualize the impact of media technology upon politics, society and economics of the state and put more analytically the idea of a 'culture industry'. They found an increasing use of media technology for inducing consent and indoctrination for generating consumer society.

Slowly by the 1960s the coming of computers had changed the way corporates designed their managerial systems and with the coming of internet and satellite technology during the 1960s economy was certainly moving faster. But the 1973 slump and ensuing stagflation began search for a new technology to cut cost of production and marketing. These new forms of economic practices which depended upon fast track service delivery systems to consumers and capitalists were transnational and designed to help the capitalists firm in increasing profits[7].Thus critical theorists of the 1920s and technology promoters of the 1980s share some form of technological and economic determinism which has prevented a more open debate on the use of technology. Two elements would emerge in this debate: first, that new information technology is a necessary corollary of the capitalist state, and second, that this technology can also be used against the state. Media research need to focus on exploring ways in which citizens start sharing controls over the usage of this technology[8]. Some important issues raised by critical theorists in explaining culture industries, domination and consent in the capitalist consumerism in modern lives has also to answer the brain and brawn divides in media shows in which the physical assets take over the value based assets such as bodies over intellect, malls over customer controlled local markets, fashionable office spaces over service delivery, Anglo-American lifestyles to divert resources for golf-courses, centrally air-conditioned clubs, highly upgraded technological systems even though irrelevant and berating of human resource to machines.

Thus the new ICT technology which combines authoritative controls over both knowledge storage and communication has started mediating choices made by people and governments. Andrew Feenberg[9] insists in all his writings on a critical theory of technology that the design of technology is an ontological decision fraught with political consequences. In all circumstances such decisions tend to exclude a large majority of citizens clustered at the lower end of the socio-economic system in every country developed or underdeveloped. This chapter would put across two comparative pictures from Australia and India, the former being a developed country with fourth position in the Human Development Index while the latter being a transitional country having 127th position in the Human Development Index. What they have witnessed with the rise of new information technology is a competitive turbulence at the upper decisional levels, wealth generation and accumulation restricted to small minority, liberation and deregulation for capital nomadic investor, knowledge banks under the control of rich. Thus technology of this sort cannot bring any fundamental change in society such as a radical poverty eradication drive unless it is democratically transformed.

Conclusions

ICT has redrawn the map of democracy and participation across the world. Originally meant to enhance managerial capabilities through computerization of records and data within offices and corporations it has increased from a scarcely million users to more than 125 m. within a decade (1990 to 2000). In the last five years it has managed to control more than a $1.5 trillion annual transactions through the internet and has been impacting education, health and consumer systems across the globe in a manner not witnessed by the world anytime in the history of its evolution. A serious research on the wide ramifications of this new technology on people has been ignored by social scientists outside the American world for two important reasons; *first,* it was primarily considered as a conspiracy of the corporations to sell and promote their software and hardware to enhance service delivery systems hence academicians preferred to keep out or look down upon any analytical study upon the processes touching this promotional market and it was thus rejected as a nuts and bolts study appropriate for management schools.

Second, that the network systems emerging out through the application of this technology were being used by academics to facilitate their communicational and ideological networks, update research abilities and improve their global opportunities, as a result of this a 'wait and watch' policy which suited them better to understand the real nature and objective of ICT.

In the first instance it would be imperative to sketch a rationale for a comparative study between the two countries placed at two opposite ends of economic and human development index. Australia is 4th in Human Development Index while India is slowly moving upwards from 127th position. Australia is a developed country which has so far managed a sustainable balance between population growth, resource consumption and employment in national policies. In contrast India is still continuing with highly unsustainable policies as a result of which even though the country is gaining in wealth this is not translating into poverty reduction and employment generation. For lack of exposure to global norms and practices India continues to carry much of the bureaucratic pathologies and corruption in public life. However the fact that despite a huge and growing population India has remained consistent with a rising growth rate in the past few years which is far ahead that of Australia and given the fact that in coming times a relatively much younger population would control technology and production this gap between the two countries may not remain as large.

As the world is more of a global village now policies cannot be formulated in isolation to each other. Especially, countries which are connected in history and geo-morphology, there are several unexplored areas where collaboration in research may simply emerge effortlessly. One factor which has helped India to come out of stagnation and negative trade balance triumphantly is the technological strides taken by her in the information and communication market. India has churned some of the best engineers, agriculture research scientists and biotechnologists in the last fifteen years who not only compensate for the weaknesses of infrastructure, machines and bad politics within the country but have withstood major challenges from global market of technology. It is this rising population behind the telecommunication revolution which stands to challenge the culture of backwardness, softness and hierarchy in global relations. It is another matter whether this new generation of technologists are able to change the rules of the game through which technological implantations occur in developing societies and this would form the core of the discourse dealt within this book.

Significant disparities in the degree of democratic development tarnish the achievement of millennium development goals (MDG). These are disparities in income, educational attainment, gender and access to resources including training in science, technology, legal frameworks and governance which keep a large majority of people out of the social net. Alienation and marginalization seeps into efforts of reform leading to a completely uneventful and ritualistic policy implementation. (see MDG in Human Development Report 2003 pp. 1–13). The report admitted that these goals cannot be realized with business as usual approach but the pace of progress must be dramatically accelerated. It was also clarified that even though a stronger economic growth was required yet growth alone will not be enough as policies also need to strengthen the links between stronger growth and higher incomes in the poorest households. (HDR, 2003, p. 5) For achieving this access to education, food, technology and health services becomes a dire requirement of sustaining growth. For Australia the issue is to sustain growth and development for a longer period of time in this competitive market system.

ICT services have played a major role in bringing India out of stagnation and economic depression. TNCs have played a major role such as American Express, British Airways, GE, Canadian Nortel Networks, US's Texas Instruments, etc. Now India's domestic market is well developed and ready for a major outflow of FDI since Tata Consultancy, Infosys, Wipro and Satyam computers are at par with foreign rivals. (McKinsey & Co 2003) Indo-Australian collaboration can safely broaden up in ICT services such as customer care, finance, human resources, billing and payments, administration and content development. Engineering, design, knowledge processing and logistics are further going to generate a major employment market which is slated to show the highest growth in coming times.

Export Oriented FDI projects reveal that between 2002 and 2003, Australia's biggest investment has been in IT Services which, however, is a meager 4 per cent share of the total but India on the other hand had 19 per cent share of total investment in IT services. This shows that India is fast emerging as an IT destination. Of the more than 300 export-oriented IT projects in developing countries, 37 per cent went to India, 19 per cent to China and 11 per cent to Singapore. Similarly, from the 80 per cent FDI in call centres in Asia, India bagged 60 projects, China 30 and Malaysia and Singapore 16 each. More than half of these projects came from IT related services. Even in shared service centres more than half of these projects came to India. It is being observed that 50 per cent of Fortune 500 companies have not yet set up any such centres but are likely to do so in near future for which India, China and Philippines are likely to be the most attractive destinations. (World Investment Report, *The Shift towards Services,* 2004: UNDP, p. 161)

What is of particular interest here is that the structure of FDI has shifted towards services. From less than a quarter of the world FDI stock in 1970 it has risen to a little less than half in 1990 and to more than 60 per cent or an estimated $ 4 Trillion in 2002. (p. xx). Therefore services account for 2/3rd of total FDI inflows. It is also seen that the dominance of US firms has now given way to Japan and EU in trade and trade supporting services but the highest concentration of FDI has been in countries such as US and Western Europe where markets attract FDI.

Looking at the composition of services FDI provide one can notice the shift from trade and finance to IT enabled corporate services including electricity, water, telecommunications and business where it has risen 14 fold. Even in telecom storage and transport the rise is 16 fold and in business services 9 fold. What is of particular interest for this paper is that FDI inflow is decreasing in developed countries while the outflow is increasing for which India is ranked as the foremost destination for reasons described in the UNDP Report as "Firms are attracted not just by its base of low cost and skilled labour, it also has first mover and agglomeration advantages." The report further states that "the growing technological capabilities of Indian firms and their rising exports, particularly IT services are driving FDI growth." This in turn has been strengthening regulatory systems, reliability of services and consumer protection laws. Thus IT enabled services have opened up doors for partnerships in legal services besides infrastructural issues.

The Australian telecommunications system has undergone a radical reform since 1991. Indeed, along with New Zealand, Chile and Guatemala, Australia is viewed as one of the leaders in telecommunications reform (Spiller and Cardilli, 1997). The former's public monopoly, comprising Telecom Australia and the Overseas Telecommunications Corporation (OTC) has been corporatised, taking the name Telstra, and partially privatised (A proposal for full privatisation was put forward in 1998, but abandoned in the face of parliamentary and public opposition). Competition has been fostered through the introduction of a private competitor, Optus in 1991 and the removal of all restrictions on entry in 1997, while Telstra has been subject to special regulation requiring the provision of network access to competitors on favourable terms in markets where it is deemed to be dominant. Australian policy was designed to ensure the survival of at least one competitor for Telstra and to encourage the emergence of as many others as possible. Compared to the reforms undertaken in New Zealand, the existing monopoly carrier was given far less favourable treatment.

Four trends towards industry wide consolidation need to be noticed which indicate prospects for across the ocean collaboration:

- Some foreign affiliates (mainly US and EU) are thinking of selling some of their operations.
- Fast growing Indian firms see acquisitions—inside and outside India—as a way to sustain growth.
- Some contract service provider TNCs such as IBM and Accenture are acquiring local service providers in the Indian market.
- Increasing consolidation is occurring among Indian companies.

The total value of Australian investments in India during the period August 1991 to August 2004 was Rs 68437.1 million or A$ 2138.7 million (A$ 1 = Rs. 32.01). This accounted for 2.34 per cent of the total approved investments in India from all countries. The number of Australian joint ventures in India approved during the period August 1991 to August 2004 was 512. Of these, 332 collaborations were financial and 180 technical. According to the accumulated total of approvals up to August 2004, Australia ranked as the 8th largest source of foreign investments in India.

Bilateral trade between India and Australia during the calendar year 2004 recorded A$ 6.54 billion. This was nearly 52 per cent or A$ 2.23 billion higher than the corresponding figure of A$ 4.31 billion in 2003. India's exports to Australia in 2004 were A$ 1.12 billion or 14.6 per cent higher than the corresponding figure of A$ 977.7 million in 2003. India's imports from Australia in 2004 recorded A$ 5.42 billion or a 62.7 per cent higher than the 2003 figure of A$ 3.33 billion. For the fiscal year July 2003-June 2004 India ranked 7th as Australia's export destination (6th export destination in calendar year 2004) with a share of 4.5 per cent in terms of overall exports. India ranked 26th as Australia's import source with 0.8 per cent market share in Australia's total imports. It ranked 13th as Australia's overall trading partner. Australia's Joint Ministerial Commission and Joint Business Council may act as strong facilitators in the process.

Behind the revival of improved trade patterns 'internet' has served as a major driving force. Between 1996 and 2000 the number of households connected to the internet in Australia grew rapidly from 260,000 to 2.7 million households, a growth from a mere 4 per cent to 37 per cent in less than four years. Another change that could be seen was that 99 per cent of households connected to the internet used computer for access. Households' ownership of computers increased over the period but not as strongly as the use of internet. Thus by 2000 around 56 per cent households owned a computer and more than two third of them were connected to the computer (ABS). Issues related to the 'digital divide' where unequal access to information and communication technology among communities and sexes raise some critical interrogations in the discourse. A change of the magnitude of what has been brought about through information and communication technology defies any classification within social movements yet by facilitating globalization, and also raising one of the most critical tirades against it justifies a critical cultural discourse on the nature of this new technology.

Endnotes

1. See, Flew, Terry, 2004, Critical Communications Research in Australia: From Radical Populism to Creative Industries, *Javnost: The Public,* Vol. 11, No. 3, 2004.
2. G. Turner, 1992, 'Of Rocks and Hard Places: The Colonised , The National, and Australian Cultural Studies' *Cultural Studies,* Vol. 6, No. 3., Mc. Guigan, J., 1992, *Cultural Populism,* London: Routledge. Sinclair, J., 2002, 'Media and Communications: Theoretical Traditions', in S. Cunnigham and G. Turner (eds.) *The Media and Communications in Australia*, 3rd edition, Sydney: Allen & Unwin.
3. Much of this emerges out of the author's personal meetings and dialogues with Deans of Cultural and Media Studies departments in Australia such as Prof. Krishna Sen and Prof. Jan Sinclaire of Curtin University at Perth, Prof. Stephanae H. Donald of University of Technology at Sydney, Dr. Andrew Hassam of Monash University, Prof. Rae Francis of the University of New South Wales (Currently at Monash University) and Dr. Julian de Roeper of the University of Southern Australia at Adelaide. Even some political scientists like Prof. Carol Johnson at the University of Adelaide have provided a critical political commentary on communications technology applications in Australia.
4. 'The strong democratic tradition contrasts with more passive or inegalitarian models of democracy that in practice tend to prevail today, so called thin democracy'. (see Barber, 1984).
5. Douglas Kellner, 1989, *Critical Theory, Marxism and Modernity,* John Hopkins University Press, Baltimore.
6. Kellner writes 'Techno-capitalism depends on an increasingly high-velocity form of capital in which money, ideas, images, technologies, goods and services can be rapidly moved from one part of the world to another and in which an international division of labour segments production and distribution in different regions and countries connected by new forms of global organization.' (1989:180–181).
7. Kellner, '—a theory of techno-capitalism should resist temptations toward either the technological or economic determinism which plague many classical and contemporary social theories.' (1989:181).
8. Transforming Technology, p. 3.

14

Education and Empowerment: Dalits and the Demand for Modern Education in Colonial India

Shashi Bhushan Upadhyay

Modern education became an important instrument of power in colonial India. Education and knowledge were always considered important. However, in pre-colonial period, there were other and more potent modes of power. The emergence of the East India Company as the dominant force in the late eighteenth century, the subjugation of non-British armed groups, the suppression of the Great Rebellion of 1857, and, finally, the establishment of *Pax Britannica* in the late nineteenth century concentrated the armed power solely in the hands of the colonial state. Education, therefore, became an important source of power by the late nineteenth century. But it had several foci. It was conceived by the colonizers to establish their ideological hegemony over the colonized. On the other hand, the colonized also used it to their advantage in many ways. The modern education not only produced clerks, but it also produced leaders who began mass movements against British rule. In recent times it has been pointed out that education as such is important for the people. Amartya Sen and Jean Dreze, in an important study, deal extensively with the significance of education for the community. They consider education as an important resource which can provide tremendous help in human development. It has also been considered as a crucial "enabling factor" which facilitates not only economic development but also human freedom. Education is considered an important achievement in several ways, for example, "for getting a job and more generally for being able to make use of economic opportunities". Moreover, it may also help in political mobilization, in formulation of collective demands and in resisting oppression.[1] Dreze and Sen attach great importance to basic education. According to them,

> Literacy is an essential tool of self-defence in a society where social interactions include the written media. An illiterate person is significantly less equipped to defend herself in court, to obtain a bank loan, to enforce her inheritance rights, to take advantage of new technology, to compete for secure employment, to get on the right bus, to take part in political activity – in short, to participate successfully in the modern economy and society.[2]

It is considered so by the disadvantaged groups also. Dreze and Sen point out that "a common finding of village studies and household surveys is that education is widely perceived by members of socially disadvantaged groups as the most promising means of upward mobility for their children'[3]. They also assert that the states, like Kerala, which have a wider educational base, are also more advanced in basic human indicators.

This traces the historical antecedents of the demand for modern education, particularly with regard to Dalits in colonial Indian society. A few preliminary remarks are required in this connection. Firstly, the terms Dalit, depressed classes and untouchables are used interchangeably and according to context. Secondly, Phule has been discussed extensively because his thoughts as well as the non-Brahman movements were, in many senses, foundational to Dalit thinking. Thirdly, the Dalit thinking has a Maharashtrian and South Indian bias as most of the important Dalit leaders in colonial period came from these areas and were rooted in regional discourses. These were also the regions which witnessed strong non-Brahman movements. In these areas, the Brahmans had a more privileged position in the pre-colonial period. Even during the colonial period, their better access to modern education strengthened their position in colonial bureaucracy and officialdom. Their representation in the colonial offices was quite disproportionate to their number in society. In other parts of India, the situation was not so lop-sided. Moreover, the relative importance of the powerful Muslim and non-Brahman upper castes in pre-colonial India also presented a different picture.

II

British policy on the education of Indian masses, including Dalits who faced specific discrimination, was deeply ambivalent. The British, as colonizers, had come to take money away from India, and not to invest it in putatively non-profitable ventures like education. At the same time, they required low-level functionaries at cheaper rates to man their offices as well as public works. For this purpose, the target group was the already initiated and somewhat literate population with a tradition of learning. Moreover, the paltry funds would be allocated mainly in higher education. As a self-justification, it was believed that such classes would act as leaders and impart education to those below them. Hence the so-called 'downward filtration theory'. However, the reality turned out to be true to its situation. The system did initiate those groups in the modern education which were economically and socially in a position to do so. But they did not fulfill their roles as educational leaders as the project had unrealistically envisaged. The education remained the privilege of a few and it was those groups who had already enjoyed access to education in pre-colonial times.

On the other hand, the colonial project needed a wider resource base for its success as a modern state. It also had a genuine liberal urge to seek equal opportunities for all without any social discrimination. However, the urge for equality could not go far along with the broader project of domination, control and exploitation. Therefore, the colonial educational project, in both its Orientalist and Anglicist versions, became a project of acquiring and consolidating power[4]. Colonial education served as a tool of imperial hegemony. One aspect of it was that the production and control of knowledge took place in the metropolis whereas the colony served as a place for its transmission. The real knowledge was created by the British and other Europeans and the Indians at best played the role of 'native informants' for gathering the local knowledge. Until the last quarter century of the British rule, there was "no space in the colonially sponsored system for other kinds of research by Indians in India. The three major Universities founded in 1857–58 were designed as examining authorities, not as centres of studies to advance knowledge"[5]. The curriculum in the educational institutions was novel at two levels. It preached the superiority of the English culture and values, and the inferiority of the Indians. And, secondly, it now had no relation to the lived reality of the learner. This dissociation of knowledge and life was further strengthened by the use of English as the medium of instruction[6]. Thus the native needed to be educated and brought up near to the level of the Western civilization in an effort to create the "colonial citizen". This enterprise envisaged the role of adult for the colonizer and that of a child for the colonized[7].

As the Western institutions and knowledge were considered infinitely superior to the Indian ones, the pre-colonial educational institutions and knowledge-system were marginalized. Macaulay's well-known statement that a single stack in any good European library contained more knowledge than the entire Oriental knowledge sounded the death-knell of pre-colonial system. The new system differed from the old system in many regards. It required a high level of centralization in both the administrative and academic matters. Decision-making, employment, curriculum and examination which earlier existed in a decentralized form, now acquired a centralized structure as the new system totally depended on government grants for its survival. Similarly, while in the old system the teacher enjoyed substantive autonomy, the new system made the teacher "a subordinate functionary of the superior officers of the education department"[8].

Despite colonial rhetoric about educating the masses, the investment in elementary education remained very low. Higher education cornered most of the already low disbursement by the government. This benefited mostly the higher castes and classes in colonial society and it endeavoured to initiate the "native mind into categories and values constructed by the colonizer"[9]. The inequality in the access to modern education remained quite pronounced and there was a "convergence of privileges" in terms of class, caste and gender[10].

It was this situation which attracted sharp criticism from the non-Brahman and Dalit leaders.

III

It is a well-known fact that the untouchables were the most discriminated groups in pre-colonial India. This discrimination did not cease under the colonial rule, when racial discrimination was added to earlier social ones. In fact, the move towards unified administration and law made the conditions of such discrimination more general across the country. Education was another area where this discrimination was evident.

The British paid little attention to the education of the Indians in the early years of their rule. The Charter Act of 1813 made the Company somewhat responsible for the education of Indians. However, it was assumed that the best way to do so was by promoting education among the so-called community leaders. The British Parliament stated in 1813:

> Out of the surplus revenues of India, a sum of not less than one lakh of rupees in each year shall be set apart and applied to the revival and improvement of literature and the encouragement of the learned natives of India, and for the introduction and promotion of knowledge of the sciences among the inhabitants of British territories in India, etc.[11]

The elitist bias in education remained strong. It was also pragmatic because it required much less investment than the mass education would demand. Thus the Court of Directors of the Company wrote in 1830:

> The improvements in education, however, which most effectively contribute to elevate the moral and intellectual conditions of the people, are those which concern the education of the higher classes of the persons possessing leisure and natural influence over the minds of their countrymen. By raising the standard of instruction amongst these classes, you would eventually produce a much greater and morally beneficial change in the ideas and feelings of the community than you can hope to produce by acting directly on the more numerous classes.[12]

Macaulay's Educational Minutes of 1835, with its 'downward filtration' theory, further strengthened this upper-class bias. This theory, which was later refined by John Stuart Mill, envisaged that initially a very small number of Indians would receive modern education in English. After completing their studies, this group of educated Indians was supposed to transmit this knowledge to the groups lower to them by acting as "teachers and translators of useful books, through which they would communicate to the native literature and to the native community 'that improved spirit' they had imbibed from the influence of European ideas and sentiments. The theory required the few to teach the many"[13]. Apart from the practical consideration of the expenses involved in imparting education to the masses, there was the class ideology at work here. The few who would receive education would be from the "leisured classes". John Stuart Mill declared in one of his dispatches that "the character which may be given to the classes possessed of leisure and natural influence, ultimately determines that of the whole people"[14]. In formulating this distinction between the few and many as between the leisured and labouring classes, J.S. Mill was reiterating his father's position. James Mill, in his writing on education, had earlier stated that "There are certain qualities, the possession of which is desirable in all classes. [And] There are certain qualities, the possession of which is desirable in some, not in others". He went on to explain:

> As we strive for an equal degree of justice, an equal degree of temperance, an equal degree of veracity, in the poor as in the rich, so ought we to strive for an equal degree of intelligence.... It is absolutely necessary for the existence of the human race, that labour should be performed, that food should be produced, and other things provided, which human welfare requires. A large proportion of mankind is required for this labour. Now, then, in regard to all this portion of mankind, that labours, only such a portion of time can by them be given to the acquisition of intelligence, as can be abstracted from labour.... There are degrees, therefore, of intelligence, which must be reserved to those who are not obliged to labour.[15]

In line with these arguments, the Court of Directors wrote to the Madras Government in 1830:

> It is our anxious desire to afford to the higher classes of the Natives of India the means of instruction in European sciences and of access to the literature of civilised Europe. The character which may be given to the classes possessed of leisure and natural influence ultimately determines that of the whole people.[16]

To this class bias were added the general discriminatory attitudes towards the masses, particularly the Dalits. Mountstuart Elphinstone referred to them as the "most despised" section of society and feared that "if our system of education took root among them, it would never spread farther, and in that case we might find ourselves at the head of a new class superior to the rest in useful knowledge, but hated and despised by the castes to whom these new attainments would always induce us to prefer them"[17]. Thus it was clearly assumed that the educational opportunities would be restrictive and it would be offered to those who were socially superior and belonged to the "leisured classes".

Who were these 'upper classes' in India? The Report of the Board of Education of the Bombay Presidency for the year 1850–51 outlines these as follows:

- *First* – The landowners and Jaghirdars, representatives of the former feudatories and persons in authorities under Native powers and who may be termed the Soldier class.
- *Second* – Those who have acquired wealth in trade or commerce or the commercial class.
- *Third* – The higher employees of Government.
- *Fourth* – Brahmins, with whom may be associated, though at long interval, those of higher castes of writers who live by pen such as Parbhus and Shenvis in Bombay, Kayasthas in Bengal provided they acquire a position either in learning or station.[18]

Out of these classes eligible for education, the above Report indicated, the Brahmins were socially most influential. However, they were "wretchedly poor; and in many parts of India, the term Brahmin was synonymous with 'beggar'". Therefore, "a very wide door should be opened to the children of the poor higher castes, who are willing to receive education at our hands". So far as the poor among the lower castes are concerned, the Report put the entire onus on the social prejudices and decided that it would not be judicious to do anything about it.[19]

The educational scenario witnessed some changes in the 1850s. Two important government measures were responsible for this. The Caste Disabilities Removal Act of 1850 and Wood's Educational Despatch of 1854 tried to overcome both the hindrances to Dalit education – the state's reliance on the upper classes and the upper caste opposition to Dalit education. However, both these policy formulations remained at the level of ideas and very slow movement in the direction of Dalit education took place and that too due mostly to non-state agencies. The Wood's Despatch did not altogether abandon the Filtration Theory, even though it diluted its unadulterated upper-class and Euro-centric biases. Lord Ellenborough, President of the Board of Control, in a letter to the Chairman of the Court of Directors, wrote in 1858 that "Education and civilization may descend from the higher to the inferior classes, and so communicated may impart new vigour to the community, but they will never ascend from the lower classes to those above them."[20]

The Hunter Commission of 1882 also vacillated between the Macaulay's earlier emphasis on the teaching of pure forms of European thought and English literature, and provision of practical knowledge[21] . At another level, it proposed that "no boy be refused admission to a Government college or school merely on the ground of caste". But it simultaneously stressed that "this principle be applied with due caution"[22] The nationalist intelligentsia criticised the elitist bias in government's education policies and demanded that education be provided to masses. Jugannath Sunkersett in Bombay, Bankim Chandra Chatterjee in Bengal, Dayanand Saraswati and G.K. Gokhale were some of the early nationalists and reformers who spoke in favour of mass education[23]. However, their concern remained mainly at the level of ideas. In the context of Maharashtra, Eleanor Zelliot remarks that "although the Brahmans did not initiate educational institutions, they were an important source of support"[24].

Thus, despite colonial government's occasional pronouncements in favour of a non-discriminatory educational policy, in actual practice the scales were weighed against the Dalits. In Bombay Presidency, the foundation of the Bombay Education Society in 1815 may be said to have started the process of state's initiative in education. In Bombay, four separate schools for the Indian students were opened, and, by 1855, there were 15 English colleges and schools with about 2850 students and 256 vernacular schools with 18,883 students[25]. However, before 1855, no schools for the depressed classes were opened because, as Ambedkar commented, "the deliberate policy of the British Government was to restrict the benefits of education to the poor higher castes, chiefly the Brahmins"[26]. Even after 1854 the development of the education among the Dalit castes was not much. In the 28 years between Wood's Despatch and Hunter's Commission (1882), the percentage of the Dalit and tribal students in primary education was respectively 0.87 and 0.87, in middle schools 0.14 and 0.05, and in high schools and colleges it was zero[27]. In Madras Presidency, Thomas Munro, as Governor from 1820 to 1827, did important work towards gathering information about the existing state of education. According to his findings, the untouchable classes like Pariahs, Malas and Madigas were virtually excluded from education. Munro's efforts also contributed towards opening of government schools in some small towns. But it was insignificant and his policy towards promotion of popular education was soon abandoned in favour of English education and Filtration doctrine[28]. In the wake of the Wood's Despatch, 'Rate schools' were started in Madras Presidency. In this scheme, it was the responsibility of the peasants to pay for the education of their children and maintain schools in their villages. Since the untouchables were often very poor, they could not pay and, therefore, could not derive any benefit from the scheme. In any case, this system could not continue its voluntary character and was brought under government umbrella[29]. Hunter Commission, in its report in 1884, paid little attention to the education the Dalits. The government was still wary of doing anything special for the education of the socially discriminated groups. The result was that even in 1923 there was great disparity in the level of education among different strata of population.

However, the Commission had recommended the establishment of separate schools for untouchables wherever the situation warranted. In some places, this was done in more organized manner. In 1893, the Madras Government formulated a broad scheme along these lines. However, due to the social prejudices of high caste government officials and the difficulty in getting trained teachers limited the success of these schools[30].

Table 1: School and Tertiary Education

Classes of population	*Primary education, students per 1000 of the population of the class*	*Secondary education, students per 100,000 of the population*	*College education, students per 200,000 of the population*
Advanced Hindus	119	3,000	1,000
Mahomedans	92	500	52
Intermediate class	38	140	24
Backward class	18	14	Nil (or nearly one if at all)

Source: Ambedkar, 1993:109.

IV

Among the non-state actors in the field of education the Christian missionaries were the first. By 1780s, Christian Friedrich Schwartz and his associates were running several mission schools in South India which were attended mostly by the students from upper castes.[31] During the initial decades of the nineteenth century, there were many more primary schools started by the missionaries which were open to the education of all groups, including Dalits.[32]. In fact, the missionaries were particularly interested in the education of Dalits as they offered "a most fertile ground for proselytization"[33]. However, despite their obvious interest in proselytization, the missionaries opened new vistas in the area of elementary education which would encourage other non-state initiatives. Important among these were those associated with non-Brahman and Dalit movements. Jotirao Phule, himself a product of a mission school, was the pioneer and a radical activist in this regard. Inspired by the missionary initiative, he opened a school in Pune for the girls of lower and Dalit castes. He himself and his wife, Savitribai, began teaching in the school as it was difficult to get high-caste teachers and, moreover, the school suffered from shortage of funds. The project was sustained with utmost efforts, more so because his father, upset by such unconventional move, turned him and Savitribai out of house[34]. He criticised the traditionalists who were opposed to the education of women:

> In their opinion, women should forever be kept in obedience, should not be given any knowledge, should not be well educated, should not know about religion, should not mix with men, and they bring out extracts from our Shastras in which women are so deprecated in support of these idiotic beliefs, and ask whether anything written by the great and learned sages be untrue.[35]

In 1852, he established a school for untouchables where "reading, writing and grammar, geography of the world and of India particularly, and the history of the Marathas" were taught[36]. In 1853, Phule, along with his high caste colleagues, formed a "Society for increasing education amongst Mahars, Mangs, and others". Two more schools for untouchables were opened under its auspices. Soon, however, Phule fell out of the other members of the committee over what was to be taught. Phule's increasing radicalism was evident in the nature of disagreements. According to him,

> when I started to expose the hidden cunning in the crafty books of their ancestors, they started to disagree with me. They seemed to think that there was absolutely no need to educate the atishudra students. If at all they have to be educated, giving them the basic literacy skills is enough. I was of the opinion that we should give them good education, which would give them the ability to discern between good and bad.[37]

Thus even in the mid-nineteenth century Phule was concerned about the content of education and not just about imparting any kind of education. In a memorial addressed to the Education Commission of 1882 he was very critical of "the present system of education, which, by providing ampler funds for higher education, tended to educate Brahmins and the higher classes only" and which left "the masses wallowing in poverty and ignorance"[38]. Even earlier, in his very important essay, 'Slavery', he criticised the government for "providing ampler funds and greater facilities for higher education and neglecting that of the masses"[39]. This "pernicious system of high class education"[40] had resulted in the domination of the upper classes and castes and the degradation of the lower ones. He believed that "A good deal of their poverty, their want of self-reliance, their entire dependence upon the learned and intelligent classes, is attributable to this deplorable state of education among the peasantry."[41]

Phule considered education as the most important factor for the miserable condition of peasantry and workers, or in his own diction, the Shudras and Atishudras. The opening lines of his another important essay, 'Cultivator's Whipcord', were:

> Without knowledge, intelligence was lost, without intelligence morality was lost and without morality was lost all dynamism! Without dynamism money was lost and without money the shudras sank. All this misery was caused by the lack of knowledge.[42]

The modern education and consequent knowledge was necessary to lift the masses, particularly the Shudras and Atishudras, from centuries of imposed illiteracy and ignorance on them. Without the knowledge of "Western ideas and civilization" which would erode centuries of "superstition and bigotry"[43], real enlightenment was not possible and "until real education and knowledge is available to them, the strong imprint of the scheming brahmans will not be erased from their minds. And until this is done, the farmer will not come to his senses"[44].

However, according to Phule, the problem with the colonial education was not only its upper-class orientation, but also its impractibility and its distance from the life of the people. In his memorial to the Education Commission, he pointed out that the "character of instruction given in the Government higher schools, is not at all practical, or such as is required for the necessities of ordinary life. It is only good to turn out so many clerks and schoolmasters"[45]. The teachers were "all unpractical men, and the boys who learn under them generally imbibe inactive habits and try to obtain service, to the avoidance of their hereditary or other hardy or independent professions"[46]. Such impractical education system compel the educated persons to compete for limited number of government jobs "because the course of training they receive being not of a technical or practical nature, they find great difficulty in betaking themselves to other manual or remunerative employments".[47]

Phule put forward several ideas to overcome the problems besetting the system of education. To begin with, the education should be universalized. More emphasis should be given to the primary education and Shudras and Atishudras should be encouraged to send their children to schools. In his essay, 'Slavery', Phule declared that "Let there be schools for the Sudras in every village"[48]. In his memorial to the Education Commission in 1882, he appealed for "universal education" and "larger diffusion of knowledge in the country". He further insisted that the "higher education should be so arranged as to be within easy reach of all"[49].

Secondly, the education should acquire a practical orientation and relate to the lives of the people:

> The course of instruction should consist of reading, writing Modi, and Balbodh and accounts, and a rudimentary knowledge of general history, general geography, and grammar, also an elementary knowledge of agriculture and a few lessons on moral duties and sanitation. The studies in the village schools might be fewer than those in larger villages and towns, but not less practical. In connection with lessons in agriculture, a small model farm, where practical instruction to the pupils can be given, would be a decided advantage and, if really efficiently managed, would be productive of the greatest good to the country. The text-books in use, both in the primary and Anglo-vernacular schools, require revision and recasting as much as they are not practical or progressive in their scope. Lessons on technical education and morality, sanitation and agriculture, and some useful arts, should be interspersed among them in progressive series.[50]

Phule's suggestion was that the "government should educate all the farmers ... until they become mature enough to use machines to do the usual things on the farms like European farmers"[51]. He also proposed that the Brahman teachers were not the right kind of persons to impart education because of their exclusive and discriminatory practices towards the lower caste students, and their outmoded ideas. In a tract written in 1869, he complained that the Brahman teachers "consider it polluting to teach the children of their great enemies", that is the Mahars. They also practice blatant discrimination in classrooms:

> If the children of their own caste make mistakes, they
> repeat and explain
> And give punishments wisely
> If other children make mistakes they strike them with
> their fists
> And twist their ears sharply
> When no one is watching, they beat the Shudra children and
> Make them run away.[52]

Phule's solution to this problem was:

> Appoint teachers from other castes
> Appoint those with knowledge of the truth
> Prepare a class of schoolteachers
> Only of Malis and Kunbis
> Another for Mahars and Mangs.[53]

In 1882 also he made similar suggestions to the Education Commission:

> I think teachers for primary schools should be trained, as far as possible, out of the cultivating classes, who will be able to mix freely with them and understand their wants and wishes much better than a Brahmin teacher, who generally holds himself aloof under religious prejudices. These would, moreover, exercise a more beneficial influence over the masses than teacher of other classes, and who will not feel ashamed to hold the handle of a plough or the carpenter's adze when required, and who will be able to mix themselves readily with the lower orders of society.[54]

Throughout his life Phule remained committed to the education of the masses, particularly the peasantry, the Dalits and the women. The Satyashodhak Samaj (Truth-seeking Society) founded by him also undertook this work. One of its rules for the members was that they "will strive to give enough education to our children that they may understand their rights" and "I shall not neglect to educate my boys and girls".[55] Education, particularly Western modern education, came to acquire a very important place in the Society's aims, as it did in the non-Brahman movement as a whole. In fact, it was projected as a solution for all social and religious evils. It was believed that modern education would ideologically liberate the masses from the clutches of Brahmanism, provide occupational skills for self-sustenance, facilitate the entry into government services, and reform the popular manners and eliminate the vices like drinking, dowry and laziness. The importance attached to education can be gauged from the fact that in 1875 eighteen out of twenty-nine resolutions of the Society were concerned with education[56]. In 1889, Din Bandhu Sarvajanik Sabha, founded by one of Phule's followers, displayed a slogan during the visit of Prince of Wales to Pune:

> Tell Grandma we are a happy nation.
> But 19 crores are without education.[57]

There were other important efforts towards the education of the people, particularly the lower castes. In 1893, Sayajirao Gaikwad of Baroda opened eighteen special schools for the Dalit students in his territory. It was reported that "in these schools, no fees were charged and the slates, pencils and textbooks were provided free". Moreover, by 1893, Gaikwad made the primary education compulsory in his state[58]. Vithal Ramchandra Shinde was another pioneer in the field of depressed class education. In 1905 he opened a night school for the Dalit children. In 1906, Shinde founded the Depressed Classes Mission. It witnessed rapid growth and under its auspices, several schools and hostels for the depressed class students were started. It also began vigorous campaign for the removal of untouchability. By 1912, under the Mission, there were 23 schools in 14 towns with 1,100 students and a staff of 35 teachers. In the early 1920s, Shinde got alienated from the rising Dalit generation who were more in favour of higher education than technical education which Shinde favoured. But his efforts were pioneering for Dalit education and they, to some extent, influenced the government educational policies towards the Dalits[59].

Like Gaikwad, Shahu Maharaj of Kolhapur also promoted education for the depressed classes within his territories. Another very important educational reformer in the early twentieth century was Bhaurao Patil. He was a Jain whose source of inspiration was Phule. In 1919, he founded the Rayat Shikshan Sanstha (Peasants' Education Society) under whose auspices significant educational work was undertaken. He emphasized the elimination of untouchability and the education of the masses. He organized mixed schools and hostels for the students from all castes[60]. All these efforts were able to create an atmosphere where the education of the untouchable castes could make significant progress. In case of Bombay Presidency, Eleanor Zelliot remarks that:

> the education of the Dalits in a hundred-year period before Independence was an indigenous effort. It also was, by and large, an effort performed by individuals. And it can be said that the most effective of these experiments were integrated institutions that accepted all castes and classes, but paid special attention to the inclusion and the needs of the Dalits.[61]

In South India, the missionary efforts were particularly pronounced. The missionaries opened several institutions for imparting education to the pupils of Dalit castes in Madras Presidency. It is true that their ultimate aim was to convert the Dalits to Christianity and they were remarkably successful in this in this region. However, their pioneering attempt towards the education of the untouchables created an atmosphere which prompted many others to undertake such work. Kandukuri Viresalingam and Raghupati Venkataratnam Naidu were some of the reformers who campaigned for the removal of untouchability and worked in the field of lower caste education. The activists of Brahmo Samaj and Arya Samaj also worked in this direction. In 1907, some reformers established the Andhra Deen Sangham which worked towards the uplift of the depressed castes[62]. In the 1930s, the Harijan Sevak Sangh, founded by Gandhi, did active work in this regard. In Andhra Pradesh, between 1932 and 1934, it established 41 night schools, 11 day schools, 19 hostels and 20 libraries for Dalit students. Besides this, it opened a few vocational training schools and provided many scholarships to Dalit students[63].

The aspirations of the Dalits for modern and secular education were most powerfully articulated by the Dalit leaders themselves. The initiatives taken by the Dalit leaders were earlier and more pronounced in Maharashtra and among the Mahar caste. As early as 1880, the Khandesh Gazetteer noted that some Mahars had "begun to send their boys to school"[64]. The social change among Mahars was most noticeable in the Vidarbha region of Maharashtra. Since a significant number of Mahars joined the British Indian army in the nineteenth century, they received some education and later acted as community leaders. Gopal Baba Walangkar, Subhedar Bahadur Gangaram Krishnaji and Subhedar Savadkar were some of the early Mahar leaders who raised their voices for better educational and occupational opportunities for the Dalits and mobilized them to register their protests. In 1890, Walangkar appealed to the Shakaracharya and other Hindu leaders for facilitating, among other things, the access of the untouchables to education.

Shivram Janba Kamble in Pune, Kisan Faguji Bansode in Nagpur and G.A. Gavai from Amraoti were some of the leaders who in the 1900s and 1910s worked for the education among the Dalits. Bansode, for example, established a Dalit organization in 1903 and several educational institutions, including a school for girls, by 1907. Gavai founded a 'Mahar Library' and 'Mahar Sudharak Mandal' in his village[65] From the late 1920s onwards, the leadership of Mahars in particular and the Dalits in general shifted into the hands of one person who was to become the most important Dalit leader. B.R. Ambedkar considered education as a very important means of raising the consciousness and social status of the Dalits. In 1924, he established the Bahiskrut Hitkarini Sabha which, among other things, initiated hostels, libraries, social centres and class rooms where the untouchables could study. In 1928, he founded the Depressed Classes Education Society to provide a firm footing to the Dalit education. In 1945, he established the People's Education Society under whose auspices several institutions of higher learning, including the Siddharth College, were opened. Ambedkar's belief in education and political power as the means for Dalit empowerment remained unwavering.

It was reflected in the slogan he coined for his followers: 'Educate, organize and agitate'[66].

In Hyderabad, a Dalit movement developed under the name of Adi-Hindu. Bhagyareddy Varma and Arigay Ramaswamy were its important leaders. Varma was even earlier involved in educational activities for the untouchables. About 26 primary schools with about 2,500 Dalit students were functioning under the auspices of the Adi-Hindu movement by the 1930s[67]. The content of education also came up for criticism. One Dalit poet in Andhra, Gurram Joshua, expressed it:

> Our books are as meaningless as the crops of our forefathers.
> If we confine reading to these books
> The posterity will be as learned as the trained bull
> That shakes or nods its head to the prompting of its master
> Thrust such decadent books on the heads of people
> And the tree of knowledge will never flower.[68]

V

Despite all these efforts, however, the educational status of the Dalit castes did not register any significant improvement. The situation in Bengal, Maharashtra and South India was somewhat better. For the Chamars of the United Provinces the literacy rates in 1901 and 1931 were 0.10 and 1.00 per cent. The corresponding figures for the Mahars in Maharashtra were 0.4 and 2.00 per cent[69]. In Andhra Pradesh, the literacy rates of the Dalit castes (Malas and Madigas) were 0.3 in 1901 and 1.9 in 1931.[70] The situation in other places would not have been better, except in Bengal where the literacy rate was about 5.0 per cent in 1931. Thus, although the general literacy rates in colonial India was already quite low (5.35 and 9.50 per cent in 1901 and 1931 respectively), those of the Dalits was much lower.

Table 2: Literacy and participation of depressed classes in schools in 1931

	% of total population	*% of literacy among dalits*	*% of dalits in schools*	*Literacy in general population*
India	14	1.9	NA	9.5
Bengal Presidency	14	5.0	5.4	11.1
Bihar & Orissa	15	0.6	0.4	5.3
Bombay Presidency	8	2.8	3.6	10.8
Madras	15	1.5	4.8	10.8
United Provinces	23	0.5	1.1	5.5
Central Provinces & Berar	18	1.5	1.5	6.6

Source: Modified version of table given in Nambissan, 2002:88–89.

During the post-independence period the general literacy situation, including that of the Dalits, became much better. But even then the gap between the general population and the Dalits remained significant and kept increasing.

Table 3: Literacy rates

Year	*General*	*SC*	*ST*	*Rest of population* *SC*	*ST*	*Gap*
1931	9.5	1.9	–	–	–	–
1961	24.0	10.27	8.53	27.86	17.59	19.33
1971	29.0	14.67	11.30	33.80	19.13	22.50
1981	36.17	21.38	16.35	41.22	19.84	24.87
1991	52.21	37.41	29.60	57.69	20.28	28.09

Source: Chatterjee, 2000:22.

VI

The reasons for this situation were many. To begin with, the Dalits had the weight of history against them. The Brahmanical texts had debarred them from acquiring any formal education and the mostly non-Brahman kings applied these decrees, particularly with regards to the untouchable castes. The colonial rule was beset by a dilemma. In the nineteenth century particularly, it swore by the rule of Reason and Equality. At the same time, its *raison d'etre* was exploitation of the resources of the colony and domination over its people. At some crucial points, both these streams joined. In the hands of the colonialists, the post-Enlightenment discourse of Reason and Civilization became the discourse of domination and creation and maintenance of hierarchies. Such a project sought cooperation and alliance with the locally dominant groups. In India particularly, where the British were far outnumbered, their attempt was to seek alliance with and provide patronage to the dominant social and political groups. They were extremely wary of disturbing existing social relations. Therefore, although they aroused the desires of the Dalits by their occasional rhetoric of equality, they did little in practice to enforce the norm of social equality. Till 1813, the colonial government did not bother about education at all. When, after the Charter Act of 1813, it was compelled to undertake the responsibility for education, the investment was limited to the minimum and it was consciously decided to limit the education to the higher classes of Indian society. Even when they realized that the access of the Dalits to the education was negligible due to poverty and social discrimination, nothing was done to support them, or even to provide them equal opportunities. Even after 1850s, when the law formulated that social/caste discrimination should not be permitted in schools, the government dragged its feet and when it failed to enforce the law in common schools, it opened some separate schools for the Dalits. But its reluctance to invest in education resulted in extremely slow development in Dalit education. Where the government failed, the non-government actors succeeded to some extent. The missionaries, the non-Brahman and Dalit activists, the nationalists and reformers, and some other individuals opened and ran common schools where students of all castes studied together. They also provided special support to the socially discriminated and poor students. Their efforts were also successful in stimulating the government in the 1930s to formulate certain schemes for the education of socially disadvantaged sections of society, which included the Dalit castes. But, despite all these, the actual progress of education in general and for the Dalits in particular remained extremely limited in colonial India.

References

Ambedkar, B.R. (1993), *Dr. Babasaheb Ambedkar: Writings and Speeches*, vol. 12, edited by Vasant Moon, Education Department, Government of Maharashtra.

Bhattacharya, Sabyasachi (2002), 'Introduction: An Approach to Education and Inequality', in Sabyasachi Bhattacharya (ed.), *Education and the Disprivileged: Nineteenth and Twentieth Century India*, Orient Longman, New Delhi.

Chatterjee, S.K. (2000), *Educational Development of Scheduled Castes: Looking Ahead*, Gyan Publishing House, New Delhi.

Dreze, Jean and Sen, Amartya (2002), *India: Development and Participation*, OUP, New Delhi.

Kumar, Krishna (1991), Political Agenda of Education: A Study of Colonialist and Nationalist Ideas, Sage, New Delhi.

Mendelsohn, Oliver and Vicziany, Marika (1998), The Unouchables: Subordination, Poverty and the State in Modern India, CUP, Cambridge.

Nambissan, Geetha (2002), 'Equity in Education? The Schooling of Dalit Children in India', in Ghanshyam Shah (ed.), *Dalits and the State*, Concept Publishing Co., New Delhi.

Nancharaiah, G. (2002), 'Dalit Education and Economic Inequality', in Sabyasachi Bhattacharya (ed.), *Education and the Disprivileged : Nineteenth and Twentieth Century India*, Orient Longman, New Delhi.

O'Hanlon, Rosalind (1985), Caste, Conflict, and Ideology: Mahatma Jotirao Phule and Low Caste Protest in Nineteenth-Century Western India, CUP, Cambridge.

Omvedt, Gail (1994), Dalits and the Democratic Revolution: Dr. Ambedkar and the Dalit Movement in Colonial India, Sage, New Delhi.

Phule, Jotirao (2002), edited by Deshpande, G.P., *Selected Writings of Jotirao Phule*, LeftWord Books, New Delhi.

Pinto, Ambrose (2002), 'Culture, Values and Dalits in Higher Education', in Sabyasachi Bhattacharya (ed.), *Education and the Disprivileged: Nineteenth and Twentieth Century India*, Orient Longman, New Delhi.

Satyanarayana, A. (2002), 'Growth of Education among the Dalit-Bahujan Communities in Modern Andhra, 1893–1947', in Sabyasachi Bhattacharya (ed.), *Education and the Disprivileged : Nineteenth and Twentieth Century India*, Orient Longman, New Delhi.

Satyanarayana, A. (2005), Dalits and Upper Castes: Essays in Social History, Kanishka, New Delhi.

Viswanathan, Gauri (1989), Masks of Conquest: Literary Study and British Rule in India, OUP, New Delhi.

Yagati, Chinna Rao (2002), 'Education and Identity Formation among Dalits in Colonial Andhra', in Sabyasachi Bhattacharya (ed.), *Education and the Disprivileged: Nineteenth and Twentieth Century India*, Orient Longman, New Delhi.

Zelliot, Eleanor (1998), From Untouchable to Dalit: Essays on the Ambedkar Movement, Manohar, New Delhi.

Zelliot, Eleanor (2002), 'Experiments in Dalit Education : Maharashtra, 1850–1947', in Sabyasachi Bhattacharya (ed.), *Education and the Disprivileged: Nineteenth and Twentieth Century India*, Orient Longman, New Delhi.

Endnotes

1. Jean Dreze and Amartya Sen, *India: Development and Participation* (New Delhi: OUP, 2002), pp. 38–39.
2. Ibid, p. 143.
3. Ibid, p. 144.
4. Gauri Viswanathan, Masks of Conquest: Literary Study and British Rule in India, (New Delhi: OUP, 1989), p. 167.
5. Sabyasachi Bhattacharya, 'Introduction: An Approach to Education and Inequality' in Sabyasachi Bhattacharya (ed.), *Education and the Disprivileged: Nineteenth and Twentieth Century India* (New Delhi: Orient Longman, 2002), pp. 4–5.
6. Krishna Kumar, Political Agenda of Education: A Study of Colonialist and Nationalist Ideas (New Delhi: Sage, 1991), pp. 14–15.
7. Ibid, pp. 23–24.
8. Ibid, p. 189.
9. Ibid, p. 192.
10. Bhattacharya, 'Introduction', pp. 13–15.
11. Quoted in G. Nancharaiah, 'Dalit Education and Economic Inequality', in Bhattacharya (ed.), *Education and the Disprivileged*, p. 164.
12. Quoted in B.R Ambedkar, *Dr. Babasaheb Ambedkar: Writings and Speeches*, vol. 12, edited by Vasant Moon (Education Department, Government of Maharashtra, 1993), p. 96.
13. Viswanathan, *Masks of Conquest*, p. 149.
14. Quoted in ibid, p. 149.
15. Quoted in ibid, pp. 149–150.
16. Quoted in Ambedkar, *Writings and Speeches*, vol. 12, p. 98.
17. Quoted in ibid, 152.
18. Quoted in ibid, p. 99.
19. Given in ibid, pp. 99–101.
20. Quoted in ibid, p. 104.
21. Viswanathan, *Masks of Conquest*, pp. 154–155.
22. Quoted in Geetha Nambissan, 'Equity in Education? The Schooling of Dalit

Children in India', in Ghanshyam Shah (ed.), *Dalits and the State* (New Delhi: Concept Publishing Co., 2002), p. 81.
23. Bhattacharya, 'Introduction', pp. 9–10.
24. Eleanor Zelliot, 'Experiments in Dalit Education: Maharashtra, 1850–1947', in Sabyasachi Bhattacharya (ed.), *Education and the Disprivileged*, p. 47.
25. Ambedkar, *Writings and Speeches*, vol. 12, pp. 93–94.
26. Ibid. p. 101.
27. Ibid, pp. 102–103.
28. A. Satyanarayana, 'Growth of Education among the Dalit-Bahujan Communities in Modern Andhra, 1893–1947', in Bhattacharya (ed.), *Education and the Disprivileged,* p. 65. Also, Chinna Rao Yagati, 'Education and Identity Formation among Dalits in Colonial Andhra', in Bhattacharya (ed.), *Education and the Disprivileged* pp. 88–89.
29. Yagati, Ibid, p. 90.
30. Ibid, pp. 91–92.
31. Ibid, p. 88.
32 . Satyanarayana, 'Growth of Education among the Dalit-Bahujan Communities in Modern Andhra', p. 64.
33. Rosalind O'Hanlon, Caste, Conflict, and Ideology: Mahatma Jotirao Phule and Low Caste Protest in Nineteenth-Century Western India, (Cambridge: CUP, 1985), p. 6.
34. Ibid, p. 118.
35. Quoted in ibid, p. 119.
36. Eleanor Zelliot, 'Experiments in Dalit Education : Maharashtra, 1850–1947', in Sabyasachi Bhattacharya (ed.), *Education and the Disprivileged*, p. 36.
37. Jotirao Phule, edited by G.P. Deshpande, *Selected Writings of Jotirao Phule*, (New Delhi: LeftWord Books, 2002), p. 94.
38. Ibid, p. 103.
39. Ibid, p. 33.
40. Ibid, p. 35.
41. Ibid, p. 105.
42. Ibid, p. 117.
43. Ibid, p. 33.
44. Ibid, p. 173.
45. Ibid, p. 111.
46. Ibid, p. 107.
47. Ibid, p. 112.
48. Ibid, p. 35.
49. Ibid, p. 111.
50. Ibid, pp. 107–108.
51. Ibid, p. 180.
52. Quoted in O'Hanlon, *Caste, Conflict and Ideology*, p. 214.
53. Quoted in Ibid, p. 215.
54. Phule, *Selected Writings*, p. 107.
55. O'Hanlon, Caste, Conflict and Ideology, p. 231; and Eleanor Zelliot, From Untouchable to Dalit: Essays on the Ambedkar Movement, (New Delhi: Manohar, 1998), p. 40.

56. O'Hanlon, *Caste, Conflict and Ideology*, pp. 233–235.
57. Zelliot, *From Untouchable to Dalit*, p. 39.
58. Zelliot, 'Experiments in Dalit Education', p. 38.
59. Ibid, pp. 39–42.
60. Ibid, pp. 43–46.
61. Ibid, p. 48.
62. See, Yagati, 'Education and Identity Formation among Dalits in Colonial Andhra'.
63. Satyanarayana, 'Growth of Education among the Dalit-Bahujan Communities in Modern Andhra', pp. 71–72.
64. Zelliot, *From Untouchable to Dalit*, p. 35.
65. Ibid, p. 65; and Gail Omvedt, Dalits and the Democratic Revolution: Dr. Ambedkar and the Dalit Movement in Colonial India, (New Delhi: Sage, 1994), p. 109.
66. Zelliot, *From Untouchable to Dalit*, p. 159; and Geetha Nambissan, 'Equity in Education? The Schooling of Dalit Children in India', in Ghanshyam Shah (ed.), *Dalits and the State* (New Delhi: Concept Publishing Co., 2002), pp. 84–85.
67. Omvedt, *Dalits and the Democratic Revolution*, p. 121; and Yagati, 'Education and Identity Formation among Dalits in Colonial Andhra', pp. 105–106.
68. Quoted in Yagati, p. 105.
69. Oliver Mendelsohn and Marika Vicziany, *The Unouchables: Subordination, Poverty and the State in Modern India* (Cambridge: CUP,1998), p. 141.
70. A. Satyanarayana, *Dalits and Upper Castes: Essays in Social History* (New Delhi: Kanishka, 2005), p. 52.

15

Recent Developments in Indian Migration to Australia

(with Special Reference to Academics)

Graeme Hugo and Gouranga Lal Dasvarma

Indian migration to Australia has a long history but it has experienced substantial change in recent years. Indian migration to Australia has increased in scale and diversity which has important implications for the development of linkages between the two countries. The present paper outlines some of those developments and discusses some of the implications. After analyzing the major changes in migration between Australia and India in recent years it focuses on an important and growing component of Indian migration to Australia – that of academics, scientists and researchers. It is shown that there will be an unprecedented increase in demand for academics in Australia over the next two decades due to a highly imbalanced age structure among Australian university staff and that the Indians will be particularly well placed to compete in this market. Finally, some observations are made of the implications of the study for future migration between India and Australia.

The paper draws upon a number of sources of data. Australia has some of the most comprehensive and accurate data on international migration in the world. Firstly, the Australian population census has a set of questions relating to international migration and these are used to show the changes in the stock of India-born population in Australia and some of the features of Indian university staff. All persons entering or leaving Australia are required to complete a card so there is excellent flow data on all arrivals and departures. These are divided into three categories:

Permanent Movements

- Immigrants are persons arriving with the intention of settling permanently in Australia.
- Emigrants are Australian residents (including former settlers) departing with the stated intention of staying abroad permanently.[1]

Long Term Movements

- Overseas arrivals of visitors with the intended or actual length of stay in Australia of 12 months or more.

- Departures of Australian residents with intended or actual length of stay abroad of 12 months or more.

Short Term Movements

- Travellers whose intended or actual stay in Australia or abroad is less than 12 months.

These data allow detailed analysis by age, birthplace, sex, occupation, origin and destination to be undertaken. The secondary data is currently being augmented by a survey of Indian academics in Australia and a number of in-depth interviews with Indian members of the staff of Australian universities. However, at the time of writing this survey was still in process so its results cannot be employed in this paper.

Indian Migration to Australia

Table 1 shows the growth of Australia's India-born population.[2] The first two post-war decades saw a very slow growth of the India-born but the bulk of the immigration was of Anglo-Indians and persons with two European origin parents. This saw a doubling of the India-born population. However, with the breaking down of the White Australia policy in the 1960s and its eventual total abolition in the early 1970s the tempo of Indian immigration to Australia increased so that Australia's India-born population doubled in the 1960s and increased by 47 per cent in the 1970s. This pattern of rapid growth continued

Table 1: India-born persons in Australia, 1861–2005

Census Year	*India-born population*	*Intercensal per cent per annum growth*
1861*	2,500	
1901*	7,760	+2.9
1947*	8,162	+1.1
1954	11,957	+5.6
1961	14,167	+2.5
1966	15,754	+2.1
1971	29,212	+13.1
1976	37,586	+5.2
1981	42,930	+2.7
1986	47,820	+2.2
1991	61,602	+5.2
1996	77,551	+4.7
2001	95,452	+4.2
2005	138,662	+8.5

* Refers to the former British colony of India (i.e. present day India and Pakistan).

Source: Australian censuses.

in the 1980s (43.5%) and 1990s (55%). However, the growth has been even more substantial over the 2000–2005 period when the India-born population of Australia increased by 45 per cent to reach 138,662 in mid 2005.

There have been, however, considerable annual fluctuations in the flow of Indian settlers to Australia as Figure 1 demonstrates. This shows that the numbers were quite small in the overall high immigration years of the first two post-war decades but the revocation of the White Australia regulations in the late 1960s and early 1970s saw an upsurge of immigration.

The overall downturn of immigration to Australia in the mid-1970s was also experienced by Indians but the tempo increased in the 1980s and reached unprecedentedly high levels in the 1990s. A similar pattern is evident when we examine the proportion which Indians have made up of the total immigration inflow over the post-war period (Figure 2). However, it has been in recent years that the largest settler inflows occurred with the numbers arriving in Australia increasing from 5,091 in 2001–02 to 11,286 in 2005–06.

The settler flows shown in Figure 1, however, only represent part of the contribution of Indian migration to Australian population growth in recent years. It is shown later that there has been a substantial increase in non-permanent migration from India to Australia over the last decade. One of the impacts of this has been an increasing number of persons who enter Australia initially as temporary residents but subsequently apply for and gain permanent residency. Indeed in 2005–06 26.8 per cent of the immigrant gain in the Australian population was due to onshore migration.

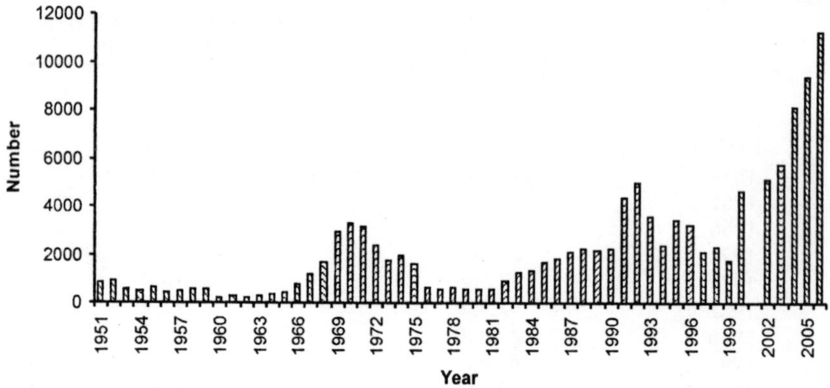

Figure 1: Australia: Immigrants from India, 1951–2006

Note: Data from 1999–2000 comprise immigrants by country of birth. Data prior to this date comprise immigrants by country of last residence. From 1960, data are for financial years. Prior to this data are for calendar years. Data for 2001 are not available.

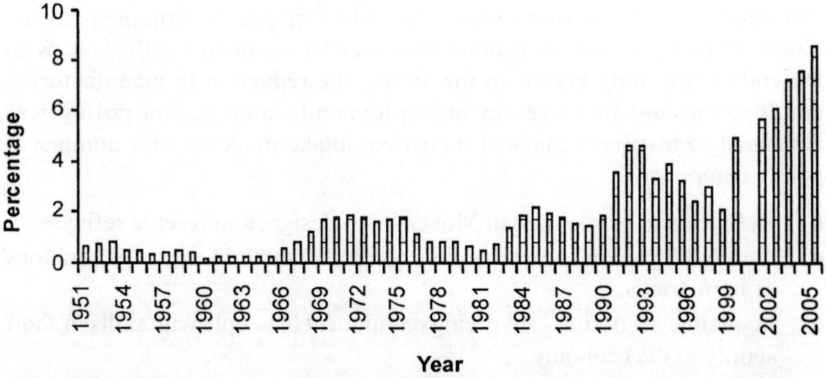

Figure 2: Immigrants from India as a percentage of total immigrants, 1951–2006

Source: CBCS Demography Bulletins; DIMIA Australian Immigration Consolidated Statistics and Immigration Update; ABS Migration Australia.

Note: Data from 1999–2000 comprise immigrants by country of birth. Data prior to this date comprise immigrants by country of last residence. From 1960, data are for financial years. Prior to this data are for calendar years. Data for 2001 are not available.

Table 2 shows that "onshore" arrivals for India have increased significantly in recent years. In 2005–06 India was the third largest origin nation for settler arrivals (after United Kingdom and New Zealand) and the third largest origin nation for onshore arrivals (after China and the United Kingdom).

Source: CBCS Demography Bulletins; DIMIA Australian Immigration Consolidated Statistics and Immigration Update; ABS Migration Australia

Table 2: Australia: Permanent additions to Australian population from India, 2001–2006

Year	*Onshore*	*Offshore Arrivals*
2001–02	2,696	5,091
2002–03	2,503	5,783
2003–04	3,224	8,135
2004–05	3,464	9,414
2005–06	4,012	11,286

Source: DIMA Immigration Update, various volumes.

Immigration to Australia is a highly planned and controlled process. In the first three post-war decades the imperatives of Australian immigration policy were both economic and demographic. On the one hand, there were massive labour shortages in the post-war boom period and labour – skilled, semi-skilled and unskilled – was needed for the massive growth in manufacturing. Also, there was a 'populate or perish' argument in the aftermath of the nation being almost invaded by Japan during the war. With the end of the 'long boom' in the 1970s, the reduction in manufacturing employment and increases in unemployment, immigration policy was redefined to involve a planned numerical intake made up of a number of policy components:

- Refugee and Humanitarian Movement – designed to resettle refugees.
- Family Migration – enabling family members to join earlier generations of immigrants.
- Economic Migration – involving recruitment of people with skills in short supply in the economy.
- Special Categories – involving mainly New Zealanders, people with special talents, etc.

Over the years there has been a fluctuation in the significance of the various components of immigration. In the most recent period there has been a deliberate policy to increase the proportion of skilled workers in the immigration intake as is apparent in Figure 3.

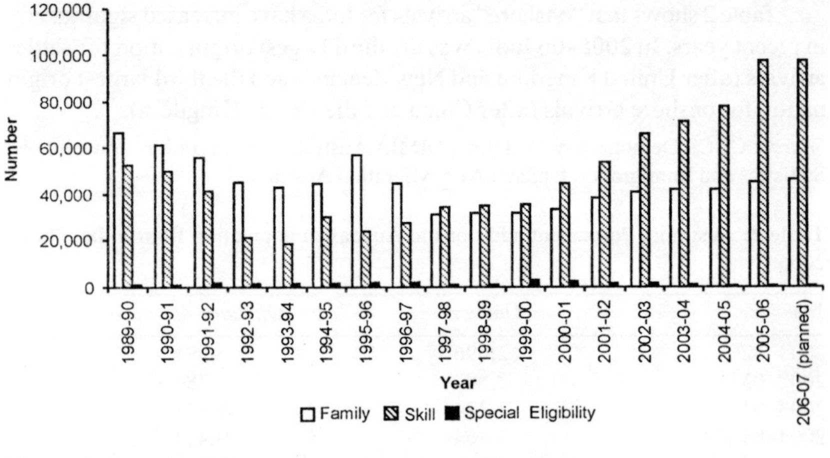

Figure 3: Australia: Migration program outcomes by stream

Source: DIMIA Population Flows: Immigration Aspects, various issues; http://www.immi.gov.au/media/statistics/statistical-info/visa-grants/migrant.htm, accessed 24th October 2006

Settler arrivals from India have a disproportionately large group of skilled migrants as Table 3 demonstrates. Almost three quarters of settler arrivals from Southern Asia are skilled migrants.

Table 3: Australia: Visa categories of settler arrivals from Southern Asia and total, 2005–06

	Settler Arrivals from Southern Asia		*Total Settler Arrivals*	
Migration Stream	*No.*	*%*	*No.*	*%*
Family Migration	3,833	23.9	34,771	26.4
Skill Migration	11,690	72.9	59,507	45.3
Special Eligibility	—	—	104	0.1
Humanitarian	23	0.1	12,113	9.2
Non-Program Migration	496	3.1	25,098	19.0
Total	16,042	100.0	131593	100.0

Source: DIMA Immigration Update.

Non-Permanent Migration

In post-war Australia there has been bi-partisan agreement that permanent settlement of a significant number of overseas migrations is desirable and accordingly each post-war government has had an active Immigration Program while the non-permanent labour migration encouraged by some other OECD nations during this period was strongly opposed. There has been no challenging the notion that the permanent settlement paradigm dominated Australian thinking and policy regarding international migration. However, there has been a change. In response to major changes in the Australian economy, internationalization of labour markets and globalization forces more generally, there has been a major shift in policy which has allowed entry of large numbers of people who have the right to work in Australia on a non-permanent basis. It is argued elsewhere that this represents a parametric change in Australian immigration policy. Nevertheless, this type of visa entry has not been extended to unskilled and low skilled areas and has been strictly only open to people with skills in demand and entrepreneurs. The growth of the main temporary migration visa categories in Australia since 1996 is shown in Figure 4.

The Temporary Business Visa category was introduced in 1996 and a DIMA points out:

> The employer sponsored temporary business visas allow employers to fill skill shortages from overseas and assess new ideas, skills and technology. The visa holders tend to be highly skilled and have relatively high income levels and therefore able to contribute to economic growth through improved productivity and increased demand for goods and services. The entry of managers and skilled specialists under these categories can also enhance Australia's ability to compete in international markets.

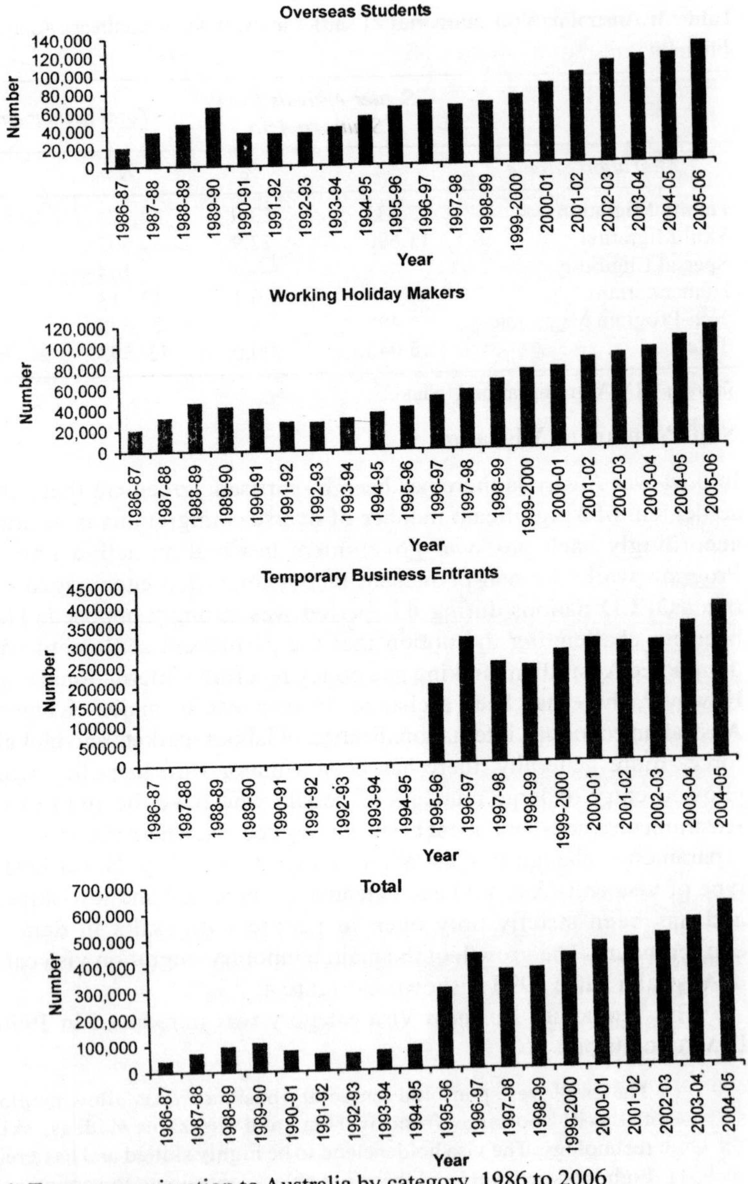

Figure 4: Temporary migration to Australia by category, 1986 to 2006

Source: DIMIA Population Flows: Immigration Aspects, various issues. http://www.immi.gov.au/media/statistics/study/_pdf/2006_visa_grants/oct_Offshore_Grants.pdf and http://www.immi.gov.au/media/statistics/study/tempentstat.htm, accessed 24th October 2006.

The Indian population have been an important part of the temporary business migration to Australia. An important temporary entry group which has greatly increased in significance is that of students. Australia has a greater ratio of overseas to local students in its tertiary education institutions than any other OECD nation. In 2005, 163,930 students were studying in Australian tertiary education institutions and Table 4 shows the main origin countries of these students in recent years.

Table 4: Total overseas students by top 10 source countries in higher education in Australia, 1999–2005

Country	*1999*	*2000*	*2001*	*2002*	*2003*	*2004*	*2005*
Singapore	8,109	8,647	8,712	10,815	10,317	9,229	8,349
Malaysia	9,545	9,866	9,467	12,443	13,781	15,895	15,375
Hong Kong	5,922	6,502	6,790	9,304	10,969	10,974	10,703
Indonesia	7,799	9,283	9,516	11,088	10,748	10,542	9,543
China	2,870	3,712	6,268	13,466	19,368	30,203	40,054
India	3,143	4,374	5,568	7,716	10,513	17,853	22,279
Thailand	2,398	2,716	3,031	4,598	5,300	5,721	5,252
Taiwan	2,232	2,440	2,677	3,342	3,512	4,165	3,964
Korea, South	1,883	2,174	2,365	3,230	3,594	4,976	5,380
Japan/USA/ Bangladesh*	1,605	1,762	1,875	7,868	8,913	3,371	3,657
Sub-Total	45,506	51,476	56,272	83,870	97,015	112,929	124,556
Other Countries	15408	21241	25465	35012	39792	38375	39374
Total	60914	72717	81737	118882	136807	151304	163930

Source: Tan.

In 2005 there were 22,279 Indian tertiary students in Australia, second only to China as major origins of foreign students. It will be noted that the numbers have increased sevenfold since 1999 and over that time India has gone from being the fifth largest to the second largest foreign student group.

What are the causes of the steep increase in the numbers of students coming to Australia from India after 2001? There are a number of hypotheses that could be put forward and all undoubtedly have played a part. Firstly, and obviously, the effects of 9/11 may have had an influence both in encouraging students to avoid the United States as a destination as well as a tightening of entry criteria for studying in the United States.[3] Secondly it may have been in response to initiatives taken by the Australian Government to facilitate foreign students in Australia on temporary visas applying for and getting permanent residence in Australia:

- Since 1999 a series of reforms have made it possible for completing overseas students to apply for permanent residence without returning to their home country.

- In 2005 overseas students who studied at a "regional"[4] university would be given an extra five points in the Points Assessment Test sat by applicants for permanent residence as skilled migrants in addition to extra points for an Australian qualification. To what extent are Indian students seeing student migration as an initial preliminary stage in permanent migration to Australia is not known at present although it undoubtedly operates to some extent.
- A further factor, which explains the upturn in Indian student migration to Australia undoubtedly, is the upturn in recruitment activity of individual Australian educational institutions as well as the Australian Government in India. Other factors may include a network effect of students following relatives and friends who moved earlier and increased significance of study in Australia being significantly cheaper than in the United States and several other OECD nations.

Table 5: Australia: Long term movement to and from India and Australia, 1993–94 to 2005–06

Period	*Long Term Resident*			*Long Term Visitor*			*Total Long Term Net Migration*
	In	*Out*	*Net*	*In*	*Out*	*Net*	
1993-94	607	510	97	915	563	352	449
1994-95	704	550	154	1,453	701	752	906
1995-96	696	626	70	2,441	1,006	1,435	1,505
1996-97	712	694	18	2,903	1,596	1,307	1,325
1997-98	711	699	12	4,461	2,300	2,161	2,173
1998-99	631	687	-56	5,321	2,330	2,991	2,935
1999-00	718	643	75	6,048	3,459	2,589	2,664
2000-01	600	691	-91	5,871	3,973	1,898	1,807
2001-02	755	622	133	5,216	2,410	2,806	2,939
2002-03	758	641	117	7,100	3,009	4,091	4,208
2003-04	813	673	140	11,212	3,356	7,856	7,996
2004-05	1,041	866	175	13,718	5,113	8,605	8,780
2005-06	1,118	1,057	61	18,628	6,598	12,030	12,091
Total	9,257	8,449	808	84,372	35,851	48,521	49,329

Source: DIMA unpublished tables.

It is apparent that India has participated in the substantial expansion of temporary migration to Australia, although until recently this was not to the same extent as some other Asian groups. Table 5 shows that there has been a major increase in the number of India-born persons visiting Australia on a long term basis. The numbers doubled between 1992 and 1996, between 1996 and 1998 and again between 1998 and 2000 and there was a levelling off after the September 11 incident which dampened international migration generally. Table 5 shows, however, that there was a major increase long term movement of Indians from 5,217 in 2001–02 to 7,100 the following year and then to 11,212 in 2003–04. However the exponential increase continued and in 2005–06 there were 18,628 long term visitor arrivals from India. Hence there has been a very rapid uptake of the temporary settler visa categories by Indians in the last two years.

There has been a significant increase in the numbers of Indians living temporarily in Australia on temporary resident visas. Table 6 provides some insights into the recent rapid growth of Indians temporarily resident in Australia. It shows a substantial growth in all categories between 2005 and 2006. It is important to stress that the temporary residents are an even more skilled group than permanent migrants since the eligibility criteria are even more selective on skill than is the case for permanent migration.

Table 6: Changes in numbers of Indians with temporary residence permits in Australia, 2005–06

Visa category	*2005*	*2006*
457 visas	4,007	5,889
Students	17,034	23,43
Other Temporary Residents	5,947	7,443
Visitors	5,952	7,540

Source: DIMA 2006.

Table 7: Australia: Short term movement to and from India and Australia, 1993–94 to 2005–06

	Short Term Resident		*Short Term Visitor*	
Year	*Return*	*Depart*	*Arrive*	*Depart*
1993-94	25,000	26,257	10,614	10,419
1994-95	29,224	28,101	14,566	13,940
1995-96	33,169	38,296	19,022	18,263
1996-97	35,966	35,404	23,951	22,023
1997-98	37,998	38,806	28,088	27,111
1998-99	39,863	40,281	31,326	30,409
1999-00	37,810	41,242	38,614	37,919
2000-01	46,081	48,517	45,620	45,875
2001-02	Data not available for 2001-02			
2002-03	48,954	46,653	41,247	37,697
2003-04	60,565	60,555	53,818	52,707
2004-05	80,261	84,040	59,231	59,814
2005-06	93,217	99,186	78,903	78,612

Source: DIMA unpublished tables.

It is also interesting to note shifts in short term movement in recent years. Table 7 shows that there has been an increase in both Australian movement to India and that in the opposite direction. In particular, Indian short term movement (involving primarily tourists and short term business visitors) to Australia has increased substantially – doubling between 1995 and 2000. The post-September 11 period saw a lull in movement but it increased substantially in 2005–06.

In sum there has bee a substantial increase in all forms of movement from India to Australia in the last few years.

Movement from Australia to India

There is a tendency for Australia to be categorised as a purely immigration country but, in fact, it is also a country of significant emigration. Figure 5 shows that in recent years, departures on a long-term or permanent basis have been very substantial in relation to the intake of immigrants. Former settlers have formed a major part of the outflow as scene in Australia and the fluctuations in its numbers are very much related to earlier levels of immigration. With an increase in the skill profile in immigration we can expect an increase in settler loss since skilled migrants have a greater chance of remigrating than Family migrants.

In 2005–06 permanent and long-term departures (258,141) reached unprecedented levels and the proportion which was Australian-born among the permanent departures reached its highest ever levels (55%). It has been demonstrated elsewhere that the emigration outflow is slightly more skilled than the immigration intake. Table 8 shows that both permanent (settler) and long term arrivals from India are highly concentrated in the most skilled categories.

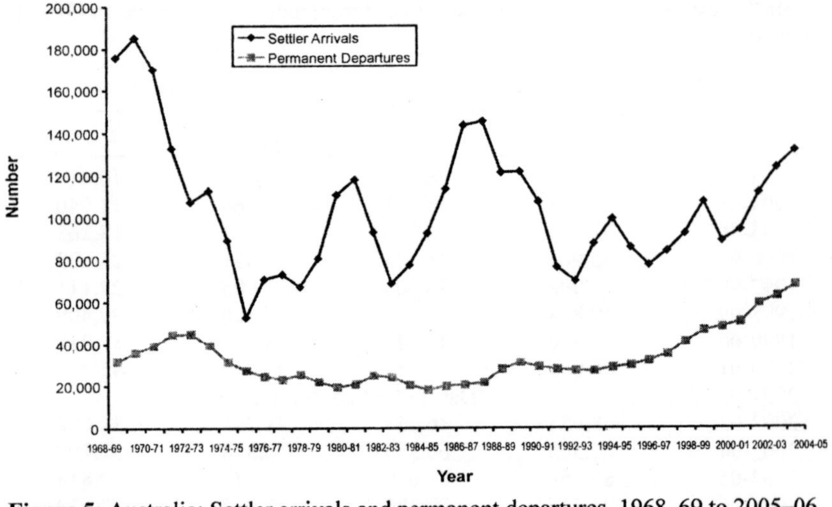

Figure 5: Australia: Settler arrivals and permanent departures, 1968–69 to 2005–06

Source: DIMA.

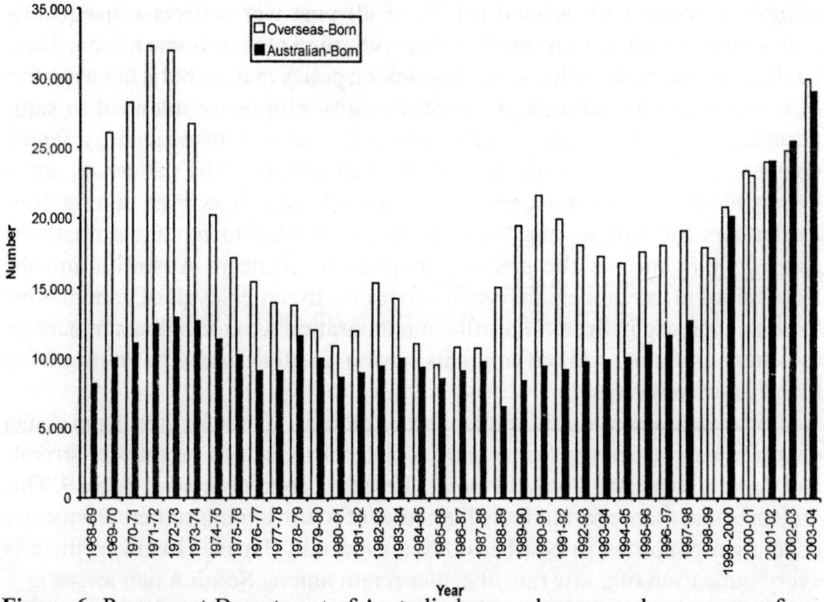

Figure 6: Permanent Department of Australia-born and overseas-born persons from Australia, 1959–60 to 2003–04

Source: DIMA.

Table 8: Australia: Occupation of permanent and long term arrival from India, 1997–98 to 2005–06

	SettlerArrivals		*Long TermArrivals*	
	No.	*%*	*No.*	*%*
Managers & Administrators	1,061	5.9	1,994	10.0
Professionals	11,110	62.1	12,329	62.0
Associate Professionals	1,561	8.7	2,254	11.3
Tradespersons	2,092	11.7	886	4.5
Advanced Clerical and Service Workers	351	2.0	145	0.7
Intermediate Clerical, Sales and Service	995	5.6	1,094	5.5
Intermediate Production and Transport Workers	80	0.4	106	0.5
Elementary Clerical, Sales, Service Workers	581	3.2	997	5.0
Labourers	59	0.3	92	0.5
	17,890	100.0	19,897	100.0

Source: DIMA unpublished data.

Settler loss has been an important feature of the post-war Australian migration scene with around a fifth of all post-war settlers subsequently emigrating from Australia, most of them returning to their home nation. There has been concern about this settler loss among policy makers but it has a number of components including a group of migrants who never intended to settle permanently in Australia as well as people who are influenced by family changes, are not able to adjust to life in Australia, etc. The pattern of settler loss while it varies between birthplace groups (e.g. it is high among New Zealanders but low among Vietnamese) has tended to remain a relatively consistent feature of the post-war migration scene in Australia and the fluctuations in its numbers are very much related to earlier levels of immigration. With an increase in the skill profile in immigration we can expect an increase in settler loss since skilled migrants have a greater chance of re-migrating than Family migrants.

A rough indication of contemporary patterns of settler loss from Asian countries can be derived from comparing the birthplace of permanent arrivals and departures to and from Australia. These data are presented in Table 9. This indicates that there are relatively high rates of return among settlers from more developed countries in Northeast Asia, especially Japan. However, there is every indication of a low rate of settler return among South Asian arrivals.

Table 9: Australia: Selected Asian country – overseas and Australia-born permanent arrivals and departures, 1994–95 to 2004–05

Region/Country of Origin	*Settler Arrivals*	*Overseas-born Departures*	*Australia-born Departures*	*Total Departures*	*Permanent Departures as Per cent of Settler Arrivals*
South East Asia					
Cambodia	4,995	282	177	459	9.2
Thailand	11,814	2,700	2,817	5,517	46.7
Viet Nam	24,382	3,855	1,284	5,139	21.1
Indonesia	26,879	4,928	3,891	8,819	32.8
Malaysia	23,049	2,666	2,807	5,473	23.7
Philippines	34,579	1,608	1,103	2,711	7.8
Singapore	29,843	7,658	11,403	19,061	63.9
Total South East Asia	158,977	24,357	24,593	48,950	30.8
North East Asia					
China	66,172	13,223	4,099	17,322	26.2
Hong Kong	33,905	23,206	11,042	34,248	101.0
Taiwan	13,473	5,737	758	6,495	48.2
Japan	7,754	3,063	3,855	6,918	89.2
Korea, Rep of	7,854	2,461	674	3,135	39.9
Total North East Asia	129,846	47,896	20,618	68,514	52.8

(*Contd.*)

(*Contd.*)

Region/Country of Origin	*Settler Arrivals*	*Overseas-born Departures*	*Australia-born Departures*	*Total Departures*	*Permanent Departures as Per cent of Settler Arrivals*
Southern Asia					
Bangladesh	4,312	66	21	87	2.0
India	38,279	712	450	1,162	3.0
Pakistan	12,209	154	84	238	1.9
Sri Lanka	12,992	273	127	400	3.1
Afghanistan	1,289	25	18	43	3.3
Total Southern Asia	69,910	1,259	792	2,051	2.9
Total Asia	358,733	73,512	46,003	119,515	33.3

Source: DIMA.

It will be noted that permanent departures to India over the last few years has been very low especially when compared to the number of permanent additions from India to the population in these years (11,359; 12,878 and 15,294). There are more overseas-born than Australia-born reflecting the fact that the bulk of the outflow is of former Indian settlers returning home, although the proportion of settlers who return is one of the smallest of all nations. It is interesting however that the number of India-born leaving Australia, while still small, is substantially larger than the numbers of overseas-born moving to India. This reflects an interesting pattern in Indian migration to Australia, namely the onward migration to a third country following a "transit" stay in Australia. This was found to exist in a very interesting field study of Indian Information Technology workers in Australia. This found a pattern of IT workers from India migrating to Australia, gaining permanent residency but then seeking to move to the United States. However, Australia was seen as more than a means of getting to the United States. It was seen also as a form of insurance whereby workers who were not successful in the US or who were victims of the collapse of the IT industry could return to Australia.

Table 10: Permanent migration from Australia to India, 2003–06.

Year	*Total Departures to*		
	Australia-born	*Overseas-born*	*India-born*
2003–04	71	94	339
2004–05	75	122	426
2005–06	121	144	446

Source: DIMA 2006.

There is then a clear pattern that the great majority of Indians settle down in Australia. It is however still relatively early in terms of high levels of migration to

Australia and return migration can be expected to increase in the future although it seems likely that they will have one of the lowest return rates of any group of settlers. It is apparent however that there has been a considerable amount of travel on a temporary basis back to India building the Australian Indian community.

Figures 7 and 8 show the large and increasing volume of long term and short term movement from Australia to India in recent years. This connection between settlers maintaining strong linkages with their home country is an important dimension for the future.

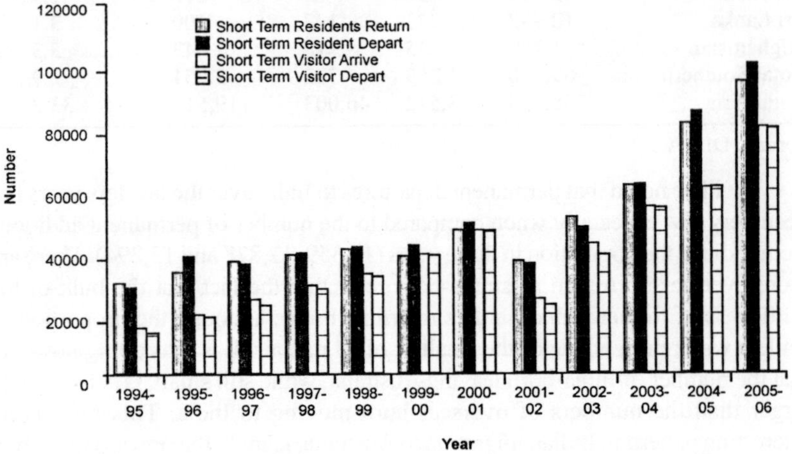

Figure 7: Short term movement to and from India, 1994–95 to 2005–06

Source: DIMA unpublished data.

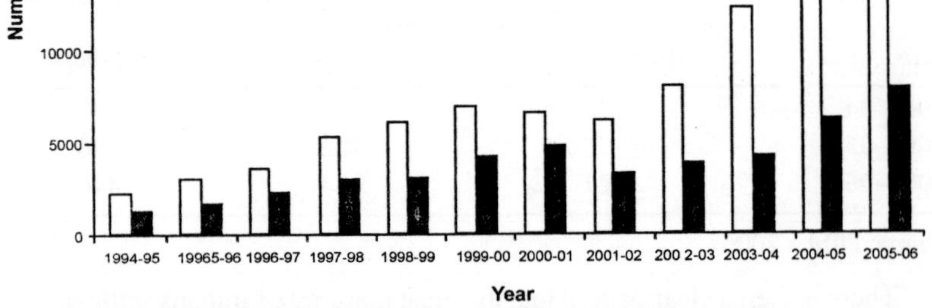

Figure 8: Long term movement to and from India, 1994–95 to 2005–06

Source: DIMA unpublished data.

Migration of Academics and Researchers from India to Australia

The focus will now turn to a discussion of the migration of one occupational sub-group from India to Australia – that of university teachers and researchers. Although there is some difficulty in identifying this group in the movement data base, some indicative information can be obtained.

Figure 9 shows the long term and permanent migration of academic teachers and researchers to and from India between 1997–98 and 2005–06.[5] All told over this period there were 278 and 541 permanent arrivals of teaching university lecturers and tutors and researchers respectively while the numbers of long term arrivals were 207 and 321. There are contrasting patterns. With respect to university teachers it is clear that universities have switched from using permanent settlement to temporary business visas to bring in staff. This is partly a function of the increased number of contract positions in Australian universities but also is partly a function of the speed and relative simplicity of the 457 Temporary Business Visa compared with gaining permanent residency. It would seem certain that many of the long term arrivals will seek permanent residence at some stage. Researchers on the other hand are predominantly coming to Australia as permanent settlers.

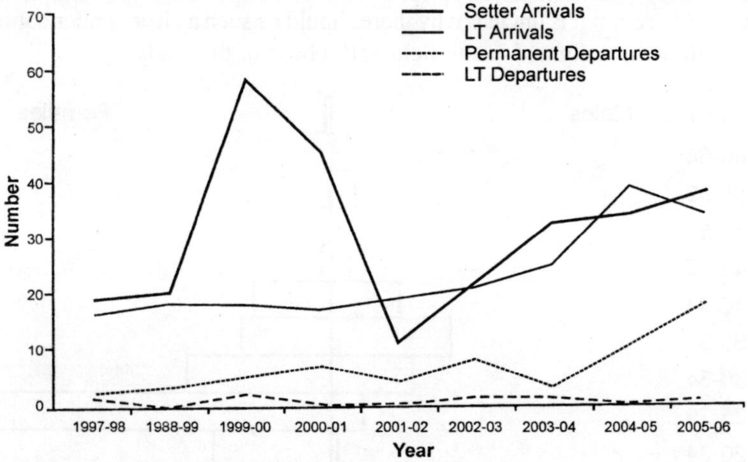

Figure 9: Australia: Permanent and long term movement of university lecturers and tutors to and from India, 1997–98 to 2005–06

Source: DIMA unpublished data.

Clearly there are significant numbers involved in this movement but a key issue is the fact that there is likely to be a substantial increase in the flow over the next decade. This is not only due to the increasing internationalization of academic and researcher labour markets associated with globalization. It is shown elsewhere that academics are one of the oldest occupational sub-groups in the Australian workforce. At the 2001 census, some 19 per cent of the university academic workforce were aged 55 years and over and 51.2 per cent 45 years and over. This was due to a large influx of young academics in the 1960s and 1970s associated with a massive increase in student numbers due to the entry of post-war baby boomers into university studies and increases in university participation rates. This was followed by a period of slow growth in academic staff numbers due to reduced student growth together with increasing student-staff ratios. Hence, there will be a high level of recruitment in Australian universities over the next two decades and it is unlikely that this demand will be met by the Australian labour market. Accordingly the opportunities for Indian academics and researchers in Australia will increase.

Figures 10 and 11 show that the permanent and long term arrivals among lecturers and tutors from India are very young with the largest group being in their late 20s. Among permanent arrivals 80 per cent were aged less than 40 while among the long term arrivals 70 per cent were aged less than 40. The most striking pattern in the figures however is the dominance of women among settler arrivals and the dominance of males among those coming as long term arrivals. At present it is unclear why there should be such a clear gender contrast but it will be investigated in the fieldwork phase of the study.

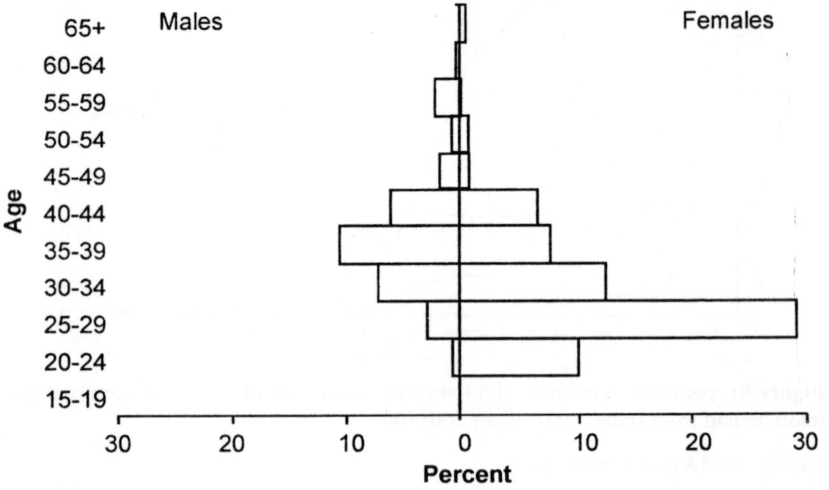

Figure 10: Australia: University lecturers and tutors, settler arrivals from India, 1997–98 to 2005–06

Source: DIMA unpublished data.

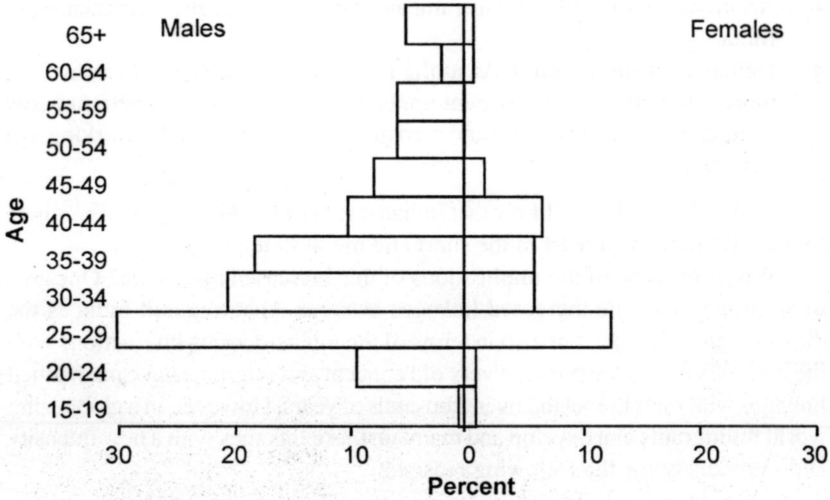

Figure 11: Australia: University lecturers and tutors, long term arrivals from India, 1997–98 to 2005–06

Source: DIMA unpublished data.

Discussion

It has been shown that Indian migration, both permanent and temporary, has experienced an unprecedented increase in the last few years so that the Indian community in Australia has almost doubled in size in the last decade. The immigration is an especially selective one of persons with high levels of skill and qualification. Moreover it is likely that this rapid growth will continue into the foreseeable future. This is likely for a number of reasons:

- The increasing shortage of skilled workers in Australia will ensure that visas for temporary and permanent migration from India to Australia will be keenly sought.
- The doubling of Indian student numbers in Australia in recent years will undoubtedly result in a high proportion taking advantage of new regulations which allow (and in some cases encourage) students to apply for permanent residence without first returning to their home country.
- The high level of ability of Indians in English language gives them a significant advantage over many of their Asian counterparts as desirable skilled migrants for Australia. Language issues are becoming important barriers for example to Chinese migration to Australia.
- The greatly increased size of the Indian community in Australia and the linkages established between India and Australia will in themselves encourage more movement both in terms of family networks but also more Indians being in the labour force and recruiting more migrants.

- An increasing profile of Australia as a potential migration destination in India.
- Demand for migration in Australia is likely to increase but there will be more competition for those migrants as more countries experience low fertility, population ageing and zero growth or decline of the working age population.

Hence it would seem likely that Indian migration to Australia will continue to increase rapidly at least in the short and medium term.

What are some of the implications of this increased migration? One area of significance is the increased linkages between Australia and India as the diaspora grows in size but also in terms of the intensity of its interactions with the home country. Diaspora is a very old concept and migrants have maintained linkages with their homeland over thousands of years. However, in a globalizing world immigrants can develop and maintain these linkages with a new intensity and immediacy for the following reasons:

- The revolution in Information Communication Technology has meant that whereas migrants previously kept in contact with their homeland through letters they now regularly (daily, weekly) telephone or email family in the homeland. Moreover the internet means the migrant can keep up with events in the homeland through reading newspapers and other media at the same time as their homeland based counterparts.
- The reduction of the real cost and travel times of international travel means that regular visiting by the diaspora and their families is feasible and at times of family emergency the family can be readily assembled.
- It is increasingly possible to be bi-national in that one can lead active economic and social lives in both origin and destination.

There is a growing appreciation in the development literature that "a highly skilled diaspora may play several important roles in promoting development at home". In terms of academics in the diaspora it is their role in transmitting information and in facilitating technology transfer which is most significant. It has been shown how professionals in origin and destination countries have maintained strong linkages so that ideas flow freely in both directions. In the scientific world, flows of information are of utmost significance and it may be that diaspora can play a role in technology transfers. The potential for such interaction to accelerate diffusion of new ideas, products, processes, etc. is considerable. Undoubtedly, the ethnic linkages between Taiwan and India with Silicon Valley have had a major impact on the development of the information technology in the home countries. There has been an increasing recognition that there is considerable potential for linking expatriate researchers and scientists with colleagues in their home countries to facilitate knowledge transfer and the development of tertiary research and teaching organization in the home nation.

One of the strongest findings of a survey of Australian Chinese Academics was that they maintained strong linkages with China. Nearly half of the sample (43.1%) has contact with China several times a week and 72.3 per cent visit China at least once a year. In addition more than half of the respondents (51.4%) had active joint research projects with colleagues in China. Half of these projects receive at least some funding from Chinese sources. Hence, there are strong professional linkages being maintained by Chinese academics in Australia with their homeland. This is attested to by the fact that the majority of respondents (84.7%) indicated that they would like to have a joint position between Australia and China.

It is likely that it will be found that Indian scientists, academics and researchers in Australia maintain similar linkages with their homelands. Clearly the potential for them to return regularly to interact with colleagues in India – both through temporary visits and virtually through ICT is huge. There has been an increasing recognition in the literature that the existence of a diaspora of researchers, scientists and technologists can provide a "brain gain option" without returning to their home nation since they can be avenues for technology transfers, information spread and training for people in their home country. China has used administrative means in order to encourage such networking. It will be interesting to find whether the diaspora of Indian academics in Australia have maintained strong connections with colleagues and institutions in India which would facilitate this non-return brain-gain phenomenon.

Conclusion

Australia's immigration has undergone parametric changes in the last decade. The first sweeping shift was the transformation of the national Immigration Program from being one dominated by permanent settlement to one where each year several hundred thousand people are granted a visa to live and work on a temporary basis in Australia. The second was the increasing workforce/economic orientation of the program so that skill, education, Australian qualifications, ability to speak English and work experience became the dominant criteria in selecting both settlers and temporary migrants. A third and related element has been the increasing share of Australian settlement which has involved "onshore" migration whereby temporary residents are granted permanent residency.

While these changes have occurred, India has become Australia's largest origin country of Asian immigrants. Moreover there are a number of reasons why India is to become an even more significant source of migrants in the near future as was discussed earlier.

There are some additional factors which are likely to see an even greater movement of Indian academics and researchers to Australia. Firstly there has been an increasing focus in Australian universities on recruiting Indian students. This together with increasing prosperity in India is likely to lead to a continuation of the upward trajectory over the next few years. Moreover, over the last few years the Australian government has introduced a number of changes to its immigration regulations to facilitate overseas students obtaining permanent residence in Australia. A second factor is the ageing of the staff of Australian universities. This will result in an increased demand for academics and researchers in Australian universities. This will be occurring at a time when the Australian labour market in this area has tightened. Australian higher degree graduates have shown a greater propensity than in the past to seek careers outside of the university sector and have increasingly sought positions outside Australia, especially the United States and the United Kingdom. Hence, there will be more opportunities for academics and scientists from countries like China and India. Another particularly important finding is the strength of linkages maintained by Indian academics in Australia with their homeland. This suggests that there is considerable scope from the Indian perspective of enhancing the flow of information and encouraging technology transfer.

References

Australian Bureau of Statistics (ABS), 2005. *Migration Australia 2003–04*, Catalogue No. 3412.0, Canberra: ABS.

Barré, R., Hernandez, V., Meyer, J-B., Vinck, D. 2003. *Diasporas scientifiques/Scientific Diasporas*, IRD Editions, Paris.

Biao, X., 2006. 'Towards Sustainable "Brian Circulation": What India and China Can Learn From Each Other'. Paper Presented at the International Conference on Population and Development in Asia: Critical Issues for a Sustainable Future, Phuket, Thailand, 20–22 March.

Birrell, B., 2005. *Immigration Rules and the Overseas Student Market in Australia*. Report prepared for IDP, December.

Department of Education, Training and Youth Affairs (DETYA). Students: Selected Higher Education Statistics, Various issues, Australian Government Publishing Service, Canberra.

Department of Immigration, Multicultural and Ethnic Affairs (DIMIA). Australian Immigration: Consolidated Statistics, Various issues, Australian Government Publishing Service, Canberra.

Department of Immigration, Multicultural and Ethnic Affairs (DIMIA). Immigration Update, various issues, Australian Government Publishing Service, Canberra.

Hugo, G.J., 1999. "A New Paradigm of International Migration in Australia", New Zealand Population Review, vol. 25, Nos. 1–2, pp. 1–39.

Hugo, G.J., 2004. "Recent Population Movements Between India and Australia: Trends and Implications", in D. Gopal and D Rumley (eds.) India and Australia: Issues and Opportunities, Authorspress, Delhi. pp. 229–298.

Hugo, G.J., 2004. "Australia's Most Recent Immigrants 2001". Australian Census Analytic Program, Catalogue Number 2053.0, Australian Bureau of Statistics, Canberra.

Hugo, G.J., 2005. "Some Emerging Demographic Issues on Australia's Teaching Academic Workforce", *Special Issue of Higher Education Policy*, vol. 18, no. 3, pp. 207–230.

Hugo, G.J., 2006. "An Australian Diaspora?" *International Migration*, vol. 44, no. 3, pp. 105–132.

Hugo, G., Rudd, D., and Harris, K., 2001. "Emigration from Australia: Economic Implications". (Second report on an ARC SPIRT Grant). *CEDA Information Paper No. 77*; CEDA, Melbourne.

Hugo, G.J, Rudd, D., and Harris, K., 2003. "Australia's Diaspora: It's Size, Nature and Policy Implications", *CEDA Information Paper No. 80*; CEDA, Melbourne.

Khoo, S., Voight, C., Hugo, G. and McDonald, P., 2003. 'Temporary Skilled Migration to Australia: the 457 Visa Sub-Class', *People and Place*. Vol. 11 no. 4. pp. 27–40.

Lucas, R.E.B., 2001. "Diaspora and Development: Highly Skilled Migrants from East Asia". Report prepared for the World Bank, Boston University, November 2001.

Meyer, J-B et al., 1997. "Turning Brain Drain into Brain Gain: The Colombian Experience of the Diaspora Option", *Science, Technology and Society*. vol 2. no. 2. pp. 285–317.

Meyer, J. and Brown, M., 1999. "Scientific Diaspora: A New Approach to the Brain Drain". (World Conference on Science). Discussion Paper No. 41, UNESCO – ICSU, Hungary, 26 June – 1 July.

Meyer, J-B 2001a. "Network Approach versus Brain Drain: Lessons from the Diaspora". *International Migration.* Vol. 39: Issue 5, Special Issue 2. pp. 91–110.

Meyer, J-B 2001b. "Les diasporas de la connaissance: atout inédit de la compétitivité du sud". *La Revue Internationale et Stratégique*, vol. 55. pp. 69–76.

Meyer, J-B., Kaplan, D., Charum, J. 2001. "Scientific nomadism and the new geopolitics of knowledge". *International Social Sciences Journal/Revue Internationale des Sciences Sociales*. Vol. 168. pp. 341–54.

Saxenian, A.L., 1999. *Silicon Valley's New Immigrant Entrepreneurs*. Public Policy Institute of California, San Francisco.

Yao, L., 2004. "The Chinese Overseas Students: An Overview of the Flows Change". Paper presented at 12th Biennial Conference of the Australian Population Association. Canberra, 15 – 17 September 2004.

Endnotes

1. However, before 1974 former settlers were not classified as emigrants unless they had been in Australia for at least 12 months.
2. The Indian population in this section are not all ethnic Indians in Australia but those born in India. The ethnic Indian population is considerably larger including substantial numbers born in Australia but also many from the Pacific and Asia. Hence, at the 2001 Australian census there were 95,452 India-born persons enumerated but some 156,624 persons indicated they had Indian ancestry. This

includes all first and second generation migrants who identify themselves as having Indian ancestry including the Australia-born children of parents born in India.

3. The number of United States educational institutions authorized to admit foreign students fell from 77,000 before 9/11 to 7,000 after (*Migration News*, January 2005).
4. Defined as any place with less than 200,000 residents or a population growth rate less than half that of Australia as a whole over the last decade.
5. The occupation coding system in the DIMA data was changed in 1997–1998.

Cultural Diversity in the Australian Classroom and the Experience of Arab-Muslim Students

Sally Percival Wood

This article reports on the Diversity – An Educational Advantage Project, a collaboration between Deakin University's Centre for Citizenship and Human Rights and Victorian Arabic Social Services. The Project came about in response to a growing number of Arab-Muslim refugees arriving in Australia, in parallel with a growing distrust of this cultural group due to international events, and concerns over the impact on secondary school students of Arabic-speaking background (ASB). Despite Australians' affirmation of a long-standing and easy-going commitment to cultural diversity as a national attribute to be celebrated, the inter-cultural dynamic within schools, the (in)effectiveness of State and Federal multicultural policy, and negative stereotypes propagated by the media, can undermine ASB families and students resulting in a sense of cultural and social isolation. The Project's three tiered approach: conducting research and focus group discussions with students; engaging ASB parents in school activities and information sessions; and working with teachers on understanding cultural diversity in pedagogical practice, seeks to effect structural transformation in schools, support ASB parents in guiding their children through the Australian education system and improve the educational outcomes of ASB students.

By way of background and contextualisation, the paper will begin with a broad overview of Australia's national and State educational policies to establish how, and whether, current policy is adequate in its response to cultural diversity in Australian schools. This will be followed by an overview of the Project, its longitudinal research findings, and its achievements to date to illustrate the effectiveness and durability of its three tiered approach.

Education and Multicultural Policy in Australia

At the time of Australia's federation in 1901, education was the province of the individual colonies and, in turn, a responsibility largely borne by the church. Though the States retained constitutional authority over education policy after 1901, the Federal Government has always played a significant role in steering policy towards initiatives it deems to be of national concern. For example, foreign language study is considered "an important cultural and economic asset for Australia", and the Federal Government asserts certain priorities in its funding for language studies.[1] Similarly, joint policy initiatives are negotiated between Federal and individual State Governments in relation to children with special needs, including migrant students.

While Australia has moved on from the imperatives of cultural uniformity implicit in the education policies of the 1950s and 1960s, a level of national standardisation is still evident in schools' learning priorities, curricular structures and pedagogy. Indeed, at the time of writing this paper, a debate which has arisen spasmodically since the 1970s, that curriculum should be formulated on a national level, has re-emerged for public debate. Of particular interest to the Diversity – An Educational Advantage project, which seeks to understand the experience of Arab-background students in the post–9/11 environment, is the re-invigoration of debates over multiculturalism, which in turn is placing renewed emphasis on concepts of citizenship and democracy, and more specifically, shared national "values" in education.

Since the return of the conservative Liberal-National Party Coalition in 1996, the term "multiculturalism" has lost favour in Federal Government circles. Indeed, Prime Minister John Howard has made it clear that he favours the term "cultural diversity" over "multiculturalism": "It's not a word I use a lot, but there is no other word. I mean, I tend to talk about cultural diversity. I tend to talk about people's different heritage."[2] Whichever term might be favoured, the 1999 Adelaide Declaration on National Goals for Schooling in the Twenty-first Century acknowledged the inevitability of a continually evolving local cultural environment, enforced by the complexities of globalization, noting that:

> This world will be characterized by advances in information and communication technologies, population diversity arising from international mobility and migration, and complex environmental and social challenges.[3]

To manage these changes, the task of assisting young people to develop a fuller understanding of their rights and responsibilities as Australian citizens was identified as a core goal of the Declaration. A better understanding and acknowledgement of "cultural and linguistic diversity"[4] ; and the view that a student's school experience ought to be "free from the effects of negative forms of discrimination based on sex, language, culture and ethnicity, religion or disability"[5] were outlined as core goals. More broadly, however, the Declaration places primary emphasis on fostering the individual's capacities to develop their "Australian-ness", rather than on an accommodation of the diversity of values present in an increasingly multicultural society. Indeed, the issue of a generic set of "values" in Australia's plural setting continues to pose a challenge to policy-makers and educators, as it becomes more urgent in an environment increasingly charged with the politics of difference.

Federal Policy

In the 10 years since 1996, the Howard Government has instigated several studies which have served as guiding principles for State education policy. The central themes underpinning national education priorities include citizenship and democracy studies in secondary school curricula, and the broad question of "values". Values were identified as an education priority by Brendan Nelson, former Federal Minister for Education Science and Training, in 2002 when a comprehensive report was commissioned to evaluate values education in Australian schools. The Values Education Study Report (August 2003) positions values as central to curriculum development initiatives in State education policy. The Federal Government's Ministerial Council on Education, Employment, Training and Youth Affairs (MCEETYA) National Report on Schooling in Australia 2003, reiterated this focus in national civics and citizenship education, drawing upon the findings of the Values Education Study; as does the Discovering Democracy programme which spanned 1997 to 2004. In 2004, a National Values Education Forum organised by the Department of Education Science and Training (DEST) convened to assess the progress of the Federal Government's values initiative and to launch the draft National Framework for Values Education in Australian Schools.

The Values Education Study was reflective of a much broader move internationally to arrive at a framework of generic or universal values that could be embraced by school communities, in an increasingly complex global society, which could somehow transcend culturally or religiously inscribed values. In designing and implementing values education processes for the Values Education Study, a range of well established programmes framed around a variety of psychological and philosophical approaches became the base point for the Study. For example, The Virtues Project,[6] the Living Values Educational Programme,[7] Dr. William Glasser's "Choice Theory",[8] the Victoria-based Philosophy for Schools,[9] and You Can Do It! Education[10] were all also accessed as entry points into values in education. PeaceBuilders[11] was central in developing respect and civic responsibility for one group of schools which had utilised this model for some years. Various other initiatives drawn from overseas designs were utilised as guiding frameworks, including: the Tribes Teaching Learning Community programme,[12] Costa's Habits of Mind[13] or the Sathya Sai[14] schools programme. A more secular approach, with human rights as its central objective, is the framework developed by UNESCO's Asia Pacific Network for International Education and Values Education (APNIEVE).[15] One particular school, confronted with "challenging behaviours" from students who "do not fit the stereotypical pattern for successful schooling ... [and] tend to become caught up in the punishment cycle"[16] used the Real Justice Programme.[17] Other schools looked to the values structure inherent in their school philosophy, for example, Christian schools adopted the values defined by their faith and traditions, such as those found in the Gospels. Where no such specific values framework underpinned a schools' identity, they had to wrestle with the broader challenges of their schools' cultural diversity. In such instances, input was sought from the wider school community – students, parents and teachers – through questionnaires and workshops to form a generic or holistic approach. Where deep cultural dissimilarities existed, outside consultants such as Griffiths University's Centre for Leadership and Management in Education,[18] were invited to assist.

When school communities were subsequently surveyed for the study it was found that values were clearly a high priority for recognition within the school community and inclusion in the curriculum. While a majority of students (58%) thought that values should be taught in all subjects across the curriculum, only 35 per cent believed that values should be taught as a separate subject. Parents and staff were overwhelmingly in agreement – over 97 per cent – that values should be taught in schools as part of the day to day curriculum and that parents ought to have input into values education.[19] Overall, the survey found that the majority embraced the idea of values in education, that it should be a high priority for schools, and nine values for Australian Schools emerged:

1. Care and Compassion: Care for self and others;
2. Doing Your Best: Seek to accomplish something worthy and admirable, try hard, pursue excellence;
3. Fair Go: Pursue and protect the common good where all people are treated fairly for a just society;
4. Freedom: Enjoy all the rights and privileges of Australian citizenship free from unnecessary interference or control, and stand up for the rights of others;
5. Honesty and Trustworthiness: Be honest, sincere and seek the truth;
6. Integrity: Act in accordance with principles of moral and ethical conduct, ensure consistency between words and deeds;
7. Respect: Treat others with consideration and regard, respect another person's point of view;
8. Responsibility: Be accountable for one's own actions, resolve differences in constructive, non-violent and peaceful ways, contribute to society and to civic life, take care of the environment; and
9. Understanding, Tolerance and Inclusion: Be aware of others and their cultures, accept diversity within a democratic society, being included and including others.

This set of values has now become a focal point of Australian curricular design, as is illustrated in the recently-developed Victorian Essential Learning Standards (VELS), currently being rolled out into government schools.

State Policy

The platform for the State of Victoria's school curriculum in the areas of multiculturalism and the teaching of languages other than English (LOTE) are centred on two policy documents: the Multicultural Policy for Victorian Schools developed in 1997 and the Guidelines for Managing Cultural and Linguistic Diversity in Schools established in 2001. Since then, the Blueprint for Government Schools (2003) and the Victorian Curriculum Assessment Authority's (VCAA) Victorian Curriculum Reform Project (2004) have more generally provided the framework for Victorian Government schools' curriculum. In addition to these, on 1 January 2005, the new Multicultural Victoria Act 2004 came into effect enshrining principles of access, participation and contribution, for all Victorian citizens, to services made available by the Victorian Government. Schools are encouraged to be aware of the Act and advice as to how it is to be applied to school councils, principals, school staff and students, asking them to enshrine multicultural principles in school charters (or Strategic Plans as they are now referred to), codes of conduct and to be generally absorbed into school community awareness.[20]

The Multicultural Policy for Victorian Schools 1997 was a collaborative effort between the Victorian Government's then Department of Education, the Ministerial Advisory Councils on Languages Other Than English (MACLOTE) and English as a Second Language (ESL). The policy was developed in response to the Multicultural Victoria Inquiry of 1995, which identified "the need to develop a specific multicultural education policy for schools, to provide intercultural education in primary and secondary schools, and to develop strategies to combat prejudice, racial tension or misunderstanding in schools."[21] It sets out a range of recommendations intended to move multicultural initiatives from the periphery of education policy, into the mainstream of the State's school curriculum. The primary target of the policy was to ensure that:

By 2006 all students P–12 will have multicultural perspectives delivered across all eight key learning areas (The Arts, English, Health and Physical Education, LOTE, Mathematics, Science, Study of Society and Environment, and Technology) and incorporated into all aspects of school life.[22]

The policy, nevertheless, only embodies a set of "recommendations" and while an Implementation Strategy has been set out by the Victorian Department of Education and Training (DET), this is limited to links to written support materials rather than through strategies to develop ways to incorporate the policy into Key Learning Areas (KLAs).

In November 2003, a Blueprint for Government Schools was released, identifying three priority areas for government school reform:

- Recognising and responding to diverse student needs;

- Building the skills of the education workforce to enhance the teaching-learning relationship; and
- Continuously improving schools.

Under the Blueprint's Flagship Strategy 1, community partnerships – between schools, community agencies and industry – are encouraged in defining schools as the learning centres of communities. As well as this acknowledgement of a greater need for cross-community engagement, in its conclusion the Blueprint acknowledges that education inequities exist:

The Government's case for further reform has been built on the understanding that current inequities across the system are unacceptable. Every government school student, irrespective of the school they attend, where they live or their social or economic status, is entitled to a high-quality school education and a genuine opportunity to succeed.[23]

To this end, completion of Year 12 or its equivalent by 90 per cent of young Victorians is targeted by 2010.[24] In achieving this objective of success and equity, the Blueprint encourages school self-management and endorses the strengthening of teacher-student-parent and community engagement. In other words, the need to bridge inequity is recognized but achieving educational equality is constrained by limited resources in areas with high populations of refugee families with limited cultural, social and financial capital. Government schools are frequently forced to seek assistance from local industry and non-government organizations to meet the complex demands of their school communities to fund initiatives, such as homework clubs for students without after-school parental supervision.

This leads us to the core question: Is policy working? And, for the Diversity – An Educational Advantage project, two issues of primary importance emerge from the current policy platform. First, how, and indeed whether, "cultural diversity" is being managed within Federal and State policy frameworks; and second, how, and who, is taking up responsibility for the realisation of the entitlement to equity prescribed by policy? The policy discourse tends to avoid explicit debates over the impact and implications of cultural difference in education, sidestepping the complex issues of negotiating cultural difference by rhetorically falling back on liberal notions of tolerance. The emphasis on common values evident in recent initiatives such as the Discovering Democracy initiative suggests that policy-makers favour a uni-dimensional approach to integration, which de-emphasises curricular incorporation of cultural difference as a mode of encouraging broader participation, in favour of encouraging acculturative adaptation among culturally and linguistically diverse (CALD) students. This discourse is being ramped up by the current Federal Education Minister Julie Bishop in her calls for a national, standardised curriculum that further homogenises the delivery of education across increasingly complex communities.

Decentralisation, the placing of increased emphasis on communities in solving their own problems, is the subtext of initiatives such as the Blueprint's Flagship Strategy 1. Both State and Federal policy invocations of flexibility and responsibility emerge from policy discourse that place increasing pressures and responsibilities on: (i) local school management structures and teachers; and (ii) on learners and their families. Arguably, this shift towards loosely defined values and emphasis on flexibility reflects a broader political trend of governments toward shifting responsibility for outcomes and management of diversity onto local communities, and individual schools. This trend is tied to the broader decline of the welfare state and emergence of neo-liberal "governance" models of educational reform. These shifts highlight the critical need for local level intervention involving school executives, teachers, parents and students in the management of cultural diversity in educational environments.

The Diversity – An Educational Advantage Project

The Project was established in 2003 in the wake of terrorist attacks on New York in September 2001 and the subsequent pressures being felt by many Muslims in the West, including Australia. The New York attacks were followed by two more recent events closer to home: the Bali bombings in October 2002, in which 202 people died, 88 of whom were Australian; and the bombing of the Australian Embassy in Jakarta in September 2004, which killed 10 Indonesian civilians and injured 200 people. This signalled the first ever attack on an Australian diplomatic mission, and both events suddenly brought the spectre of terrorism closer to home. While Australians, by and large, remain committed to a culturally plural society, the US-led "war on terror" has been appropriated by some to exacerbate ethnic tensions and to turn the clock back on Australia's long-standing commitment to "multiculturalism" as a national attribute to be celebrated. This manifested on the beaches of Cronulla in December 2005, when "white Anglo" Australians and Australians of Arabic origin, many second or third generation, engaged in riots which lasted several days.

This backdrop, along with the often emotive media attention given to the trial of Australia's "jihad Jack" Thomas, the intermittent arrests of suspected terrorists accused of plotting attacks on Australian soil, and the controversial five-year detention of Australian David Hicks at Guantanamo Bay, have served to maintain anxieties and detrimental stereotyping of Muslims in the public eye. The debate about Muslims and their integration into Australian society have rarely been out of the news since the Project's inception. Such public imagery poses significant challenges for young people of Arabic and Muslim backgrounds, some of whom are identified as being "at risk", many of whom strive but struggle to complete secondary school, and too few of whom successfully compete for tertiary places. The Project, which focuses on students in Years 9 and 10 (aged 14 to 17), is not prescriptive, advocating rigid instructions on how to manage schools or teach students. Rather, it is a partnership project that seeks to work collaboratively with school communities. It also engages with community organizations in order to effect tangible positive change, not only at the level of learning outcomes for students, but also at the level of school inter-cultural relations, and community support for and involvement in school life and activities.

The Project is framed within a "four P" approach: Policy, Parents, Professional Development and Practice. In order to affect this approach within an "active research" model, quantitative and qualitative analysis was drawn from three areas of practice:

- *Cultural diversity facilitator* – an Arabic-speaking community development worker who, in close collaboration with VASS and the Project team, worked within the partnership schools to: function as a cultural mediator between staff and students; clarify curriculum issues with parents, some of which take on a sensitive nature around, for example, mandatory secondary-level health studies; facilitating parent consent for school camps, student work experience, sporting events and after school programs such as the A.R.A.B. (anti-racism action band) hip-hop dance initiative.
- *Research and evaluation* – surveys, interviews and focus groups among Year 9 and 10 students, ASB parents, teachers and staff; close work with the CDF and parent groups on the structure and expectations of the Australian education system; professional development programs with teachers and staff on managing cultural diversity within the extant policy frameworks and collaboratively developing pedagogical strategies.
- *Teacher resource materials* – working with the material gleaned from the above activities, development of an on-line resource database that draws together a diverse range of resources for teachers and schools to use including: theoretical approaches to teaching in culturally diverse settings; various links to programs developed elsewhere; lesson plans; Strategic Plans for school-wide management of diversity; vignettes from the Project research.

Rather than provide a theoretical analysis of the Project, the purpose of this paper is to provide a glimpse of its longitudinal outcomes which demonstrate a practical, active approach to managing cultural diversity in schools to effect positive change. The Project's research with ASB students from 2003 to 2005 has yielded clear indicators that shifts in the migrant population of the study region, and in student attitudes across the life of the Project, have taken place.

The first most noticeable shift in the student cohort from 2003 to 2005 was the increased number of ASB students born overseas. In 2003, the majority of ASB students surveyed (72%) were born in Australia of ASB background, that is, one or more of their parents were born overseas. Two years later, in 2005, this number had more than halved, with just under one third of the cohort (31%) born in Australia. The clear shift was in the number of Iraqi migrants arriving in Australia across that period and settling in the areas nominated for the Project research. Just 8 per cent of students surveyed in 2003 were born in Iraq. The number of students born in Iraq had grown sixfold to 47 per cent in 2005. Not only does this represent a significant shift in the cultural composition of the lower socio-economic communities in north-west Melbourne, a high concentration of whom are enrolled in the Project partnership schools, it also represents a rapidly growing number of students who have limited experience of English-language learning and of the Australian education system. Several of these students spend one to two years of English language tuition before being immersed in mainstream classes. The significant challenges they face in competing at senior high school level with students who have experienced English-language learning since primary level, however, must be recognised. The educational challenges in this region across the study period, therefore, have increased, rather than decreased since the Project's inception.

Key indicators in the student surveys included: experiences of cultural diversity at school; issues of identity and belonging at school, in the community, and as Australians; relationships with teachers; family involvement at school; future ambitions and study motivation; and community interaction. It would be over ambitious to attempt to report the findings from each of these areas. However, one very positive outcome has been the level of confidence demonstrated by students in their relationships with teachers. In 2003, the CDF had only recently begun her activities at the schools. Therefore interventions on behalf of ASB parents had not been coordinated in any systematic way. ASB parents infrequently attended school functions or parent teacher evenings due to their inability to access information or unfamiliarity with school procedures. The Project found that the presence of the CDF as a liaison point between students, parents and teachers, relieved pressure from students as "go-between" between school and home. Parents' increased engagement with the school and improved levels of understanding around school expectations appears to have been a contributing factor in positively effecting student confidence. This graph shows that in 2003 only 3 per cent of students "always" felt comfortable approaching teachers or staff members with difficulties. While more students in 2005 reported that they only "sometimes" felt comfortable, there was a dramatic increase in the number of students who were "always" comfortable approaching staff with problems at school. The other striking feature of this result is that, in 2003, the majority of the ASB students who were asked this question (39%)

said that they were "not at all" comfortable approaching teachers. In 2005, this number had shrunk to just 2 per cent of ASB students who felt this. Given the shift in the educational backgrounds and country of origin of students by 2005, this represents a very positive attitudinal shift since the interventions of the CDF in the partnership schools in the region.

Although the majority of ASB students both in 2003 and 2005 believe that racism is a problem in Australia either "very much" or "somewhat" – a combined result of 87 per cent in 2003 compared to 73 per cent in 2005 – the balance tilted away from the stronger response in 2005. 27 per cent less students in 2005 believed that racism in Australia is "very much" a problem; 14 per cent more students believed it to be "somewhat" a problem in 2005; and twice as many believed that racism is "not at all" a problem – 8 per cent in 2003 compared to 20 per cent in 2005.

Students were less inclined to view racism as a problem at school, where most had developed a strong sense of belonging, and more inclined to project it as a community issue, recognising that it is often exacerbated by the media. In discussion, most agreed on a clearly defined hierarchy of "wogs" (migrants) in Australia, starting with "pure wogs" of Arabic background (themselves), "other wogs" (second, third or fourth generation Europeans) and "full Aussies", people of Anglo-Celtic background. The students acknowledged that their identities were "hyphenated", for example, that they sometimes feel "Lebbo" and sometimes "Aussie". It is this multiplicity of identities in culturally complex environments that the Project has worked to shape into an opportunity, and to activate its potential for positive change, in education.

Conclusion

One of the vital purposes of education is to ensure that all students – irrespective of race, gender or religious background – benefit from learning in ways that facilitate their full participation in public, community and economic life. When this Project started in its current multidimensional form in 2003, the preliminary research findings (that is pre-testing) suggested that ASB students exhibited negative tendencies in key areas relating to teacher-student relations, perceptions of interethnic relations at school, confidence in achieving a tertiary place, beliefs about whether racism affects learning and behaviour, and family emphasis upon and attitudes towards education. More worrying perhaps was the fact that ASB students were more likely to express distrust towards teachers, particularly based around a perceived lack of cultural understanding. They were less confident in their abilities to achieve education or training beyond secondary school, and were more likely to hold more limited educational ambitions than students from other backgrounds. While all students tended to think that their parents regarded education to be of importance, ASB students were less likely to discuss their education with their parents.

In order to address these negative trends, this Project with its various elements ("four P" approach: Policy, Parents, Professional Development and Practice) aimed to provide sustainable yet complementary educational and structural resources. To this end, the Project has made significant progress in facilitating positive change. The research and evaluation undertaken in the participating schools shows clearly that there has been significant and measurable improvement in students' attitudes towards schools, teachers and their surrounding communities. The positive attitudinal change detected among Years 9 and 10 students has taken place within an integrated action plan that involved parents' workshops; teachers' professional development sessions and community liaison and case management performed systematically through the Cultural Diversity Facilitator. These attitudinal, cultural and societal shifts have contributed to improved educational outcomes as reported by the schools independently.

The second level of intervention commenced through this Project relates to teacher training and curriculum resources, or as they are referred to here Teacher Support Materials (TSM). This part of the Project is concerned with professional development and practice in the classroom. To this end, a number of structured focus group discussions took place in both schools where a collaborative approach towards this complex was established. Indeed, teachers' views on various aspects of multicultural education and cultural diversity were gauged and their input into the basic architecture and content of the TSM was also sought. Linking the key questions and issues arising from students' focus groups and interviews to wider educational themes as defined in Victorian Essential Learning Standards, the TSM aims to build relevant yet inclusive teaching resources that address and reflect the students' interests and concerns. This is done within the existing curriculum framework, hence providing teachers with cutting edge resources that fall within the policy and curriculum standards. The TSM will be housed on the internet and will allow teachers to navigate various cultural vignettes and cross-reference these against educational resources, policy documents and other relevant links.

A third level in this multidimensional Project has focussed on parents and their involvement in and contribution to their children's schooling. This has been supported by the role of the Cultural Facility Facilitator whose work in bridging communication and cultural gaps between the schools and the parents/communities has seen improvements in parental attendance at school events, more proactive attitudes towards their children's education and a willingness to form permanent parent-teacher forums. These are all indicators of positive change that is reflected in their children's responses on family/ parents interest in education.

The multidimensional model adopted in this study recognises the inter-dependent nature of the learning experience and the critical role of social and cultural factors in shaping the educational achievements of ASB students and CALD students in general. The Project findings have confirmed the basic principle of the model, namely, that the comparative lower achievements of ASB students generally reflect their attitudes towards their social and cultural environment and their parents' understanding of schooling policies and attitudes towards education achievements. The positive views expressed regarding the community-based facilitator support the model's focus on the importance of bridging the gap between schools and their immediate communities, particularly where these communities are facing considerable economic and social obstacles. The model adopted in this study has been useful in analysing the many factors influencing educational outcomes for ASB students in addition to providing a 'transformative' model to effect positive change in the school environment, both at the social and the educational levels.

Now in its final stages, the Project is working through the handover phase. A series of modules developed to orient ASB parents to the Australian school system are being refined so that they will be applicable to a variety of CALD groups; a "model of best practice" for managing cultural diversity in schools is being finalised; the online Teacher Support Materials which can be used across cultural groups using the ASB experience as a model is ready for release; and finally, the development of lesson plans based around the active research findings, tying in with the VELS and values policies, that are responsive to the schools' cultural composition are being developed. The integrated approach adopted, interlocking the experience of students, teachers and parents, has aimed to diminish the perceptions of cultural difference as a barrier and reframe it as an educational advantage.

Endnotes

1. Federal support is provided through programmes giving priority to 10 languages, six of which are European, two Asian (Thai and Vietnamese), Aboriginal languages and Arabic. From 'The Australian Education System', Australian Government website (as at January 2005). http://www.education.gov.au/goved
2. Megalogenis, George, 'Multicultural Australia examined: the full text of the John Howard interview.' *The Australian* 6 February 2002. See also David Hollinsworth, *Race and Racism in Australia*, Social Science Press, Sydney, 1998, pp. 269–276.
3. *The Adelaide Declaration on National Goals for Schooling in the Twenty-first Century* were developed at the 10th Ministerial Council on Education, Employment, Training and Youth Affairs (MCEETYA) in Adelaide, 22–23 April 1999 by State, Territory and Federal Government Ministers. See http://www.dest.gov.au/schools/adelaide/adelaide.htm
4. Ibid, Goal 3.5.
5. Ibid, Goal 3.1.
6. The Virtues Project is founded upon the values of the Baha'i Faith and was developed as a neutral values teaching programmes by Canadians Linda Kavelin

Popov, Dan Popov and John Kavelin. It's focus is upon moral and spiritual development across cultures in schools, the community, corporations and for couples. See http://www.virtuesproject.com

7. Living Values Education, sponsored by UNESCO, has very much a global focus operating in 74 countries. Its focus is to nurture positive teacher-student and student-student relationships through twelve universal values. See http://www.livingvalues.net
8. William Glasser's Choice Theory, based on the premise that we choose all that we do, is used widely across industries for people who manage, teach, counsel or supervise others. It has been developed into the Quality Schools Programme. See http://www.wglasser.com
9. The Victorian Association for Philosophy in Schools promotes the teaching of philosophy in primary and secondary schools. It is aimed at stimulating children to think about philosophical ideas, rather than values specifically. See http://www.jcsav.vic.edu.au/vaps/info.htm
10. Dr. Michael Bernard, an educational psychologist, developed the You Can Do It! Education programme to address mental health issues – emotional, behavioural and academic – affecting school age children. See http://www.youcandoit.com.au/about.html
11. PeaceBuilders is an anti-violence campaign funded by the U.S. *Safe and Drug-Free Schools Act*. Its focus is on eradicating miscreant behaviour to create a safe school environment for primary and secondary school children. See http://www.peacebuilders.com
12. Tribes is an American-based organization developing 'character education' values through a 'resiliency-building' model that is neither a programme nor a curriculum, but a 'process'. It is used in response to the *Improving America's Schools Act* of 1994. See http://www.tribes.com
13. The 16 habits of mind developed by Arthur Costa and Bena Kallick, based in California, are less about values and more about teaching skills, such as, effective thinking, intelligent behaviour in the face of difficulties, reasoning and creativity. See http://www.habits-of-mind.net
14. This international organization is built around the spiritual teachings of Sri Sathya Sai Baba, whose philosophy is framed by the Indian tradition. This organization takes a more spiritual approach to its Human Values in Education programme, embracing five 'Ds' – devotion, discipline, duty, discrimination, determination. Sri Sathya Sai Baba's motto is 'the end of education is character'. See http://www.sathyasai.org/saieducation/content.htm or http://www.saieducare.org/html/index.html (under construction).
15. APNIEVE was established at a meeting in Seoul to form the Network of Regional Experts in Education for Peace, Human Rights and Democracy in 1995. Its overall strategy is to recognise the indivisibility and interdependence of all rights – civil, cultural, economic, political and social. See http://portal.unesco.org/education/en/ev.php-URL_ID=4920&URL_DO=DO_TOPIC&URL_SECTION=201.html
16. *Values Education Study*, op.cit., p. 85.
17. Real Justice is a part of the International Institute for Restorative Practices. In response to juvenile crime it developed conferencing (structured meetings and role plays) with victims, offenders, families and friends. The Real Justice

programme is used by schools, but also the courts, police, correctional and treatment facilities, and the workplace generally. See http://www.realjustice.org/

18. The Centre for Leadership and Management in Schools at Griffiths University is more focussed upon professional development for teachers and principals than students. It is currently addressing the issue of ethics for school principals. See http://www.griffith.edu.au/centre/clme
19. *Values Education Study*, op.cit., Appendix III: Report of the Online Survey of community views on values for Australian schools, pp. 213–228.
20. See Appendix A of this document, but also http://www.sofweb.vic.edu.au/lem/multi/mpol.htm#implications
21. *Multicultural Policy for Victorian Schools*, Department of Education MACLOTE and ESL, Department of Education, Victoria, 1997, p. 7. The policy can be found at http://www.sofweb.vic.edu.au/lem/multi/mpol.htm
22. *The Adelaide Declaration*, op. cit., p. 9.
23. See 'Conclusion', ibid.
24. See Appendix 2: the Goals and Targets for Education and Training, ibid.

17

Working Australia Efficiency and Equity

Liz Hall

Australia—Culturally and Linguistically Diverse

Australia has one of the most multicultural workforces in the world. Australians come from over 232 countries and speak over 200 languages. Also, there are an estimated 250 Indigenous languages that are spoken. 2.5 million People speak a language other than English at home.

The vast array of cultures, religions and languages that are represented in Australia include immigrants and Australian-born people. 25 per cent of the population was born overseas and 27 per cent of Australian-born people have at least one parent who was born overseas.

This diversity serves to strengthen the Australian population as well as the Australian workplace.

Culturally diverse workplaces have more potential to solve problems due to the greater number of perspectives and increased number of options, alternatives and creative solutions generated.

Having a more culturally diverse workforce enables organizations to reach a larger marketplace that reflects the changing Australian population. Organizations are tapping into their diverse workforce to respond to the needs of a multilingual and integrated marketplace.

Various employers are now using diversity as an efficiency gain to their business bottom-line. However there are many definitions of 'diversity' in a workplace sense, and numerous terms are used to describe essentially the same thing. For instance, there are various definitions of 'productive diversity', 'diversity management' and 'workplace diversity' 'cultural diversity' 'linguistically diverse'. In a pragmatic sense, the common ground in these definitions that generally appear in a workplace includes:

- acknowledge the reality that people differ in many ways;
- identify implications for the workplace, or society generally, that arise because of the diversity; and
- they suggest or imply strategies to ensure that these issues are addressed, in the interest of the workplace, or society generally.

Workplace diversity is a tool for capturing the diversity dividend by focusing on and managing the difference within a company's workforce, capitalising on the benefits of diversity and minimising workplace challenges.

Companies who encourage diversity management find that it contributes significantly to the bottom line for their overall profitability.

- improving the effectiveness and efficiency of Human Resource Management functions;
- fostering superior decision-making, problem-solving, creativity, and innovation; key factors in the creation of knowledge companies;
- developing cross-cultural capabilities that facilitate operations in culturally complex environments at home and abroad; and
- implementing new product/service developments and new sales/marketing strategies for diverse customer bases.

There are two main areas of managing diversity in the workplace which will lead to superior company performance.

1. Tap into the benefits that flow from effectively managing diversity.
2. Develop strategies to address ineffective diversity management, which imposes costs.

Effective workplace diversity leads to improved individual and organisational performance. However, having a diverse workforce does not, in itself, translate into bottom-line benefits for companies. Diversity must be managed in order for companies to reap a diversity dividend. Companies must commit to effectively managing diversity to ensure that the unique skills, perspectives and knowledge of their workforces are channelled into producing a diversity dividend. Companies that recognise the financial benefits of a culturally diverse workforce are using internal talent, companies save money by contracting less external translators and experience the financial effects of extending their accessible market. In addition, employees feel appreciated and valued for their uniqueness that increases morale and creates an organizational culture that is supportive of difference.

Equity for employees on an individual level has principally been equal pay for equal work with equal opportunities to employment and advancement. However statistical information below show this is not correct.

- Workers from non-English speaking backgrounds hold only 3 per cent of senior executive positions in Australian companies.
- 85 per cent of Australian companies have either 0 or 1 board member from a Non-English Speaking Background.
- 82 per cent of companies had either 0 or 1 person from a Non-English Speaking Background in the Senior Executive Management Group.

- Over 70 per cent of job vacancies are not advertised, and are therefore not accessible to migrants who have not yet built up social and professional networks.
- Many migrants are refused employment because of a lack of local experience and referees.
- Some migrants find that employers will not consider them due to their accent.
- Skilled migrants who have internationally recognised qualifications are sometimes rejected by Australian professional and trade bodies.
- Migrants from English speaking backgrounds are 3-times as likely to earn more than $1500 a week.
- However, those from non-English speaking backgrounds were half as likely to earn a high income.

Debate has arisen from some authors on the statistical in balance of migrant workers on our industrial relations system not supporting cultural diversity through limited opportunities to bargain and negotiate employment conditions and fare wages.

Bargaining Changes in Australia

The industrial relations system in Australia has evolved in recent decades from a "centralised" and "collective" model of conciliation and arbitration, to one which places primary responsibility for determination of wages and conditions of employment with the parties at the enterprise and workplace levels. Successive federal and state governments in Australia have, since 1988, introduced reforms to labour law regimes which aim to encourage the parties to the employment relationship to "bargain" and negotiate over employment conditions to best suit the needs of the employer and employee. These changes have been viewed by some as disadvantaging particular groups of workers in disadvantaged positions as they can easily be over looked in obtaining equitable employment conditions. I will outline industrial relations in Australia in three parts – firstly, an analysis is provided of the industrial relations reforms introduced by the Keating government in 1993.

Secondly, overview of the industrial relations system during the first 10 years of the coalition government since 1996.

Finally the recent "WorkChoices" legislative reforms with a summary of the likely impacts on Australian industry and all workers.

Further, future directions in federal industrial relations are discussed with a focus on enterprise bargaining regulation effecting workers. A central focus will be made on a bargaining regime which primarily exists at the federal level in Australia and is developing better ways to promote outcomes which are both equitable and efficient for the employer and employee, and assist in those workers least able to bargain better terms and conditions through education programs.

Industrial Relations in Australia and the Growth Enterprise Bargaining

The Australian Industrial Relations system has undergone significant change since the 1980s, towards a model both unions and employers have deemed more suitable to meet the challenges of global competition and changing workplace and industrial needs. Collective bargaining in many industrialised societies had been seen by 'groups of employees and left-wing political groups…as a way of replacing unilateral decision-making by the employer and of overcoming the weaker bargaining position of individual employees'.[1] Employer groups since the 1980s, have similarly advocated a "decentralisation" and "deregulation" of industrial relations systems at both state and federal levels. The degree to which the industrial relations system in Australia should be deregulated, along with the necessity for collective forms of bargaining, has however remained a matter of significant debate. The introduction of enterprise bargaining in Australia was unique in that 'it is unlike other nations where a decentralisation of bargaining has occurred. The union movement contributed to the changes through two industrial campaigns and the Australian Industrial Relations Commission (AIRC) to introduce enterprise bargaining'.[2] The Industrial Relations Act 1988 (Cmth) ("IRAct 88") provided for the making of enterprise agreements whereby 'if the parties to an industrial dispute or any of them agree on terms for the settlement of all or any of the matters in dispute, they may make a memorandum of the terms agreed on'.[3] Stackpool describes how the 1988 reforms stopped short of the recommendations of the Hancock Report to allow 'direct employee negotiations on awards and conditions'.[4] The IRAct 88 required that 'if the Commission is of the opinion that the agreement is in the interests of the parties immediately concerned, the Commission shall… certify the agreement unless it is of the opinion that it would be contrary to the public interest to certify the agreement'.[5]

The Australian Industrial Relations Commission (AIRC) took a cautious approach to these reforms in its February 1989 Review (1989) 27 IR 196 decision. The AIRC determined that 'before certifying an agreement pursuant to s 115 of the Act, the Commission much be satisfied that the agreement…is not a device to circumvent the general wage fixation principles and thus threatens the orderly operation of the industrial relations system'.[6] In the 1991 national wage case decision[7] the Commission noted that the government's 'enterprise bargaining proposals challenged a long established principle of wage fixation in Australia, namely that the benefits of increased productivity should be distributed on a national, rather than an industry or an enterprise, basis'.[8] Amendments to the IRAct 88 made in the Industrial Relations (Legislation Amendment) Act 1992 facilitated a greater emphasis and importance on enterprise bargaining to wage determination in Australia than permitted in AIRC decisions. Pittard and McNaughton (2003) outline how the amendments aimed to ensure that 'where the bargaining was between a trade union (the employees representative) and a single business or single place of work, the Industrial Relations Commission had very limited powers to refuse to certify an agreement'.[9] An important distinction between the IRAct 88 and future industrial relations reform initiatives was that it retained 'the system of conciliation and arbitration as the [primary] means by which Australia's industrial relationships are regulated'.[10] Further, that a role for trade unions in awards and enterprise bargaining was maintained ensuring that employees covered by these instruments could be assured of working conditions regardless of their association or membership with industrial bodies. (ie: union membership).

The Industrial Relations Reform Act 1993

The industrial relations reforms of 1993 made extensive amendments to the IRAct 88 and introduced non-union forms of collective enterprise agreements, underpinned by section 51(20) of the constitution (the "corporations power"). Considered the most radical aspect of the Industrial Relations Reform Act 1993 (Cmth) was that 'awards were to play a subsidiary role by acting as safety nets for those workers who were unable to access enterprise bargaining'.[11] Before the 1993 reforms it was evident that 'enterprise bargaining provisions have been a mechanism whereby the industrial parties might 'opt-out' of the centralized and dominant award structure'.[12] Many of the provisions of the Workplace Relations Act 1996 (Cmth) ("WRAct 96") have been adopted from the 1993 reforms including the form and constitutional basis for the making of enterprise agreements. McCallum presents that as the non-union stream of certified agreements was underpinned by the corporations power, 'many employers, especially in the small business sector, [were] unable to take advantage of the non-unionised stream even where they were already bound by federal awards'.[13] This situation has continued under the present industrial relations regime whereby most forms of certified agreements[14] and individual Australian Workplace Agreements are only generally available to employees of the Commonwealth or corporations.[15]

The 1993 legislation represented an innovative reform agenda in many other aspects. The Industrial Relations Reform Act 1993 and to a lesser extent legislation introduced by the conservative government in 1996 made use of the external affairs powers of the constitution to underpin various minimum employment rights and provisions, including termination of employment and parental leave. The right to strike was expressly permitted in the legislation through the introduction of "protected" action during specified bargaining periods. These changes assisted with diversity growth by encouraging women to remain engaged in the workforce and assist in meeting family needs.

Non-union certified agreements introduced by the Industrial Relations Reform Act 1993 were, along with s.170LK certified agreements and Australian Workplace Agreements (AWAs) introduced in 1996, were slow to be taken up by both large and small business in Australia. Enterprise Flexibility Agreements (EFAs) were designed to make 'enterprise bargaining accessible to enterprises which, although covered by federal awards, are not unionised, thus encouraging the spread of bargaining into those workplaces'.[16] Unlike non-union certified agreements available under the WRAct 96, the AIRC imposed additional checks and reviews on EFAs based on the fact that trade unions had not been involved in their development or negotiation. Coulthard (1996) stated however that 'it was inaccurate to describe Division 3 [agreements] as providing only for non-union bargaining, given that unions can become involved in the process of negotiating and formalising an enterprise flexibility agreement'.[17] No such statutory guarantee of trade union involvement exists with s.170LJ certified agreements under the present industrial relations regime, which causes concern for some groups as inequitable.

However despite the push from employer groups for the need for non-union statutory bargaining options, most firms that negotiated collective agreements were bound by union certified agreements. Between 1994 and May 1996 only 181 EFAs were approved – a figure argued to be due to 'the possibility of unions being involved in the process [deterring] employers with non- or little-unionised workforces from utilising the system'.[18] When reviewing the proportion of employees on federal statutory agreements under the WRAct 96 however, it is clear that the argument of union involvement in collective bargaining "deterring" employers from using statutory agreements (as with EFAs) has not proven accurate. While non-union s.170LK and AWA options under the present regime have been more popular than EFAs, the vast majority of employees, covered by statutory agreements under either legislative regime, had remained on options the under union collective agreements.

The Conservative Reforms – 1996 Onwards

The WRAct 96 was introduced with a view to 'ensuring that the primary responsibility for determining matters affecting the relationship between employers and employees rests with the employer and employees at the workplace or enterprise level'.[19] To facilitate this, the Act introduced a range of "choices" available to the parties in terms of statutory collective and individual agreements. The rhetoric of the government in introducing choice in agreement options was to 'allow the natural cooperation between employers and employees to flourish and ultimately build better relationships increasing employee satisfaction and increased profitability.[20] Lee (2004) presents, however, that 'in pursuit of these objectives, the Act bristles with coercive, punitive and compensatory remedies'.[21] While the conservative reforms of 1996 substantially maintained many provisions and underpinning constitutional bases of the Industrial Relations Reform Act 1993, the WRAct 96 represented a radical departure from traditional industrial relations regulation in the federal jurisdiction insofar as it sought to alter the role of trade unions in workplace, its membership of employees and tribunal industrial relations processes and practices.

Many authors have presented that the WRAct 96 contributes little to the "deregulation" of industrial relations and has in fact introduced new levels of regulation of employment (primarily with regards to trade unions), and is framed on an ideological opposition to collectivism and trade unionism, and its effect on balancing equity in the workforce by placing barriers in assisting disadvantaged workers. Changes in the content of the legislation where no reference is made to the term "trade union" – rather, the Act introduces new terminology of "bargaining agent" or "organizations of employees".

The enterprise bargaining framework established under the WRAct 96 has however been successful in comparison to other federal and state initiatives in terms of facilitating a move to agreement-making from state or federal award coverage. This is demonstrated by the fact that in the period from July 2001 to July 2004 the AIRC certified nearly 22,000 collective certified agreements covering several million workers some of these agreements not only included terms and conditions of employment but also included workplace values and principles of behaviour expected of all employees encouraging an understanding in diversity.[22] The WRAct 96 established a range of "choices" open to the parties to the employment relationship (in effect, the "choice" of agreement utilised largely rests with the employer). Division 2 s.107LJ of the WRAct 96 provides for collective certified agreements which cover an employer and "one or more organisations of employees" which must be 'entitled to represent the industrial interests of the member in relation to the work that will be subject to the agreement'.[23] Division 2 s.170LK provides for certified agreements between an employer and 'a valid majority of the persons employed at the time whose employment will be subject to the agreement'.[24] Section 170LK "non-union" certified agreements specifically effective trade union involvement in that while employees may request the participation of a union in the agreement making process, the legislation only requires that an employer meet and confer with the "organization of employees" whose interests they are "entitled to represent".

Division 3 certified agreements are made between employers and unions, in circumstances where the Commission certifies an agreement in settlement of an industrial dispute or where certification of the agreement would 'prevent industrial situations from giving rise to industrial disputes'.[25] A further limited option is provided under the WRAct 96 to the AIRC to settle protracted negotiations which may have involved industrial disputation in the form of s.170MX awards. The full bench of the AIRC may only make s.170MX awards where the 'negotiating parties have not settled the matters that were at issue during the bargaining period' and 'it is not likely that further conciliation will result in the matters being settled within a reasonable time'.[26] However very few s.170MX awards have been made since 1997.

Although industrial action is permitted under the legislation, it may only be undertaken during a bargaining period as defined in Division 8 of the Act. The AIRC has powers to stop or prevent industrial action under s.127 of the WRAct 96 such that 'the AIRC can, by order, direct that the industrial action stop or not occur'.[27] The WRAct 96 can increase industrial disputation in that 'while in terms s.127 it extends to all industrial action, orders made under the section will not apply to industrial action that is protected action, that is action in relation to negotiation of a certified agreement'.[28] The WRAct 96 has also extended the ability of employers to use lockouts as a means to advance claims. Legislative provisions which allow lockouts as "protected" industrial action have been introduced at a time when 'a resurgence of lockouts has been observed by industrial relations academics'.[29]

The provisions of the WRAct 96 regarding industrial action 'generally represent a considerable reduction in the circumstances in which industrial action may be taken without exposure to adverse legal consequences'.[30] Given that most industrial action is taken by employees rather than employers, these provisions affect employees' ability to effectively pursue their interests in enterprise bargaining. With regards to industrial action and negotiations, many authors have argued that the Act introduces more complexity and legalism. In many areas with regards to industrial action and collective bargaining, the Coalition's industrial relations regime encourages a situation where trade union capacities are diverted from 'organizing workplaces' and the core union activities of improving wages and conditions for their members and generally protecting and enhancing workers' rights'.[31]

The WRAct 96 also introduced statutory individual agreements in the form of Australian Workplace Agreements (AWAs). Part VID of the Act provided for the filing and approval of AWAs. It gives primacy to these individual agreements and through them operating to the exclusion of awards, state legislation and any future certified agreements.[32] AWAs have in several publicised cases been used to avoid bargaining with trade unions, (for instance, the mining and telecommunications sectors). Van Barneveld & Nassif (2003) present that 'despite the rhetoric of choice, AWAs are primarily a tool for employers, rather than a tool used to the benefit of both parties to the employment relationship'.[33] However some defended AWAs saying they are largely used to 'foster positive employer/employee relations without the need for third party involvement and to give true choice, with a balance of suitable working conditions and wages to employees. Alternately others view AWAs use to avoid unions, and to reduce labour costs'.[34]

Despite their potential strategic importance, AWAs to date cover only a small percentage of the current labour force. The Office of the Employment Advocate (OEA) recently announced the approval of 1,000,000 AWAs since 1997 – while this represents a nominal figure of approximately 10 per cent of the labour force, it is estimated that a reasonable percentage of these agreements has no longer remained in force.[35] McCallum presents that 'instead of being the centre piece of the WR Act... AWAs may be relegated to the sleepy back-water of Australian Industrial Relations law'.[36] However others agree there will always be niche market for AWAs especially for small business and business with good work life balance policies and principals. Merlo (2000) noted that 'the fact that AWAs regulate conditions only for a smaller percentage of the workforce, it is not surprising considering that like EFAs, AWAs were always likely to be of marginal practical significance, largely because of the elaborate procedural and substantive criteria to be satisfied before they could become operative'.[37]

Numerous legislative reform initiatives have been undertaken since the introduction of the WRAct 96. Of these the most comprehensive reform proposal, the Workplace Relations Amendment (More Jobs, Better Pay) Bill 1999. "More Jobs Better Pay", failed to pass the Senate as the Labour and minority parties had strong reservations about the effect of the proposal on labour market equity and trade union activities. As with the original legislation and future proposed amendments, the "More Jobs Better Pay Bill" was introduced with a justification to 'improve outcomes, to lower transaction costs, to improve opportunities for enterprise level innovation and flexibility, to have a more effective safety net, to provide impetus for organizational change and to provide a flexible labour market capable of meeting the competitive challenges facing Australia'.[38] Further initiatives were introduced during the 38th, 39th and 40th parliament of which only a few eventually passed through the upper house. These included amendments to the Workplace Relations Act 1996 which prohibited pattern bargaining, union bargaining fees and attempts to exempt small business from unfair dismissal laws. The Workplace Relations Amendment (Genuine Bargaining) Act 2002 provided additional responsibilities to the AIRC to terminate bargaining periods where it was viewed the parties were not genuinely negotiating. Trade unions presented that the Act was in fact a narrowing of the AIRC's discretion to deal with the conduct of the parties engaged in a bargaining period such that the 'effect of the [legislation] is to direct the Commission to consider a number of matters and, where it is established that one or more of the circumstances exist, to find that this tends to indicate that the first party is not genuinely trying to reach agreement with the other negotiating party'.[39] Further, it has been presented that this and other legislative amendments and proposals 'will create greater inequality in bargaining outcomes and ... women and weaker/vulnerable groups in the labour market will be further disadvantaged'.[40] During 2003 and 2004 the government introduced a significant number of bills primarily aimed to curtail union activity and promote AWAs, including secret ballots for protected action, further prohibitions on union bargaining fees and to "simplify" AWA processes and agreement making.

The attempts to further reform the federal industrial relations system since 1996 and the legislative initiatives have focused on changing trade unions core functions, i.e., collectively represent groups of employees'.[41]

The No Disadvantage Test in Federal Industrial Law – A Case Study

The Industrial Relations Reform Act 1993 introduced a "no-disadvantage test" to both union certified agreements and non-union enterprise flexibility agreements. The AIRC was required 'in the certification of an agreement to identify the employees who are covered by the agreement but whose interests may not have been sufficiently taken into account in the negotiations for, or within the terms of, the agreement'.[42] It is widely held that the "flexibility" available to employers under the WRAct 96 is greater than that available under the previous legislation, when considering "flexibility" in terms of the ability to change fundamental terms and conditions of employment including work/life balances.

An important case highlighting the difference in practice and application of the no-disadvantage test under the 1993 and 1996 legislation is the decision of the AIRC in Automotive, Food, Metals, Engineering, Printing and *Kindred Industries Union* v. *Tweed Valley Fruit Processors Pty Ltd* (1995) 61 IR 212 ("Tweed Valley Processing"). In this appeal decision of the full bench of the AIRC, the union contended that the AIRC had erred in approving an Enterprise Flexibility Agreement which among numerous reductions to "core" terms and conditions of employment, provided for no paid personal leave entitlements. It was submitted that the AIRC had 'misconstrued or misunderstood the test [the AIRC] was obliged to apply to the application'.[43] The federal government intervened in the decision submitting that 'the Commissioner failed to exercise the public interest discretion as required by the no disadvantage test'.[44] The full bench considered the direction and intentions of the government in introducing the no disadvantage test in the 1993 legislation, and reviewed the Minister's second reading speech in parliament such that:

> '...the provision is intended to protect well established and accepted standards which apply across the community—standards such as maternity leave, hours of work, parental leave, minimum rates of pay, termination change and redundancy provisions and superannuation...'[45]

The full bench accepted that sick leave is a community standard and must be substantially taken into account in the no-disadvantage test. Further, that the Commissioner was in error in concluding that the implementation of the agreement would not result in an overall reduction in entitlements when compared to the relevant award. An appeal to the Industrial Relations Court of Australia by the employer, where it was contended that the Full Bench of the AIRC had no jurisdiction to overturn the certification of an agreement, failed to overturn the decision.[46]

The Tweed Valley Processing case highlights important distinctions between the no-disadvantage test under the 1993 legislation and the WRAct 96. Firstly, although the Tweed Valley agreement was a non-union EFA, the appropriate trade union was entitled to appear before the AIRC and make submissions regarding the effect of the proposed agreement on employees' terms and conditions of employment. This case clearly highlights the effect of trade union participation in agreement making such that substantive conditions of employment are more likely to be protected or properly compensated for in any overall "package" of employment conditions proposed in an enterprise agreement. No such right for trade union participation exists under the present legislative regime in terms of s.170LK non-union certified agreements or Australian Workplace Agreements. Secondly, the prevalence of agreements which reduce or abolish conditions considered "community standards" is much higher under the WRAct 96, as this legislation (and the policy directions of the government) provide for a more "global" assessment. Section 170XA of the WRAct 96 provides only minimal regulation of the no disadvantage test in that an agreement passes the test 'if it does not disadvantage employees in relation to their terms and conditions of employment'.[47] The likelihood of such conditions being reduced or abolished in enterprise agreements is again much higher in non-union statutory options than in union certified agreements. Merlo (2000) presents that the legislative framework for the no disadvantage test assessment under the Industrial Relations Reform Act 1993 indicate the 'government's intention to maintain a strong NDT'.[48]

Many authors contend that the authorities which apply the no-disadvantage test under the WRAct 96 may not properly consider the true effect of the loss of such entitlements on the overall terms and conditions of employment of relevant employees.[49] Pittard & Naughton (2003) present that 'even though the 'no disadvantage test' [under the WRAct 96] is arguably more flexible than the one which existed under the IR Act, the test may still prevent employers from modifying or removing terms and conditions of employment from agreements, where they have the status of 'community standards'.[50] Some suggest however that the maintenance of 'community standards' in many agreements has not increased outside collective bargaining with trade unions. Following the changes to awards of twenty allowable matters, many AWAs and enterprise agreements have expanded to cover issues dropped from awards, however some have not'.[51] Merlo (2000) describes how the WRAct 96 has relinquished the aim of protecting community standards and has allowed through both individual and collective agreement certification an 'erosion of community standards'.[52] Mitchell & Fetter (2003) presented in their research findings of the content of Australian Workplace Agreements that there was 'little to indicate that the individualization process through AWAs was demonstrating any sort of a managerial shift towards the new employment paradigm'.[53] Further, that their research showed 'a substantial number of agreements were simple in construction, and sought to achieve a limited objective such as the liberalization of the ordinary hours of work'.[54] Van Barneveld presents (with reference to AWAs referred to the AIRC for review where decisions were published) that 'all of the decisions published by the Commission highlight cases of AWAs being used for cost-cutting purposes'.[55] Further, that the motivation for many employers in using "non-union" statutory agreements is to achieve greater flexibility in employment terms and conditions (including 'community standards') than possible in union collective agreements.

The former Workplace Relations Minister, Reith, contended that the proposed new Workplace Relations Act facilitated a situation where 'employers and employees are now at liberty to strike genuinely innovative agreements without any contrivances or artificial restrictions'.[56]

The High Court and Electrolux

The High Court of Australia has a long tradition of taking conservative views of the federal industrial relations power and regulations. In the decision of Electrolux Home Products Pty Ltd v Australian Workers' Union [2004] HCA 40 (2 September 2004), following the Electrolux decision, aspects of federal certified agreements and Australian Workplace Agreements (AWAs) were cast in doubt as the High Court ruled that agreements must only contain matters pertaining to the relationship between employers and employees. The Electrolux High Court decision emerged from a full bench Federal Court determination[57] ruling in favour of the Australian Workers' Union claim that a s.170LJ certified agreement could legitimately contain a "bargaining fee clause" and that this clause pertained to the relationship between the employer and employees as trade union members.

The effect of the Electrolux decision cast into doubt the AIRC's ability to certify a collective agreement which contains provisions considered "ancillary" or "organisational" in nature such as bargaining fees. Following this ruling, such matters were not considered to be pertaining to the employer-employee relationship and therefore may not legitimately be certified in a collective agreement. It was possible that the Electrolux decision may also have affected AWAs.

The AIRC then took a broader interpretation of the Electrolux decision and 'rejected employer-group arguments that a raft of provisions in a comprehensive NUW agreements do not pertain to the employment relationship, allowing clauses covering a prohibition on offering AWAs, site rates for casual labour hire workers, union right of entry, trade union training leave, and paid leave for union delegates'.[58] In this decision Vice President Iain Ross determined that 'a certified agreement may contain provisions which are machinery in nature or are ancillary or incidental to a matter pertaining to the requisite relationship'.[59]

Efficiency and Equity in Labour Law

The proper role of labour law in Australia is to promote productivity and efficiency in private and public enterprise, and to protect and develop the industrial rights and entitlements of employees. In the absence of such regulation, the system would be characterized by sharply divided and unequal standards across the community, an unfettered managerial prerogative over all facets of work (and even private) life, and ultimately, become a poorer and unjust society. A system which can properly balance the often competing priorities of capital and labour is one which provides fairness to both employers and employees, and seeks to re-distribute economic wealth and power from those who possess it to those who are unable to access the rewards of an industrialized nation. The views presented in this paper demonstrate very different schools of thought and some say that the federal industrial relations regime at present has contributed to greater inequity, a power shift to employers, and more broadly, to the abandonment of principles of equality in favour of short term rationalist economic ideology. The law surrounding enterprise bargaining is a critical element in how labour law either promotes or reduces the level of equity across the labour force.

Many industrial relations and pluralist human resource management authors have contended that an industrial relations system based on common law principles and precarious (or conflictual) notions of the employment relationship is not an "efficient" system. The "high trust" model of employment relations is suggested to be one which most effectively involves workers in the business of the enterprise, and at the same time provides fair rewards for employees. Prevailing economic ideology promotes that workplace cooperation and enterprise "efficiency" is linked to the labour regulation which requires more equal allocation of rewards or better work practices increasing a work/life balance, or in other ways, restricts the ultimate capability of management to make decisions. A cooperative employment relation is in no way necessarily linked to labour de-regulation. Labour de-regulation simply allows employers to unilaterally adopt employment practices they deem most suitable, whether this be a high trust or a precarious relationship with employees. The federal system in Australia, promoted a more cooperative industrial relations, directly between employer and employee. However some author's debate that it has simply shifted power and decision making responsibilities from employees and independent government authorities, and possibly to the ultimate detriment of those employees least able to bargain better terms and conditions for themselves especially NESB or vulnerable employees. Others debate that the federal industrial relations system has, balanced efficiency with fairness (an essential element of the high trust cooperative model) and simply given the ability to employees to improve their own terms and conditions of employment.

Conclusion

This paper has reviewed the legislative framework for enterprise bargaining and its effects on employees and employers. Evidence has been provided which offers outcomes which are generally more equitable for workers that are able to bargain with their employer. However, in general terms employees in weaker bargaining positions will not get employment in their area of expertise nor advance at the same rate within an organization. Given that the support for enterprise bargaining is primarily founded on economic & productivity improvement concerns, it has been suggested that, when considering efficiency to be simply the number of agreements registered, the federal model since 1996 has been successful in achieving efficient outcomes. When viewing efficiency as a balance of interests, which ultimately contribute to an equitable workforce improvement is needed either through community or employer, education programs or a clearer understanding of the benefits of a diverse workforce to Australian businesses and the community. The Industrial relations system needs to ensure for all parties, a demonstrated greater "equity & efficiency" in agreement making. With the new expansionary changes to the federal system, it is apparent that workers and trade unions in NSW will face a further divergence of these standards and potential challenges to their industrial interests and rights. Companies however need to capitalize on diversity and extract the value to the business that can be gained from acknowledging, valuing and developing diversity to enhance and create business opportunities that arise from this difference.

Bibliography

ACCI (2002) Submission to the Senate Employment, Workplace Relations, Small Business and Education Legislation Committee. (Inquiry into Workplace Relations Amendment Bills). Sourced from: www.acci.asn.au

ACTU (2002) Submission to the Senate Employment, Workplace Relations, Small Business and Education Legislation Committee. (Inquiry into Workplace Relations Amendment Bills). Sourced from: www.actu.asn.au

AMWU (2002) Submission to the Senate Employment, Workplace Relations, Small Business and Education Legislation Committee. (Inquiry into Workplace Relations Amendment Bills). Sourced from: www.amwu.org.au

Bamber, G. & Sheldon, P. (2001) 'Collective Bargaining'. *Comparative Labour Law and Industrial Relations in Industrialised Market Economies*. Kluwer Law International. The Hague. 7th Edn.

Bennett, L. (1994) *Making Labour Law in Australia – Industrial Relations, Politics and Law*. The Law Book Company Limited. North Ryde.

Boreham, P. et al. (1996) 'What Does Enterprise Bargaining Mean for Gender Equity'. *Labour & Industry*. 7(1). June 1996. pp. 51–68.

Bray, M. & Waring, P. (1998) 'The Rhetoric and Reality of Bargaining Structures Under the Howard Government'. *Labour & Industry*. 9(2). December 1998. pp. 61–79.

Briggs, C. (2001) 'Australian Exceptionalism: The Role of Trade Unions in the Emergence of Enterprise Bargaining'. *Journal of Industrial Relations*. 43(1). March 2001. pp. 27–43.

Briggs, C. (2004) The Return of the Lockout in Australia: A Profile of Lockouts Since the Decentralisation of Bargaining. AIRAANZ Conference Paper – Noosa Australia 2004. Sourced from: www.griffith.edu.au

Callus, R. & Lansbury, R. eds. (2002) *Working Futures: The Changing Nature of Work and Employment in Australia.* The Federation Press. Sydney.

CFMEU (1999) Submission to the Senate Employment, Workplace Relations, Small Business and Education Legislation Committee – Inquiry Into "More Jobs Better Pay'. Sourced from: www.aph.gov.au

Coulthard, A. (1996) 'Non-Union Bargaining: Enterprise Flexibility Agreements'. *Journal of Industrial Relations*. 38(3). September 1996. pp. 339–358.

Coulthard, A. (1999) 'The Decollectivisation of Australian Industrial Relations: Trade Union Exclusion Under the Workplace Relations Act 1996'. *Employment Relations, Individualisation and Union Exclusion: An International Study*. The Federation Press. Sydney.

CPSU (2002) Submission to the Senate Employment, Workplace Relations, Small Business and Education Legislation Committee. (Inquiry into Workplace Relations Amendment Bills). Sourced from: www.cpsu.org.au

Creighton, B. & Stewart, A. (2000) *Labour Law – An Introduction*. 3rd Edn. The Federation Press. Sydney.

Dabscheck, B. (2001) 'The Slow and Agonising Death of the Australian Experiment with Conciliation and Arbitration'. *Journal of Industrial Relations*. 43(3). September 2001. pp. 277–293.

Department of Employment and Workplace Relations (2002) Submission to the Senate Employment, Workplace Relations, Small Business and Education Legislation Committee. (Inquiry into Workplace Relations Amendment Bills). Sourced from: www.dewr.gov.au

Electrolux Home Products Pty Ltd v. *Australian Workers Union* [2001] FCA 1600 (14 November 2001). Sourced from: www.austlii.edu.au

Electrolux Home Products Pty Ltd v *Australian Workers Union* [2004] HCA 40 (2 September 2004). Sourced from: www.austlii.edu.au

Giudice, J. (2002) Our Industrial Relations System – What Makes it Unique? Address to the Sydney Institute. 12th February 2002. Sourced from: www.airc.gov.au

Hancock, K. (1998) 'The Needs of the Low Paid'. *Journal of Industrial Relations*. 40. pp. 42–62.

Hammond, S. (2002) Submission of the Women's Electoral Lobby to the Senate Employment, Workplace Relations, Small Business and Education Legislation Committee. (Inquiry into Workplace Relations Amendment Bills). Sourced from: www.aph.gov.au

Industrial Relations Act 1996 (NSW). Sourced from: www.austlii.edu.au

Lansbury, R. (2004) 'Kingsley Laffer Memorial Lecture – Work, People and Globalisation – Towards A New Social Contract for Australia'. *Journal of Industrial Relations*. 46(1). March 2004. pp. 102–115.

Lee, M. (2004) Shaping a Preferred Bargaining Paradigm: Labour Law Remedies, the Scope of Agreements and Union Influence. AIRAANZ Conference Paper – Noosa Australia 2004. Sourced from: www.griffith.edu.au

Lee, M. & Peetz, D. (1998) 'Trade Unions and the Workplace Relations Act'. *Labour & Industry*. 9(2). December 1998. pp. 5–22.

Loudoun, R. & Harley, B. (2001) 'Industrial Relations Decentralisation and the Growth of 12-Hour Shifts in Australia'. *Journal of Industrial Relations*. 43(4). December 2001. pp. 402–421.

MacDermott, T. (1997) 'Industrial Legislation in 1996: The Reform Agenda'. *Journal of Industrial Relations*. 39(1). March 1997. pp. 52–76.

MacDonald, D. et al. (2001) 'Ten Years of Enterprise Bargaining in Australia: An Introduction'. *Labour & Industry*. 12(1). August 2001. pp. 1–25.

Marks, Hon Keith. (1989) 'Australia's New Federal Industrial Laws – The Industrial Relations Act 1988 and The Industrial Relations (Consequential Provisions" Act 1988'. *Australian Journal of Labour Law*. 2(1). March 1989. pp. 66–74.

Merlo, O. (2000) 'Flexibility and Stretching Rights: The No Disadvantage Test and Enterprise Bargaining'. *Australian Journal of Labour Law*. 13.

McCallum, R. (1997) 'Australian Workplace Agreements: An Analysis'. *Australian Journal of Labour Law*. 10. pp. 50–61.

McCallum, R. (1997) 'Crafting a New Collective Labour Law for Australia'. *Journal of Industrial Relations*. 39(3). September 1997. pp. 405–422.

McCallum, R. (2002) Good Faith Bargaining, Protected Action and the Need for a Statutory Trade Union Recognition Procedure. Address to the Tenth Annual Labour Law Conference. Thursday 21st March 2002. Sydney.

McCallum, R. (1995) 'Our Changing Labour Law' in McCallum, R. (ed) *Enterprise Bargaining, Trade Unions and the Law*. The Federation Press. Sydney.

McCallum, R. (2002) 'Trade Union Recognition and Australia's Neo-Liberal Voluntary Bargaining Laws'. *Relations Industrielles*. pp. 225–251.

McCarry, G. (1997) 'Industrial Action under the Workplace Relations Act 1996 (Cmth)'. *Australian Journal of Labour Law*. 10(1). April 1997. pp. 133–155.

McCarry, G. (1998) 'Relationships Between the Federal and NSW Industrial Relations Systems'. *Australian Journal of Labour Law*. 11(2). August 1998. pp. 69–94.

McGrath, S. (2004) Enterprise Bargaining and Australia's New Regional Economies: The Effects of Rescaling Wage Regulation. AIRAANZ Conference Paper – Noosa Australia 2004. Sourced from: www.griffith.edu.au

Mitchell, R. & Fetter, J. (2003) 'Human Resource Management and Individualisation in Australian Labour Law'. *Journal of Industrial Relations*. 45.

Moore, B. (1994) 'The Industrial Relations Reform Act 1993: A New Era for Industrial Relations in Australia'. *Australian Journal of Labour Law*. 7(1). March 1994. pp. 69–76.

Naughton, R. (1995) 'Bargaining in Good Faith – The Asahi Decision'. *Australian Journal of Labour Law*. 8(2). August 1995. pp. 166–168.

Naughton, R. (1994) 'The New Bargaining Regime Under the Industrial Relations Reform Act'. *Australian Journal of Labour Law*. 7(2). August 1994. pp. 147–169.

Nelson, L. & Firth, A. (2001) 'The Process of Enterprise Bargaining in a Manufacturing Organisation'. *Journal of Industrial Relations*. 43(4). December 2001. pp. 462–469.

Nolan, D. ed. (1998) *The Australasian Labour Law Reforms – Australia & New Zealand at the End of the Twentieth Century*. The Federation Press. Sydney.

Peetz, D. (2002) 'Individual Contracts, Bargaining and Union Membership'. *Australian Bulletin of Labour*. 28(1). March 2002. pp. 39–52.

Peetz, D. (1998) 'The Safety Net, Bargaining and the Role of the Australian Industrial Relations Commission'. *Journal of Industrial Relations*. 40(4). December 1998. pp. 533–553.

Pittard, M. & Naughton, R. (2003) *Australian Labour Law – Cases and Materials*. 4th Edn. LexiNexus Butterworths. Chatswood.

Pittard, M. (1997) 'Collective Employment Relationships: Reforms to Arbitrated Awards and Certified Agreements'. *Australian Journal of Labour Law*. 10(1). April 1997. pp. 62–88.

Pragnell, B. & O'Donnell, M. (1997) 'A Failed Experiment? Enterprise Bargaining under the New South Wales Industrial Relations Act 1991'. *Journal of Industrial Relations*. 39(1). pp. 3–20.

Pyman, A. (2001) 'Workplace Relations and Other Legislation Amendment Act 1996 (Cmth): Experiences of Five Trade Unions'. *Journal of Industrial Relations*. 43(3). September 2001. pp. 340–348.

Reitano, R. (1994) 'Legislative Change in 1993'. *Journal of Industrial Relations*. 36(1). March 1994. pp. 57–73.

Reith, Hon P. Approaches to Dispute Resolution: A Role for Mediation? Ministerial Discussion Paper.

Reith, Hon P. (1999) The Continuing Reform of Workplace Relations: Implementation of More Jobs, Better Pay. Implementation Discussion Paper. May 1999. Sourced from: www.dewr.gov.au

Reith, Hon P. (1999) Workplace Relations Legislation Amendment (More Jobs, Better Pay) Bill 1999. Regulation Impact Statement.

Riley, J. (2000) 'Individual Contracting and Collective Bargaining in the Balance'. *Australian Journal of Labour Law*. 13. pp. 92–98.

Riley, J. (2004) 'Industrial Legislation in 2003'. *Journal of Industrial Relations*. 46(2). June 2004. pp. 184–194.

Riley, J. et al. (1997) *Workplace Relations – A Guide to the 1996 Changes*. LBC Information Services. North Ryde.

Rimmer, M. (1989) 'Transforming Industrial Relations in New South Wales – A Green Paper'. *Australian Journal of Labour Law*. 2(2). August 1989. pp. 188–196.

Roan, A. et al. (2001) 'Australian Workplace Agreements in Practice: The 'Hard' and 'Soft' Dimensions'. *Journal of Industrial Relations*. 43(4). December 2001. pp. 387–401.

Shaw, J. (1996) 'A Balanced Industrial Relations Reform Package for New South Wales'. *Journal of Industrial Relations*. 38(1). March 1996. pp. 57–69.

Shaw, J. (1997) 'In Defence of the Collective: New South Wales Industrial Relations in the 21st Century'. *Journal of Industrial Relations*. 39(3). September 1997. pp. 388–406.

Shaw, J.Q.C. (1996) 'The Industrial Relations Act 1996 (NSW): Some Legal Aspects'. *Australian Journal of Labour Law*. 9(3). December 1996. pp. 273–281.

Shaw, J. & Walton, M. (1989) 'The Niland Report and Labour Law: A Critical Response'. *Australian Journal of Labour Law*. 2(2). August 1989. pp. 197–205.

Smith, G. (1992) 'Industrial Legislation in 1991'. *Journal of Industrial Relations*. 34(1). March 1992. pp. 113–127.

Stackpool, J. (1989) 'Industrial Legislation in 1988'. *Journal of Industrial Relations*. 31(1). March 1989. pp. 93–100.

Stewart, A. (2002) 'Federal Labour Law and New Uses for the Corporations Power'. *Australian Journal of Labour Law*. 14. pp. 145–168.

Suwa, Y. (2003) 'The Actors of Collective Bargaining: Is the System Really Sustainable in the Future?' Bulletin of Comparative Labour Relations. 51(23).

Van Barneveld, K. & Arsovska, B. (2001) 'AWAs: Changing the Structure of Wages'. Labour & Industry. 12(1). August 2001. pp. 87–108.

Van Barneveld, K. & Nassif, R. (2003) 'Motivations for the Introduction of Australian Workplace Agreements'. Labour & Industry. 14(2). December 2003. pp. 21–37.

Waring, P. & Lewer, J. (2001) 'The No Disadvantage Test: Failing Workers'. Labour & Industry. 12(1). August 2001. pp. 65–86.

Watson, I. (2002) 'Wage Inequality and Underemployment in the 1990s'. *Journal of Industrial Relations*. 44(1). March 2002. pp. 88–107.

Watts, M. Mitchell, W. (2004) 'Wages and Wage Determination in 2003'. *Journal of Industrial Relations*. 46(2). June 2004. pp. 160–183.

Wooden, M. (1999) 'Individual Agreement-Making in Australian Workplaces: Incidence, Trends and Features'. *Journal of Industrial Relations*. 41(3). September 2004. pp. 417–445.

Wooden, M. (2000) *The Transformation of Australian Industrial Relations*. The Federation Press. Sydney.

Workplace Express (2004) 'Andrews Reveals IR Priorities'. 22nd October 2004. Sourced from: www.workplaceexpress.com.au

Workplace Express (2004) 'Electrolux: The Ramifications'. 3rd September 2004. Sourced from: www.workplaceexpress.com.au

Workplace Express (2004) 'How Low Can The Bar Go? ACTU's Response to Andrews'. 28th October 2004. Sourced from: www.workplaceexpress.com.au

Workplace Express (2004) 'Matters Pertain: Win for Unions in Post-Electrolux Case'. 22nd October 2004. Sourced from: www.workplaceexpress.com.au

Workplace Express (2004) 'Munro Labels Electrolux High Court Bench "Blind Assassins"'. 25th October 2004.

Sourced from: www.workplaceexpress.com.au

Workplace Express (2004) 'WA Court Case Shaping Up As Next Electrolux Test'. 27th October 2004. Sourced from: www.workplaceexpress.com.au

Workplace Express (2004) 'Will Howard Pursue Radical IR Agenda?'. 14th October 2004. Sourced from: www.workplacexpress.com.au

Workplace Relations Act 1996 (Cmth). Sourced from: www.austlii.edu.au

Endnotes

1. Bamber, G. & Sheldon, P. (2001) 'Collective Bargaining' – Chapter 22 in Blainpain, R. & Engels, C. eds *Labour Law and Industrial Relations in Industrialized Market Economies*. Kluwer Law International. The Hague. 7th Edn. p. 551.
2. Briggs, C. (2001) 'Australian Exceptionalism: The Role of Trade Unions in the Emergence of Enterprise Bargaining'. *Journal of Industrial Relations.* 43(1). March 2001. p. 27.
3. *Industrial Relations Act 1998* (Cmth) – s.115(1).
4. Stackpool, J. (1989) 'Industrial Legislation in 1988'. *Journal of Industrial Relations*. 31(1). March 1989. p. 95.
5. *Industrial Relations Act 1998* (Cmth) - s.115(4).
6. *February 1989 Review* (1989) 27 IR 196 – at 204 & 205. Sourced from Pittard, M. & Naughton, R. (2003) *Australian Labour Law – Cases and Materials*. 4th Edn. pp. 713-714.
7. *National Wage Case 16 April 1991* (1991) 36 IR 120.
8. *National Wage Case 16 April 1991* (1991) 36 IR 120 – sourced from Pittard, M. & Naughton, R. (2003) *Australian Labour Law – Cases and Materials*. 4th Edn. p. 718.
9. Pittard, M. & Naughton, R. (2003) *Australian Labour Law – Cases and Materials*. 4th Edn. p. 723.
10. Marks, Hon Keith QC. (1989) 'Australia's New Federal Industrial Laws – The Industrial Relations Act 1988 and The Industrial Relations (Consequential Provisions) Act 1988'. *Australian Journal of Labour Law*. 2(1). March 1989. p. 66.
11. Pittard, M. & Naughton, R. (2003) *Australian Labour Law – Cases and Materials*. 4th Edn. p. 723.
12. Naughton, R. (1994) 'The New Bargaining Regime Under the Industrial Relations Reform Act'. *Australian Journal of Labour Law*. 7(2). August 1994. p. 148.
13. McCallum, R. (1994) 'The Internationalisation of Australian Industrial Law: The Industrial Relations Reform Act 1993'. *Sydney Law Review*. 16 (122).
14. This includes Division 2 Certified Agreements made under s.170LJ, s.170LK and s.170LL of the *Workplace Relations Act 1996* (Cmth). Division 3 Certified Agreements relate to agreements made in settlement of an industrial dispute – the traditional "conciliation and arbitration" process and function of federal industrial relations regulation.
15. Except in Victoria, where the *Workplace Relations Act 1996* operates as the primary industrial statute following referral of state industrial relations powers by the Kennett coalition government in 1996.
16. Coulthard, A. (1996) 'Non-Union Bargaining: Enterprise Flexibility Agreements'. *Journal of Industrial Relations.* 38(3). September 1996. p. 340.
17. Ibid, p. 355.
18. Ibid, p. 356.
19. *Workplace Relations Act 1996* (Cmth) – s.3(b).
20. Bray, M. & Waring, P. (1998) 'The Rhetoric and the Reality of Bargaining Structures Under the Howard Government'. *Labour & Industry*. 9(2). December 1998. p. 67.

21. Lee, M. (2004) *Shaping a Preferred Bargaining Paradigm: Labour Law Remedies, the Scope of Agreements and Union Influence*. AIRAANZ Conference Paper – Noosa Australia 2004. p. 1.
22. Australian Industrial Relations Commission (2004) *Annual Report of the Australian Industrial Relations Commission 2003-2004*. p. 12.
23. *Workplace Relations Act 1996* (Cmth) – s.170LJ (1)(b).
24. Ibid, s.170Lk (1).
25. Ibid, s.170LN (b).
26. Ibid, s.170MX (3)(a) & (3)(b).
27. McCarry, G. (1997) 'Industrial Action under the Workplace Relations Act 1996 (Cth)'. *Australian Journal of Labour Law*. 10(1). April 1997. p. 143.
28. Ibid, p. 143.
29. Briggs, C. (2004) *The Return of the Lockout in Australia: A Profile of Lockouts Since the Decentralisation of Bargaining*. AIRAANZ Conference Paper – 2004. p. 1.
30. McCarry, G. (1997) 'Industrial Action under the Workplace Relations Act 1996 (Cth)'. *Australian Journal of Labour Law*. 10(1). April 1997. p. 153.
31. Lee, M. & Peetz, D. (1998) 'Trade Unions and the *Workplace Relations Act*'. *Labour & Industry*. 9(2). December 1998. p. 13.
32. This issue was contended by the ACTU with the International Labour Organisation (ILO). The ILO found that the Australian government had contravened the *Right to Organize and Collective Bargaining Convention* (no. 98) 1949 in promoting individual agreement making over collective bargaining through the *Workplace Relations Act 1996*.
33. Van Barneveld, K. & Nassif, R. (2003) 'Motivations for the Introduction of Australian Workplace Agreements'. *Labour & Industry*. 14(2). December 2003. p. 22.
34. Ibid, p. 32.
35. AWA approval figures are sourced from www.oea.gov.au
36. McCallum, R. (1997) 'Australian Workplace Agreements: An Analysis'. *Australian Journal of Labour Law*. 10(1). April 1997. p. 61.
37. Merlo, O. (2000) 'Flexibility and Stretching Rights: The No Disadvantage Test in Enterprise Bargaining'. *Australian Journal of Labour Law*. 13(3). December 2000. pp. 220-221.
38. *Workplace Relations Legislation Amendment (More Jobs, Better Pay) Bill 1999* (Cmth). Regulation Impact Statement. p. 2.
39. ACTU (2002) *Submission to the Senate Employment, Workplace Relations and Education Legislation Committee Inquiry*. p. 10.
40. Hammond, S. (2002) *Submission of the Women's Electoral Lobby to the Senate Employment, Workplace Relations and Education Legislation Committee Inquiry*. p. 2.
41. AMWU (2002) *Submission of the Women's Electoral Lobby to the Senate Employment, Workplace Relations and Education Legislation Committee Inquiry*. p. 1.
42. Reitano, R. (1994) 'Legislative Change in 1993'. *Journal of Industrial Relations*. 36(1). March 1994. p. 66.

43. *Automotive, Food, Metals, Engineering, Printing and Kindred Industries Union v Tweed Valley Fruit Processors Pty Ltd* (1995) 61 IR 212. Sourced from Pittard, M. & Naughton, R. (2003) *op cit.*, p. 754.
44. Ibid, p. 754.
45. Ibid, p. 757.
46. *Tweed Valley Fruit Processors Pty Ltd v Ross and Others* (960149) (1996) Industrial Relations Court of Australia. Decision Number 149/96. The functions of the Industrial Relations Court of Australia were subsumed by the Federal Court of Australia following the introduction of the Workplace Relations Act 1996 – based clearly on the intention and belief of the conservative government that the more "commercial" Federal Court would deliver outcomes more favourable to business than to trade unions.
47. *Workplace Relations Act 1996* (Cmth) – s.170XA (1).
48. Merlo, O. (2000) 'Flexibility and Stretching Rights: The No Disadvantage Test in Enterprise Bargaining'. *Australian Journal of Labour Law*. 13(3). p. 212.
49. The Office of the Employment Advocate (OEA) applies the no-disadvantage test to proposed Australian Workplace Agreements (AWAs). The AIRC applies the no-disadvantage test to certified agreements, and also AWAs referred to the AIRC by the OEA where the parties fail to provide satisfactory "undertakings" to redress no-disadvantage test concerns.
50. Pittard, M. & Naughton, R. (2003) *op cit.*, p. 747.
51. Bray, M. & Waring, P. (1998) 'The Rhetoric and Reality of Bargaining Structures Under the Howard Government'. *Labour & Industry*. 9(2). December 1998. p. 77.
52. Merlo, O. (2000) 'Flexibility and Stretching Rights: The No Disadvantage Test in Enterprise Bargaining'. *Australian Journal of Labour Law*. 13(3). p. 228.
53. Mitchell, R. & Fetter, J. (2003) *The Individualisation of Employment Relationships and the Adoption of High Performance Work Practices – Final Report*. Centre for Employment and Labour Relations Law, University of Melbourne. p. 11.
54. Ibid, p. 11.
55. Van Barneveld, K. & Nassif, R. (2003) 'Motivations for the Introduction of Australian Workplace Agreements'. *Labour & Industry*. 14(2). December 2003. p. 31.
56. Pittard, M. & Naughton, R. (2003) *op cit.*, p. 747.
57. Australian Industry Group v Automotive, Food, Metals, Engineering, Printing & Kindred Industries Union [2003] FCAFC 183 (15 August 2003).
58. Workplace Express (2004) 'Matters Pertain: Win for Unions in Post-Electrolux Case'. 22nd October 2004.
59. Ibid.

18

North-East India's Cultural Diversity: Trends of Unrest and Marginalization

Sudhir Jacob George

North-East India is Asia in miniature, a place where the brown and yellow races meet and mingle. It is home to seven states, part of a great tropical rain forest that stretches from the foothills of the Himalayas to the tip of the Malaysian Peninsula and the mouth of the Mekong river as it flows into the Gulf of Tonkin. The jungles of South East Asia extend from Bhutan and Arunachal Pradesh to seven other nations – Bangladesh, Myanmar, Thailand, Laos, Kampuchea, Malaysia and Vietnam, spanning political boundaries, irrevential even of physical frontiers. Here men and women, with common origins but different nationalities, share a racial, historic, anthropological and linguistic kinship with each other that is more significant than their links with the mainstream political centres, in particular at Delhi, Dhaka and Yangnon. India's North-East is a misshapen strip of land, linked to the mainland by a narrow strip known as the Chicken's Neck. The region has been the battle ground for generations of sub-national identities confronting insensitive nation-states and their bureaucracies as well as of internecine strife. It is a battle that persists of ideas and arms, new concepts and old traditions.[1]

The North-East of India is a culturally rich and diverse region encompassing several tribes/communities singularly distinct and also alienated from the mainstream Indian society. The several tribal groups and few non-tribal ethnic groups, viz. the Meties of Manipur valley and the Ahoms of upper Assam belong to the Mongoloid stock and few, viz. the Jaintia's and Karbis to the Austric. The ethnically distinct tribal groups reside in the hills while the non-tribals dominate the plains and the valley. Around 12 per cent of India's tribals live in the seven states (Assam, Nagaland, Manipur, Meghalaya, Mizoram, Tripura and Arunachal Pradesh). The principal tribes of the region are the Naga(s) – Angamis, Ao's, Chekasang, Lotha, Rengma, Sema, Tanghkul, Zeilanrong besides the Kukis and other smaller tribes inhabiting Nagaland and the Hill areas of Manipur; the Bodos, Dimasas, Karbis, Koch-Rajbansgs of Assam, Khasis, Jaintias and Garos of Meghalaya; the Mizos of Mizoram, Tripuris, Reangs of Tripura besides the several tribes, viz. Monpas, Sherdukpens, Membas, Khambas, Singphos, Adis, Akas, Apatanis, Bangnis,

Nishis, Mishmis, Mijis, Thongsas, Noctes and Wanchos of Arunachal Pradesh. Whereas the tribals are over 80 per cent of the population in Nagaland, Meghalaya and Mizoram and two thirds of Arunachal but are small in number in the otherwise populous states of Assam, Manipur and Tripura.[2]

The cultural diversity of the North-East is buttressed by the fact that each of the tribe inhabiting the region is very particular and conscious of protecting and upholding its cultural trait and tradition(s). It is significant to note that every tribe in the North-East maintain(s) its distinct identity by its own dialect, dress, ceremonies during marriage and celebration of their own and distinct festivals round the year.[3]

Brief History of the North-East

Until the entry of the British into the region in the 19th Century the tribes led a life of pristine isolation and resisted the dominance of the Kacharis and subsequently the Ahoms who ruled the Assam valley prior to the British entry. With the arrival of the British, change occurred. Although they did not disturb the tribal communities in their lifestyle, overtime the British gradually extended their control over the remote hill areas of the region. The hill areas of the North-East were uniformly administered until 1937 as a backward tract exclusively under the Chief Commissioner. However, in April 1937 there was a bifurcation of the administrative pattern. The Lushai Hills (present Mizoram), Naga Hills, North Cachar and North-East Frontier Agency (NEFA) tracts were designated as excluded areas, excluded from ministerial jurisdiction. The Garo Hills, the British portion of Khasi and Jaintia Hills and Mikir Hills (Karbi Anglong) were partially excluded areas. The excluded areas were guarded by the Inner Line Regulation of 1873 that restricted the entry of outsiders without permit. As a matter of fact the Line System was introduced by the British to prevent and guard their soldiers and officials from inadvertently foraying into the wild tribal areas. However overtime, the British used this Inner Line system to restrict the entry of people from the plains and this is one of the major causes that has led to the isolation of the tribal areas and the tribes of the N.E. in particular, with mainstream India. In fact, it is significant to note, it was only the Assamese who actively participated in the anti-British mainstream Indian National Movement besides the Manipuris who were exposed to the movement due to the entry of the Indian National Army of Subash Chandra Bose into the North-East and Manipur in particular, from Burma.

Notwithstanding this fact the tribes of the North-East did oppose and resist the white man's rule and administration and the most virulent in this regard were the Nagas who since the British era regarded themselves as an independent entity. Besides the Nagas, the Khasis under U Tirot Singh and the Mizos did raise their own flag of resistance to British authority. The Meities of Manipur valley one of the Princely states of the North-East have questioned the very accession of Manipur state to India in 1949 and its rebel groups primarily the Peoples Liberation Army of Kangleipak and Peoples Revolutionary Party of Kangleipak have been in the thick of a struggle to liberate the people of Manipur and beyond from the clutches of the overarching Indian state since few years. Today these two rebel groups are down, though not out, and as their struggle is based on Metei nationalism bordering on fanaticism and Mao's doctrine of armed revolution, it is a major challenge to India's effort to establish a genuine democratic, plural nation-state. Most of the tribal communities in the region nurse the feeling that their autonomous territories/kingdoms have in fact been annexed by the Indian State and no effort was ever made to secure the opinion of the tribal people prior to the so called accession of their territories by democratic India.

Separatist Tendencies in the North-East

The tendencies of separatism/ethnic assertion in the North-East can be delineated as follows:

a) Sections and groups asserting for greater autonomy within the existing regional/state framework, viz. the Bodos (who have been accorded a Territorial Council under the VI Schedule); the Dimas, Karbis, Hmars and Misings.
b) Sections and groups aspiring to carve/carved out new centres of power, i.e. attaining status of separate states within the federal set up, based on the principle of ethnicity/and being distinct tribes (Khasis, Jaintias and Garos who attained a separate state on this basis, i.e. Meghalaya in 1971), Bodos who have attained a Territorial council in early 2000 and the Hmars of Mizoram who continue to be in ferment for autonomy.
c) Sections and groups which desired to break away from India and establish sovereign entities. The Mizo National Front (MNF) pre-1986; the Tripura National Volunteers (TNV) pre-1988; Peoples Liberation Army (PLA); Manipur, United National Liberation Front UNLF, Manipur; United Liberation Front of Asom (ULFA); Nationalist Socialist Council of Nagaland (NSCN), Nagaland broadly fall in this category.[4]

The major challenge to the federal arrangement in India is from the PLA, PREPAK, UNLF in Manipur; ULFA (Hard Core) in Assam and NSCN in Nagaland. In fact the goal of the PLA has been to unite all nationalities including the Chins, Kukis, Meteis, Nagas, Mizos and to arouse the neighbouring states of India so that India's federal set up can be destabilized through their joint forces. PREPAK aims to install a socialist sovereign state in Manipur by suppressing all counter revolutionaries. UNLF floats the plan for the long term national liberation movement in Manipur by armed revolution even with external assistance. The ULFA seeks the establishment of scientific socialism in independent Assam. It reckons the 1886 Yandabo Treaty between Burma and Britain in India that incorporated Assam into British India as the episode that marked the end of Assam's independence. ULFA vows to restore that lost independence.[5] The NSCN, by far the most powerful rebel group active in the North-East aims at the creation of a sovereign Xian Socialist State (Nagalim) incorporating all the Naga areas/tribes of Nagaland and beyond.[6]

The Naga rebellion, movement, struggle for independence began in the 1950s and during its heyday the NNC led by Angami Zapu Phizo held complete sway over the struggle against the Indian State and its security forces. However, with some of the moderate Nagas supporting and opting for the formation of the state of Nagaland in 1963, the Naga National Council led by Phizo was weakened and in over a decade several of its cadres came over ground and signed the Shillong Accord in 1975. However some of the hardcore among the NNC rejected the Shillong Accord and formed the NSCN in the early 1980s led by Isak Chisi Swu, Th. Muivah and Kaphlang. Subsequently Kaphlang who happens to belong to the Naga tribe inhabiting Mynmar broke away from Chisi Swu and Muivah and formed the NSCN (K). However, overtime it is the NSCN led by Swu and Muivah which has been in the forefront of the Naga insurgency through the 1980s and 1990s. The beginning of a dialogue between the Government of India and the NSCN (IM) in the early 1990s during the regime of P.V. Narasimha Rao, in Geneva, and Bangkok led to the signing of a holding ceasefire in 1997 which has been extended periodically since then. This ceasefire has given some respite to the Nagas who were under the shadow of armed conflict since over 5 decades. In fact the decades of unrest and turmoil in Nagaland and the North-East led by the NSCN and the counter action by the security forces has been the cause of immense suffering for the Nagas who in a way were caught in between the fire of the insurgents and armed forces of India. The long deployment of the armed forces and their extended presence in civilian areas in Nagaland has virtually marginalized the autonomy and identity of the tribes of Nagaland which the state seeks to uphold.

The ceasefire agreement of August 1997 with the NSCN (IM) and NSCN (K) 2000 April, is a landmark that has ushered in the process of peace making. However while New Delhi has tried to work out a solution within the ambit of the Constitution, the NSCN (IM) has pushed for the unification of all Naga inhabited areas in the North-East into a single politico-administrative unit. This has been virulently opposed by the Manipuris who will stand to lose two fifths of Manipurs territory and Assam a sizeable area of its own if the NSCN's demand of greater Nagaland (Nagalim) which it seems to be set on, is conceded. To attain peace within Nagaland one cannot afford to disturb the status-quo and peace in the neighbouring states. This is bound to lead to serious repercussions in the entire North-Eastern region as also in the other states of the country.

The other major ongoing challenge that India faces in its effort to establish a democratic/federal/multicultural society is from the United Liberation Front of Asom (ULFA).

The ULFA was established in April 1979 at Sibsagar the former ruling centre of the Ahoms. ULFA's objective on its founding was to establish scientific socialism in an independent/culturally distinct Assam and to use the states natural resources for the benefit of its people. After the failure of the Asom Gana Parishad government and the 1985 Assam Accord to live up to its promises, the people of Assam lost faith in the electoral process and ULFA obtained space to pose a radical solution to the ills besetting Assam. It advocated a long term militant approach and not non-violent protest to arrest the attention of the Federal Government. ULFA's primary goal is to liberate Assam through armed national liberation struggle and rid it of the stranglehold of occupation of the Indian State and to establish a sovereign independent Assam[7]. ULFA does not consider its movement to be separatist or secessionist because it reckons that it was never a part of India. It contends that Assam has been occupied by India which has exerted its colonial will on the Assamese by permitting illegal immigration from neighbouring Bangladesh to persist, and extraction of the valuable resources of the state. It also opines that the Federal Government has persisted with the erstwhile British colonial policies and has passed a series of repressive laws that include the Armed Forces Special Powers Act of 1958 and the Disturbed Areas Act (Assam) of 1980.[8] The movement for national self-determination—it contends—was made necessary in 1979 after the failure of peaceful demonstration.

Strategy and Tactics of ULFA

Though not pronounced by the organization itself it has been pursuing tactics to internationalize its cause, form extensive intelligence networks, undermine the legitimacy of the state—by its social agenda and methods of parallel governance, obtain control of resources, terrorize and eliminate outside migrant workers from other parts of the country eking out a living in Assam of and on, espouse the cause of the indigenous local population and secure their all round support essentially in the rural areas. Over the past two decades ULFA has held sway over the middle class Assamese and the state perse. Although ULFA reached its peak in the early 1990s with its threats and extortion and destruction of public property, viz. oil pipelines, trains and other government installations, two major military operations Operation Bajrang, though not successful, and operation Rhino almost broke the back of ULFA. However since then it has been operating intermittently and causing much pain and destruction in the North-East. During the past few years efforts have been made to bring ULFA to the negotiating table but its rigid stance on sovereignty has brought this effort to nought. The recent spurt of violence when ULFA militants (1/07) resorted to the killing of migrant Bihari workers in Assam has shocked all right thinking people both within the North-East and the country and this act has been condemned by one and all. Whether such acts can lead to the protection of any community and its interest is the question to be asked of ULFA? Further do the efforts of ULFA to preserve its distinct culture by the Assamisation of Assam have the support of the other singularly distinct tribal communities of Assam, viz. Bodos, Rabhas, Karbis, Misings, Deuris and Morans? It is important that ULFA and its leadership introspect in this regard posthaste.

In Manipur the majority of its populace have since its incorporation into the Indian Union been questioning the manner in which the erstwhile Princely State became a part of India with its ruler being made to enter into the instrument of accession in 1949. This undemocratic action, sans the consent of the people of Manipur has been the refrain of the insurgent groups of Manipur. The major insurgent groups, which have been operating in Manipur, are the PLA, PREPAK, UNLF that have been proscribed. Though these groups approach the national liberation movement in Manipur from different platforms and perspectives, their premises for insurgency are not different from the other major groups operating in the North-East. The PLA aims at organizing a revolutionary front covering Manipur, Nagaland, Mizoram, Assam, Tripura, Meghalaya and Arunachal.[9] The PLA aims to unite all nationalities including Nagas, Mizos, Chins, Kukis and Meteis to arouse the neighbouring states of India so that the Federal set up at Delhi can be destabilized through their joint force. The PLA guided by Marxism/Leninism and Mao's thought aim at mobilizing the entire population to rise up in armed revolt. The Revolutionary Government of Manipur, established in the 1970s, collapsed in the 1980s. According to the PLA, this was due to a failure to achieve the goal of a sovereign Manipur. This was due to an ideology that was based on Metei fanaticism, chauvinism and revivalism. The PLA regards Indians as the Mayans (outsiders) but it clarifies that all Indians are not its enemy. The Indian working class is regarded as its ally. The PLA stands for Metei National question seeking support from the Indian working class in the struggle against the ruling Indian bourgeoisie.

The PREPAK aims at installing a socialist sovereign state in Manipur by the suppression of all counter revolutionaries, destruction of class enemies including politicians, bureaucrats who are corrupt, contractors who are very corrupt and all anti social elements.[10] The PREPAK defies the bureaucratic set up of state, which they feel has exploited the traditional economy of Manipur, supported outsiders and unleashed military force against Kangleipak (Manipur) as neo-colonialist economies. It envisages the setting up of collectivized farming, nationalization of all trade and business and a system of Peoples Courts, as judiciary. The PREPAK concept believes in armed protest against the postures of the Federal Government. "The PREPAK extremists aim at converting their activities into a pan-mongoloid movement. They aim at establishing an independent sovereign state embracing geographically all the North-Eastern states. They have had links with the other insurgent outfits active in the North-East".[11]

The UNLF (Manipur) floated the plan for a long term national liberation movement in Manipur, propagates the imperative need for armed revolution and promises to liberate Manipur from the federal rule of New Delhi with Chinese assistance. The UNLF in its several proclamations emphasizes its commitment to the emancipation of the subjugated working class, the oppressed nationalities in India, and they seek to promote the emancipation of the suppressed nationalities elsewhere where their movement cannot reach. Their universal appeal makes their cause a part of the human emancipation movement, they condemn the oppression from which they suffer. Manipur thus has been beset with several problems, over the years, insurgent activity, transborder illegal trade, unemployment and above all rampant drug addiction among the youth; besides the continuous presence and action of the armed/ security forces are a major cause for the alienation of the Manipuri from the Indian state. In fact the law and order situation in the state has been going from bad to worse day by day. However the people seem to have accepted these as part o the general bane of a remote, marginalized border state, but the death, albeit killing of Manorama Devi on the fateful day, 11th July 2004 angered and shocked one and all, in particular the women of Imphal, Manipur who protested in a manner never seen before in independent India. They stripped outside the gates of the Assam Rifles headquarters at Imphal. The objective was to shame and shock the world; it worked. This protest awakened the usual reticent national media vis-à-vis issues of the North-East. The Centre and the State and its respective governments all became concerned about the anger engulfing the people of Manipur. In fact it led to the commencement of mass protests in the state, which virtually paralyzed normal life in the state. The self-immolation of one of the student leaders in Imphal in mid-August 2004, further represents the pathos surrounding the people of Manipur since the killing of Manorama Devi. The protests in Manipur persist, with calls for bandhs and sporadic violence reported from different parts of the state since the incident in '04. One of the major demands of the protesters is to secure the repeal of the Armed Forces Special Powers Act 1958, applicable to Manipur since 1980.

The Armed Forces Special Powers Act

The key provisions of the Act are ironically rooted in the Armed Forces (Special Powers) Ordinance, 1942 promulgated at the time of the quit India Movement that virtually placed the state under an undeclared emergency. After independence the Government of India went further by making it an Act of

Parliament, and extending its powers even to non-commissioned officers. Under the Act, the Armed forces can conduct search, destroy places and shoot to kill – at will – without warrant. The only requirement is that the officer should be satisfied that all this is necessary for the maintenance of public order. Suspicion is recognized by this acts a legitimate ground for exercising its draconian powers. By ensuring that proceedings can not be brought against any member of the Armed Forces without permission of the Centre, the Act virtually denies the right to Constitutional remedies under the Article 32 of the Indian Constitution. As the right to life cannot be suspended even under emergency, the opinion is existent that enforcing the Act amounts to a *de facto* emergency. The recent alienation of the Manipuris was aggravated after the killing of Thangjam Manorama (an alleged IED expert in the PLA as stated by the men in uniform) by the security forces after arresting her from home in the small hours of 11th July 2004. Her body riddled with bullets was found on a roadside. Post-mortem reports could not establish whether the injuries to the body might have destroyed any evidence of rape or sexual assault. What is the legal truth; this will unravel long after the incident is virtually forgotten. But the fact remains that the violent agitation against the security forces that followed Manorama's killing is rooted in the conception of security that obtains in our country's North-East. Security here is equated with the integrity of the state. While there is no denying the primacy of territorial security, but what is questionable is the inherent tendency to dismiss and degrade other considerations. The territorial boundaries of a state are secured by the Armed Force against external threats to the nation; within its territory, it requires the forces to exercise sovereignty and secure uniformity to ensure that the nationals remain secure. That is the rationale behind the injunction that the Armed Forces should not be deployed for security in civilian areas. Can security be pursued by ignoring human emotions and rights? Should a system of legal redress not be made a part of the larger plan of counter insurgency? Has insurgency become the black hold into which all injustices dissolve and cannot be pulled out to face justice? The scenario prevailing in Manipur, Nagaland, Assam as also the other states in the North-East underscores the urgency of coming to terms with these issues. It is erroneous to argue that the Act has helped contain insurgency and rescued the administration from catharsis over the last two decades. On the contrary insurgency has mushroomed and taken deep roots and the administration remains non-challant.[12]

Besides the insurgency, trends of separatism/secessionism and its consequences, the most important being the violation of the Human Rights of the general populace because of the activities of the rebels and the counter action of the armed/security forces, the region stands neglected and alienated due to the overall backwardness of the region. Despite being abundant in resources, the economy of the region has metamorphosed into a dependent one. The Centre is no doubt pumping in crores of rupees every year but there is no sign of its being appropriately utilized on the ground. The region is devoid of proper infrastructure, roads, rail network, medical facilities and adequate employment opportunities essentially due to the lack of planned development of region specific industries. External investment into the region has been limited especially because of the uncertainty prevalent in the core state, Assam, besides Nagaland and Manipur. Economic backwardness, deprivation and overall neglect has in fact not only compromised with the legitimate rights of the marginalized communities of the North-East as equal citizens of Democratic India, but has also alienated them from mainstream India.

The neglect of the region in particular Assam is reflected by the annual flooding of the mighty Brahmaputra. In fact for almost three months or more during the monsoon season, thousands lose their hearth and home and seek shelter of both sides on the National Highway which ironically many a time remains submerged during the monsoon. It is such apathy and neglect that prompts groups like the ULFA to project this fact and state "if Asom is independent it can manage, control and harness the power of the Brahmaputra for the benefit of the people of Asom".

Another major issue which is of concern to the people of Assam and the North-East is the attempts of the Chinese to divert the Tsangpo in Tibet (the origin of the Brahmaputra) to meet the requirement of the Chinese mainland. If this project is executed it is bound to have serious consequences for the lower riparian states and their water needs which have been taken care of abundantly by the river Brahmaputra. The Government at the Centre needs to address this issue post haste with the Chinese and protect the environment security of the North-Eastern States, in particular Assam and Arunachal Pradesh.

Another major issue which merits attention is the deprivation of daylight hours in the region due to the standardization of time and adherence to Indian Standard Time. It is needless to state that the Sun rises hours before in the North-East than it does in the mainland and it sets very early too. To enable the people of the North-East take advantage of daylight hours, it is imperative that the Government should seriously look into the need for providing an appropriate Time Standard for the region. This act will go a long way in progress and development in all realms as also uphold the 'natural' rights of the communities of the region.

It has to be accepted that the North-East is a distinct region with distinct people, culture and problems which merit handling post haste. It appears that the region, society and economy have reached the threshold. It is time the actors and participants concerned, be they at the Centre or at the region/state level have to work out a clear development perspective that spells out the needs of the region. There is also an absolute need to develop a pragmatic development scenario, which can be implemented despite the political and social change that may emerge in the regional/national scenario. Development on a firm basis of the economy and its sustainable nature alone will provide solutions to the several problems, which confront the North-East.

Conclusion

The culturally diverse North-East is distinct and unique in every sense of the term. The region with its colourful people of simple, honest and cheerful demeanor is in fact an epitome of India's concept of 'unity in diversity'. The North-East and its people are blessed with singular socio-cultural traits that merit emulation by the masses in mainland India. The honour and respect bestowed to women, the absence of dowry, the care rendered to the old and infirm by the community is unique and does merit acceptance and adherence by the divergent communities in the other parts of the country. India is a land of pluralities, of communities and groups all over. In this scenario it is imperative that the culturally diverse North-East with its unique position and history needs to be handled with care and sympathy. No attempt should be made to impose strands of cultural hegemony by the mainstream. If the people are to accept some of the cultural traits that is 'Indian', it should be voluntary and even this should be a two way process with the mainstream accepting and adopting the best traits of the North-East culture. Imposing any time of a pan-Indian culture is bound to be counterproductive especially in this frontier region of India. It is appropriate at this juncture of Indian federalism to advert to Jawaharlal Nehru's formulation of the five principles more popularly known as Panchsheel in relation to the North-East Frontier (NEFA). He stated:

> "People should be enabled to develop along the lines of their own genius and we should avoid imposing anything on them. There should be encouragement in every way for their own tradition art and culture. Tribal rights in land and forests should be protected and respected. Efforts should be made to build a team of the indigenous people to do the work of administration and development. Some technical personnel from outside will no doubt be needed, especially in the beginning, but the introduction of too many outsiders into tribal territory must be eschewed. These areas should not be over-administered nor should they be overwhelmed with a multiplicity of schemes. We should work through and not in rivalry to their own social and cultural institutions. Results of growth and development should not be judged on the basis of statistics or the amount of money spent but by the quality of human character that is evolved".

In view of the ever-increasing tensions and demands of several groups/ communities, in particular in the peripheri(es), of democratic India with its efforts to establish a truly plural and culturally diverse society in the 21st century should take into account the specificities of the socio-cultural space and history of communities, (especially the marginalized ethnic minorities of the North-East) The process must be an evolving one of changing relationships, openness, respect for democratic norms, establishment of the process of dialogue into the socio-political fabric and dispensing the goal of homogenization and the all encompassing federal state. This alone can ensure stability and peace that is indispensable for speedy development and growth of the region. Further, the establishment of stable peace in the North-East is imperative to equip the youth of the region to grapple with the ever increasing challenges of globalization and liberalization. It is imperative that the North-East and its varied ethnic inhabitants should be provided with all opportunities to be a part and parcel of the mainstream both at the national and international arena. This can lead to the over all progress of not only the marginalized communities in the periphery but also make them equal partners in the endeavour to make India a truly democratic, plural and all inclusive culturally diverse united nation.

Endnotes

1. Sanjoy Hazarika, Strangers *of the Mist: Tales of War and Peace from India's North-East*, New Delhi, Penguin, 1995, pp. xv-xvi.
2. Walter Fernandez, "Conflict in the North-East: A Historical Perspective", *Economic andPolitical Weekly,* Mumbai, 1999, Vol. 34, No. 5, December 18–24, pp. 3579–3582.
3. *The Seven Sisters of North-East India: A Profile,* Guwahati, North-East Social Science Research Centre, Aaranyak, 2004, pp. 1–2.
4. Sudhir Jacob George, "Separatist tendencies in North-East India" in Kousar J. Azam(ed) *Federalism and Good Governance: Issues Across Cross Cultures,* New Delhi, South Asian Publishers, 1998, p. 247.
5. Sanjib Baruah, "The Stae and Separatist Militancy in Assam: Winning a battle and losing the war, *Asian Survey*, Berkley, California, 1994, Vol. 10, No. 34, October, pp. 863–877.
6. *The Statesman*, New Delhi, 17 July, 1981.
7. http//www.geocities.com/capital/congress/ulfa/thm, 1774.
8. ulfa/geocities
9. *New Delhi,* 9–22 June, 1990, pp. 14–15.
10. *The Sunday*, Kolkatta, Vol. 3, No. 25, 21 February, 1980.
11. *The Sunday*, 21 February, 1980.
12. Bidhan Laishram, "Manipur and the Paradox of Security" New Delhi Institute of Peace and Conflict Studies, www.ipcs.org, Article No. 1456, 9 August, 2004.
13. See Jawaharlal Nehru's views on administration of the tribal areas of the North-East and their analysis in Hassan, Amir, The Tribal Administration in India, New Delhi, B.R. Pubn., 1958, pp. 55–56.

19

Socio-economic Inequities of Tribal Communities in India

Priti Singh

Today, we all are talking of a new India – using epithets like 'Rising India', 'India Shining' and 'Incredible India' – epithets which are no doubt applicable. We are following the formula which has been laid down by the 'developed' world – a sure-shot road to prosperity, success and higher living standards. An India that is moving towards the eradication of the main problem dogging its steps – poverty. However, while we are on this one-way road to development, we claim that we are doing so while ensuring that we retain our rich and diverse cultural heritage. What is development? What is poverty? What is our culture?

Author discusses the inequity prevalent in the new 'Shining India' by talking about the issue of the socio-economic inequalities plaguing the tribal communities in India and the impact of government induced 'development' policies meant to alleviate poverty and at the same time help preserve our cultural heritage. The question is whose poverty are we alleviating, and whose heritage are we preserving? While this paper focuses on issues of tribal peoples, I talk alongside about problems faced by tribal women in particular, as it further explains the repercussions of socio-economic impact of 'development' and tribal 'welfare' programmes on the sustenance of these cultural groups.

Hypothesis

The presentation is premised on the following working hypotheses/ propositions:

One: All too often, problems of social-economic inequalities are discussed upon which policies are devised without consideration being given to the existing cultural diversities in a society.

Two: When a culturally distinct minority participates actively in the economic life of a country, its cultural differences and peculiarities are less likely to be rejected.

Three: Where a culturally distinct minority remains for long economically deprived and socially excluded, more often it takes recourse or resorts to asserting/reconstructing its cultural identity.

Four: Women form the backbone or foundation of a group's identity and the effect of government policies on the women in that group have not been addressed seriously thus affecting the entire cultural group.

Evolution of Tribal Governance in India

About five hundred communities with a population of nearly 8.50 crores (85 million) are designated as tribal peoples in India. Since India's independence they have been made a part of the 'national' development process. According to the 2001 census, Scheduled Tribe members represented only 8 per cent of the total population of India (about 68 million). There are 533 tribes (with many overlapping types in more than one State) as per notified Schedule under Article 342 of the Constitution of India in different States and Union Territories of the country with the largest number of 62 being in the State of Orissa. In proportion, however, the populations of states in the northeast have the greatest concentrations of Scheduled Tribe members.

Under the colonial administration the British adopted a policy based on segregation and isolation of tribal communities.

But since Independence, a mixed policy of isolation and integration has been followed within the broad framework of constitutional provisions and principles of *panchsheel.* Broadly defined these principles are:

1. Tribal people should develop along the lines of their own genius;
2. Respect for tribal rights on land and forests;
3. Minimum involvement of non-tribal people in the development of tribal areas;
4. Tribal areas to be administered on the basis of tribal cultural-social institutions; and
5. Evaluation to be made on the quality of 'tribal' life – emphasis on tribal life.

In spite of the principles on which tribal governance in India is based, without doubt tribal peoples live in more abject poverty situations than the general population in India.

The poorest among the poor are largely the tribals. According to an estimate of the Planning Commission, the incidence of poverty among the scheduled tribes continued to be higher with 46 per cent and 35 per cent living below the poverty line in rural and urban areas respectively as compared to 27 per cent and 24 per cent of the general population.[1] As a consequence, they are affected by poor health, have limited access to basic services, their communities are marked by social disintegration and abject poverty. The tribals in India constitute 7 per cent of the landless people in India which is the second-largest section after the Scheduled Castes (10%) and they own only 3 per cent of the large landholdings. While they have less chronically unemployed persons than the non-tribals, their monthly per capita expenditure is the lowest (Rs. 387.69) even worse than that of the Scheduled Caste population (Rs. 418.51).

The policy initiatives undertaken by the government of India have been admittedly modest. Besides protecting the identity and general welfare of the tribal peoples as enshrined in the preamble of its Constitution, India extended subsequently limited self-government to select tribal communities only.

Upon India's independence, the Constituent Assembly considered the question of what to do with tribal regions, which under the British rule were 'excluded' (or as the Crown had designated them as 'non-regulated' areas in respect of colonial administration) and, finally, decided to rename them as 'scheduled areas' in order subsequently these areas could be considered for being granted self-government rights.[2] Nonetheless at the Constituent Assembly there was intense discussion and disagreement between those who espoused "assimilation" as a policy approach and so argued for only special representation rights (poly-ethnic rights) for tribal peoples, and the liberals on the other hand championing the Nehruvian ideals argued in support of self-government rights to the tribal peoples. A compromise that was arrived at finally provided for the Sixth Schedule that would grant self-government to those who were considered culturally "far out" and geographically peripheral to the mainstream society and thus originally limited the right to self-government to the *Nagas* in Assam[3]. At the same time, the Constituent Assembly provided for the Fifth Schedule for all other tribal peoples granting them the right to participate in a duly appointed tribal advisory council. Its main objective was to establish special development zones in tribal areas. Its measures were considered temporary with the ultimate goal of bringing tribal assimilation into the mainstream society. It is with these objectives in view the founding fathers of the Constitution of India had also envisaged a special scheme of administration in the scheduled areas where general laws would not be applicable unless the governor of the state where the tribal peoples are in sizeable number deemed fit to enforce such laws.[4]. Today there are as many as ten such states in the Indian Union with 'scheduled' tribal peoples.[5]

The duality in approach as evidenced in the contrasting rights granted in the Fifth and the Sixth Schedules respectively has placed the tribal peoples in a fix regarding their right to self-government. For, the differentiation between these two categories seems to be based on the debatable principle of the degree of cultural difference that determined whether tribal peoples fell under the Fifth or the Sixth Schedule at least when these constitutional provisions were initially conceived.

Ostensibly, to resolve the anomaly, the Union government sought an amendment to the Constitution decades after. Under the provisions of the 73rd Amendment to the Constitution made in 1992 on *panchayat* bodies (local self-government at the village level) which among others included setting up *gram sabhas*. Based on this historic constitutional amendment the Panchayats (Extension to the Scheduled Area) Act was enacted in 1996, which further recognised the rights of tribal communities over natural resources, respecting their traditional institutions and gave vast powers of self-governance to the tribal communities. Proclaimed as landmark legislation it is the first-ever enactment to empower the tribal people to redefine their own administrative boundaries as it attempted to vest legislative powers in *gram sabha* (village assembly) specifically in matters relating to development planning, management of natural resources and adjudication of disputes in accordance with prevalent tribal traditions and customs. In turn, it is claimed that this legislation would usher in far reaching changes in the social, economic and cultural lives of the tribal peoples paving the way for self-government. As the Union Minister of Panchayati Raj stated recently:

> This revolutionary law has, at one stroke, provided for empowerment of tribal communities and their political participation and strengthened their healthy traditional practices. By providing that at least 50 per cent of the members in Panchayat are tribals and the Chairperson is always a tribal, this law gives them the necessary critical mass to ensure that decisions taken in Panchayats are not indifferent or opposed to their interests.[6]

Nevertheless the minister himself admitted that the implementation of this law requires "much more hard work as it entails the loosening of political and bureaucratic control over natural resources in tribal areas".[7]

No doubt, it is a candid admission. For, although to operationalise and to conform to the letter and spirit of this legislative initiative the scheduled states were given one year to amend their respective *panchayat* acts (as the subject: 'local government' figures in the State List under the Indian Constitution) yet this "revolutionary" federal legislation has produced no transformative change on the terrain of the tribal peoples of India. For one, the law stipulates that almost all powers under the new dispensation are subject to rules/further orders "as may be prescribed by the State Governments". The control over prospecting of minor minerals, planning and management of water bodies, control and management of minor forest produce, prevention of alienation of land are all subject to rules in force or as may be prescribed by the State. The fact that the enabling rules are not in place even more than a decade after the adoption of the legislation only suggests reluctance by the state governments to operationalise the mandate. Besides, the wording of the new legislation leaves much to be desired. For instance, on land acquisition the *gram sabhas* would only be consulted by the other tiers of the government which could as well mean that there is no prior consent that is needed for tribal land acquisition by government agencies or their appointed representatives. Some of the rules and prescriptions that have been formulated following the promulgation of the law have been over-ruled and revoked by official orders of the state governments which in turn have made these additional provisions inoperative. According to one observer: "The operative provisions being not in place, a promising radical law has been reduced largely to a paper law".[8]

Despite the laudable objectives with which the Panchayats (Extension to the Scheduled Area) Act was passed to pave the way for tribal self-rule, built-in ambiguities and omissions in the law have subverted the basic intent and objective of the law. For reasons of its inefficacy and inadequacy, the Union Government of India proposed yet another legislative initiative called the Scheduled Tribes (Recognition of Forest Rights) Bill. The Bill was purported to contribute towards tribal self-government as the pending bill in its present formulation provides for laying down "procedure" for "recognition and vesting of forest rights in the forest dwelling Scheduled Tribes" so that it "reinforces and utilizes the rich conservation ethos" of the tribal communities. The draft legislation spelt as many as 12 rights to tribal peoples ranging from inheritable rights to forestland, rights of ownership to minor forest produce, and rights to traditional knowledge. Major highlights of the proposal are as follows: (i) giving 2.5 hectares of land to each tribal family occupying forestland since or before 25 October 1980; (ii) empowering fully the *gram sabha* to determine the extent of forest rights to the inhabitant; (iii) converting forest villages into revenue villages to bring modern development; and (iv) providing access to traditional seasonal resources.

The bill, earlier tabled in December 2005, was referred to a joint parliamentary committee (JPC) to look into the issue of resettlement of tribals who had "encroached" on forestland.[9] The Committee (JPC) made three vital recommendations. First, the bill should deal with all forest dweller groups, and not just scheduled tribes. Second, the cut-off date for deciding who can be vested with rights should be pushed to December 2005, when the bill was first tabled, instead of 1980 – the year the Forest Conservation Act, 1980, was enacted. Third, the ceiling of 2.5 hectare (ha) of land given to each settler family needs to be done away with. It has also recommended several other changes regarding the procedure for settling land and forest rights. It suggests that *gram sabha*s or village councils delineate such rights in their respective areas. The first right of appeal extends to a sub-divisional committee, which can only suggest changes to the *gram sabha*, giving them the upper hand to reject such changes. The second right of appeal may be made to the district committee. That decision will be final.

Proponents of the legislative initiative felt that it was a right step and remedy to the grave historical injustice that had been inflicted on tribal peoples from times immemorial. They felt that tribal peoples need land to sustain their culture, and by giving them their rights, the legislative proposal was an attempt to undo the injustice done to them in the past. Moreover, it was felt that as tribal peoples know their surroundings well, they are better equipped to safeguard and protect their flora and fauna. It was also argued that the legislation only sought to recognize and regularize ground reality by granting legal entitlement to those millions of families who are today seen as encroachers and thus empower and improve livelihood chances of a historically marginalized people.

Yet, the legislative proposal drew a lot of criticism and controversy both from within the government (e.g., the Ministry of Environment and Forests) as well as from the tribal communities and social activists.[10] The most contentious issue had earlier been that the proposal left out many forest dwellers, such as tribes not scheduled in the Constitution, creating circumstances for their eviction from notified areas. With the new proposal of the joint parliamentary committee, the improved Scheduled Tribes and Other Traditional Forest Dwellers (Recognition of Forest Rights) Bill 2006, this issue was addressed to a certain extent, but in turn raised other crucial issues. The Ministry of Environment and Forests objected to it on grounds that it would hinder efforts to conserve India's dwindling forest cover and subsequently its biodiversity. Moreover, those who were opposed expressed lack of confidence in the ability of the *gram sabhas* to carry out this mandate. They felt that without adequate levels of literacy, it would not be possible to expect the tribal *gram sabhas* to understand the rules/provisions and at the same time feel bold enough to take action. It was feared that *gram sabhas* will fall prey to the local traders and *mafias*. The conservation lobby, on the other hand, felt strongly that protected areas in particular will be jeopardized as a result of this initiative and should not be considered within its purview. The procedure of including more tribal groups in the schedule list is a lengthy procedure and was last done in 2002 after amendment to the 1950 Act. The Scheduled Tribes and Other Traditional Forest Dwellers (Recognition of Forest Rights) Act was finally passed in 2006 almost unanimously by the Lok Sabha as well as the Rajya Sabha. This has been at least a significant admission of the historic injustice done to forest dwellers even if it is believed that in reality, the Act assures pitifully little.

Problems

Tribal peoples, particularly those living in forest and hill areas, are extremely marginalized, many having lost access to traditional forest livelihoods and food resources through the creation of Forest Reserves, and many remain without food ration cards or access to government services. Tribal peoples also suffer disproportionately from displacement because of development projects such as dams, power plants, coal mines and mineral industries.[11] There are no official statistics on the number of people displaced, but NGOs and academics estimate that dam projects alone have displaced up to 33 million people who have lost their lands and livelihoods. Around 40–50 per cent of the displaced are tribal people even though they make up only 8 per cent of the population, reflecting the serious discrimination against tribal peoples.[12]

Despite the enormity of the problem, India does not have a national rehabilitation policy. One is being formulated since 1993 but is yet to be promulgated. The latest draft of 1998 has many positive points but is weak on questions concerning women. Most projects that have a resettlement package show the same weakness. In most of them the DPs are taken as a homogeneous group. Recent projects give some importance to categories like tribals, but women are by and large ignored. And yet, studies indicate that they pay the highest price for development. While this is true about tribal groups in general, the situation of women is the worst among the marginalized.

The impact of displacement and deprivation on tribals is much more. Estimates show that no fewer than 40 per cent of the DPs/PAPs of five decades of planned development are from the tribal communities that formed only 8.08 per cent of the country's population in 1991 (Fernandes, 1998:265). In Andhra Pradesh, they are a little over 6 per cent of the state's population, but constitute 27 per cent of its 3.2 million DPs/PAPs between 1951 and 1995 (Fernandes, et al. 2001:79). In Orissa they are 22 per cent of the population, but account for 42 per cent of its DPs/PAPs (Fernandes and Asif, 1997:112). Similar data come from other states like Jharkhand, West Bengal and Kerala.

Recent critiques offered by Nobel laureate Amartya Sen on the question of development strategies and poverty alleviation do underline the need for such an approach or recourse. According to him changes in property rights regimes and shifts in natural resource use due to economic, social, political, and environmental reasons impact negatively on peoples' welfare. So much so, he specifically focuses on legal issues of 'entitlement' in the study of development. Based on a set of rights of "ownership, transfer and rectification", Sen brings in law as an important mediating agency in his 'entitlement' approach. It centres on an individual's entitlements, which depends not only on the endowment that an individual starts with, but is also related to exchange relations. Sen further states that "production opportunities, trade possibilities, legal rights to the produce, and social conventions" all affect entitlements or, what he calls the "e-mapping". Upon this, he makes the argument that poverty results from both a "fall in the endowment" and "unfavourable shifts in exchange mapping".[13]

Analysis of legal shifts with reference to natural resources ownership and control enable us to understand how for instance, the decline in access to, and the degradation of common property resources can result in change of ownership endowments, and consequent entitlement failures. Thus, Sen underlines the role of laws and legality both in bestowing and transferring endowments, and in providing an individual with entitlements to meet her/his needs. Implicit at least in this line of argument is the recognition of legal pluralism that accommodates customary laws of the tribal peoples rather than the dominant legal systems suppressing traditional or customary rights of these segments of the population.

Three aspects concerning tribals are rarely attended to in policy-making and while discussing development-induced deprivation. First, the natural resources from which development projects alienate them are the foundations of their economy, culture, social systems and political structures, and of their very identity. Second, these natural resources are common property resources (CPRs), not individual property. Third, the status of women in their societies. While these traditional societies could be patriarchal, women do have a higher status than in general Indian society and culture. What is important to note is that both their relatively high status and children's upbringing depend on abundant resources and the partial control that they exercise over them. This is possible as long as their lands were CPRs. Given this close link to land, alienation from these resources results not merely in economic impoverishment but also in deprivation of social support, i.e. weakening of their community systems and the displacement of women from their traditional positions and occupation in society. Downward social mobility follows from this process. However, the few rehabilitation packages that exist do not extend beyond the economic factor to encompass community and cultural support, particularly in ways that concern women.

In discussing development, the need to protect certain of the rights have to be kept in mind: (Medha Patkar)

> the rights to resources comes first especially for indigenous peoples. Rehabilitation is a question that can be raised only if displacement is inevitable.

The issue of the right to resources is invariably linked to the right to decide what should be done with those resources such as a mineral resource that is underground, or on the surface. If the community is granted that right by the law or if the community asserts its right, then the decision related to a mine or dam becomes the community's decision. This can change the entire development dynamics. This kind of power helps to minimise displacement, destruction and degradation of the environment. This would also hopefully, minimise economic expropriation and exploitation and, of course, political exclusion. In such a situation, issues of gender, caste-related inequities and differences in natural resource ownerships within the community will not be acute.

> The real conflict is between natural resource based communities and urban industrial societies. This conflict needs to be our basis not just for the struggle but also for economic and political analysis of development and

displacement. Today, the richer the community in natural resources, the more vulnerable it is to attack, encroachment and expropriation.

Change in the Economic Status of Women

Tribal women owe their relatively high status both to the abundance of resources and a clear division in their societies between the family and social spheres. The man represents the family in society and the woman is the main decision-maker in the family economy, production and social relations. Shifting cultivation, the traditional sustenance of about 25 per cent of Indian tribals, is an example of her control over the family economy and her work outside her home was socially recognized. In settled agriculture, the man, as landowner, takes most decisions concerning production and division of work. With the alienation of the CPRs, the woman is unable to work outside the home. The project that deprives her of these resources does not give her a job. Thus she is reduced to being a housewife alone. Even when resettled, she cannot continue her economic autonomy. If resettlement is land-based, land is allotted in the name of individuals considered heads of families (invariably men, except in women-headed households). With the individual becoming the norm of land ownership after resettlement, power is transferred to the man and from him to his son. The woman ceases to be the main decision-maker in the family economy.

Rehabilitation – Jobs for Skilled

Even when a project which causes displacement gives a job (which is very rare), it is limited to one job per family. This means that jobs go to men, considered heads of families. Till 1986, industries and mines came under the 'T.N. Singh Formula 1967' that stipulated that the displacing public sector industry or mine should give a job to every family it displaced. The formula had many shortcomings. One of them was that it did not take women into consideration. Modern privileges were a prerogative meant only for men. In the Koraput district of Orissa, for example, the literacy of tribal men in our sample was around 20 per cent and that of women was 2.3 per cent. Similar is the situation in our sample of 618 respondents from 14 projects in Andhra Pradesh, 725 respondents from 14 projects in West Bengal, and 900 respondents from 18 projects in Jharkhand (Fernandes and Ganguly Thukral, 1989:5–6).

As a result, the few jobs the tribals and dalits got were by and large unskilled ones, often temporary or on daily wages. The NALCO unit of Damanjodi is among the few to give semi-skilled jobs to a few tribal men because a voluntary agency trained them in some skills. Even in this case no woman got a job. In most other places, skilled jobs go almost exclusively to persons from the dominant castes. [14]

The T.N. Singh Formula was scrapped in 1986 because after mechanization very few jobs are created.

In the mid-1980s, the company began to mechanize its mines and started transferring employees to other mines instead of giving jobs to the persons it displaced. The impact of this is seen, among others, in the 25 mines under construction in the Upper Karanpura Valley of Jharkhand. They are expected to displace 100,000 persons, over 60 per cent of them dalits and tribals. The first five of these mines each gave a job to only 638 (10.18%) of the 6,265 families they displaced till 1992 (BJA and NBJK, 1993:36). Our studies in various states confirm that the trend of project-related employment is constantly declining. [15] However, the woman's role as caretaker of the family remains unchanged. She has to buy even the family's basic needs like food that she used to get earlier from land and forests.

Compensation for Land

The project authority provided compensation for the land and homestead plots but not for the CPRs on which tribes greatly depended. That was because the land laws in India considered them as state property. From many accounts, tribal DPs became more deprived than others. For example, in Andhra Pradesh, the predominantly middle- and high-caste DPs/PAPs of the Industrial Development Area, Kakinada, received an average compensation of Rs. 74,614.43 per acre in 1992. Most of their land was individually owned. The predominantly tribal and dalit losers of the land acquired for VUDA Housing in Visakhapatnam were paid an average of Rs. 13,000 per acre of *palla* land in 1996.

Most of what the dalits and tribes lost were CPRs. In 1994 the Vasavi Steel Plant in Srikakulam district acquired many tribal CPRs without any compensation. For the little private land they owned, they received an average of Rs. 4,151.41 per acre (Fernandes, et al. 2001:90). Thus they receive very little compensation, which is inadequate for them to begin life anew. In our study of 11 projects in Orissa we have seen that the dalits (SCs) and tribals (STs) spend most of the compensation on daily consumer needs. Those among them who have not been resettled have to spend much of their compensation on house building.

Resettlement

Most resettlement packages hardly give importance to women's needs. The main reason for these problems is that the project authorities bear almost exclusively economic aspects in mind at the time of displacement. They ignore some other important needs of the people they deprive, particularly of the subaltern groups and of women among them – ignoring their social and hygienic needs.

Apart from all this, displacement and deprivation, more often than not, result in additional workload for the woman but less food for the family, particularly for girls and women especially with deforestation. The distance of forests from resettlement areas increase and the consequent extra workload impacts more on women. In Orissa and Chhattisgarh, the distance from the forests had increased from around 1 km from the village in the 1960s to more than 5 km in the 1980s (Fernandes and Menon, 1987:72). The resources from forests were the source of their high status and of their economic utility. With their disappearance they feel that their community does not have any use for them. They are reduced to being housewives alone.

Change in Social Status

This in turn leads to their social status being affected. The tribal women had complained of overwork because of the distance of forests. But the decrease in their workload, affected their morale just as much as additional workload did. The fact of being forced to remain at home and the decline in their contribution to the family economy become factors in the deterioration of their social status. Men become the only or main income earners since most jobs go to them. Or they leave home looking for jobs. This is not purely an economic decision. The state in modern times had taken over the traditional role of men in society that of being hunters, guardians and village council leaders thus creating a vacuum and providing no alternative for their loss in social status.

When the man is away from the scene, the housewife is forced to look after the household on her own. Other men, particularly moneylenders and merchants, exploit her powerlessness by occupying her land, thus depriving her of the family's livelihood (Menon, 1992). In other cases, the husband absorbs the value system of another society and returns with a second, younger wife. In the traditional tribal system in which divorce was allowed, the woman would have walked out of the house and got married again. Being deprived of sustenance by the project, she has no choice but to put up with this deviation and accept her subordinate status as the *de facto* second wife (Menon, 1995).

Since poverty is the consequence, many of them are forced to migrate once again in search of jobs. In some cases, men migrate alone, leaving women at home. In other cases, the whole family goes to the urban slums. In either case, women face the negative impact more than men do. Because of their low exposure to the external society, the tribes are able to cope with migration much less than other social groups do. The woman, being illiterate and less exposed to the external world, is forced to accept only very low status jobs at exploitative wages. Men and children often absorb the value system of the dominant culture to which they are exposed through the workers from outside the region coming to the new industrial townships. So they spend more than they did in the past on clothes, entertainment and other trivia, thus making a relatively small amount available for the woman to run the household. Drunkenness or accepting status symbols like expensive clothes and other trinkets are ways of coping with this tension. We found that drunkenness is very common among the displaced and the deprived whose situation we studied in Orissa, Andhra Pradesh and Jharkhand.

Besides, as mentioned above, they often internalize upper-caste practices, like the housewife eating after feeding the elders, her husband, his brothers, boy children and girl children, in that order. The other new practice is dowry in place of bride price. Out of our 400 respondents, 80 respondents confirmed paying bride price before migration; 55 per cent of them said that after moving to the city they had either given or would give dowry at their daughters' marriages and 70 per cent wanted to receive dowry for their sons (Fernandes, 1990:148–149)

Effect on Culture

Cultural contact with caste society induces among tribals a mode of upward mobility in which the family with the man as its head adopts the mainstream upper-caste customs to which women's subordination is basic. The process is called Sanskritisation, in which over a generation or two the low castes adopt upper-caste gods and customs such as vegetarianism (Srinivas, 1966:52). In a survey carried out on Why Women Get Unskilled Jobs both tribal men and women stated that the woman's place is in the house and that she should not aspire for anything more than that. Some men insisted that women did not contribute to the household since they worked neither on land nor in the project. So they should obey men, who alone earned their livelihood. Among them were tribal women among whom the woman has a higher status than in caste societies. Time and again several men as well as women justified the subordinate status of women as being natural.

Development in terms of economic growth ignores the other important aspects of the social sector. The development project that ignores rehabilitation and attends only to its financial and technical components represents exactly the same trend. This neglect ensures the marginalization of the powerless classes in general and of women among them in particular. It affects even women from the dominant classes and is felt much more by dalits and tribals.

Policy-makers pay very little attention to the situation of the displaced woman. They take her subordinate role for granted even in the few rehabilitation schemes that exist. The Narmada Award, the Karnataka, Maharashtra and Madhya Pradesh Rehabilitation Acts and others are among the examples. Thus, displacement runs the risk of playing the double role of weakening tribal society and further marginalizing tribal women. So one should take a new look at the process of displacement as well as the rehabilitation policy.

Compensation cannot be calculated according to market principles. The people lose their whole livelihood, not merely individual assets. One has to move away from the principle of eminent domain that considers all CPRs as state property. One has to recognize that CPRs are the livelihood of the tribal and other rural poor communities. As such they have a right to their replacement. The people have to be involved in the decision concerning the project and not merely in rehabilitation (Sherman 1993). Finally, rehabilitation has to be total. What is called rehabilitation today is in reality resettlement. It is physical relocation with or without other economic, social and cultural components. True rehabilitation means re-establishing the livelihood, culture and the remaining social inputs.

Conclusion

Inequality has persisted in the socio-economic life of the tribal peoples in India in terms of access to land and its resources, education, employment, and health services.

While the programmes have mainly been concerned with issues such as nutrition, health, and education, the emphasis is varied in the policies over the years. Each successive Five Year plan shifted emphasis – from general welfare schemes to family oriented development schemes. Or, subsequently it shifted to reduction of gap between tribal and non-tribal people and further to social empowerment.

Whereas earlier the policy thrust was social equity and growth, currently it is substituted by political empowerment through local self-government: *panchayats*.

However, throughout the five decades what has been attempted at is to deal with social and economic needs of the tribal peoples narrowly defined by the mainstream development policies. "Quality" of life measured in terms of their cultural identity and the needs thereof have either been ignored or overlooked.

As an institutionally implemented principle, policies purported to manage cultural diversities are basically characterized by a built-in dichotomy. Being bisected, the policies are implemented by two separate sets of logic – one of which tends to be social and economic, and the other cultural, whereas it has to be integrated and should go hand in hand.

Where it tends to remain disintegrated/disjointed, then the issues, which it claims to deal with, will never be met.

This is why it calls for a wider policy, one, which is both social and cultural, or itself a combination of social and cultural measures capable of breaking the link between poverty/exclusion and ethnicity.

If recognition of cultural identity is crucial and problematic for the most deprived groups, any policy device to be effective has to combine social and cultural aspects.

For, what could cultural recognition mean for populations who are subject historically to intense exploitation in employment, or are relegated to poor urban/rural areas and massively excluded?

Or, if multiculturalism is restricted to a policy of cultural recognition alone, then the question that needs consideration is whether should it not come after the fight against social discrimination or simultaneously?

In fact, if multiculturalism is limited to culture alone, there is the constant danger that it will appear as a policy in the service of groups, which are already well situated socially.

These are issues that call for serious and careful discussion in crafting appropriate policy mix.

Failing to do so would lead to the kind of the ongoing policy debate in India and the resulting policy initiatives. Such of the currently dished out affirmative policy initiatives devoid of the vital cultural inputs appear simply as quick-fix political strategy to deal with social inequality based on, or reinforced by, ethnic discrimination. In fact, already it has come to mean explicit additional quotas for jobs and opportunities for higher education adjusted to culturally oriented means to anti-discriminatory ends.

In which event, these initiatives towards marginalized sections of the population including the tribal peoples would move the policy rationale from 'protective discrimination' to 'discrimination protected'.

Endnotes

1. See *Tenth Five Year Plan Draft 2002–2007*, Planning Commission, Government of India, New Delhi, Chapter 4.2, p. 455.
2. The 'schedule' in 'scheduled areas' refers to the Fifth and Sixth Schedules of the Indian Constitution, both of which address accommodation of 'tribals'.
3. The state of Nagaland was established in December 1963.
4. For the Constituent Assembly debate see Government of India, *Constituent Assembly Debates, 1946–1950, Official Report*, 3rd edn., (New Delhi: Lok Sabha Secretariat, 1999), pp. 980–997.
5. These states are Andhra Pradesh, Bihar, Chattisgarh, Gujarat, Himachal Pradesh, Jharkhand, Madhya Pradesh, Maharashtra, Orissa and Rajasthan. The widely used Indian term for tribals is '*adiva*sis'. It carries the connotation of aboriginal, living in geographically and topographically isolated areas (usually in forest-jungle areas). Tribal/adivasi also carries the connotation of being culturally different. The President of the Indian Union under the Constitution notifies these as Scheduled Tribes.
6. From the text of the speech of the Minister of Panchayati Raj on "The Panchayat System: A Major Innovation in Empowering People" presented at the Conference on "Making Democratic Governments Work—connecting Principle and Practice" at Ash Institute for Democratic Governance and Innovation, Harvard University, 13 April 2005.
7. Ibid.

8. Sanjay Upadhyay, "Tribal Self-Rule Law and Common Property Resources in Scheduled Areas of India: A Paradigm Shift or Another Ineffective Sop?" Paper Presented at the 10th Biennial Conference of the International Association for the Study of Common Property (IASCP), Oaxaca, Mexico, 9–13 August 2004.
9. B.G. Verghese, "Tribal Rights and Wrongs", *Deccan Herald*, 8 July 2006.
10. Ashish Kothari, "Rights and Promises", *Frontline*, vol. 24, Issue 14, July 15–28, 2006.
11. Planning Commission, *Mid-Term Appraisal of 10th Five-year Plan*, 2005.
12. Harsh Mander, Ravi Hemadri and Vijay Nagaraj, *Dams, Displacement, Policy and Law in India*, 1999.
13. See Amartya Sen, *Resources, Values and Development* (Delhi: Oxford University Press, 1984); and *Poverty and Famine and Social Exclusion* (Delhi: Oxford University Press, 1999).
14. In West Bengal, only eight permanent jobs went to women. Of the 45 semi-skilled jobs, none went to tribals or dalits, and only two jobs went to women from dominant castes. In Andhra Pradesh, 90 per cent of the jobs given to tribals were unskilled, often temporary. In the Jagannathpur mines of Talcher in Orissa and the Piparwar mines of Palamau in Jharkhand, a family is entitled to a job for every 3 acres of land lost. Later the Piparwar mines reduced it to 2 acres for providing a job if the claimant had completed matriculation (Sherman 1993). Some projects are ready to give technical training to the DPs/PAPs who have adequate educational qualifications. Only dominant-caste boys qualify for this.
15. One can find similar examples from other projects like NALCO in Koraput district of Orissa. Its mines are built on a hill that served the natural resources needs of 72 villages around it. Transport of minerals is fully mechanized and has created about 300 skilled and semi-skilled jobs that have gone to outsiders. The tribals who were deprived of their livelihoods have not been provided any alternative in the form of jobs or other sources of income (Pattanaik and Panda 1992).

20

Reinventing Australian Identity

D. Gopal

The world is passing through a crucial phase in its evolution. Since the end of the Cold War the traditional issues like nationality and identity, are replaced by globalization, borderless world and global village. The latter have been projected by an active role played by multinational corporations, new media of communications such as internet and e-mail, and most important foreign direct investment. Yet related issues like terrorism, Afghanistan and Iraq wars, and social unrest in Africa, refugee inflow proved instrumental in undermining the national borders and identities. In this game of globalization, no doubt, the economically developed countries have an added advantage whereas the developing countries stand on the receiving end. A bigger challenge is posed to the middle powers, whether to open the societies to the free flow of globalization or strengthen their national identities and values.

Australia in its wake is aimed at diluting the multicultural aspect of society and establishing an order to install Australian values. An attempt is made in this paper to trace the formative stage of the Australian population policy since the advent of British arrival, indicate the circumstances and the antecedents that resulted in a multicultural policy in the early 1970s and analyze the shift to the Australian values and their impact on the broader society in the 21st Century.

Evolution of Australian Identity

Starting with the British settlement in Australia in 1788, the flow of migrants and settlers continued at varying paces as per the economic and political circumstances both in Australia and Europe. The Gold Rush in 1850s added a new impetus to migration which in addition to White British category added the Chinese category, though for a short duration. A consistent policy for migration intake was developed in 1901 with the formation of the Federation. The White Australia Policy or the Immigration Restriction Bill based on the dictation test was introduced to retain "the noble idea of a White Australia – a snow white Australia if you will. Let it be pure and spotless".[1] The first Prime Minister Edmund Barton endorsed the policy which was aimed at "controlling the leakage of coloured immigration".

Geographically placed in the Asia Pacific region and culturally attached to Europe, Australia was quagmired between the emotional attachment and geographical reality. Against this backdrop, to evolve a policy to regulate the migration intake, guard security and assert dominion mono-culture was a great challenge. Firstly, to maintain the Britishness and Whiteness; and secondly, to face the geographical and strategic challenges posed by the surrounding Asian countries. To overcome the above challenges, Australia charted out a basic framework of the society and the core values to be achieved. The new settlement of white people charted out the core values for the future development of the society that included "democratic and egalitarian, predominantly Christian, capitalist but maintaining a healthy balance between capital and labour, and high standards of living".[2] A major emphasis was put on the egalitarian nature of the society to maintain coherency and peaceful coexistence in the society and to avoid domination of one section over the other.[3]

This policy continued successfully until the outbreak of the First World War in 1914. Between 1905 and 1914 some 390000 new settlers arrived, mainly from the British Isles. After the war, though majority of migrants continued from UK and Ireland but people from Italy, Greece and Yugoslavia also joined. The migration intake was further diversified by accepting refugees before the Second World War from Germany. This was a major sway from Britishness.

After the end of the Second World War several factors contributed in re-thinking about nature of the population policy in Australia. In the backdrop of the heavy Australian causalities during the Second World War, Japanese advances towards Australian mainland, vulnerability of Australia to a rising Japanese power, joining the allies against Hitler's racist policies, depleting source of migration from Europe and defending the Australian mainland, all these issues attracted attention of the political leadership and intellectuals of the country alike. Artur Calwell, the first Minister for Immigration after the end of the Second World War, highlighting the predicament in which Australia was placed in the context of defense emphasized "Populate or Perish" policy. He expressed the programmes philosophy in a speech to the House of Representatives in November 1946: "The call to all Australians is to realize that, without adequate numbers, this wide brown land may not be held in another clash of arms, and to give their maximum assistance to every effort to expand its economy and assimilate more and more people who will come from overseas to link their fate with our destiny".[4] At the same time, conscious of the migration intake, he suggested "maximum effective absorption capacity in any expanding country is usually two per cent of its numbers".[5] The aftermath of the Second World War proved a benchmark in Australian thought process about migration intake. Major changes included a diversion from mono-culturalism to multiculturalism, Whiteness, Britishness to acceptance of previously feared Asians. This was witnessed when a big influx of large number of Asian refugees were accepted in Australia in the wake of Japanese invasion. Though they were given space to settle but with an understanding that they would return after the War ended. Witnessing the depleting source of migration from Europe, lack of labour supply, unwillingness of Asians to return (association with Australia) and moralist and liberal education all contributed in considering the Asian people for settlement.

From 1947 onwards, the Australian Government relaxed many of the rigid restrictions on non-European settlement that had existed since the Immigration Restriction Act 1901. For the first time it involved attracting non-English speaking immigrants. Substantial numbers were recruited from refugee and displacement camps across the Europe. As a result, a wide area was focused that ranged from Britain to Southern Europe (Italy, Greece).

With the new government of Robert Menzies in office in 1949, there were not many alternatives left apart from accepting people from throughout Europe and Asian continent; however Menzies believed that Australia was emotionally and sentimentally linked to Britain. In his words: "Australian and Englishmen and South Africans and Canadians and the New Zealanders…are one people, with one ancestry…who met on the footing of an ancient alliance…an ancient brotherhood…created out of roots, that go deep into the history of our race".[6] Witnessing the multi racial nature of the Australian immigrant population several opinions were expressed in 1960s for multi-cultural nature of the society but the concept of multiculturalism was taken as alien. Billy Snedden, Minister of Immigration, spoke of 'multi-culture' in 1969, but only to reject the idea in favour of 'monoculture'.

Transition to Multiculturalism

The word Multiculturalism has its origin from two Latin words, 'Multus' meaning many and 'Cultura' meaning cultivation. So Multiculturalism can mean many different racial groups with their own culture mixing into one nation. The Australians came from around 200 different country origins which have brought their own cultures. In sum, a statement from the federal Office of Multicultural Affairs defined multiculturalism as "the character of relationships existing between groups within the Australian community".[7] The concept of multiculturalism imported from Canada was fitted in Australian framework by Al Grassby during the Gough Whitlam government from 1972–1975. In a statement entitled *A Multicultural Society for the Future in 1973*, he outlined and elaborated on ethnic heterogeneity and cultural pluralism in Australian context. He emphasized that without a multicultural society, NES (Non-English Speaking) migrants would become 'non-people'. He further asserted that the concept of "the family of the nation" was necessary to recognize and accept the culture that migrants carried with them rather than dismissing their distinctiveness. The concept of cultural pluralism and multiculturalism was developed further by the academies. The Australian Ethnic Affairs Council (AEAC) argued that there were three principles of a multicultural society, that is, social cohesion, cultural identity, and equality of opportunity and access. After five years, Australian Council on Population and Ethnic Affairs (ACPEA), AEAC, and Australian Population and immigration Council (APIC); agreed that multiculturalism was "the most suitable model for relation between all ethnic groups in Australia and as the preferred basis for government ethnic affairs policies". The ACPEA added the fourth principle to Multiculturalism, that is, equal responsibility for, commitment to and participation in society.[8]

To make a conducive environment to implement multiculturalism, the Gough Whitlam government removed all the vestiges and declared the White Australia policy as "dead and buried".[9] Witnessing the high return rate of the migrants in 1977, Zubrsyeky argued that one of the cause of the high departure rate of migrants was the lack of equality of opportunity for migrants in Australia.[10]

However, the policy of multiculturalism was extensively implemented for the first time by Prime Minister Malcolm Fraser's Liberal National Country Party coalition government of 1976–1983. Though it is a subject of debate why the multicultural policy was implement by a Liberal government. However, Fraser had three main objectives in adopting the multicultural policy; one – to fold the migrant voters into his vote bank; two – feeling the tremors in the social cohesion, directing the society towards inclusiveness; three – de-shelving the government financial burden of managing ethnic affairs to the communities themselves.[11]

At the same time, there are scholars who argue that Australia had reached a precipice stage where it was no more able to afford to neglect the migrants so the multiculturalism was a force to reckon with and had a natural evolution: "Australia's transformation into a multiracial (and not just multicultural) society was an unintended consequence of developments beyond the nation's own control; it was not something actively willed by the Australian community itself".[12]

Impetus to multiculturalism was given by the Fraser Government by creating a special category for Lebanese and Vietnamese immigrants in 1970s. Taking a step forward in 1981, Bob Hawke Government added new vistas to the immigration policy by providing special status to Soviet Jews, Chileans, Sri Lankans and others. This indicated a global nature of the immigration intake. A caveat in the migration law was created to cover this wide geographical intake under Global Humanitarian Programme.[13] Finally, a Special Assistance Programme was introduced in 1991 to reunite the people fleeing Yugoslavia with their family members and relatives in Australia. However, this programme was abolished by the Howard Government in 1996.

Taking a serious note of the opposition Hawke faced from different sectors of Australian society about multiculturalism, in May 1984 in a major statement to the Parliament on immigration policy while affirming that Australia was susceptible to fracture the stability and social fabric, he indicated that there were mechanisms in vogue to assess and analyze the size and composition of intake and provisions to integrate and promote racial tolerance.[14] Though skeptical in 1984 but by 1987 he firmly believed that multiculturalism was the future of the country. Re-confirming his commitment and outlining the advantages of multiculturalism, Hawke emphasized in 1987 that his government was totally committed to the concept of Australia as a truly multicultural society. He said, Australia "has been immeasurably enriched by the contribution of immigration to our national life and by the success of the immigration program. It is one of our nation's greatest achievements that people have been accepted from a wide and diverse range of backgrounds, race, religion and culture".[15]

Notwithstanding Hawke's strong support for multiculturalism and underlining multi-benefits of multiculturalism, John Howard and Geoffrey Blainey in Opposition Party endorsed caution about Asian immigration in 1984. In other words: "Howard has always felt uncomfortable about multiculturalism – an idea he only accepts reluctantly, as if it were an inevitability or a necessary nuisance".[16]

Howard frequently described himself as the most conservative Prime Minister in Australian history. Perhaps taking a que from the conservatives in United States, he took multiculturalism affront. In an article entitled Multiculturalism: A Strategic Threat to International and National Security, Samuel P. Huntington is quoted as stating that multiculturalism was instrumental in "erosion of American national interests". Huntington further stressed that "diaspora interests are increasingly triumphing over American and Western national strategic security interests.... Media driven self-appointed and unelected ethnic lobbyists are positioned to subvert the democratic process".[17] Impetus to this idea was added by a group of journalists, supporting Howard, who aired the opinion that "multiculturalism denied Australian culture, the British inheritance and social cohesion."[18] Even John Howard had reservations in endorsing the word multiculturalism, he "refused to use the word 'multiculturalism' in public until 1999 and replaced the term 'Non-English-speaking background' (NESB) with 'culturally and linguistically diverse' (CALD)". After winning the election in 1996, his government not only abolished the Bureau of Immigration, Multicultural and Population Research, and merged its remnants into the Immigration Department in mid-1996 but emphasized the need for "ensuring that cultural diversity is a unifying force".[19] It forewarned that diversity and unity were two different issues and the latter may be achieved even at the cost of diversity. Perhaps an anti-thesis of the core values of multiculturalism. In 1996 Howard government abolished the Office of Multicultural Affairs and in its place constituted a Council for Multicultural Australia three years later.

Multiculturalism Challenged

The 1996 federal election appeared to be different than previous elections in the sense that Pauline Hanson, an Independent from Oxley, put forward a new agenda before the electorate. The newness in the agenda included an elaborate list of what Australia should do and not do. Some of the major issues included: challenge from Asians, multiculturalism and liberal multiracial society be abolished, no privileges or reconciliation for the aborigines, repudiate international obligations, free trade and economic rationalism, cease foreign aid – all aimed at building Australia as 'One Nation'.[20]

Pauline Hanson clarified her fear as: "If we were to have too many of one race coming in that weren't assimilating and becoming Australians, it would take over our culture, our own way of life and our own identity, and that's what I'm protecting."[21] To avert the damage that the ongoing influx of Asians was causing under the cloak of multiculturalism, Hanson focused on the assimilation process. Moreover, she strongly emphasized the need for controlled migration: "Of course, I will be called racist but, if I can invite whom I want into my home, then I should have the right to have a say in who comes to my country".[22]

Hanson's warning that the time was running out and only 10–15 years were left, perhaps she hinted at consequences of Asian migration to Australia. The Asian migrants settling in the cities and developing their ethnic groups mushroomed in isolated colonies. In a policy document she stressed that immigrants (Asian) "will lead to the bizarre situation of largely Asian cities on our coast which will be culturally and racially different from the traditional Australian nature of the rest of the country."[23] However, the 2001 Census indicated that the composition of the Asians in Australian population constituted only 12 per cent, whereas UK and Ireland constituted 26 per cent, Europe 26 per cent, North Africa and Middle East 12 per cent, Oceania 11 per cent, the Americas 4 per cent and Sub-Saharan Africa 3.5 per cent. Aborigines constituted 2.2 per cent. At a later stage Pauline stated more than once that she was not against Asians per se but only against their forming ghettos (segregational clusters). As of the 2001 Census the Australian population consisted of 18,769,074 people. Of this population: 23 per cent were born overseas, 43 per cent were either born overseas or had at least one parent born overseas. The top religions indicated constitute Christianity 12,763,880; Buddhism 357,814; Islam 281,586; Hinduism 95,448; Judaism 83,990. Perhaps a major concern for Pauline was the 23 per cent of Australians born outside the country, more than in any other nation apart from Israel, however the debate about how far Australia should bend to accommodate the values of new arrivals, or how far they should assimilate to Australian values, was not new.

Hanson a common person with the common person's issues tapped the pulse which was probably difficult to side track. As Ann Curthoys and Carol

Johnson have remarked: "Hansonite politics, in one form or another, whether or not it revolves around Pauline Hanson herself, or around One Nation specifically, is a form of politics of the future not the past.... It is a politics that is here to stay at least as a significant minority factor in Australian political life".[24]

Pauline Hanson opened a Pandora's box that was not only difficult for the Labour Party to respond but more so for the Liberal (coalition) ruling party of John Howard. Moreover, Hanson phenomenon took the Australian society a step back by initiating an open debate on racism which had been taken by the political parties and political elite groups as an 'untouchable' issue, mainly since 1970s. It was imperative for the ruling party to respond to One Nation agenda. John Howard while criticizing the racism issue, responded to Pauline Hanson: "I defend to the death your right to say it because a lot of voters agree with you".[25] This gave a chance to the ruling party to encourage public debate on the issue of racism, without being labeled as racist. Keeping the other issues aside (such as political, social and economical) raised by Hanson, John Howard pursued vigorously on the issue of migration and multiculturalism.

In 2001 to avoid the undesirable boat people, Howard introduced the "border protection bill aimed at having absolute control over who should be allowed to enter. This was evidenced when the *Tampa* people were not allowed to touch the Australian soil. Even Howard boasted in 2001 election campaign: "We determine who comes into this country and the circumstances under which they enter!", a statement very close to that of Hanson.[26] Even in June 2002 the government further tightened up the border protection policy by excising all small islands off Australia's northern mainland from its migration zone to stop boat people off shore. This appeared as 'Pacific Solution' to avert boat people reaching the Australian mainland or its peripheral islands. The boat people were given three years Temporary Protection Visa (TPV) and subject to extension depending on the home country situation. As a result, the Howard government instead of considering refugees under the Refugee Convention and providing shelter without any discrimination or how they reached the country considered them only for the Temporary Protection Visa for three years, subject to extension based on home country situation of the applicant. In this backdrop the Kosovars were sent back to their homeland.

Since 1954 with the signing of 1951 United Nations Convention by Australia, more than 599,000 people have arrived in Australia under humanitarian programmes, initially as displaced persons and more recently as refugees but the policy under the Howard government changed direction in the sense that instead of general intake of the refugees, it was government's prerogative to choose from overseas refugees waiting in the queue, rather than accepting the refugees who fled their home countries and reached Australian waters or land. In addition, the people on TPV had no provision for family reunion or welfare services. In this case the refugees from Iraq and Afghanistan were the worst hit.

Facing the criticism nationally and internationally, only after entering into refugee return agreements with China, Vietnam and Iran, and in the wake of Federal election in 2004, the then Immigration Minister Amanda Vanstone adopted a flexible approach to grant TPV holders, who had been already considered as refugees, a chance to apply for permanent residency. Commenting on the people detained in the Baxter and Woomera Detention Centres for years a leading expert on immigration compared the detention with Second World War situation: "Not since the Second World War had any Australian government had so many people locked up without charge and without any crime being committed which would stand up in the court".[27]

With increase in people from the Middle East and Asian countries, they better organized themselves and entered into some sort of lobbying and managed a major chunk of the family reunion intake. Parents and spouses with limited or no English and minimal professional skills had an easy entry in Australia. As a consequence, instead of mixing in the society at large, they formed their own groups. This was further highlighted by the Fitzgerald Inquiry in its report: *Immigration: A Commitment to Australia*. The report highlighted that the quality of immigration to Australia was declining and that multicultural policy was causing concern.[28]

Immigration Minister, Phillip Ruddock in order to improve upon the existing lacunae made strenuous efforts to get immigration policy 'back on track'. The 'back on track' appeared as an important improvement upon Whitlam, Hawke, Keating and Fraser's policies "especially multiculturalism and generous humanitarian and family reunion programs".[29] The policy shift was witnessed in the form of emphasis on points testing (education qualifications; skills and experience; age and English language compatibility), encouraging overseas students to apply for permanent residency visa onshore, initiating working holiday visa programme, expansion of temporary entry for short term employees. Overall, the points test enabled only the qualified people to migrate to Australia to overcome the shortage in skills. In this case, international students had an added advantage in the sense that during a period of two years as students they acclimatized and became acquainted with the culture and society better with Australian academic qualifications. Yet the temporary visa holders and working holiday visitors were an added advantage in the sense that they visited Australia and contributed in the work force without government liabilities. These measures indicated giving impetus to the economy of the country. Though this programme has been quite successful but having focus on the skills test and boost on the economy there may be long term repercussions. However, a leading expert on Australian immigration and multicultural affairs has questioned the viability of this programme in long terms:

> It also limited other avenues into Australia such as family reunion or seeking asylum. The potential of immigrants was thus judged by their visa eligibility, rather than their overall potential. This denied the experience of history, which is that human cannot always be predicted by measures which are currently relevant, but may be outdated in a few years. Many have prospered from unpromising beginnings while others, however well endowed, have fallen by the wayside.[30]

This policy fitted very close to Hanson's fear of emerging ghettos of Asian hordes. In addition, some of the other issues raised by Hanson such as special status and treatment awarded to the Aborigines and measures initiated for reconciliation were also meted when the Aboriginal and Torres Strait Islander Commission was dissolved in 2004 and so was the fate of reconciliation issue.

Hanson out rightly opposed the Human Rights and Equal Opportunity Commission (HREOC) as it constituted one of the MAJOR pillars of multiculturalism. Subsequently the powers and jurisdiction of HREOC were curtailed, even issues like detention of children in Baxter and Woomera detention centres went unheard for a long time. According to a critic, what the Howard government has achieved is not something innovative but has put a sweet coat on Hanson agenda:

> Indeed, one could say that one of Howard's...achievements has been to make Hanson's crude white populism respectable by translating it into mainstream common sense – a mainstream unwilling to seriously address reconciliation with Indigenous Australia and deeply suspicious of immigration and multiculturalism, especially when it is seen as a threat to 'Australian way of life'.[31]

In a similar vein, recently Hanson justifying the publication of her book *Untamed & Unashamed – The Autobiography* she expressed her pain and anguish loud and clear and questioned about branding her as a racist by the current government. She further argued: "Another reason why I wrote this book was the frustration of being castigated as a racist by the media and major political parties after my inaugural speech. Yet the very same policies I advocated back then are now almost populist policy, being advocated today by the federal government".[32]

Australian Values Invented

Australia's Centenary of Federation in 2001 celebrated with great fanfare projected a number of achievements during a period of one hundred years. One of the biggest achievements projected was the multicultural aspect of the society. Over the hundred years Australia grew into a big "melting pot", mainly since it abandoned White Australia policy in the 1960s and 70s and accepted multiculturalism. With a quarter of its population born overseas, made it the country with the second highest such proportion in the world, and second only to Israel. Around the same time, The National Multicultural Advisory Council in its report entitled Australian Multiculturalism for a New Century: Towards Inclusiveness submitted its report. The Council in its recommendations highly appreciated the vibrant multiculture of Australia:

> Australian culture is dynamic. It starts with and retains its links to our total heritage, but is not a fossilised entity...it is a living, changing and interacting set of life patterns. It has been modified and enhanced by the arrival of many migrant groups. It continues to be developed by the evolution of ideas and customs within Australia and by global influences.[33]

Further emphasising the inclusive nature of Australian multiculturalism it stated: "Multiculturalism is about and for all Australians....our original inhabitants, the Aboriginal and Torres Strait Islander peoples, as well as all other Australians, whether born here or overseas and whether of English or non-English-speaking origin". The Council **recommended** that "future multicultural policies and strategies give high priority to outreach strategies that build bridges of understanding and mutual interest among individuals and groups of different cultural backgrounds, including between groups whose members are drawn from specific ethnic and indigenous cultures and more general community bodies".[34]

However the Council's recommendations for future policies proved short lived. Sending the Afghan and Iraqi refugees to Nauru and Manus (so called Pacific Solution) and finally urging them to return home, national political campaign highlighting terrorism as Islamic oriented and support to wars in Afghanistan and Iraq created a tense environment mainly in the Muslim community in Australia. Moreover after 11 September 2001 and Bali Bombings, massive psychological pressure was put on the Muslim community. This situation can be summed up as: "A state of unease, fed by images in the media and political sub-texts, now permeates Australian society. Equally, Australian Muslims are worried that they have become the 'other' who is being unfairly labelled and targeted".[35] The furry of Muslim community was further enhanced in a December 2005 incident when a mob of white Australian youths, incensed by what they saw as offensive behaviour by Lebanese youths, gathered on Cronulla, a south Sydney beach, and went on a rampage, beating up anyone they could find of Middle Eastern appearance. The riots and claims by the local youths that Cronulla was their ancestral place and outsiders were subject to entry restrictions left deep scars on the multicultural fabric of the society in general and Muslim community in particular. In response, the Islamic religious leadership not only reacted sharp and hard and challenged the British legacy and claims on Australia soil. Sheikh El Hilaly went to the extreme extent of accusing British ancestry by stating:

> They are the biggest liars and the most unjust, the Western people, especially the English people. The Anglo-Saxons arrived in shackles in Australia, while

> we paid for our tickets from our own pockets and we went there free. So we are more entitled to Australia than them. Australia is not Anglo-Saxon. Islam is deep rooted in the soil and it preceded the English arrival there.[36]

In addition, in another incident in a You Tube video made by Lebanese Muslim youngsters in Sydney while glorifying notorious gang rapist Bilal Skaf predicted that Australia would one day be a Muslim country.[37]

This resulted in counter attacks from the ruling party. Even senior leadership was no exception. *The Age* published several statements that came in the wake of Hilaly's claims on Australian land. Treasurer Peter Costello warned that people thinking of coming to Australia who did not like Australian values and preferred a society that practised Sharia Law should go elsewhere. In a similar vein, the Education Minister Brendan Nelson bluntly warned (Islamists): "We want them to understand our history and our culture, the extent to which we believe in mateship and giving another person a hand up and a fair go. And basically, if people don't want to be Australians and they don't want to live by Australian values and understand them, well basically they can clear off".[38]

According to Acting Race Discrimination Commissioner Dr. William Jones, Australians who appeared as Arab or Muslim by their dress, language, name or appearance have been: "abused, threatened, spat upon, assailed with eggs, bottles, cans and rocks, punched and even beaten….People reported being fired from their jobs or refused employment or promotion because of their race or religion. Children have been bullied in schoolyards. Women have been stalked, abused and assaulted in shopping centres. Private homes, places of worship and schools were vandalized and burned. 'terrorist', 'dirty Arab', 'murderer', 'bloody Muslim', 'raghead', 'Bin-Laden', 'illegal immigrant', 'black c..t' are just some of the labels and profanities that we were told have been used against Arabs and Muslims in public places".[39]

Branding of Muslims as 'other' in a multicultural society like Australian "it leaves a lasting impression that contributes to a sense of alienation, distrust and fear of future discrimination and attacks".[40]

Australia proud of its multiculturalism that allowed its residents/citizens to celebrate both their heritage and the Australian culture for over three decades sent the nerve feeling deep down in the society. Against the evolving debate on who has better claims on Australia, the Howard government took tangible steps that were witnessed on 23 January 2007 Cabinet reshuffle. The name of the Department of Immigration and Multicultural Affairs (DIMA) was changed to Department of Immigration and Citizenship (DIAC). Moreover, the government also revised immigration regulations that extended the waiting period before applying for citizenship from the current two-year period to four years and a tough new citizenship test to assess proficiency in English, knowledge of Australian history and the applicant's grasp of civic responsibilities. The renaming of DIMA from DIAC represents a much deeper change in government policy: a shift of emphasis from celebrating the cultural diversity of its immigrant population to promoting an Australian cultural unity. In addition, the government supported that Australia and Australians must have commitment to core Australian values that include: liberal democracy, rule of law, sexual and racial equality, and a common language, English. The declaration of Australian Values appeared a justifiable measure to overcome the debate about who had what claims on the country. Howard indicated that the path for new settlers would be "you come to this country, you embrace its customs, its values, its language, you become a citizen".[41]

Conclusion

The issue of Australian Values is taking place against the backdrop of intense debate about how these values will shape the future of the Australian society.

A school of thought headed by intellectuals like James Jupp believes that the change in name from DIMA to DIAC conveys a significant message to the society: "The new message is that this is a liberal, democratic, English-speaking society which has been well established and it is up to people who come from other cultures to adjust their behaviour accordingly".[42]

Other school of thought that supports immigrants' perspective stresses that Australian Values are exclusive in nature and promote racism. According to Keyser Trad, head of the Islamic Friendship Association of Australia: "I love these values, but when he [John Howard] talks about them, they are little more than clichés; they tend to be exclusive....They are encouraging racism through national pride. It's a recipe for a highly polarized society". In his attempts to highlight on the implications of the Australian Values, Trad added: "There's an attitude that if you are not white, you are somehow less equal".[43] *In a similar vein,* the Greens warned of a slide back to White Australia policy in parliament and labeled the current changes aimed at colour-blind immigration policy. Greens leader Bob Brown argued: "It's going to be harder to come to Australia if you don't have an Anglo background".[44]

Yet another school of thought that supports status quo finds no faults with multiculturalism and recognizes that even if some issues appear, these instances alert the society about the contradictions in multiculturalism, and as forward-looking multiculturalist Australia needs to address them instead of back-pedaling. According to a free lance journalist:."It seems to me that this paranoid nationalism is a reaction to some choice words emitted by one or two members of our Muslim community, yet there is little evidence that our country is about to be swamped by extremist Muslim values".[45] *More precisely, T.S. Eliot commenting on the multicultural nature of the society supported that the* "country which receives culture from abroad without having anything to give in return, and the country which aims to impose its culture on another, without accepting anything in return, will both suffer from this lack of reciprocity".[46]

Though Australia politically a vibrant and stable democracy, economically a buoyant economy endowed with ample resources and socially a melting pot admixture of the population has a strong and straightforward trajectory of over overcoming contentious and conflicting issues. The Australian Values though a landmark in nature and scope, and a major deviation from the concept of multiculturalism attracted a healthy intellectual debate in media. Except the Islamic religious leadership, the response remained quite reticent and yet it is not clear how the society as such will react to the Australian Values. However, the late 2007 federal election with Labour Party's rejuvenated leadership may prove as a referendum to government's policy.

Endnotes

1. H.I. *London, Non-White Immigration and the 'White Australia' Policy* (New York: New York University Press, 1970), p. 12.
2. John Kane, "Racialism and Democracy: The Legacy of White Australia" in Geoffrey Stokes (ed), *The Politics of Identity in Australia* (Cambridge: Cambridge University Press, 1997), pp 121–133.
3. For a detailed explanation on Australian society and egalitarianism see Hugh Mackay, *Reinventing Australia: The Mind and Mood of Australia in the 90s* (Sydney: Angus & Robertson, 1993), pp. 138–142.
4. *Australia and Immigration 1788 to 1988* (Canberra: Department of Immigration, Local Government and Ethnic Affairs, 1988), p. 27.
5. Arthur Calwell stated in August 1945, Ibid, p. 29.
6. Quoted in Meg Gurry, "Identifying Australia's 'Region': From Evatt to Evans", *Australian Journal of International Affairs*, vol. 49, no. 1, May 1995, p. 119.
7. Quoted in K S Inglis, *Observing Australia: 1959 to 1999* (Melbourne: Melbourne University Press, 1999), p. 204.
8. For details see_http://www4.gu.edu.au./ext/civics/cv02/mod03/cv02m03t02.htm
9. Gough Whitlam, *The Whitlam Government, 1972–1975* (Ringwood: Viking, 1985), p. 501.
10. For details see www.petra.ac.id/asc/people/multiculturalism/historical/theory.html-4k-
11. For details see http://www4.gu.edu.au./ext/civics/cv02/mod03/cv02m03t02.htm
12. Ien Ang "From White Australia to Fortress Australia: The Anxious Nation in the New Century," in eds, Laksiri Jayasuriya, David Walker and Jan Gothard, *Legacies of White Australia: Race, Culture and Nation* (Crawley: University of Western Australia Press:, 2003, p. 62).
13. For details see Australia and Immigration 1788 to 1988 (Canberra: Department of Immigration, Local Government and Ethnic Affairs, 1988), pp. 62–72.
14. Ibid, p. 78.
15. Ibid, p. 89.
16. Ang, n. 12, p. 65.
17. *National Observer* (Melbourne), Summer 2002, Issue 51, p. 7.
18. Betts Quoted in James Jupp, "Immigration and Multiculturalism" in eds, Chris Aulich and Roger Wettenhall, *Howard's Second and Third Governments*(Sydney: UNSW Press, 2005), p. 175.

19. For details see Ibid, p. 178 and also see *Australian Multiculturalism for a New Century: Towards Inclusiveness* (Canberra: AGPS, 1999).
20. For details see http://www.paulinehanson.com.au/pauline-maiden-speech.pdf
21. Sydney Morning Herald, 23 July 1998.
22. Pauline Hanson Maiden Speech, p. 8.
23. Pauline Hanson, *One Nation, Immigration, Population and Social Cohesion Policy Document,* 1998, p. 11.
24. Ann Curthoys and Carol Johnson, "Articulating the Future and the Past: Gender, Race and Globalisation in One Nation Discourse", *Hecate*, vol 24, no 2, 1998, p. 97.
25. John Howard quoted in Jupp, n. 18, p. 180.
26. www.safecom.org.au/orwellian.htm - 45k –
27. Jupp, n.18, p. 185.
28. For details see Fitzgerald, S, *Immigration: A Commitment to Australia* (Canberra: AGPS, 1988).
29. Jupp, n.18, p. 174.
30. Ibid, p. 175.
31. Ang, n.12, p. 65.
32. *Untamed & Unashamed-The Autobiography* http://www.paulinehanson.com.au/buy-untamed-unashamed-online.php?nav=4
33. www.dimia.gov.au/media/publications/multicultural/nmac/prelim.htm - 13k -
34. www.dimia.gov.au/media/publications/multicultural/nmac/prelim.htm - 13k -
35. Mohamed Abdalla, "A Fair Go: A Muslim's Perspective", in ed, Patty Fawkner, *A Fair Go in an Age of Terror*(Melbourne: David Lovell Publishing, 2004), p. 64.
36. Australian Muslim, Sheikh El Hilaly on Egyption Television , 11 January 2007.
37. *Gulf Times* (Doha) 26 January 2007.
38. Quoted in theage.com.au/news/war-on-terror/.../2005/08/24/1124562921555.html -
39. Quoted in Abdalla, n.35, p. 64.
40. Ibid, p. 64.
41. www.pm.gov.au/media/Interview/2007/Interview2339.cfm - 15k -
42. Quoted in *International Herald Tribune*, 28 January 2007.
43. Ibid.
44. phastidio.net/2007/01/26/from-multiculturalism-to-integration-weekend-open-trackback/ - 94k
45. Masako Fukui, "Diversity breeds a stronger identity", The Australian, 4 February 2007.
46. T.S. Eliot, "*Notes Towards the Definition of Culture*", ed, Frank Kermode, *Selected Prose of T S Eliot*, (London: Faber and Faber, 1975), p. 303.

    As Charles Taylor has rightly stated "Though ethnic and religious diversity trouble some Australians", but "the real task is…to ignore the great diversity that prevails on peripheral matters and to make sure that the over-arching framework of core values is sound, strong and flexible. Then, whatever our ethnic and religious origins, we can all feel that sense of identification with Australia". (Quoted in K S Inglis, Observing Australia: 1959 to 1999 (Melbourne University Press: Melbourne, 1999, p. 218). One Nation?

21

Identity and Rights of the Diaspora in the Post-colonial Era

R. Narayanan

The article examines the diasporic communities globally and raise a few theoretical issues regarding its study in respect of identity and rights in the current context of globalization.

A proposition that was made by a media expert, which pithily stated reads as follows: "We no longer have roots, we have aerials; we no longer have origins, we have terminals". (Mackenzie Wark, *Virtual Geography: Living with Global Media Events* (Bloomington: Indian University Press, 1994)

Author's reasons for invoking this proposition are obvious. Though relevant to any analysis on cultural diversity and related issues of representation and rights, the question of identity is largely treated too imprecisely in the current social science discourse and policy debates.

Although one should not exaggerate the degree of globalization and the attendant deterritorialization, these and other material transformations have rendered the rigidities of the modern socio-spatial triad of the inter-state system (i.e. nation-state sovereignty, territorial integrity and community identity) increasingly problematic in the study of Diaspora. No doubt, this heavily mythologized triad of state-territory-community was never perfectly set in the past. But its instability and precariousness are becoming more and more pronounced as places are increasingly denationalized and globalized by transnational flows of all kinds – capital, skills and information. This implosion, however dramatic or gradual, as one perceives it, has caused a crisis in socio-spatial identities, thus provoking an experience of vertigo.

But every deterritorialization creates in turn conditions for an order using fragments of the beliefs, customs, practices and narratives of the old splintered world order, leading either to re-territorialization or multi-territorialization not necessarily of course in spatial terms.

Instead of the socio-spatial triad, if the cultural diversity framework is adopted for diasporic studies, then the analytical ambience of Diaspora does assume considerable significance. Yet, admittedly it is riddled with some methodological nuances. For one, there are the conceptual problems such as the notion of culture itself. I, therefore, take what some social scientists would describe as the 'billiard ball' view of culture being in a state of continuous flux. Nevertheless boundaries are to be drawn and redrawn across space and time around particular cultures because social relations cannot be explored without taking into account wherever differences between cultures are manifest in the everyday life of communities. Defining these differences, in my view, is at the heart of the problematique of diasporic culture in the present era.

Before raising a few theoretical issues for an analysis of diasporic identity based on my case study of Indian Diaspora, let me briefly delineate four sequential phases of the Indian emigration overseas.

First, the phase when ancient and medieval monarchs and traders from the east and west coast of peninsular India reached out and established contacts and outposts in Southeast Asia, West Asia and eastern and northern Africa. Of these, the medieval period was marked by trade exchanges, accounts of which are well documented by historians and also sensitively delineated by creative writers such as (Amitav Ghosh in *In an Antique Land* and Salman Rushdie in *The Moors Last Sigh*).

The second phase spans most part of the 19th Century under the guise of indentured labour triggered by British colonialism to plantation economies of the colonial world including Australia, though here, in Australia, numerically speaking, it was only a fraction compared to other parts of the British colonies. This phase also included traders and white-collared workers to the British, Dutch and French colonies.

The third phase is the emigration from India in the 20th Century, more so, since India's Independence, and in that sense may be characterized as the post-colonial phase of skilled professionals and their kin.

Lately, especially in the wake of economic liberalization reforms unleashed in 1990s, debate on Indian Diaspora has acquired considerable stridency among policy-makers and scholars. Also, perceptions on Indian Diaspora are undergoing changes. No more, the Indian exodus to the industrially advanced Western countries is treated as 'braindrain'. Instead, it is labelled as 'brainbanks', in the hope that such edification would encourage generous remittances and capital flows from the overseas Indians to their homeland. Subtle distinctions, therefore, are made between 'non-resident Indians' (NRIs) and the 'people of Indian origin' (PIOs) with offer of incentives and special economic rights including dual citizenship to overseas Indians. However, on the choice of who among them – NRIs or PIOs – should be conferred such rights are as of now debated. While the Government of India is disposed to extend dual citizenship status to the NRIs based in the more developed countries such as Australia, Britain, Canada, New Zealand and the United States, resident Indians elsewhere and their lobbies in India are clamouring for extension of such rights to all overseas Indians. According to them such distinctions of NRIs and PIOs are not only tenuous but also unjust. Or, as some put it, the government is favourably disposed to the NRIs as against the PIOs because in its reckoning Non Resident Indians the NRIs are as the 'newly rich Indians' as against the People of Indian Origin, the PIOs who are the 'poor Indians overseas'!

Scholars, at least some of them, engaged in the study of Indian Diaspora too tend to justify such distinctions. According to them, admittedly different groups of people claim Indian identity and, in turn, attach different kinds of significance to their claim. In support of their line of argument, they say that the 'construction' of Indian identities in the Caribbean, south Pacific islands and eastern Africa is different from the construction of such identities in the West Asian region and also among the post-colonial diasporics resident in the metropolitan regions of the West. Thus, they claim that the problem of identity construction remains unresolved and by and large therefore remains "untheorised".

Demographic studies on Indian Diaspora largely based on the numbers, fertility among the immigrant population, the role of linguistic and religious variables raise a set of additional issues. While the quantum of Indian Diaspora globally is evident (nearly 10 million live outside South Asia region), mind you these are direct migrants, their concentration vary from country to country – the largest in Britain followed by Malaysia and South Africa and in countries such as Guyana, Surinam, Trinidad & Tobago in the Caribbean, and in Mauritius and Fiji, Indians constitute nearly half of the total population.

Demographic data on Indian immigrants in Australia throw up some socio-political issues. According to the 1991 census, a little more than 40 per cent of the total number of Australians was born overseas or had one or both parents born overseas. Of this, the Asia-born constituted 4.6 per cent. The percentage of Asians in the population has since steadily increased and of these, nearly two-thirds of the second-generation immigrants were marrying outside their ethnic group – all of this is melting the predominantly celtic demographic profile of Australia of yesteryears. As one friend in Sydney quipped: "Today there are less celts as against the 'melts' in Australia!"

A comment on Indians in Australia

First, building on the demographic profile of Indians in this country, it is interesting to note that the 'geographically indirect' or 'twice migrants' and that too from geographically proximate Fiji predominate the Indian ethnics.

Second, the Hindu Indians cut across nationality by birth – Malaysia, Sri Lanka, India and Fiji.

Third, the Tamil-speaking Hindus are again cutting across the same nationalities by birth.

Upon this, what kind of a 'construct' of Indianness can be made? Are there, therefore, slippages? If so, where do the 'slippages' occur? What is their significance when a notion like Indian culture is deployed in a context where Indians are not culturally hegemonic? Can the Tamil-speaking Hindu Indian ethnics constitute a potent force to encourage Tamil nationalism elsewhere in South Asia? These and related questions are themes that need careful attention both in respect of policy debates and academic discourse both in the host and home countries.

Cultural-anthropological studies on Indian Diaspora are aplenty and varied depending on the different approaches:

1. "cultural persistence" framework (as evidenced in Morton Klass' empirical study of Indian ethnics in Trinidad),
2. "cultural adaptation" approach (as evidenced in the work of R.K. Jain on Malaysia), and
3. "structural-functional" study (on the urban-based Indians in Britain by Tambs-Lyche).

More perhaps are under way with a new line of approach that seems to cut across the disciplinary boundaries. Here, mention may be made of a recent anthropological study by Katherine Verdery who inclines to put the rise of ethnicity and the nation-state in an evolutionary order by stating:

> It is not from ethnic identities that national identities develop; rather the latter creates the frame that generates the former – the frame within which ethnicity *qua* difference, in its broadest sense, acquires social significance.

What is suggested in this line of approach is that the process of ethnicity emerging from the nation-building becomes pronounced in the present globalized world in which people with their pre-constituted national identities migrate elsewhere and become ethnic groups – a behaviour pattern very visible and pronounced in places like the MCC grounds. In a sense, it is an extension of what Benedict Anderson calls the "ethnicisation of existing nationalities" practicing "long distance nationalism".

Yet another genre in the studies on Indian Diaspora – both sociological and anthropological – relates to their location differentiated between what are called the settlement societies and civilizational societies. (J.S. Furnival's celebrated study brings to fore the characteristics of the settlement societies.)

Culturally, it comprises of groups, which are institutionally disparate and do not share the same basic values and ways of life. Economically, these separate social groups have interaction mainly in the market place. Politically, the colonizing authority holds these culturally disparate but economically interacting groups together. Though plural in appearance, they lack common social will and to that extent the constituent segments 'mix' in limited contexts and confines but do not 'blend'.

Such settlement societies share one or all of the following historical and geo-political antecedents:

1. a short history marked by massive immigration;
2. presence of native population variable in numbers;
3. colonialism or dependent status of one kind or another;
4. a correlation between economy and ethnic relations in such a way that if the economy is buoyant inter-ethnic relations are better or vice versa;
5. the settlement society is also a geopolitical entity for example, Mexico and South America can be contrasted with Australia, Canada, the Caribbean and the United States of America – the former provide instances of civilizations and the latter of settlement societies.

In the Old World, when much of Europe, India and China and parts of Africa are contrasted with island societies, the former are seats of civilizations while the latter the settlement societies.

Here, some have drawn attention to a distinction to be made between 'non-modern' and 'modern' civilizational societies basing the differentiation on the technology factor.

Again, in respect of settlement societies distinctions are drawn between elementary settlement societies such as Mauritius, Fiji, Trinidad & Tobago, etc. and the more complexly structured settlement societies like the US, Canada and South Africa.

These distinctions are useful for differentiating the settlement societies from the civilizational societies while examining the issues of identity and rights of the diasporic communities. However, when the political economy framework is applied in the context of the settlement societies, the elaborate and subtle differentiations made of them become less rewarding as a methodological tool.

It is here, discourses (of John Rex and others) blending the sociological analysis with political economy framework merit mention – in the context of study of Indian diaspora especially of the 19th and 20th Centuries and even more so, in the current context of Indian emigration. According to this, post-modern world migratory movements take place according to the different imperatives of economies for labour. Consequently, major movement of people such as specialized skilled labour and professionals takes place from post-colonial to metropolitan societies, irrespective of their settlement/civilizational antecedents. When this happens, metropolitan labour movements seek to place barriers to a movement of a racist kind. Political parties supporting their cause engage in a vitriolic, which smacks of downright racialism – what in the context of Australia may be described as the "Pauline Hanson phenomenon". In so far as these are effective, even if it were for a brief spell, what one sees is stark racial/ethnic discrimination directly impinging on the diasporic identity and its rights exacerbating thereby social distancing in an otherwise functional multicultural settlement societies.

Besides these, in the current context yet another kind of diasporics is emerging which are outside the familiarly known models. This relates to the legal category of refugee migrants. Citing the example of Tamil minority from Sri Lanka, Oivind Fuglerud, a Norwegian scholar in his recent study describes how these people comprehend their emigration through a complex relationship to the Tamil homeland or the *Eelam*. They enter into a complex set of relationship with an ideal and a non-existing reality of the homeland. This then transforms our understanding of what it means to be a refugee-migrant and how ethnic-national conflicts are constructed at home through their translation abroad.

At its most transparent level, Fuglerud's study traces the history of Tamil migration, from the arrival of the economic migrants of the 1960s to the "asylum seekers" of the mid-1980s onwards. Against this history he draws parallels between the status of the Tamil community in Sri Lanka, as a beleaguered and persecuted minority waging a war of liberation, and as a displaced, marginalized and excluded refugee community. Between them they have only tenuous links to the "host country" and a fierce but often contradictory attachment to revolutionary politics and to Tamil customs and rituals. In the process of displacement, Fuglerud argues, particular aspects of Tamil culture marriage – dowry, chastity and ritual – acquire a heightened significance: tradition, literally, is consolidated in exile, and inextricably bound up in the violent struggle for independence in Sri Lanka. The contradictions and inconsistencies which characterize the Tamil refugee communities, and the success of revolutionary Tamil nationalism in exile, highlight the transnational nature of identity politics and demonstrate why the fumbling attempts by the state to integrate these diasporic communities are doomed to failure. For the Tamils, displacement is not so much a question of geography as a state of mind. As he says:

> The future of *Eelam* depends on the Tamil diaspora as much as the future of the diaspora, in a certain sense, depends on the fate of *Eelam*.

Major implications diasporic rights – cultural and economic.

First, it pertains to issues involved in translation and translatability of identity upon which diasporic cultural rights are premised. But these issues are not peculiar to a multicultural or plural society made up of diasporic communities. Rather it is a phenomenon wherever socio-cultural stratification is pronounced, be it civilizational or settlement societies.

Second, it pertains to hybridity or its elementary structure, creolisation. Here again, what matters in respect of its efficacy are the factors of stratification in the settlement society. Regarding Indian diaspora, more often comparisons are made between Guyana and Fiji – the success of hybridity in Guyana is often attributed to the free inter-mixture between East Indians and the Africans whereas its failure in Fiji is attributed to the 'divide and rule' policy adopted by the colonial power.

Finally, multiculturalism. Here the major snag is also the same as in the discourses of translation and hybridisation. If multiculturalism is not cultural relativist, then the universal values have to be of a certain cultural cast governed by dominant strand in the modern history of a particular society. As James Jupp puts it where minorities are excluded in the multicultural model, then it degenerates into cultural racialism.

No gainsaying then that any analysis of identity and rights of the diasporics need to transcend the theoretical constructs in which they were made in the colonial past. What is suggested here is that social scientists need to pay attention to post-colonial concepts and theories of migrant identity and of their rights. Such an inquiry would shift the focus from looking at an immigrant's acculturation as governed by singular developmental end states such as integration and assimilation to a more process-oriented notion of acculturation which could account for situated, negotiated and often contested developmental trajectories. In other words, what is imperative is a theoretical construct that could go beyond national and cultural boundaries and allow us to think more in terms of moving cultures where, here and there, past and present, homeland and hostland, self and other are constantly being negotiated with each other.

By way of elucidation, here let me quote Rhoda Reddock, an African Trinidadian feminist scholar in her paper on *Conceptualising Difference in the Caribbean.*

In our society, African and Indian women were constantly being defined in opposition to each other.... This within the racial contestations of the society, served to narrow the options and spaces to manoeuvre for the women concerned. It was for this reason that in my own historical research my efforts to understanding of the experiences of Indian women was as important to me as was my understanding of that of the African women.... I felt that our differences had in some way contributed to what we had now been constructed to be. In other words, it was impossible to know myself if I did not know my other/s.

Put differently, what Reddock suggests in this passage is the importance of understanding the "other" within "ourselves".

In a similar vein Espin, in her book entitled *Women Crossing Boundaries* emphasizes the importance of personal narratives to understand the inner experience of migration of women in relation to gender and sexuality. Not that she intends to create a grand narrative but rather to present a window into the individual life narratives developed by women who have been immersed in the transformations brought about by the migrants. By counterposing narratives of women from diverse backgrounds, Espin allows us to appreciate how the social and political constructions of gender, ethnicity, race and nationality are crucial to any discussion of the migrant self.

Even more revealing is the inner experience of the post-modern migrant portrayed in a more recent study on Iranian diasporics by Naficy in his book *The Making of Exile Cultures* where he discusses how the Iranian diasporic community uses television media as a source for resisting cultural messages both from the dominant American host culture as well as the culture of the homeland. Through an eleven-year ethnographic study, he demonstrates that the relationship between the mainstream culture and the subcultures is fraught with ambivalence and contestation on the one hand and the enrichment and assimilation on the other.

These and similar other studies offer useful insights enlarging the framework for the study of the diasporics and of their cultural needs and expectations. Developments of diasporic identities in the current context therefore need to ask and answer such critical questions as: Do all immigrants traverse the same routes in their acculturation process? Can we relegate colonial history, gender, and race to the status of variables and overlook how identity is embedded in a network of multiple and often contested cultural practices? Are there multiple endpoints to this process? How are we then to understand and explain how millions of migrant children living in diasporic contexts negotiate their sense of identity *vis-à-vis* the larger mainstream culture? One can add a host of other related questions to these basics. In finding the answers to these questions perhaps we have to go back to the invocation with which I began my presentation; However, with some modifications.

We no longer have roots, but we *should* have aerials; we no longer have origins, we have to look for the terminals.

22

Understanding Cultural Diversity: Reflections from the Americas

Satya R. Pattnayak

The debate over the future of American culture has intensified in recent years as the country faces unprecedented legal and illegal immigration from overseas. The percentage of the US population of European ancestry is projected to decline to 62 per cent by 2025 from 74 per cent in 1995. During the same thirty year period, the shares of Americans with Latino and Asian ancestries are likely to increase to 18 per cent from 10 per cent and to 6 per cent from 3 per cent respectively.[1] At the center of this debate is of course a sweeping uneasiness over the characterization of the United States as a culturally diverse nation. "Cultural Diversity" is defined for the purpose of this essay in the broadest possible way. A society may be considered culturally diverse if: It is inhabited by multitudes of groups who claim cultural, ethnic, racial, or religious heritage from the outside of the country's borders; is associated with a heterogeneous occupational structure where statuses may be defined by the individual occupation of such positions; and consists of residential neighbourhoods that are generally segregated by race, ethnicity, religion, and/or income.

It is indeed true that the discussion of cultural diversity in the United States has been emotional and polarized in recent years. On the one hand, Huntington, Brimlow, and others have become alarmed over the explosion of non-European immigration, both legal and illegal, to the United States.[2] As estimates go, the United States on average absorbs about 1 million new immigrants each year, the majority of whom are from Latin America and Asia.[3] Furthermore, another 12 to 15 million illegal immigrants, mostly Mexican, are estimated to live and work in the United States currently.[4] According to alarmists such as Huntington, the challenges of incorporation of foreigners, mainly from Latin America but also from Asia, would have deep ramifications for American values, work-ethic, and democratic way of life, as these newer immigrants are prone to competing values, life styles, and a more authoritarian political and social structure. Writes Huntington in a much publicized essay in Foreign Policy:

> "...The persistent inflow of Hispanic immigrants threatens to divide the United States into two peoples, two cultures, and two languages. Unlike past

> immigrant groups, Mexicans and other Latinos have not assimilated into mainstream American culture, forming instead their own political and linguistic enclaves…and rejecting the Anglo Protestant values that built the American dream."[5]

On the other hand, the proliferation of studies singing the praises of "cultural pluralism" has also exploded.[6] The primary emphasis of cultural pluralists is to recognize diversity as it exists in its multiple forms and shapes. Essentially, cultural pluralism entails a high level of tolerance for differences in race, religion, ethnicity, political aptitudes, moral orientation, and lifestyles. Testifying to the diverse nature of the American body civic, Nathan Glazer declared triumphantly in as early as 1997 that "we are all multiculturalists now."[7]

Theoretical Underpinnings

For a long time, the analysis of cultural diversity in the United States has been much influenced by two dominant theoretical perspectives: "cultural assimilationist" and "cultural pluralist." The cultural assimilationist position has adhered to the belief that in immigrant societies, such as the US, cultural legacies of the various ethno-cultural groups pass through later generations in progressively diminished forms and eventually disappear.[8] This "melting pot" orientation rests on the assumption that the importance of ascribed cultural traits and influence would decline with increasing incorporation into American society. The associated modernization of new groups would instill the socially acceptable traits of universalism and achievement.

The cultural pluralist paradigm, on the other hand, emphasizes the persistence of cultural heritage, notwithstanding the changes in major areas of society, such as the labour market, patterns of interaction between groups in informal settings, and increased educational opportunities.[9] According to this position, cultural identity or consciousness tends to emerge and manifest itself most acutely in the drive toward modernization, as diverse groups come in contact and compete for scarce items like power and privilege in society. The major question then is: Do cultural groups continue to maintain their distinctiveness in the destination societies in the face of long term structural changes in technology, industrial development, residential settlement patterns, increased urbanization, and the nature and extent of their labour market participation?

In this essay, it will be argued that both extreme positions have not been corroborated by empirical evidence. It is to be demonstrated that eclectic forms of culturally-assimilationist and culturally-pluralist tendencies have always persisted in the evolution of societies throughout the Americas and they continue to flourish with appropriate modifications by "labour market conditions," "ethno-cultural community," and "ethnic identity" in specific contexts. In particular, examples will be used from the US, Guyana, and Trinidad to corroborate the various arguments.

Importance of the Labour Market

Stanley Lieberson's work on immigrant groups in the US suggests that the location of these groups in the occupational structure contributes immensely to a particular definition of their ethnic culture.[10] The meanings that other groups assign to a particular cultural group are likely to change as the group progresses through various positions on the occupational hierarchy. In the beginning of this process, of course, the group's cultural background as Irish, German, or, more recently, as Mexican or Asian Indian would play a major role in framing a definition of the respective sub-culture in the context of the United States.

The sweeping predictions of the "melting pot" hypothesis under the broader rubric of "cultural assimilationism" about the historical success of the model has been consistently criticized since the 1970s by sociologists, anthropologists, and even economists.[11] It is inevitably true that the cultural belonging from an overseas society brought on board by immigrants to the United States would have its preponderance in the beginning. The persistence or complete disappearance of such traits over time would depend on several contextual factors, such as the dynamics of the US society, politics, and economy, as well as the extent of interaction with the culture of origin. The last mentioned attribute has a particular salience in today's increasingly globalized world as travel and lines of communications with relatives and friends in the country of origin are being sustained without much difficulty. Research on societies that are multi-ethnic with considerable migrant populations, such as the US and Canada, suggests that much of cultural identity changes directly as a result of occupational changes experienced by the successive generations.[12] In other words, it may have been true that the status of the arriving Irish, Jewish, and other European immigrant groups in the 19th century US was relatively homogeneous in the new country. But once the occupational changes occurred it was inevitable that the ethnically based cultural identity also underwent change. These changes occurred not only through occupational structural changes but also over time through inter-marriage and residential mobility.

In other examples, even in societies characterized by the absence of a significant number of inter-ethnic marriages, such as the former British colonies of Guyana and Trinidad in the Caribbean, the cultural identity of migrants from India changed over time not only in terms of how others perceive them but also on the basis of how they perceive themselves.[13]

Ethno-occupational mobility data from the past three decades in the US confirms to an ever expanding cultural diversity and change. For example,

Kingston argues that different labour market status of spouses has produced an eclectic mix of class consciousness, which implies different cultural consciousness within the family.[14] Furthermore, such cross-statuses are complicated by the ethnic and cultural boundaries that have continued to change as members move their residences directly as a result of upward or downward occupational mobility. Unlike the late 19th and early 20th century trends, when European ethnic immigrants settled around the manufacturing centres of the Eastern and Mid-Western sections of the United States and produced quite distinct working class cultural cleavages, the later immigration of Latin American and Asian cultural groups since the late 1960s have produced different types of occupation-centreed cultural segmentation, largely around service sector niches.[15]

No society is occupationally homogeneous. Classical theorists, such as Smith and Durkheim, have indeed based their arguments about economic growth and development on the basis of inter-dependent occupational roles played by members of divergent cultural groups in modern society.[16] Tensions over the negotiations of such roles notwithstanding, the material or instrumental basis of cultural diversity would contribute to differences in political and social practices by members commensurate with these occupational roles. Even in relatively ethnically homogeneous societies, such as Japan and South Korea, occupational diversity projects political and cultural differences that manifest in the proliferation of a diverse society.[17]

During the days of slavery, the definitional fiat was superimposed by the Southern planter aristocracy and upheld by the Federal administration in Washington DC until the Civil War of the 1860s. The cultural identity of African Americans was construed as synonymous with enslavement, although a tiny free slave population always existed in the south and a much larger one in the North Eastern part of the United States.[18] Enslaved occupational roles were performed by most Americans of African heritage until after the end of the Civil War, and it fostered a type of culture that was absent in the rest of society. But after the Civil War and the emancipation proclamation by President Lincoln, the changes occurred in the occupational roles played by blacks in America. As the occupational roles changed, and over time more blacks entered into non-agricultural jobs, cultural diversity also proliferated within the black community as it also occurred in the larger American society with the incorporation of the European and Jewish immigration later in the 19th and early 20th centuries. Larger structural changes unleashed by aggregate forces such as industrialization and large-scale immigration also affected the status of blacks, a number of whom eventually found employment outside of the south and agriculture. Wilson's research has found that by the 1980s, the majority of blacks in America are occupied in middle-class jobs while prior to the 1930s the primary source of employment for them was agriculture.[19] The labour market conditions, then, were key determinants of cultural identity and later cultural diversity once immigrants have settled in a new society and have engaged in recurring patterns of interaction in formal and informal settings with other social groups by virtue of their participation in the work-place.

Similarly, at the outset of migration from Europe, despite wide differences in educational and regional backgrounds, most of the immigrants became part of the agricultural sector in the US early in the 19th century. However, as the labour market demands changed, many more became involved in the manufacturing sector late in the 19th and early 20th centuries. Evidence suggests that immigrant cultural identity in the recipient country was very much tied to the status in the occupational structure.[20]

In the case of other immigrant societies in the new world, such as Guyana and Trinidad, most members of the Indian community, in particular the first arrivals between 1838 and 1917, entered at the lowest point of the social stratification system. They were primarily indentured laborers tied to the plantation and were largely perceived as temporary inhabitants in these societies. The Indians also thought of themselves as such – being temporary, always keeping alive the hope that they would return to the subcontinent at the termination of their labour contracts.[21] Having entered at the lowest levels of the colonial occupational hierarchy, they inevitably pushed up those who were agricultural labourers before them, namely, African slaves. The emancipation of slaves and the importation of Indian labourers reinforced the status of Indians as the occupants of the lowest status jobs in society. In a sociological sense, the cultural identity of Indians as Indians saw it and the cultural identity of Indians as other groups saw it were much different. The Indian self-cultural identity in the beginning refused to accept the status, which was imposed on them and one that signified that they were the lowest of the low. Of course, Indians themselves were fully aware of the diversity that existed among themselves, particularly in terms of the place of origin, language, and ritualistic status. From their vantage point, the cultural legacy that they had brought with them arguably provided them with hope and dignity, which other groups in the larger society did not properly comprehend.[22]

Similarly, to understand the occupational concentration of European immigrants to the United States, it is necessary to consider the diversity of the groups at the time of their arrival in terms economic skills, which many groups capitalized on as opportunities arose during the processes of industrialization of the country. It is true that in Illinois, Wisconsin, Indiana, New York, and Pennsylvania, ethnic cleavages were strong in burgeoning industrial and manufacturing centres but that was largely because the ethnic-cultural groups could only access these opportunities afforded to them by the expanding industrial economy.[23]

Although cultural assimilation was argued to have occurred indiscriminately across ethno-cultural subgroups of European immigrants in the late 19th and early 20th centuries, a careful scrutiny points to the contrary. It is true that the generation of scholars writing in the 1930s and 1940s wanted carbon copies of assimilation patterns, and accepted even limited forms of unlearning of previous ways of life by newly incorporated groups as strengths of American cultural uniformity.[24] But this line of research loses sight of the fact that American society never was homogeneous in a structural sense and that it was as much affected by the arriving immigrant groups as the groups were affected by it. For example, as Sowell argues, some typical American pastimes such as the Sunday cook-outs and bowling originate not from the original Anglo predecessors but from America's German immigrants.[25] In another example, when European ethno-cultural groups moved from the older ethnically based working class neighbourhoods of the city to the more middle class and mixed suburbs in the second half of the twentieth century, their sense of cultural diversity also underwent significant transformation.[26] It is these mutually affecting processes of cultural identity that enforce diversity but take on different shapes and forms for different ethno-cultural groups, largely depending on the ways in which they sought to respond to the labour market conditions.

Ethno-cultural Community

Historically, the influence of residential patterns on the development and maintenance of ethno-cultural communities of immigrants was very important in the Americas in the nineteenth and early twentieth centuries. In these decades, occupational segregation was reinforced by residential segregation. But that has undergone significant change and has added to the mosaic of diversity of American social ethos. For example, in Alba and Logan's study of neighbourhoods, Asians and Latinos of the same income range lived in close proximity. For these individuals, it is the similarity of income that portrays sufficiently similar cultural life style which neither solely Asian nor primarily Latino ethnic heritage can attest to. Much linguistic assimilation has also taken place in these neighbourhoods despite the persistence of some ethno-cultural differences.[27]

Let us take the Caribbean societies as a case in point. The rural neighbourhoods in which Indians lived in the nineteenth century contained the major institutions of work, religion, family, leisure (of which there was very little), and structures of colonial and internal social control. The colonial authorities eagerly controlled the movements of Indians outside of the sugar plantations. Many scholars have noted that those Indians who ventured out and traveled to urban areas faced considerable harassment and discomfort[28]

By the third decade of the twentieth century, pretty much by the time indentured labour contracts were made illegal, the city culture was also being sustained in Georgetown and Port of Spain. While urban areas in these two cities contained more institutions, because of the late arrival of Indians in urban areas they were unable to obtain gainful employment in significant numbers in the burgeoning bureaucracies and other urban-related occupations. Since few residential areas contained large concentrations of Indians, it established a certain ethno-economic identity. What pluralist scholars have noted was actually a combination of these two identities. In the beginning, certainly between 1838 and 1917, these two identities were mostly collapsed into one. But this did not last in the second half of the twentieth century. The very reason the two identities disentangled themselves was because of the internal occupational diversity among Indians. This internal diversity would force others also to perceive that diversity as the emergence of a new Indo-Caribbean ethno-cultural identity, which is different from the earlier ethno-economic super identity. In that sense, increased cultural diversity was seen within the larger Indian immigrant community as a response to increased occupational diversity of its members.

The effect of residential community on ethnic identity is directly relevant to the pluralist argument that Indians have been able to maintain their separate ethno-cultural identity, largely because of their distinct cultural origin. It is true that in the cultural pluralist studies in the United States, scholars have noted increasing patterns of religious endogamy but considerable ethnic exogamy in marital relations. For example, inter-marriages between the Irish and Italian families represented religious endogamy since both pertained to the Catholic religious identity. However, in the ethnic sense, the marriages represented exogamy.[29]

In the case of the Caribbean, the reverse had occurred. Indians, both Hindus and Muslims, should be considered exogamous in the religious sense, but endogamous in the ethnic sense. In that context, many scholars have noted that as early as the beginning of the twentieth century considerable number of inter-marriages between Hindus and Moslems had taken place.[30] This is very much in line with research conducted in the United States which argues that ethnic communities become crystallized in recipient countries largely as a response to local conditions, and not because they all came from another culture.[31]

Glazer's study in the case of the United States suggests that some ethnic groups evolve from a smaller, more parochial existence into more regional and national bases of organizations. The evolution of *La Raza* in the US represents such evolution, as the critical mass of mobilized Latinos grew by leaps and bounds. The demand for their organized entry into the political process was initially launched by *La Raza*, which subsequently grew from being primarily a regional entity focusing in the south-west to a more national entity, catering to the demands of Latinos in Miami, New York, Chicago, Washington DC and elsewhere.[32]

Similar examples can be had from the Caribbean as well. Indians in both

Guyana and Trinidad are a case in point. As most of them did not go back after their indentured tenure-ship had expired, they gradually developed a new orientation, which was more than just ethnic; it was more cultural. This is consistent with Neilli's research in Chicago which concludes that the community and group consciousness among southern Italians in the US, although of diverse origins, formed a relatively new identity even though pretty much like the Indians they were mostly from the agricultural-rural regions of Italy and they were characterized by greater loyalties to their tribe, clan, or village.[33]

The ethno-cultural identities over-time become more cultural than ethnic, as local conditions interact with the characteristics brought on board by immigrants. In the case of Indians in the new world, it was much more Caribbean than Indian over time. Ethnic cultures may evolve in a series of different directions, largely due to an ever-continuing interaction between the nature of the local communities, including villages and indentured-communities, available economic opportunities, and the national religious or cultural heritage of the group.[34] In that respect, cultural pluralists did not account for the importance of the labour market and economic opportunities or the lack of them in the Caribbean for Indians. Old world traits, such as food, language, rituals, and other aspects of human behaviour may persist, but that is not to say that changes did not take place as a result of the economic and administrative restrictions and opportunities accorded to the Indian communities in the Caribbean.

Similar arguments can be developed in the case of many immigrant communities in the United States. The Irish immigration to the US, although consisting of a large ethno-cultural community that was mostly Catholic surrounded by a sea of Protestant groups and constellations, over time merged with the larger society still dominated by the broader Anglo-Saxon values. This was attained largely through occupational mobility and inter-marriage with non-Irish groups. In the current setting, although a celebration of St. Patrick's Day does remind the Irish heritage in the US, it does not represent any specific Irish ethno-cultural identity. It is just one of many celebrated days in the year for the entire country. Of course, all immigrant groups have not attained this status in the larger American society. This is a matter of time. But the speed at which it is likely to occur would depend on a series of factors as described above.

Let us elaborate a bit more on the point of social or occupational mobility, and how the rate of such mobility may contribute to the formation of various types of ethno-cultural communities. If one can consider the fact that most Indians in Guyana started in the time period around the 1850s at the very bottom of the Guyanese society, then it is important to note some changes that subsequently took place in their structural conditions. Data from the World Bank for the 1990s suggest that in terms of the poverty data the status of the

Indo-Guyanese is not the worst; the incidence of poverty among the Indo Guyanese is 34 per cent. This is significantly lower than the 43 per cent for the Afro-Guyanese and 88 per cent for the Guyanese of Indigenous origin. By any measure, such change represents social and occupational mobility over 150 years.[35] In the case of Trinidad, whose ethnic composition is similar to that of Guyana, comparable data may be cited. The incidence of poverty among Indo-Trinidadians is 17.3 per cent, compared with 25 per cent among Afro-Trinidadians. Altogether, Afro-Trinidadians constitute 47 per cent, Indo-Trinidadians 36 per cent, and the mixed races 18 per cent of the poor population.[36] Trinidad & Tobago in general has less poverty than Guyana, and Indo-Trinidadians have taken advantage of the greater opportunities available in Trinidad and Tobago. The oil sector accounts for a big part of that difference. Although there has been some indication that in the mid-to-late 1990s, the poverty index worsened in both Trinidad and Guyana, it is important to note where the Indian communities in these societies started from. Over one hundred and fifty years, a significant portion of them have moved outside of the traditional sectors of sugar and rice into business and technical sectors of the economy.[37] This diversity has had a beneficial impact on group poverty rate. It would be naive under such circumstances to assume that ethnic identity remained static under conditions of increased mobility and movement.

Similar mobility data can be sited in the case of the Polish and Italian immigrants in the US. Over a period of one hundred years, these communities have been much mobile occupationally and thereby have increased their perceived ethno-cultural status in American society.[38]

Ethnic Identity

The studies on cultural assimilation have implied a supposed predominance of the English-language based culture in the US.[39] A significant number of socio-linguistic studies have shown that within three generations, various ethnic group members speak English primarily at home at the expense of their respective native tongues.[40] In all likelihood, the acquisition of English occurs more rapidly now than before largely due to the availability of multiple channels of communication and dialogue, either through television or radio. Although this primacy of speaking English occurs, the prevalence of other spoken languages is also widespread in the US. Spanish is the dominant language spoken in many metropolitan regions stretching from Miami to New York to Chicago to Los Angeles. What to make of this coexistence? The primacy of English coexists with other spoken languages, in particular Spanish. Does that indicate greater cultural diversity and lesser ethnic identity? It probably signifies both in the sense that a greater acquisition of English has occurred at the same time that ethno-cultural groups also maintain their linguistic traits. Portes and Rumbaut's study in particular has found that in Miami metropolitan region, the academic achievement of fluently bilingual Cuban students far exceeds that of monolingual Anglos or other ethnics.[41]

Unlike the United States and Canada, in Guyana and Trinidad, linguistic heritage has lost its ground to the Caribbean languages, in particular the Creole version of the English language. But large-scale migration to Guyana and Trinidad & Tobago did not materialize in the second half of the twentieth century. In the absence of such migration, the changes in the character of ethno-cultural diversity among Indians primarily evolved around several local factors: (a) the extent of occupational diversity experienced by the community; (b) the extent to which the community became urban-centreed, and (c) the context of reception of Indians at these urban centres. Much research in the Americas points to the fact that ethno-cultural identity was strongly sustained by formal and informal interactions fomented through the work place and residential neighbourhoods. Working class neighbourhoods were vibrant in sustaining ethnic identity of their members in cities as far apart as Philadelphia, Chicago, and Milwaukee.[42] But at the end of the Second World War, significant changes appeared. Due to the continued development of transportation and communication networks, industries no longer needed to stay-put in the cities of the Northeast and the Midwest. In search of low cost cities, the movement gravitated toward many cities of the southwest and southeast of the country. Houston, Atlanta, and Charlotte deserve attention in that regard.[43] But such movements are only possible in larger countries like the United States. No such movement occurred in the Caribbean. Since the two economies of Guyana and Trinidad remained planted in their urban-industrial centers of Port of Spain and Georgetown, it was important for Indians to break the structural barriers to entry. Such barriers had long been erected in both countries in the areas of public sector employment. The schools and the governmental bureaucracies were disproportionately populated by Africans and the mixed races with the few whites at the top of these structures. For example, by 1931, Indians in Guyana were 16 per cent of all professionals and about 1/3rd of all merchants and shopkeepers.[44] This is a far cry from the turn of the twentieth century when the overwhelming majority of Indians were either in sugar, rice, or both. These changes reflect their drive toward greater affinity with the local society by increased interaction in schools and local businesses.

Since the Second World War, with the advent of increased automobile use, the close relationship between the location of employment and that of residence was greatly loosened in the US; however, no such development was greatly felt in the Caribbean, meaning that the strength of the tie that had been formed between places of work and residence was not significantly disrupted. Hence, the process of change was much slower, but it happened nonetheless, much faster in Trinidad & Tobago than in Guyana. The increased importance of the petroleum sector and the momentum it provided in the local economy in terms of creating extended job opportunities proved catalyst for the rupture between the location of employment and that of residence.[45]

The rural village setting of Indians with priests, temples, and extended families, characterized by extensive use of the Indian languages and rituals no doubt sustained a sense of Indianness, but that sense no doubt changed with the passing of successive generations, as they sought to identify and integrate with the host society. The dreams and hopes of returning to India had largely faded by the end of World War II. Marital relationships were largely endogamous but scholars have noted with the passage of time an increased number of marriages across caste and religious lines. Marital ties with non-Indians were largely constrained because of not only the limited nature of informal contacts but also the restricted mobility patterns on the part of the Indian.[46] Even in the rural settings, what others commonly characterize as typically Indian behaviour was also largely a function of their peculiar participation in the economic life. Peasant occupation demanded certain types of family interaction and extended family links. The motive was primarily to accumulate social and financial capital. These cultural foundations were largely used by Indians to get to that goal. Based on the above, how can one argue that ethno-cultural diversity did not change in its manifestation? New forms appeared. Many times they existed side by side with the old ones; in other cases, they replaced the older traits.

Berger's study in the Boston area demonstrated this salient point quite well.[47] If one translated his arguments to Indians in another context it would read like this: For other social groups, in particular the Africans and the whites in the Caribbean the image of Indians working in sugar and rice fields was coloured by ethnic glasses. Even though the villages were largely recognized as Indian communities, the argument could be made that the effect of ethnicity was secondary to that of community and class. In other words, in the eyes of those others in the Guyanese and Trinidadian societies community and ethnicity were one and the same, while in actuality they were distinct, not only in their theoretical construction but also in their content. With the passage of time, as the indentured labour contract was eventually declared illegal, a sense of new ethno-cultural identity developed that was quite distinct from the old ethno-cultural identity.

There are parallels to this in the experiences of Blacks and Puerto Rican immigrants in the United States. Since most of these communities of Blacks and Latinos were far removed from the best economic opportunities, their informal networks regarding job availability were considered critical.[48] These networks were not tied to economic opportunities but to social and kinship ties. But segregation of residential patterns was facilitated by the economic nature of their group existence, and not because of any special ethno-cultural solidarity. Therefore, even in the beginning, at the time of the arrival of Indians, the very construction of villages and settled communities on and around the sugar plantations were as much economic as they were social. The argument that the labour market conditions then existent only afforded them limited opportunities to participate, and that too mostly as agricultural laborers, still holds as an important determinant of ethno-cultural identity and not the other way around.

The importance of ethno-cultural identity in the formation of Indian communities was not really a simple process of large groups of people from various regions of India settling in or around the sugar plantations in the nineteenth century; the type of settlement was also partly a reaction to the marginal social and political existence. Some ethno-cultural behaviour can be maintained regardless of the type of occupation and the type of settlement one is in.

Research on the Jewish population despite their tremendous economic resilience in the US has found evidence of some ethnic cultural sustenance.[49] Ethnic salience and identification can be maintained through the family and friends whether or not the members live in the same neighbourhood. But in the context of the Caribbean, fresh inputs from India were not a factor after 1917, and not until after independence significant political and cultural contacts with India were re-invigorated. Therefore, whatever ideas people had originally brought with them from India were undoubtedly beginning to take on a new twist, largely as a response to the interaction with the local factors in the Caribbean. The maintenance of ethnic organizations manifested itself in a big way around the date of political independence from Britain. More temples and mosques were built. But these were also indications of greater financial and social strengths of these communities. *Poojas* and parades and the celebrations of other Indian rituals intensified; they were not exclusively ethnic but a manifestation of their increased cultural diversity as an ethnic group. Most of that diversity can be understood as occupational diversity. The argument proposed here, then, is this: Ethno-cultural identity should not be construed primarily as an ascribed status that is static but rather as a dynamic variable. The extent of ethno-cultural identity is likely to vary depending on the specific situation of a group.

Cultural pluralists have used the historical facts that the African and the Indian populations in Guyana and Trinidad have been clashing with each other. Some have characterized it as a clash of cultures. It is true that at some point in history, Indians were mostly an agrarian group whereas the Africans were mostly semi-skilled and skilled professionals who settled in urban areas. The mutual suspicion of these groups was further exacerbated in the post-independence period. Many pluralist writers have contended that political patronage and clientelistic politics have played a big role in the respective ethnic mobilizations.[50] But that should not be misconstrued as expressions of separate identities as ethnic groups. Conflicts could be a function of structural dissimilarities in conditions. For example, Bissessar has noted that there is considerable ethnic imbalance in the public sector employment in both Guyana and Trinidad & Tobago.[51] For example, in large public sector enterprises in Guyana, there have been only 5 Indian Chairmen of Boards compared to 50 for the Afro-Guyanese. As members of Boards and Commissions of major public sector companies, the Afro-Guyanese outnumber Indo-Guyanese 487 to 6. Similar imbalances have also been noted in the Directorship of financial institutions, where the ratio favours the Afro-Guyanese over Indo-Guyanese by a ratio of 34 to 6.[52] Of course, restrictive barriers in the case of public sector employment have indeed contributed to many Indo-Guyanese attempting to develop their talent in the private business sector.

Many studies have noted in recent years that as Indians have moved into close proximity of Africans, increased interactions have resulted in even cultural and political solidarity activities between African Muslims and Indian Muslims. There have been some instances of inter-marriage as well.[53]

Conclusion

In the case of the Caribbean, cultural pluralists have maintained that the salience of ethno-cultural identity in Guyana and Trinidad & Tobago has proven the importance and staying power of the Indian culture. However, assimilationists have maintained that over time ethno-cultural identity would change and loose its initial character, and is likely to be part of a larger Caribbean cultural identity. The experiences of these two notions in the Caribbean suggest that we are probably finding more support for considerable variations in the expression of ethno-cultural identity. Cultural pluralists have vehemently maintained the importance of portable heritage, which moves around with groups but stays strong regardless of the conditions in which communities find themselves. It is no doubt much more dynamic than that. It is always necessary to understand the relationship between the ethnic group members with larger macro social processes in society such as schooling, occupational participation, and political organization. Yes, places of residence matter, but they do indeed interact with the external conditions, one of which corresponds to the context of reception. In the post-independence period, it is also useful to bring in the role of the state. State policies became critical in both Caribbean countries as power struggle intensified in the post-independence period.[54]

Much research has been done on the salience of race, ethnic identity and community in sustaining cultural diversity in the Americas. Yet, there is evidence to support both forms of theoretical hypotheses. Cultural assimilationist trends are salient in the sense that these occur in small steps, and not overnight, but that does not mean that all ethno-cultural traits completely disappear. They interact with the new society, its contextual vicissitudes, and develop eclectic yet segmented forms. These have to be researched and brought to the fore.

It is true that the Huntingtonian conflict always existed although it has been made out to be of recent origin by his supporters due to the large influx of Spanish speaking ethnic-cultural communities into the US. American society has always been culturally diverse. Fresh immigration from overseas always adds to the mosaic of diversity as material conditions worldwide are unlikely to be exactly the same. Both theoretical paradigms in their extreme forms have infrequently been supported by the accumulation of evidence from the Americas. Although the Euro-American cultural paradigms have undergone tremendous change due to the large-scale immigration from Asia and Latin America since the late 1960s, it does not mean that all ethno-cultural groups have attained parity in terms of their roles in the occupational structure or in respective economic and political powers. Large-scale immigration is likely to make the US a more culturally diverse nation. But to the extent that diversity is translated into policy changes would very much depend on the power of human agency of the various ethno-cultural communities by reaching out to each other in collective action. In other words, the diversity in cultural existence is unlikely to make the largely puritan law in the United States more sensitive to cultural nuances in the near future.

Notwithstanding all that, a different position is proposed here. It is true that much of the behaviour commonly associated with ethno-cultural diversity is actually a function of the structural conditions under which the groups find themselves. Experiences from the United States suggest that the ethnic ghettos of Chicago and New York no doubt indicate specific ethno-cultural behaviour and identity but at the same time they also demonstrate a very different set of structural conditions. Ethno-cultural identity that is defined in terms of the presence or absence of frequent patterns of association and identification with common origins is but crystallized under conditions of residential stability and segregation, common occupational position, and dependence on local institutions and services. More specifically, ethno-cultural identity changes with new experiences with the patterns of employment. The more diverse it becomes, the more variations one is likely to see in the expression of that ethno-cultural identity. There will be an identity no doubt, but it is a fluid identity very much determined on the basis of an interaction between the local and external conditions.

It is natural to expect that ethno-cultural identity is strongest among members who are geographically clustered and have occupations that are relatively similar in terms of their status on the economic or income hierarchy. People are indeed dependent on their communities for cultural items and values if only other community members are willing to supply them and are available for that. For example, when looking for a job, when a child is born, when a person becomes old and needs care, these and other day-to-day needs may be served by neighbours or institutions from the private or the state sectors. When most people working in these areas belong to the same ethnic group, the likelihood of a certain type of ethno-cultural behaviour and identification with particular ethnic origin is more likely. But in the absence of such conditions, it would be much more culturally diverse.

Despite what critics may say, being a descendant of an Indian immigrant does not necessarily make that individual an ethnic. Ethno-culture is indeed a variable and so is the expression of that identity. Indian ethno-cultural identity is very different today in the US, Guyana, and Trinidad & Tobago than what has been presented by cultural pluralists. At the same time, it has not lost many of its distinctiveness unlike what has been expected by assimilationists.

Ethno-cultural identity is indeed a function of several processes. It is a manifestation of the way populations are organized in terms of their occupational involvement, the diversity therein, institutions and the extent of ethnic homogeneity in those institutions, and so on. Indian ethno-cultural identity in the Caribbean may have in contemporary times little to do with India but much to do with the activities of survival and mobility experiences, the structure of opportunities, and the context of reception from other actors in the Caribbean. And that includes the African, the mixed races, the small minority of whites, and the role of the state and politics. But it is much different in the US. Since Indian immigration is quite recent, many of the cultural traits seen in India are also found in the United States.

Several factors, then, interact among themselves to indicate that the Indian Diaspora does exist in the larger cultural sense but in a much more diverse way. The observed patterns of cultural existence do not conform to the ways cultural pluralists have predicted. They are dynamic and they do change and crystallize in very different forms and shapes than could have been predicted under either the assimilationist or pluralist viewpoints. That is what one would call a collection of segmented ethno-cultural identities. The Indian ethno-cultural identity in the United States, Guyana, and Trinidad & Tobago is precisely that: a collection of segmented ethno-cultural identities largely determined by the occupational and social factors of the host societies and not those of the Indian subcontinent. Needless to say, much work needs to be done to sort out many loose ends outlined above in future research.

Endnotes

1. The National Research Council Report on Racial and Ethnic composition of the US population (Washington DC: 1997).
2. Samuel P. Huntington, *Who Are We: The Challenges to America's National Identity* (New York: Simon & Schuster, 2005); Peter Brimlow, Alien Nation: *Common Sense about America's Immigration Disaster* (New York: Random House, 1995).

3. U.S. Census Bureau, Decennial Census and the Population Division, www.census.gov/popest/estimates.php. Population Bulletin. Various issues, 2003–2006.
4. Ibid.
5. Samuel Huntington, "The Hispanic Challenge," *Foreign Policy* (2004):30.
6. Edward O. Laumann, *Bonds of Pluralism* (New York: Wiley, 1973); Nathan Glazer, *We are all Multiculturalists Now* (Cambridge: Harvard University Press, 1997); Anthony K. Appiah, "The multiculturalism misunderstanding," The New York Review of Books 44 (October 9):30–36; and Michael Walzer, On Toleration (New Haven: Yale University Press, 1997).
7. Quoted in Douglas Hartmann and Joseph Gerteis, "Dealing with Diversity," *Sociological Theory* 23 (2005):218.
8. Peter M. Blau and Otis D. Duncan, The American Occupational Structure (New York: Wiley, 1967); Abnor Cohen (ed.), Urban Ethnicity (London: Travistock, 1974); Mark Granovetter, Getting a Job. A Study of Contacts and Careers (Boston, MA: Harvard University Press, 1974); Leon Mayhew, "Ascription in Modern societies," Sociological inquiry 38 (1968):105–120.
9. Stanley Lieberson, "The Impact of Residential Segregation on Ethnic Assimilation," *Social Forces* 40 (1961):52–57.
10. See Stanley Lieberson, *Ethnic Patterns in American* Cities (New York: Free Press, 1963).
11. Kristin Espinosa and Douglas Massey, "Determinants of English Proficiency among Mexican migrants to the united States," International Migration Review 31 (1997):28–50; Herbert Gans, "Symbolic Ethnicity: the future of ethnic groups and cultures in America," Ethnic and Racial Studies 2 (1979):1–20; also see Gans, "Second generation decline: Scenarios for the economic and ethnic futures of post-1965 American immigrants" Ethnic and Racial Studies 15 (1992):173–192.
12. Alejandro Portes and Leif Jensen, "The enclave and the entrants: Patterns of ethnic enterprise in Miami before and after Mariel," *American Sociological review* 54 (1989):929–949; Bryan Roberts, "social expected durations and the economic adjustment of immigrants," in the Economic Sociology of Immigration, edited by Alejandro Portes (New York: Russell Sage Foundation, 1995).
13. Ron Ramdin, *Arising from Bondage: A history of Indo-Caribbean People* (New York: New York University Press, 2000).
14. Paul W. Kingston, "Are there classes in the United States?" pp. 3–41 in Research in Social Stratification and Mobility, edited by Robert Althauser and Michael Wallace (Greenwich, Ct: JAI Press, 1994).
15. Alejandro Portes and Alex Stepick, 'Unwelcome immigrants: The labor market experiences of 1980 9Mariel) Cuban and Haitian refugees in South Florida,' *American Sociological Review* 50 (1985):493–514.
16. Adam Smith, The Theory of Moral Sentiments (New York: Book Jungle, 2001); Emile Durkheim, The Division of Labor in Society (New York: Free Press, 1997).
17. Hiroshi Ishida, Social Mobility in Contemporary Japan (Palo Alto: Stanford University Press, 1985); also see Moon-Gi Suh, Developmental Transformation in South Korea: From State-Sponsored Growth to the Quest for Quality of Life (New York: Praeger, 1998).

18. William Foot Whyte, Street Corner Society (Chicago: University of Chicago Press, 1943); also see Sam B. Warner and Colin Burke, "Cultural Change and the Ghetto," *Journal of Contemporary History* 4 (1969):173–188.
19. See William J. Wilson, *The Declining Significance of Race: Blacks and Changing American Institutions* (Chicago: University of Chicago press, 1980).
20. Sidney Goldstein, *Patterns of Mobility, 1910–1950* (Philadelphia: University of Pennsylvania Press, 1958).
21. Ron Ramdin, *Arising from Bondage: A History of the Indo-Caribbean People* (New York: New York University Press, 2000).
22. Sultana Afroz, "The Mogul Islamic Diaspora: The Institutionalization of Islam in Jamaica," *Journal of Muslim Minority Affairs* 20 (2000):271–289.
23. Beverley Duncan and Otis D. Duncan, "Minorities and the process of stratification," *American Sociological Review* 33 (1968):356–364.
24. For example, see LIoyd W. Warner and Leo stole, The Social Systems of American Ethnic Groups (New Haven: Yale University Press, 1945).
25. Thomas Sowell, Migrations and Cultures: A World View (New York: Basic, 1996).
26. Richard Alba and Victor Nee, "Rethinking assimilation for a new era of immigration," *International Migration Review* 31 (1997):826–874; and Mary Waters, Ethnic Options: Choosing identities in America (Berkeley: University of California Press, 1990).
27. Richard Alba and John Logan, "Minority proximity to whites in suburbs: An individual-level analysis of segregation," *American Journal of Sociology* 98 (1993):1388–1427.
28. Alvin M. Katz and Ruben Hill. 1958. "Residential Propinquity and marital selection," *Marriage and Family Living* 20:27–35; also see Sultana Afroz, "The Mogul Islamic Diaspora: The Institutionalization of Islam in Jamaica," *Journal of Muslim Minority Affairs* 20 (2000):271–289.
29. Harold J. Abramson, 1973. Ethnic Diversity in Catholic America (New York: Wiley, 1973); Andrew M. Greeley, Why can't they be like us? (New York: Dutton, 1971); also see Andrew Greeley, Ethnicity in the United States (New York: Wiley, 1974).
30. Ron Ramdin, *Arising from Bondage: A History of the Indo-Caribbean People* (New York: New York University Press, 2000).
31. Nathan M. Glazer, "Ethnic Groups in America: from National Culture to Ideology," pp. 158–172 In Morroe Berger, Theodore Abel and Charles Page (eds.). Freedom and Control in Modern Society (New York: Van Nostrand, 1954); also see Nathan Glazer and Daniel P. Moynihan, Beyond the Melting Pot (Cambridge: MIT Press, 1963).
32. Nathan Glazer and Daniel P. Moynihan. 1963. Beyond the Melting Pot. Cambridge: MIT Press; also see many writings on La Raza at http://www.nclr.org/.
33. Humbert S. Nelli, *The Italians in Chicago: 1880–1930* (New York: Oxford University press, 1970).
34. Sara Abraham, "The Shifting Sources of racial definition in Trinidad and Tobago and Guyana: a Research Agenda," *Ethnic and Racial Studies* 24 (2001):979–997.
35. John Gafar, "Growth, Inequality and Poverty in Selected Caribbean and Latin American Countries, with Emphasis on Guyana," *Journal of Latin American Studies* 30 (1998):591–617.

36. Ibid.
37. Winston Dookeran, "East Indians and the Economy of Trinidad and Tobago, pp. 69–83 in John La Guerre (ed.), Calcutta to Caroni: The East Indians of Trinidad (London: Longman, 1974).
38. Elliott Liebow, Tally's Corner (Boston: Little, Brown, 1967); Daniel R. Fusfield, The Basic Economics of the Urban and Racial Crisis (Ann Arbor: The University of Michigan Press, 1969); also see Edgar M. Hoover and Raymond Vernon, Anatomy of a Metropolis (Cambridge, MA: Harvard University Press, 1959).
39. For example, see Calvin Veltman, *Language Shift in the United States* (Berlin: Mouton, 1983).
40. Alejandro Portes and Richard Schauffler, "Language and the second generation: Bilingualism yesterday and today," *International Migration Review* 28 (19940):640–666.
41. Alejandro Portes and Ruben Rumbaut, Legacies: The Story of the Immigrant Second Generation (Berkeley: University of California Press, 2002).
42. Raymond Breton, "Institutional Completeness of Ethnic Communities and the Personal Relations of Immigrants," *American Journal of Sociology* 70 (1964):193–205.
43. William J. Wilson, When Work Disappears: The World of the New Urban Poor (New York: Vintage, 1997); also see Wilson, The Declining Significance of Race: Blacks and Changing American Institutions (Chicago: University of Chicago press, 1980).
44. Ralph Premdas, Ethnicity and Development: The Caribbean and Oceania. Working Paper # 221, pp. 1–32, The Helen Kellogg Institute for International Studies (Notre Dame: The University of Notre Dame Press, 1996).
45. See Anthony Payne and Paul Sutton (eds.), Modern Caribbean Politics (Baltimore: The Johns Hopkins University Press, 1993); also see Ann Marie Bissessar," Addressing Ethnic Imbalances in the Public Services of Plural Societies: The Case of Guyana and Trinidad and Tobago," The International Journal of Public Sector Management 15 (2001):55–68.
46. Kelvin Singh, "East Indians and the Larger Society," pp. 39–68, In La Guerre, John (ed.) Calcutta to Caroni (London: Longman, 1974).
47. Bennett M. Berger, Working Class Suburb (Berkeley: University of California Press, 1960).
48. David Ward, Cities and Immigrants (New York: Oxford University Press, 1971); also see Herbert Gans, The Urban Villagers (New York: Free Press, 1962); William F. Footwhyte, Street Corner Society (Chicago: University of Chicago Press, 1943).
49. Rudolph Glanz, Jew and Italian: Historic Group Relations and the New Immigration (New York: Klau, 1970).
50. For a brilliant review of existing studies on the relationship between ethnicity and migration, see Yancey, William L, Eriksen, Eugene P. and Juliani, Richard N. 1976. "Emergent Ethnicity: A Review of Reformulation," *American Sociological Review* 41 (1976):391–403.
51. Bissessar, Ann Marie, "Addressing Ethnic Imbalances in the Public Services of Plural Societies: The Case of Guyana and Trinidad and Tobago," *The International Journal of Public Sector Management* 15 (2001):55–68.

52. Ibid.
53. Sultana Afroz, "The Mogul Islamic Diaspora: The Institutionalization of Islam in Jamaica," *Journal of Muslim Minority Affairs* 20 (2000):271–289.
54. Henry B. Jeffrey and Colin Baber, Guyana: Politics, Economics and Society (Boulder, CO: Lynne Rienner, 1986); also see Ron Ramdin, Arising from Bondage: A History of the Indo-Caribbean People (New York: New York University Press, 2000).

Contributors

Basu, Swaraj, Professor of History, School of Social Sciences and presently Director, Distance Education Council (DEC), Indira Gandhi National Open University, New Delhi 110 068. E-mail: basuswaraj@hotmail.com

Bennett, Bruce, Member, Australia-India Council Board, Professor of English, University of New South Wales, Australian Defence Force Academy, Canberra Australia. E-mail: b.bennett@adfa.edu.au

Dasverma. G., Senior Lecturer, School of Geography, Population and Environmental Management, Flinders University, Adelaide, Australia. E-mail: gour.dasvarma@flinders.edu.au

George, Sudhir Jacob, Deptt. of Political Science, Central University of Hyderabad, Hyderabad. E-mail: sigsa@yahoo.com

Gopal, D., Professor and Coordinator, Australian Studies Programme, Faculty of Political Science, Indira Gandhi National Open University, New Delhi. E-mail: darveshgopal@yahoo.co.in

Gullapalli, Sailaja, Research Associate, Gandhi Smriti & Darshan Samiti, Rajghat, New Delhi. E-mail: sailajagullapalli@rediffmail.com

Hall, Liz, Senior Manager, Office of the Employment Advocate, Government of Australia, Sydney. E-mail: bellyboo@dodo.com.au

Andrew Hassam, Director of Australian Studies Program, National Centre for Australian Studies, School of Political and Social Inquiry, Monash University, Australia. E-mail: andrew.hassam@arts.monash.edu.au

Hugo, Graeme, Professor of Geographical and Environmental Studies and Director of the National Centre for Social Applications of Geographical Information Systems, University of Adelaide, Adelaide, Australia. Email: graeme.hugo@adelaide.edu.au

Mayne, Alan, Research SA Chair and Professor of Social History & Public Policy, Hawke Research Institute for Sustainable Societies, University of South Australia, Adelaide, Australia. E-mail: alan.mayne@unisa.edu.au

Mukherjee, Subrata, Professor, Deptt. of Political Science, University of Delhi, Delhi 110 021. E-mail: cicero@vsnl.com

Narayanan, R., Former Dean, School of International Studies, Jawaharlal Nehru University and presently Adjunct Professor, School of Social Sciences, Indira Gandhi National Open University, New Delhi.
E-mail: rnarayanan_jnu@rediffmail.com

Pattnayak, Satya R., Professor of Sociology & Political Science, Director of Latin American Studies, Villanova University, 273 St Augustine Center, Villanova, PA 19085-1699. E-mail: satya.pattnayak@villanova.edu

Ramaswamy, Sushila, Reader in Political Science, Jesus & Mary College, University of Delhi, New Delhi.
E-mail: sushilaramaswamy@hotmail.com

Roberts, David, Associate Professor, Division of Education, Arts and Social Sciences, University of South Australia, Adelaide, Australia.
E-mail: david.roberts@unisa.edu.au

Singh, Amita, Professor and Chairperson, Centre for the Study of Law and Governance, Jawaharlal Nehru University, Aruna Asaf Ali Marg, New Delhi. E-mail: amita.singh3@gmail.com

Singh, Priti, Assistant Professor, School of International Studies, Jawaharlal Nehru University, New Delhi. E-mail: priti_jnu@rediffmail.com

Trivedi, Sonu, Lecturer in Political Science, Zakir Hussain College, New Delhi.
E-mail: sonutrivedi@gmail.com

Upadhyay, B. Shashi, Reader in History, School of Social Sciences, Indira Gandhi National Open University, Maidan Garhi, New Delhi 110 068.
E-mail: sbu11@hotmail.com

Vatsyayan, Kapila, Chairperson, Asia Project, India International Centre, 40, Max Muller Marg, New Delhi 110 003.
E-mail: asiaprojectiic@yahoo.com

Vemuri, S. Ram, School of Law and Business, Charles Darwin University, Darwin, Australia. E-mail: Ram.Vemuri@cdu.edu.au

Vijapur, Abdulrahim P., Professor, Deptt. of Political Science, Aligarh Muslim University, Aligarh, E-mail: vijapur_rahim@rediffmail.com

Wood, Sally Percival, Researcher, Centre for Citizenship and Human Rights, Deakin University, Melbourne. E-mail: sallypw@deakin.edu.au

Index